STRENGTHENING FAMILY RESILIENCE

THE GUILFORD FAMILY THERAPY SERIES
Michael P. Nichols, Series Editor

RECENT VOLUMES

Strengthening Family Resilience
Froma Walsh

Treating the Tough Adolescent: A Family-Based Step-by-Step Guide
Scott P. Sells

The Adolescent in Family Therapy:
Breaking the Cycle of Conflict and Control
Joseph A. Micucci

Latino Families in Therapy: A Guide to Multicultural Practice
Celia Jaes Falicov

Working with Families of the Poor
Patricia Minuchin, Jorge Colapinto, and Salvador Minuchin

Essential Skills in Family Therapy:
From the First Interview to Termination
*JoEllen Patterson, Lee Williams, Claudia Grauf-Grounds,
and Larry Chamow*

Case Studies in Couple and Family Therapy:
Systemic and Cognitive Perspectives
Frank M. Dattilio, Editor

Working with Relationship Triangles:
The One-Two-Three of Psychotherapy
*Philip J. Guerin, Jr., Thomas F. Fogarty, Leo F. Fay,
and Judith Gilbert Kautto*

Power and Compassion:
Working with Difficult Adolescents and Abused Parents
Jerome A. Price

If Problems Talked: Narrative Therapy in Action
Jeffrey L. Zimmerman and Victoria C. Dickerson

Narrative Solutions in Brief Therapy
Joseph B. Eron and Thomas W. Lund

Doing Family Therapy: Craft and Creativity in Clinical Practice
Robert Taibbi

Learning and Teaching Therapy
Jay Haley

Strengthening Family Resilience

F·R·O·M·A W·A·L·S·H

THE GUILFORD PRESS
New York   London

© 1998 The Guilford Press
A Division of Guilford Publications, Inc.
72 Spring Street, New York, NY 10012
http://www.guilford.com

Printed in the United States of America

This book is printed on acid-free paper.

Last digit is print number: 9 8 7 6 5 4

Library of Congress Cataloging-in-Publication Data

Walsh, Froma.
    Strengthening family resilience / Froma Walsh.
        p.   cm. — (The Guilford family therapy series)
    Includes bibliographical references and index.
    ISBN 1-57230-408-1
    1. Family—Mental health.   2. Resilience (Personality trait)
3. Problem families.   4. Family psychotherapy.   5. Family social
work.   I. Title.   II. Series.
    RC489.F33W34   1998
    616.89'156—dc21   98-8527
                                                              CIP

P·R·E·F·A·C·E

Resilience—the ability to overcome life's challenges—has been a valuable concept in understanding and treating individual survivors of trauma and adversity. This pathbreaking book presents the concept of family resilience and identifies key processes that enable families to rebound from crisis and persistent stress. With the overwhelming pressures on family life today contributing to a high rate of family breakdown, we need more than ever to understand and strengthen the ways in which families can survive and thrive.

Marital vows express a commitment "for better or for worse, for richer or for poorer, in sickness and in health." These vows are based in a recognition that no family is problem-free; all relationships must surmount crises over the life course. We are all aware of the high risk of divorce—nearly 50% of marriages fail. But what can we learn from the 50% of marriages that succeed? What processes enable family members to build and sustain enduring relationships through turbulent times? To cope well with an illness that can't be cured or a problem that can't be solved? To regenerate after losses through death, divorce, or other life-altering transitions (such as job loss, migration, or community disaster)? To rise above severe trauma or the barriers of poverty and discrimination? To succeed against all odds? How do families effectively integrate scarring experiences over the course of the life cycle? Studies of resilient individuals and well-functioning families shed light on the key processes that can strengthen couples and families to meet life's challenges.

Drawing together the fruits of over two decades of research and my own clinical experience, this book presents a family resilience framework for therapeutic and preventive efforts with couples and families. Rather than simply providing a set of techniques to treat or change families, this strength-based approach enables therapists and others (including family members themselves) to draw out the abilities and potential in every family, and to encourage the active process of self-righting and growth. As families increase their capacity to rebound from immediate crises and to weather persistent stress, they also gain vital resources to deal more effectively with future challenges. Thus, in building family resilience, every intervention is also a preventive measure.

MY EARLY PERSONAL JOURNEYS

I have always been intrigued by the creative and diverse ways families forge meaning and connection in confronting life challenges. Perhaps this is because my own family was multicultural: My father's Jewish parents had immigrated from Odessa and Budapest to escape the pogroms in the late 1800s, and my mother's French Catholic family, early pioneers on the Upper Peninsula of Michigan, had first settled in Quebec in the 1700s. I never knew which box to check when asked my ethnic and religious background. Indeed, my family never seemed to fit any box, fueling my curiosity about "normal" families.

My community development experience in the Peace Corps in Morocco, in the mid-1960s, gave me the opportunity not only to become immersed in a culture quite different from U.S. society, but also to travel back in time across centuries to experience family and community life that was little changed over the centuries. I came to marvel at the rich, informal kinship connections that fostered resilience in the midst of severe economic hardship, physical suffering, and early death. Families with little in material wealth taught me the immeasurable value of human connections over a glass of mint tea or gathered at dinner around a platter of couscous, sharing fully of themselves with one another. They taught me still more in times of trouble, when they drew on those strong connections to see them through.

Our Peace Corps assignment was to work in community centers for young girls and women, ostensibly teaching basic skills in cooking and sewing (we discovered that Moroccan women are masters in handicrafts and cuisine). In the early Peace Corps years, well-intentioned projects were sometimes misguided. It was hoped that our presence, as models of young American women, would foster the modernization of Moroccan women, who would get to know us and desire to emulate us. However, as we became friends with young adolescent girls and they became curious about us, strangely they stopped coming to the centers. We later learned that their families had pulled them out, considering us *bad* influences on their daughters. How could we make sense of the families' response? This "resistance" to new ways had to be understood contextually. It was an important lesson in the powerful influence of family belief systems grounded in cultural values (Walsh, 1985). Unfortunately, our assignment was based in an ethnocentric hubris that, as Americans, we were healthier models to emulate. From a Moroccan perspective, when parents looked at us, they didn't see a healthy influence. Instead, they were puzzled and appalled: What proper families would allow their daughters to travel to a foreign country unchaperoned and live there on their own? And what was wrong with us that we were still unmarried at the age of 22?

My experience also led me to reexamine my own cultural norms and assumptions about family, gender, and class through a very different lens. Upon my return, I was more aware of patterns I had taken for granted or had not even noticed. I also became more committed to a career in fostering positive social change processes. As a result, I was drawn to the field of family therapy, which was just flowering at that time.

MY PROFESSIONAL "FLIGHT INTO HEALTH"

I have always been attracted to a strength-oriented approach to working with families in distress. My clinical training provided state-of-the-art knowledge and proficiency in psychopathology, but offered few clues about healthy functioning. As I learned to identify family deficits and to understand how families fail, I became increasingly curious about identifying family strengths and learning how families succeed.

My interest in resilience was first sparked in the early 1970s, while I was recruiting a normal family control group for research on schizophrenia. I puzzled over how to find "normal families" who had somehow managed to raise all their children to adulthood without anyone's suffering a breakdown. My friends and colleagues jokingly wished me lots of luck, since, they assured me, they didn't know any families that were "normal" and certainly wouldn't recommend their own. If I did find some, they added, it would be a waste of time, because they would undoubtedly be boring. At that time there was a widespread fascination with schizophrenia and other serious mental disorders as creative expressions of rebellion against conformity to oppressive family and social structures. All families, so it seemed, were more or less dysfunctional.

Those grim preconceptions were wrong. "Normal" families could be found, but it did not mean that they were problem-free. In fact, in response to a local ad, over 100 families phoned to participate in our study. Through my research contacts with families from all walks of life, I learned that ordinary families worry about their own normality; they are bombarded with media reports of failing families and are uncertain about how to navigate the unprecedented challenges of our times. Many families that volunteered for our research were eager for confirmation that they were normal. One mother even asked, only half-jokingly, whether her family could receive a "certificate of normality" at the end of the study!

These families were far from being dull and stifling. The more of them I interviewed and observed, the more I was impressed by their vitality and diversity. Of most interest to me were those families that had experienced trauma and suffering, yet had emerged hardier. And, as I became more open to searching for strengths, I also found them in clinical families, even those with seriously troubled members. From that time on, my clinical teaching and practice became strength-oriented. Because my previous clinical training and practice experience had been steeped in pathology, I returned for doctoral studies in human development to deepen and expand my knowledge about family and social processes that foster healthy functioning, creativity, and growth. I have since looked back on those valuable research and learning experiences, over 20 years ago, as my professional "flight into health."

Yet we live in a culture that takes a dim view of most families. When our daughter, at age 9, began watching the evening news, in less than a week she'd had her fill: "They call this the *news*? They should call it the *bad news*!" The portrayal of families was "really bad news." The media have been saturated with images of dysfunctional families—unstable, failing, falling apart, damaging their children, and causing social and moral decay. In a society that claims to support "family values," most families have instead been viewed through a glass darkly; their strengths and potential have gone unseen and undervalued. A family resilience lens fundamentally alters our perspective by enabling us to recognize, affirm, and build upon family resources.

THE INTENT AND STRUCTURE OF THE BOOK

The family resilience framework presented in this book has been developed, refined, and reformulated over many years of clinical teaching, supervision, and direct practice from a strength-based orientation. This framework is grounded in systems theory and draws on a growing body of research on well-functioning families. Some might question the relevance of research on healthy families to our work with families in distress. When we only study and treat families that have broken down, we may better understand how they failed and how to lessen destructive processes; however, we are still in the dark about what their growth-promoting processes are and how to foster these. Quite simply, we have much to learn from successful families to illuminate our efforts to heal and strengthen those in distress.

A primary aim of this book is to demonstrate how the family resilience approach can be applied in practice. Key processes are identified that enable couples and families facing disruptive crises or persistent stresses to forge stronger bonds, regain functioning, and move forward with their lives. Practical guidelines are offered to assist family members in mastering a wide range of life challenges. Case illustrations draw on many varied examples of family resilience I have come to admire in my professional practice, research, and training of family therapists, as well as in my personal life. (Names and details have been altered to protect families' privacy.) Throughout this volume, I discuss ways in which couples, families, and helping professionals can identify, affirm, and strengthen ways of turning adversity into strength and growth.

In Part I of the volume, Chapter 1 lays the foundations for the family resilience approach: It clarifies the meaning of "resilience," surveys what we have learned from studies of resilient individuals, and advances a systemic view of resilience that integrates ecological and developmental perspectives. It then discusses the concept of family resilience: How a family deals with life's challenges over time can powerfully influence both the immediate and long-term well-being of the family unit and all members. Because it is so important for family assessment and intervention to be relevant to the diversity of contemporary families, Chapter 2 examines how families have been changing in a rapidly changing world, developing varied and innovative approaches to master new life challenges.

Part II integrates research knowledge and practice perspectives to identify the key processes in effective family functioning and resilience. Because clinical trainees and even seasoned therapists can be overwhelmed by the complexities of family processes in assessment and intervention, I have found it useful to organize them into a conceptual framework consisting of three domains of family functioning: belief systems, organizational patterns, and communication processes. Chapters 3–5 describe and illustrate key processes in couple and family resilience within each domain. The processes overlap and interact with one another in a synergistic way, reinforcing a family's capacities to deal effectively with stress. Chapter 6 offers practice principles, guidelines, and case examples to foster resilience in work with distressed couples and families.

In Part III, Chapters 7–9 describe and illustrate the application of a family resilience approach to varied crises and persistent stresses: they identify risk factors that heighten vulnerability, as well as the protective processes that can foster individual and relational healing and growth. Chapter 7 addresses the most profound challenges families face in death, dying, and loss. Chapter 8 applies a family resilience approach to serious and chronic physical and mental illnesses. Chapter 9 highlights the core principles of strength-based family therapy and family support programs with poor, multicrisis, highly vulnerable families. Countering common views of "severely dysfunctional" families as hopeless and untreatable, a family resilience approach builds on other strength-based models to affirm and nurture the resources and potential of these families.

Chapter 10 has been written from the heart. It offers stories from my own family experience, as well as examples of courageous engagement by others I have known in my personal and professional life, challenging the prevalent assumption that individuals wounded by past trauma and troubled relationships survive best by severing all ties to their families and the past and simply moving on. In contrast, based in the conviction that we humans survive and thrive best through connection with those who have come before us and all who have been significant in our lives, we will explore the many ways to achieve reconnection and reconciliation. I consider possibilities for forgiveness, relational healing, and growth in family-of-origin relations, couples on the verge of separation, postdivorce families, and nations torn by strife.

This book provides a useful conceptual map, practice principles, and case illustrations that can be drawn upon by all professionals who are interested in fostering human adaptive capacities, regardless of practice orientation, discipline, or level of experience. A family resilience framework can be applied to a wide range of family problems within the fields of mental health and health care, human services, child welfare, family life education, juvenile justice, community organization, family law, and pastoral counseling; by practicing professionals, trainers, and students; and by marriage and family therapists, social workers, psychologists, psychiatrists, counselors, nurses, and physicians. Although the book is written primarily for helping professionals, it can also serve as a resource for a general readership—especially for family members who have faced stressful life challenges and who are interested in understanding the relational resources they can draw upon and build to strengthen their own individual, couple, and family well-being.

The need to strengthen family resilience has never been more urgent, as families today are buffeted by stresses and uncertainties of economic and social upheaval. With increasing family diversity, no single model of family health fits all. Yet all families—even the most troubled—have the potential for repair and growth. An understanding of the keys to resilience can greatly enhance this potential. For helping professionals, the therapeutic process is reinvigorated as we bring out the best in families and practice the art of the possible.

A·C·K·N·O·W·L·E·D·G·M·E·N·T·S

In working on this book, my own resilience has been tested time and again by serious medical crises and other stressful life challenges. Many strong relationships have enabled me to persevere through strain and pain. I'm very grateful to Seymour Weingarten, Editor-in-Chief of The Guilford Press, for his abiding faith in me and his confidence that this "long-awaited" book eventually would appear. I thank Kitty Moore and Mike Nichols for their thoughtful reading of my chapters as I struggled to integrate earlier family process research with my evolving conceptualization of family resilience. Thanks are also due to copyeditor Marie Sprayberry and production editor Anna Brackett. I'm most appreciative of Rochelle Serwator's sharp eye and wise editorial feedback; she helped enormously when I was striving for coherence and clarity.

I am also very grateful to the many clients, students, and colleagues who have enriched my work immeasurably over the years. It is a joy to teach and learn from such bright, talented, and curious students at the University of Chicago and our affiliated family therapy training institute, the Chicago Center for Family Health. Faculty collegiality has been a valued source of nourishment. The Center's 1996 Conference on Family Resilience sparked all of us to push the boundaries of our clinical work through our conversations and collaboration. Rich connections with friends and colleagues near and far have been a wellspring of support in so many ways; I thank you all. I'd like to mention, in particular, those who read and shared reflections on parts of the book, including Michele Scheinkman, John Rolland, Josh Levy, Edie Heinemann, Celia Falicov, Monica McGoldrick, and Robert Jay Green. Thank you to all who cheered me on through difficult times, and to those who unwittingly spurred me on by asking, "Is it out yet?"

My family has been my greatest source of strength and encouragement. I thank my husband, John, for his steadfast love and my daughter, Claire, for her wonderful energy, her "can-do" spirit, and her ability to make me laugh at myself. Targa, our yellow lab was my constant companion at the computer and made sure that I took plenty of breaks for petting, walks, and snacks. Most of all I want to express my deepest appreciation to my parents. They gave me life—and so much more. I only wish that while they were still alive I had better understood and appreciated their courage to rise above the many adversities they faced in life. I carry their indomitable spirit in my heart.

C·O·N·T·E·N·T·S

P·A·R·T I

Overview

C·H·A·P·T·E·R   1

Foundations of a Family Resilience Approach

Come to the edge, life said.
They said: We are afraid.
Come to the edge, life said.
They came. It pushed them . . . and they flew.
                    —GUILLAUME APOLLINAIRE

We live in turbulent times, on the edge of uncertainty. Family life and the world around us have changed so dramatically in recent years that while we yearn for strong and enduring relationships, we are unsure how to shape and sustain them to weather the storms of life. Although some families are shattered by crisis or persistent stresses, what is remarkable is that others emerge strengthened and more resourceful. With widespread concern about family breakdown, we need more than ever to understand the processes that can foster family resilience—a relational hardiness. In order to support and strengthen couples and families, we need useful conceptual tools as much as techniques. This chapter lays the foundations for a family resilience approach to clinical intervention, prevention efforts, research, and family policy.

A family resilience approach aims to identify and fortify key interactional processes that enable families to withstand and rebound from disruptive life challenges. A resilience lens shifts perspective from viewing distressed families as damaged to seeing them as challenged, affirming their potential for repair and growth. This approach is based on the conviction that both individual and family strength can be forged through collaborative efforts to deal with sudden crisis or prolonged adversity.

Resilience has become an important concept in child development and mental health theory and research. However, the widely held view of resilience as residing within the individual, and the skewed focus on family dysfunction, have blinded investigators and clinicians to the resources that can be found and strengthened in distressed families. A family resilience framework fundamentally alters traditional deficit-based approaches to research and practice. Instead of focusing on how families have failed, we can direct our attention to how they can succeed. Rather than giving up on troubled families and salvaging individual survivors, we can draw out the best in families, building on key processes to encourage both individual and family growth.

This chapter begins by defining and clarifying the concept of resilience. It then surveys what has been learned from studies of resilient individuals, noting the crucial influence of relationships and social support. Next, a systemic view of resilience is advanced: Attention is shifted from individual traits to transactional processes that foster resilience over time. Finally, the concept of family resilience is presented, involving key processes that strengthen resilience in the family as a functional unit.

WHAT IS RESILIENCE?

Resilience can be defined as the capacity to rebound from adversity strengthened and more resourceful. It is an active process of endurance, self-righting, and growth in response to crisis and challenge. The ability to overcome the blows of outrageous fortune challenges our culture's conventional wisdom: that early or severe trauma can't be undone; that adversity always damages people sooner or later; and that children from troubled or "broken" families are doomed.

Resilience entails more than merely surviving, getting through, or escaping a harrowing ordeal. Survivors are not necessarily resilient; some become trapped in a position as victims, nursing their wounds and blocked from growth by anger and blame (Wolin & Wolin, 1993). In contrast, the qualities of resilience enable people to heal from painful wounds, take charge of their lives, and go on to live fully and love well.

In order to understand resilience, it is important to distinguish it from faulty notions of "invulnerability" and "self-sufficiency." As we will see, resilience is forged through openness to experiences and interdependence with others.

Human Vulnerability, Suffering, and Resilience

The American ethos of the rugged individual (Bellah, Madsen, Sullivan, Swidler, & Tipton, 1985), with its associated images of masculinity and strength, has led many to confuse invulnerability with resilience. The early use of the term "invulnerable child" contributed to an unfortunate image of survivors of destructive environments as impervious to stress because of their own inner fortitude or character armor (Anthony, 1987). These hardy children were likened to steel dolls—so constitutionally sound that, unlike glass or plastic dolls, they could withstand even the most severe adversity.

The danger inherent in the myth of invulnerability and the image of "superkids" is of equating human vulnerability with weakness and invulnerability with strength. As Felsman and Vaillant (1987) note, "The term 'invulnerability' is antithetical to the human condition. . . . In bearing witness to the resilient behavior of high-risk children everywhere, a truer effort would be to understand, in form and by degree, the shared human qualities at work" (p. 304). In advancing an understanding of personal or family resilience, we must be cautious not to blame those who succumb to adversity for lacking "the right stuff," especially when they are struggling with overwhelming conditions beyond their control.

Similarly, the capacity to rebound should not be misconstrued as simply "breezing through" a crisis unscathed by painful experience, as if fortified with a Teflon ego, troubles bouncing off without causing pain or suffering (Schwartz, 1997). With only two alternatives posed—either to shake off adversity or to "wallow" in it—too many Americans boldly "cut their losses" or declare, "I'm outta here!" Our culture breeds intolerance for personal suffering; we avert our gaze from disability, avoid contact with the bereaved, or dispense chirpy advice to "cheer up" and get over catastrophic events. Well-intentioned loved ones encourage people to move right on from personal life crises and to leap into new relationships on the rebound from failed ones. Likewise, we are urged simply to put national crises and past atrocities behind us—whether Watergate, Vietnam, or slavery—without looking back to draw meaning from them, come to terms with them, and heal as a society. This tendency to cut off from highly stressful and conflict-laden experiences is rooted in our immigrant and pioneer heritage. In order to forge a new life in a strange land, it was more adaptive for our ancestors to focus on meeting new challenges (with a curious blend of stoicism and cheerful optimism) than to dwell on the loss of loved ones and communities left behind, or on the horrific conditions they fled as refugees.

This cultural ethos influences us all. At the time of my mother's terminal illness, I was in the midst of a student clinical internship at Yale; I shuttled back and forth across the country to spend a few days at a time with my parents and still not miss a beat in my demanding schedule. The day after my mother's funeral, I flew right back and hit the ground running. I was praised by all for being so "resilient." It was only much later that the full meaning of her loss struck me to the core and I began to come to terms with it.

Unlike the image of the Energizer bunny, or the Timex watch that "takes a licking and keeps on ticking" (Schwartz, 1997), resilience involves "struggling well": experiencing both suffering and courage, effectively working through difficulties both internally and interpersonally (Higgins, 1994). In building resilience, we strive to integrate the fullness of a crisis experience into the fabric of our individual and collective identity, influencing how we go on to live our lives.

From Rugged Individualism to an Interactional View

Reflecting Western culture's heroic myth of the rugged individual, most interest in resilience has focused on the strengths found within *individuals* who have mastered adversity. These qualities have usually been viewed in terms of personality traits and coping styles that enable a child or adult to overcome harrowing life experiences. Resilience is commonly seen as inborn, as if resilient persons grew themselves up: They either had the "right stuff" all along—a biological hardiness—or acquired it by pulling themselves up by their bootstraps. This view fosters the expectation that they must become self-reliant and survive through fierce independence. The unfortunate corollary to this ethos is a contemptuous view of those who don't succeed as deficient, weak, and blameworthy when they can't surmount their problems on their own.

As will be shown, individual resilience is increasingly seen as an interaction between nature and nurture, encouraged by supportive relationships. However, few researchers have considered the family as a potential source of resilience—that is, as a resource. There are two reasons for this neglect. First, the traditional clinical perspective on family influences has been deficit-based (Walsh, 1993). Second, most studies of resilience have focused on children of a seriously disturbed or abusive parent; dismissing such a child's entire family as dysfunctional, researchers have looked for sources of individual resilience *outside* the family, in surrogate relationships—as with a teacher, coach, minister, or therapist—that counterbalance presumably destructive family influences.

Hardiness Forged through Adversity

I grew up with a view of myself as resilient. But I thought of myself as strong *in spite of* my family's deficiencies and the adversities we suffered; it was only in more recent years that I came to realize that my strength emerged *because* of those experiences. As researchers have discovered, resilience is forged through adversity, not despite it. Life crises and hardship can bring out the best in us as we rise to the challenges. As Albert Camus wrote, "In the midst of winter I finally learned that there was in me an invincible summer."

Higgins's (1994) study of resilient adults found that they became more substantial because they were sorely tested, endured suffering, and emerged with strengths they might not have developed otherwise. They experienced things more deeply and intensely, and placed a heightened value on life. Often this became a wellspring for social activism, a commitment to helping others overcome their adversities; in turn, they experienced further growth through these efforts. Of note, half of the resilient individuals studied by Higgins were therapists!

Crisis: Danger and Opportunity

The Chinese symbol for the word "crisis" is a composite of two pictographs: the symbols for "danger" and "opportunity." Although we would not wish for misfortune, the paradox of resilience is that our worst times can also become our best (Wolin & Wolin, 1993). In my experience, many families who have lost a loved one find that the most dreaded and painful end-of-life contacts were their most precious times together. Studies of strong families by Stinnett and his colleagues (Stinnett & DeFrain, 1985; Stinnett, Knorr, DeFrain, & Rowe, 1981) found that at times of crisis, 75% experienced positive occurrences in the midst of hurt and despair, and believed that something good came out of the ordeal. Many families reported that through their weathering crises together, their relationships became enriched and more loving than they might otherwise have been. A crisis can be a "wake-up call," heightening our attention to what really matters in our lives. A painful loss may thrust us in new and unforeseen directions. As the Navaho say, the end of a path is the beginning of another.

STUDIES OF RESILIENT INDIVIDUALS

In order to understand and foster family resilience, we can learn a great deal from studies of resilient individuals conducted over the past two decades. These efforts have countered the predominant view that family and environmental risk factors and negative life events inevitably produce childhood and later adult disorders. As Rutter (1985) noted, no combination of risk factors, regardless of severity, gave rise to significant disorder in more than half of the children exposed. Studies have documented, for instance, that most survivors of childhood abuse do *not* go on to abuse their own children (Kaufman & Zigler, 1987). What accounts for this resilience?

With concern for early intervention and prevention, a number of child development and mental health experts redirected attention in the 1970s and

1980s toward understanding vulnerability or susceptibility to risk and disorder (Garmezy, 1974; Murphy & Moriarty, 1976), as well as the protective factors that fortify the resources of children and encourage their resilience (Dugan & Coles, 1989; Luthar & Zigler, 1991; Masten, Best, & Garmezy, 1990; Rutter, 1985, 1987; Simeonsson, 1995). Most of these inquiries sought to understand how some children of mentally ill parents or dysfunctional families are able to overcome early experiences of abuse or neglect to lead productive lives (Anthony, 1987; Cohler, 1987; Garmezy, 1987). Wolin and Wolin (1993) described a cluster of qualities in healthy adults who showed individual resilience despite growing up in dysfunctional, and often abusive, alcoholic families.

A few studies broadened their focus to include the wider social context, examining individual risk and resilience in the face of devastating social conditions, particularly poverty (Garmezy, 1991) and community violence (Garbarino, 1997). Felsman and Vaillant (1987) followed the lives of 75 high-risk, inner-city males who grew up in poverty-stricken, socially disadvantaged families. Family life was often complicated by substance abuse, mental illness, crime, and violence. Many of these men, although indelibly marked by their past experience, showed courageous lives of mastery and competence. These men took an active initiative in shaping their lives, despite occasional setbacks and the multiple factors working against them. As Felsman and Vaillant concluded, their resilience demonstrated that "the events that go wrong in our lives do not forever damn us" (1987, p. 298). In cross-cultural studies with settings ranging from Brazilian shantytowns and South African migrant camps to U.S. inner cities, Robert Coles (Dugan & Coles, 1989) also found that, contrary to the dire predictions of his mental health colleagues, many children did rise above severe hardship without later "time bomb" effects.

The similar concept of *hardiness* grew out of another line of research on stress and coping (Murphy & Moriarty, 1976). Examining the influence of stressful life events in a range of mental and physical illnesses, a number of investigators sought to identify personality traits that mediate physiological processes and enable some highly stressed individuals to cope adaptively and remain healthy (Antonovsky, 1979; Dohrenwend & Dohrenwend, 1981; Holmes & Masuda, 1974; Lazarus & Folkman, 1984). Building on earlier theories of competence, Kobasa and her colleagues (Kobasa, 1985; Kobasa, Maddi, & Kahn, 1982) proposed that persons who experience high degrees of stress without becoming ill have a personality structure characterized by hardiness.

Grinker and Spiegel's (1945) pioneering study of men under stress in war launched still another line of research—that on the impact of catastrophic events involving trauma and loss (e.g., Figley, 1989; Herman, 1992; Wortman & Silver, 1989). This research, too, has revealed variability in response and in the capacity of individuals to recover and move on with their lives. In *Against All Odds*, Helmreich (1992) offers remarkable accounts of resilience in the lives forged by many survivors of the Nazi Holocaust. Such accounts attest to the human potential to emerge from a shattering experience scarred yet strengthened.

In one of the most ambitious studies of resilience, Werner and Smith (1982, 1992; Werner, 1993) spent 40 years following the lives of nearly 700 children reared in hardship on the island of Kauai. The children were mostly born to poor, unskilled sugar plantation workers of Japanese, Filipino, Hawaiian, Portuguese, Polynesian, and mixed racial descent. One-third (210 children) were classified as "at risk" because of exposure before age 2 to at least four additional risk factors, such as serious health problems, and familial alcoholism, violence, divorce, or mental illness. By age 18, about two-thirds of the at-risk children had done as poorly as predicted, with early pregnancy, needs for mental health services, or trouble in school or with the law. However, one-third of those at risk had developed into competent, caring, and confident young adults who were "fine human beings," with the capacity "to work well, play well, and love well," as rated on a variety of measures. In a later follow-up at age 40, all but two of these individuals were still living successful lives. Many of them had outperformed Kauai children from less harsh backgrounds: More were stably married and fewer were divorced, unemployed, or traumatized by Hurricane Iniki, which destroyed much of the island in 1992.

Individual Traits

Most resilience research has focused on individual traits and disposition. Several studies have found such traits as an easygoing temperament and a higher intelligence to be helpful, although not essential, in building resilience. Such qualities tend to elicit more positive responses from others and to facilitate coping strategies and problem-solving skills. More significant is a high level of self-esteem, characterized by a realistic sense of hope and personal control. Rutter (1985) noted that strong self-esteem and self-efficacy make successful coping more likely, whereas a sense of helplessness increases the probability that one adversity will lead to another. Similarly, Kobasa and colleagues found evidence supporting their hypothesis that persons with hardy personalities possess three general characteristics: (1) the belief that they can control or influence events in their experience; (2) an ability to feel deeply involved in or committed to the activities in their lives; and (3) anticipation of change as an exciting challenge to further development (Kobasa, 1985). In his cross-cultural observations, Coles noted the power of moral and spiritual sources of courage as a life-sustaining force of conviction that lifts individuals above hardship (Dugan & Coles, 1989). Werner (1993) similarly noted that the core component in effective coping is a feeling of confidence that the odds can be surmounted. Even with chaos in their own households, by their high school years the resilient children in the Kauai study had developed a sense of coherence, a faith that obstacles could be overcome, and a belief that they were in control of their fate. They were significantly more likely than nonresilient children to have an inner locus of control—an optimistic confidence in their ability to shape events. They developed both competence and hope of a better life through their own efforts and relationships.

Murphy (1987) also described the "optimistic bias" of resilient children. She observed that many latch on to "any excuse for hope and faith in recovery" (pp. 103–104), actively mobilizing all thoughts and resources that could contribute to their recovery. Based on extensive epidemiological research, Taylor (1989) found that people who hold "positive illusions"—selectively positive biases about such situations as life-threatening illness—tend to do better than those who have a hard grasp of reality. Such beliefs allow them to retain hope in the face of a grim situation. The healing power of positive emotions through humor and laughter was documented in Norman Cousins's (1979, 1989) account of how he survived a deadly collagen disease.

Seligman's (1990) concept of "learned optimism" has a strong bearing on resilience. His earlier work on "learned helplessness" demonstrated how people can be conditioned to become passive and give up on trying to solve problems, particularly when rewards and punishments are not predictably linked to their behavior. Seligman has proposed that if helplessness can be learned, then it can be unlearned through experiences of mastery, in which people come to believe that their efforts and actions can yield success.

The Relational Context of Individual Resilience

Increasingly, researchers have linked the emergence of resilience in vulnerable children to key protective influences in the family and social context. Children's resilience to hardship is greater when they have access to at least one caring parent, a caregiver, or another supportive adult in their extended family or social world. Even the emergence of genetically influenced individual traits occurs in relational context. As Werner (1993) has emphasized, self-esteem and self-efficacy are promoted, above all else, through supportive relationships. All of the resilient children in the Kauai study had "at least one person in their lives who accepted them unconditionally, regardless of temperamental idiosyncrasies, physical attractiveness, or intelligence" (p. 512). They needed to know that there was someone to whom they could turn, and, at the same time, needed to have their own efforts, sense of competence, and self-worth nurtured and reinforced. Encouraged by their connections with a mentor, many also developed a special hobby or skill (e.g., carpentry, art, or creative writing), which enhanced their competence, confidence, and mastery.

Only a few early studies of individual resilience looked for positive family contributions (Hauser, Vierya, Jacobson, & Wertlieb, 1985; Patterson, 1983; Rutter, 1985; Werner & Smith, 1992). Investigators who have focused on the family emotional climate note the importance of warmth, affection, emotional support, and clear-cut, reasonable structure and limits. They emphasize that if parents are unable to provide this climate, relationships with other family members, such as older siblings, grandparents, and extended kin, can serve this function. Moreover, adaptation to crisis events is influenced by the meaning of the experience, which is socially constructed. Kagan (1984), for instance, found that the effect of an emotionally significant occurrence, such as a father's prolonged absence or a bitter divorce, depends largely on how a child interprets these events, which is mediated by parental transmission of their own perceptions and understanding of what is happening.

Support for individual resilience is also provided by friends, neighbors, teachers, coaches, clergy, or other mentors (Brooks, 1994; Rutter, 1987; Werner, 1993). Resilient children in troubled families often actively recruit and form special attachments with influential adults in their social environment. They learn to choose relationships wisely and tend to select spouses from healthy families. The importance of social support in times of crisis has been amply documented (Pearlin & Schooler, 1978). Although these relationships may sometimes be a source of strain, they can also be a wellspring for positive coping resources (Rutter, 1987).

A SYSTEMIC VIEW OF RESILIENCE

From a Dyadic to a Systemic View

Taken together, the research on resilient individuals has increasingly pointed toward the importance of a systemic view. Worldwide studies of children of misfortune have found the most significant positive influence to be a close, caring relationship with a significant adult who believed in them and with whom they could identify, who acted as an advocate for them, and from whom they could gather strength to overcome their hardships (Werner, 1993). Yet most resilience theory and research have approached the relational context of resilience narrowly, in terms of the influence of a single significant person in a dyadic relationship with an at-risk child (Bowlby, 1988). For a full understanding of resilience, a complex interactional model is required. Systems theory expands our view of individual adaptation as embedded in broader transactional processes in family and social systems, and attends to the mutuality of influences through transactional processes.

If we broaden our perspective beyond a dyadic bond and early life determinants, we become aware that resilience is woven in a web of relationships and experiences over the course of the life cycle and across the generations. Both ecological and developmental perspectives are necessary to understand resilience in social context and over time.

Ecological Perspective

An ecological perspective takes into account the many spheres of influence in risk and resilience across the life span. The family, peer group, school or work settings, and larger social systems can be seen as nested contexts for social competence (Bronfenbrenner, 1979).

Rutter (1987) also emphasizes that to understand and foster resilience and protective mechanisms, we must attend to the interplay between occurrences within families and the political, economic, social, and racial climates in which individuals and their families perish or thrive. We must be cautious that the concept of resilience is not used in public policy to withhold social supports or maintain inequities, based on the rationale that success or failure is determined by strengths or deficits within individuals and their families. It is not enough to bolster the resilience of at-risk children and families so that they can "beat the odds"; we must also strive to change the odds against them.

Developmental Perspective

A developmental perspective is also essential in understanding resilience. Rather than a set of fixed traits, coping and adaptation involve multidetermined processes extending over time. Most forms of stress are not simply a short-term, single stimulus, but a complex set of changing conditions with a past history and a future course (Rutter, 1987). Given this complexity over time, no single coping response is invariably most successful. It is more important to have a variety of coping strategies to meet different challenges as they emerge (Pearlin & Schooler, 1978). The ability to choose viable options is crucial in resilience.

Researchers have explored coping and adaptation under such diverse stress conditions as chronic illness, developmental transitions and role strain, death of a loved one, divorce, economic deprivation, maltreatment and neglect, war and genocide, and community disasters. Stressful life events are more likely to affect functioning adversely when they are unexpected, when a condition is severe or persistent, or when multiple stressors generate cumulative effects. Events that occur "off-time," or out of sync with chronological or social expectations—such as early widowhood—are also more difficult (Neugarten, 1976).

A life cycle perspective on individual and family development is also necessary for an understanding of resilience. Although adaptive functioning in childhood and adolescence serves as a generally good predictor of adult outcomes, the role of early life experience in determining adult capacity to overcome adversity may be less important than was previously assumed (Cohler, 1987; Vaillant, 1995). Longitudinal studies following individuals through adulthood find that resilience cannot be assessed once and for all on the basis of a quick snapshot of early interactions. If we emphasize continuity and limited short-term perspectives, we may fail to appreciate that people are developing organisms whose life course trajectories are flexible and multidetermined (Falicov, 1988). Moreover, an adaptation that serves well at one point in development may later not be useful in meeting other challenges. Gender differences are also found in vulnerability at different developmental stages, with greater risk for boys in childhood and for girls in adolescence (Elder, Caspi, & Nguyen, 1985; Werner & Smith, 1982). Such variables underscore the dynamic nature of resilience over time.

Werner and Smith's (1982, 1992) longitudinal study of the at-risk Kauai children provides rich evidence for a complex interactional view of resilience. These investigators broke new ground by looking at multiple internal and external protective factors—sources of resilience—in these lives over time. Their findings revealed that earlier researchers focused too narrowly on maternal influence and the damage of one parent in the nuclear household, and missed the importance of siblings and others in the extended family network. The role of a wide variety of supportive relationships was found to be crucial at every age. Most got off to a good start through early bonding with at least one caregiver, although this was not necessarily the mother; it was often a grandmother, older sister, aunt, or other relative who provided the care.

Yet even a bad start did not determine a bad outcome. Many children overcame early neglect, abandonment, and developmental delays and began to blossom when they benefited from later nurturing care, through adoption or mentoring (e.g., special relationships with teachers). Throughout their school years, the resilient children actively recruited support networks in their extended families and communities. Interestingly, more girls than boys overcame adversity at all age levels. We might postulate the influence of gender-based socialization in seeking out and sustaining supportive relationships: Girls are raised to be both more easygoing and more relationally oriented, whereas boys are taught to be tough and self-reliant through life. Moreover, often *because* of troubled family lives, competencies were built when early responsibilities were assumed for household tasks and care of younger siblings.

Werner and Smith found that nothing is "cast in stone" because of early life experiences. A few individuals identified as resilient at 18 had developed significant problems by age 30. However, the most important finding was that resilience could be developed at any point over the course of the life cycle. Unexpected events and new relationships can disrupt a negative chain and catalyze new growth. Of the two-thirds of at-risk children who were troubled and not resilient as adolescents, fully *one-half* had righted themselves by age 30: Delinquent acts had not led to lives of crime, and many had stable marriages and decent jobs. In these cases, too, most reported that some adult had taken an interest in them when they drifted into trouble. They also credited a major turning point: a good marriage, satisfying work, service in the armed forces, or involvement in a highly structured religious group (Butler, 1997).

Werner and Smith's conclusions are supported by a handful of studies of at-risk children elsewhere (Masten et al., 1990; Wyman, Cowen, Work, & Parker, 1991), pointing to the beneficial effects of the web of relationships formed by extended family, friends, and neighbors. Over the years, positive interactions between persons and their environments have a constant, mutually reinforcing effect, in positive life trajectories or upward spirals. With multiple pathways in resilience, a downward spiral can be turned around at any time in life.

FAMILY RESILIENCE

The term "family resilience" refers to coping and adaptational processes in the family *as a functional unit*. A systems perspective enables us to understand how family processes mediate stress and enable families to surmount crisis and weather prolonged hardship. Patterson (1983) contends that stressors affect children only to the extent that they disrupt crucial family processes. It is not just the child who is vulnerable or resilient; more importantly, the family system influences eventual adjustment. Even individuals who are not directly touched by a crisis are affected by the family response, with reverberations for all other relationships (Bowen, 1978). How a family confronts and manages a disruptive experience, buffers stress, effectively reorganizes itself, and moves forward with life will influence immediate and long-term adaptation for every family member *and* for the very survival and well-being of the family unit.

From Family Damage to Family Challenge

In the field of mental health, most clinical theory, training, practice, and research have been overwhelmingly deficit-focused, implicating the family in the cause or maintenance of nearly all problems in individual functioning. Under early psychoanalytic assumptions of destructive maternal bonds, the family came to be seen as a noxious influence. Even the early family systems formulations focused on dysfunctional family processes well into the mid-1980s (Walsh, 1993). More recently, popular movements for so-called "survivors" or "adult children of dysfunctional families" have spared almost no family from accusations of failure and blame—as described in Kaminer's (1992) spot-on analysis, *I'm Dysfunctional, You're Dysfunctional*. With the clinical field so steeped in pathology, the intense scrutiny of family deficits and blindness to family strengths led me to suggest, only half-jokingly, that a "normal" family could be defined as one that has not yet been clinically assessed (Walsh, 1993).

Beyond the Myths of the "Normal" Family

Views of normality and health are socially constructed, influencing clinical assessment and goals for healthy family functioning (Walsh, 1993). The vision of a so-called "normal" family is largely in the eye of the beholder, filtered by professional values, personal family experience, and cultural standards. Two myths of the "normal" family have perpetuated a grim view of most families.

One myth is the belief that healthy families are problem-free. Based in the medical model, health has been defined clinically as the absence of problems. Unfortunately, this leaves us in the dark about *positive* contributions to healthy functioning. More seriously, it leads to the faulty assumption that any problem is symptomatic of and caused by a dysfunctional family. This belief has tended to pathologize ordinary families attempting to cope with the stresses and disruptive changes that are part of life (Minuchin, 1974). No family is problem-free. Slings and arrows of misfortune strike us all, in varying ways and times over each family's life course. What distinguishes healthy families is not the absence of problems, but rather their coping and problem-solving abilities.

A second myth is the belief that the idealized "traditional family" is the only possible model for a healthy family. For most, this conjures up the 1950s image of a white, affluent, nuclear family headed by a breadwinner/father and supported by a full-time homemaker/mother. Early theory and research in the social sciences and psychiatry, seeking to define the "normal" family in terms of a universal set of traits or a singular family form, reified this model of the intact nuclear family with traditional gender roles as essential for healthy child development (Parsons & Bales, 1955). In the wake of massive social and economic upheaval over recent decades, nostalgic images of a simpler past are understandable but are out of touch with the diversity of family structures, values, and challenges of our changing world, as we will see in Chapter 2. Yet families that don't conform to the "one-norm-fits-all" standard have been stigmatized and pathologized by assumptions that alternative forms inherently damage children. Families of varied configurations can be successful. It is not family *form*, but rather family *processes*, that matter most for healthy functioning and resilience.

Strengths in Families Challenged by Adversity

The skewed perspective on family dysfunction that long dominated the clinical field has begun to be rebalanced in recent years, as systems-based family therapists and researchers have shifted focus to a competence-based, strength-oriented paradigm (Barnard, 1994; Walsh, 1993, 1995a). A family resilience approach builds on these developments, enabling us to shift from seeing families as damaged to understanding how they are challenged by adversity. It also corrects the faulty assumption that family health can only be found in a mythologized ideal model. Instead, this approach seeks to understand how all families, in their diversity, can survive and regenerate even with overwhelming stress. It affirms the family potential for self-repair and growth out of crisis and challenge.

My interest in family resilience was sparked in my early research experience with families of psychiatrically hospitalized and normal young adults (Walsh, 1978, 1987b). The vitality and diversity I observed in families in the normal control group countered the image of normal families as dull and monotone. Most impressive, a number of parents had suffered serious childhood trauma and yet had grown up able to form and sustain healthy families and to raise their children well to adulthood. Along with other emerging research, these cases cast doubt on traditional clinical assumptions that those who have suffered childhood trauma are wounded for life. Particularly striking were the strengths shown by one normal control family, Marcy and Tom and their five children, whose individual and family resilience was interwoven across the generations:

> Marcy, one of three children in her family of origin, told of her father's serious drinking problem, repeated job losses, and family abandonment when she was 7. Despite financial hardship and the social stigma of a

"broken home," she emerged quite healthy. She attributed her own resilience to the strong family unit her mother forged, her close sibling bonds, and the support of her extended family.

Based on her childhood experience, Marcy had developed deep convictions about marriage and raising a healthy family. When she was asked what had attracted her to Tom, her reply was crystal-clear: "First, I knew I wanted a husband who didn't drink. Second, I wanted my children to have a father who would always be there for them." She consciously sought out and married into the kind of family that she wanted to have. She chose wisely: Tom was the son of a minister, one of six children from a solid, stable family. For his part, he was drawn to her "can do" spirit and admired her family's ability to weather hardship. Together, as they raised their children, they kept close contact and connection with both extended families, which, in different ways, offered strong parenting models and supportive kin networks.

Marcy demonstrated many qualities that other researchers have found to be characteristic of resilient individuals, such as her success in overcoming early life trauma, an ability to learn from traumatic experience to make conscious positive choices, and a determined effort to build a strong marriage and family life. Most striking to me was the central role of her family system in fostering her resilience after her parents' divorce. Her family's ability to handle crises and persistent challenges over time enabled her to survive and thrive. Moreover, strong sibling bonds through shared adversity provided a lasting mutual resource. As a couple and parental team, Marcy and Tom built a well-functioning family unit, raised their five children successfully, and continued to value and maintain vital extended family connections.

My research experience with healthy families fundamentally altered the direction of my research and clinical work, shifting my attention from family deficits toward understanding and promoting the family processes that foster health and growth over the life course and across the generations.

Contributions of Family Process Research

Identifying Core Elements in Healthy Family Functioning

Over the past two decades, a growing body of systems-based research has advanced our knowledge of the multidimensional processes that distinguish well-functioning from dysfunctional families (Walsh, 1993; Beavers & Hampson, 1990, 1993; Epstein, Bishop, Ryan, Miller, & Keitner, 1993; Moos &

Moos, 1976; Olson, 1993; Olson, Russell, & Sprenkle, 1989; Schumm, 1985; Skinner, Santa Barbara, & Steinhauer, 1983). The family resilience framework presented in this volume draws on the findings of this research to distill core components of effective family functioning, which can usefully inform our efforts to strengthen families in distress (Walsh, 1987a).

At the same time, the growing diversity of families and the complexity of contemporary life call for caution in generalizing from normative samples that represent only a narrow band on the wide spectrum of families. Most family process studies have been standardized on white, middle-class, Protestant, intact families that are not under stress. We must be careful not to pathologize families that differ in their cultural values, those that show common reactions to severe stress, or those that have developed their own creative strategies to fit their particular situation (Walsh, 1993). For instance, very high cohesion is too readily labeled as dysfunctional enmeshment; however, togetherness may be highly valued in a family's culture, or needed when family members must pull together to weather a serious crisis. The processes useful for effective functioning may vary, depending on differing sociocultural contexts and life challenges.

Resonant with a family resilience perspective, Falicov's (1995) multidimensional ecological view recognizes that families combine and overlap features of many cultural contexts based on the unique configurations of variables in their lives, such as ethnicity, social class, religion, family structure, gender roles, sexual orientation, and life stage. Conflict and change are as much a part of family life as are tradition and continuity. For example, the challenges posed by the process of migration involve profound ecological disruption and inevitable uprooting of meanings. We must be careful not to pathologize transitional distress or prolonged strains of adaptation, or to judge families by a single normative standard for family health.

To do justice to these complexities, we must assess family functioning with respect for each family's situation. The concept of family resilience offers a flexible view that can encompass many variables—both similarities and differences, and both continuity and change over time. This volume attempts to strike a balance that allows us to identify core elements in effective family functioning (see Chapters 3–5), while also taking into account the particular strengths called forth to meet varied challenges (see Chapters 7–9). In accord with Falicov's approach to culture, a resilience-based stance views each family in its complex "ecological niche": Each shares some borders and common ground with other families, as well as differences. A holistic assessment includes all of the contexts the family inhabits, aiming to understand the challenges, constraints, and resources in its position.

The Importance of a Family Developmental Perspective

An understanding of family resilience must also incorporate a developmental perspective, since varied processes are needed to meet emerging psychosocial challenges over time. We can usefully draw upon the models of vulnerability and protective mechanisms proposed by Garmezy and Rutter to explain individual resilience, as well as a growing body of research on family stress, coping, and adaptation (Boss, 1987; Cowan, Cowan, & Schulz, 1996; Hawley & DeHaan, 1996; Lavee, McCubbin, & Olson, 1987; Rapaport, 1962).

Models of Vulnerability and Protective Mechanisms. Garmezy (1987) has advocated longitudinal developmental research on high-risk groups to clarify the biological and psychosocial mechanisms in adaptiveness under stress. At each developmental stage, there is a shifting balance between stressful events that heighten vulnerability and protective mechanisms that enhance resilience. Three mechanisms have been proposed through which protective processes may mediate the relationship between stress and competence.

In the *immunity model*, protective factors are thought to serve as reserves against a decline in functioning under stress. The notion of "inoculation" has been expressed often in the resilience literature to describe preventive psychosocial interventions that boost hardiness and resistance to potentially harmful effects of stressful experiences. For instance, Seligman (1995) has proposed that through a process of "immunization," positive learning experiences that our responses matter for success can prevent learned helplessness throughout life (see Chapter 3 for a fuller discussion). Jonas Salk, who discovered the first polio vaccine, once remarked to Seligman that if he had his lifework to do over again, he would still devote it to the immunization of children—but he would do so psychosocially.

In the *compensatory model,* personal attributes and environmental resources are thought to counteract the negative effects of stressors. For instance, with aging, the decline in some aspects of mental functioning (e.g., recent memory) can be offset by the gains in wisdom and perspective accrued through life experience. In the *challenge model*, stressors can become potential enhancers of competence, provided that the level of stress is not too high. A crisis can challenge us to sharpen our skills and develop new assets. These three mechanisms may operate simultaneously or successively in the adaptive repertoire of resilient persons, depending on their coping styles and stages of development (Werner, 1993).

We can apply these protective mechanisms to the family system. Ongoing family processes can boost immunity to stress, preventing or reducing harmful impact. Family processes can be rallied as resources to compensate for negative stress effects. Family processes can even be strengthened through shared coping efforts. Let's consider the crisis situation when a mother is hospitalized with a serious illness. If ongoing family interaction is generally strong in communication and problem-solving skills, these processes can serve as psychosocial inoculation to bolster immunity to the negative stress effects (reducing its impact from severe to moderate or mild) and to sustain competence during the crisis period. To compensate for the mother's lost role functioning, the family may reorganize its daily routines and reallocate responsibilities to ensure that the children's needs are met, with the father flexibly altering his work schedule, older children helping out more, and extended family members pitching in. As they rally together to meet this challenge, family members' bonds are strengthened, and individuals may develop new areas of competence. For instance, the father's previously untapped potential to nurture his children may be developed as he is thrust into new responsibilities.

This transactional perspective and the contextual nature of resilience fit well with Michael Rutter's (1987) model of risk and protection, which emphasizes resilience processes and intervention possibilities (see Chapter 6). Resilience is fostered in family interactions through a chain of indirect influences that ameliorate the direct effects of a stressful event. Strains can be compounded by ineffective family coping efforts and heighten the risk for further complications. Positive coping strategies can reduce stress and restore well-being.

Family Stress, Coping, and Adaptation. Similarly, McCubbin and Patterson (1983) developed a family crisis framework, grounded in Hill's (1949) pioneering work on family coping in wartime. They examined family vulnerability and regenerative power to understand how some families are able to withstand stress and recover from crisis when others are not. They have emphasized the importance of "fit" and "balance" to the development of both the family unit and its individual members. Families need to achieve a functional fit between their challenges and resources and between different dimensions of family life. A fit at one system level may precipitate strains elsewhere, as in dual-earner families when efforts to manage job and child-rearing demands deplete the energy available for couple intimacy. With many adaptational paths possible, family members need to weigh and balance costs and benefits in their options. Research using family resilience as a major variable is just beginning to emerge (McCubbin, McCubbin, McCubbin, & Futrell, 1995; McCubbin, McCubbin, Thompson, & Fromer, 1995; National Network for Family Resiliency, 1996).

Family Resilience as Interactive Processes over Time. Family resilience cannot be captured in a snapshot at a single moment in time. More than immediate crisis response or adjustment, resilience involves many interactive processes over time—from a family's approach to a threatening situation, through its ability to manage disruptive transitions, to varied strategies for coping with emerging stresses in the immediate and long-term aftermath. Adaptation to divorce, for example, begins in the predivorce climate and the decision to separate; moves through legal complexities, emotional bereavement, and reorganization (of households, finances, parenting roles, and custodial arrangements). Later it involves further reconfigurations for most, with remarriage and stepfamily formation (Walsh, 1991; Walsh, Jacob, & Simons, 1995). Deterministic views that divorce inevitably has damaging effects on children (Wallerstein & Blakeslee, 1989) fail to take such process variables into account and overlook the wide variability in adaptation over time (Ahrons & Rogers, 1989; Furstenberg & Cherlin, 1991; Hetherington, 1989). The postdivorce functioning and well-being of family members, especially children, are influenced not simply by the "event" of divorce, but even more by the myriad family processes involved in dealing with the many unfolding stressful challenges and in making meaning of the experience.

Shared beliefs shape and reinforce interactional patterns governing how a family approaches and responds to a new situation (Reiss, 1981). A critical event or disruptive transition can catalyze a major shift in a family belief system, with reverberations for both immediate reorganization and long-term adaptation (Hadley, Jacob, Miliones, Caplan, & Spitz, 1974). Moreover, a family's perceptions of a stressful situation intersect with legacies of previous experience in the multigenerational system to influence the meaning the family makes of a challenge and its response (Carter & McGoldrick, 1998).

A cluster of two or more concurrent stresses complicates adaptation as family members struggle with competing demands, and emotions can easily spill over into conflict (Walsh, 1983). One family was able to cope with the challenges of their small child's severe developmental disabilities until the father's job loss and accompanying loss of medical benefits multiplied the stress. Over time, a pileup of stressors, losses, and dislocations can overwhelm a family's coping efforts, contributing to family strife, substance abuse, and emotional or behavioral symptoms of distress (often expressed by children in the family).

Psychosocial challenges of stress events vary with their circumstances, timing, and meaning. Catastrophic events that occur suddenly and without warning can be especially traumatic (Figley, 1989), such as the destruction of a whole community by a natural disaster (Erikson, 1976). Reverberations, like a shock wave, can extend throughout family networks and communities.

In their wake, some families are devastated while others are able to pull to-gether, right themselves, and move on. Recurrent stressors, such as family or community violence, may well strike again at any time, fueling anticipa-tory anxiety. The sudden, unpredictable, life-threatening nature of such events is especially unsettling. Posttraumatic complications are common.

A persistent challenge may require "hanging in" for the long haul; it poses very different demands from those of a sudden crisis, when families must mobilize quickly but can then return to regular daily life. Some families face episodic stress alternating with periods of calm, as in the case of migrant workers: Because temporary employment and repeated job layoffs are facts of life for them, such families must repeatedly switch gears and get by as best they can. Prolonged challenges face families when a member's permanent disability irrevocably alters lives. In most cases, psychosocial demands on the family change over time, with subsequent phases in the adaptation process, as in the variable course of a serious illness; at each transition, the family must readjust and recalibrate (Rolland, 1994). Therapeutic responses must be at-tuned to these varied and changing demands and tap into family resources to meet them. When a crisis looms, and in its immediate and long-term after-math, a systemic approach to intervention strengthens key interactional pro-cesses that foster healing, recovery, and resilience, enabling the family and its members to integrate the experience and move on with life.

Future Research Priorities

A redirection of research focus and funding priorities is needed, from stud-ies of dysfunctional families and what makes families fail, to studies of well-functioning families and what enables them to succeed, particularly in the face of adversity. As an analogy, after a devastating earthquake, we need to examine not only the buildings that crumbled; more importantly, we need to examine those structures that withstood the crisis and aftershocks, in order to identify the essential elements and construct more resilient structures. Rather than proposing a blueprint for any singular model of "the resilient family," our search for family resilience should identify key processes that can strengthen each family's ability to overcome the challenges they face in their particular life situations.

A FAMILY RESILIENCE APPROACH: LOOKING AHEAD

A family resilience framework can serve as a valuable conceptual map in orienting a wide range of human services. A systemic view of resilience is important in all efforts to help individuals, couples, and families to cope and adapt through crisis and adversity. The family has been a neglected resource in interventions aiming to foster resilience in children and adults. A narrow focus on individual resilience has led clinicians to attempt to salvage individual "survivors" without exploring their families' potential, and even to write off many families as hopeless. A clinical stance is called for that fosters a compassionate understanding of parental life challenges, encourages reconciliation, and searches for unrecognized strengths in the network of family relationships (see Chapter 10).

In the field of family therapy, we have come to realize that successful interventions depend as much on the resources of the family as on the skills of the therapist (Karpel, 1986; Minuchin, 1992). What we need even more than new techniques are strength-oriented conceptual tools that guide intervention. The concept of family resilience offers such tools, and is distinct in its focus on surmounting crisis and challenge. Symptoms are assessed in the context of past, ongoing, and threatened crisis events, their meanings, and family coping responses. Therapeutic efforts are attuned to each family's particular challenges and family resources are mobilized to meet them.

A resilience-based stance in family therapy is founded on a set of convictions about family potential that shapes all intervention, even with highly vulnerable families whose lives are saturated with crisis situations. Collaboration among family members is encouraged, enabling them to build new and renewed competence, mutual support, and shared confidence that they can prevail under duress. This approach fosters an empowering family climate, reinforcing the possibilities that members can overcome seemingly insurmountable obstacles by working together, and that they will experience success as largely due to their shared efforts, resources, and abilities. Experiences of shared success enhance a family's pride and sense of efficacy, enabling more effective coping with subsequent life adaptations. A family resilience approach provides a positive and pragmatic frame that guides interventions to strengthen the family as presenting problems are resolved. This approach goes beyond problem solving to problem prevention; it not only repairs families, but also prepares them to meet future challenges. A particular solution to a presenting problem may not be relevant to future problems, but the promotion of resilient *processes* can prepare families to surmount unforeseen problems and to avert crises. In these ways, every intervention is also a preventive measure.

The growing body of systems-based research on healthy family processes can serve as a useful basis for identifying strengths and vulnerabilities, informing interventions to build and reinforce core process elements in effective family functioning. Part II of this volume (Chapters 3–5) presents and integrates our knowledge and perspectives on these elements. I have found it useful to organize these findings into a conceptual framework comprising three domains: belief systems, organizational patterns, and communication processes. (Sluzki, 1983, mapped similar domains in his overview of systems-based practice.) In Chapters 3–5, key processes in family resilience are identified in each domain (see Table 1.1): These processes may be organized and expressed in different ways and to varying degrees as they fit diverse family forms, values, resources, and challenges.

To summarize, several basic principles grounded in systems theory serve as the foundations for a family resilience approach:

- Individual hardiness is best understood and fostered in the context of the family and larger social world, as a mutual interaction of individual, family, and environmental processes.
- Crisis events and persistent stresses affect the entire family and all its members, posing risks not only for individual dysfunction, but for relational conflict and family breakdown.
- Family processes mediate the impact of stress on all members and their relationships:
  - Protective processes foster resilience by buffering stress and promoting recovery.
  - Maladaptive responses heighten vulnerability and risks for individual and relationship distress.
- Family processes can influence the course of many crisis events.
- All families have the potential for resilience; we can maximize that potential by encouraging their best efforts and strengthening key processes.

TABLE 1.1. Keys to Family Resilience

Family belief systems
- Making meaning of adversity
- Positive outlook
- Transcendence and spirituality

Organizational patterns
- Flexibility
- Connectedness
- Social and economic resources

Communication processes
- Clarity
- Open emotional expression
- Collaborative problem solving

Thus, the same stressors can lead to different outcomes, depending on how a family meets its challenges. A core conviction in a family resilience approach is that there are strong advantages to family members' working collaboratively on finding solutions to shared problems. Family therapy can be most effective when it identifies key processes for resilience and encourages a family's own best efforts for recovery and growth.

Changing Families
in a Changing World

If we are to achieve a richer culture . . . we must recognize the whole gamut of human potentialities, and so weave a less arbitrary social fabric, one in which each diverse human gift will find a fitting place.
—MARGARET MEAD, *Blackberry Winter*

The concept of family resilience is especially timely as our world grows increasingly complex and unpredictable, and as families face unprecedented challenges. At a time of widespread concern about family breakdown, it is more important than ever to identify key processes that can enable family members to weather stresses and rebound strengthened as a family unit. Our understanding of family functioning and our efforts to build resilience must be relevant to the diverse challenges of contemporary families.

As the 21st century approaches, the structure of societies worldwide is in transformation. With profound social and economic upheavals over recent decades, families and the world around them are changing at an accelerated pace. It is useful to highlight four emerging trends and to place them in sociohistorical context:

- Diverse family forms
- Changing gender roles
- Cultural diversity and socioeconomic disparity
- Varying and expanded family life cycle course

This chapter first describes each of these trends; it then discusses the importance of resilience as families face the future, and it considers some of the clinical implications.

DIVERSE FAMILY FORMS

The very survival of the family has been called into question with the recon-figuration of human relationships in recent decades. Yet concern over family crisis isn't unique to our times; controversy and change have surrounded the definition of the family throughout U.S. history (Skolnick, 1991). Every generation has expressed doubts about the stability and continuity of the family. Each has thought it was witnessing the breakdown of the "traditional family"— a popular image at the time of what families were supposed to be like. Fears of the demise of the family have escalated in periods of social turbulence, as in our times.

The idealized image of intact, multigenerational family households of the distant past distorts their actual instability and diversity (Walsh, 1993). Family patterns were no more orderly and stable than today's complex and varied family structures and roles. In fact, family transitions were more unpredictable as a result of the many life uncertainties, particularly unplanned pregnancies and untimely deaths. The risk of not growing up in an intact family was high. Family units were frequently disrupted by early parental death, which led to re-marriage and stepfamilies, or to placements of children with extended family members, in foster care, or in orphanages. Most families now have greater control over the options and timing of marriage and parenting, largely due to birth control and to medical advances that have increased life expectancy.

Family households in the past, as in most cultures other than our own, were quite diverse. Their flexibility enabled resilience in weathering insta-bilities. Households commonly included non-kin boarders providing surro-gate families for individuals on their own and facilitating the adaptation of new immigrants, in addition to furnishing income and companionship for widows and the elderly. Actually, the current proliferation of diverse family arrangements and support networks, although termed "nontraditional forms," continues this tradition. For instance, when two single parents combine house-holds and resources, they strengthen their family resilience.

The predominance of the nuclear family structure arose with the indus-trial era and peaked in the 1950s. The household consisted of an intact two-parent family unit headed by a male breadwinner and supported by his full-time homemaker wife, who devoted herself to household management, raising children, and elder care. Many mistakenly perceive this model as an essen-tial, and now endangered, institution when it was actually unique to its times (Skolnick, 1991). Following the traumas of the Great Depression and World War II, U.S. prosperity was fueled by a strong postwar economy and govern-ment benefits that provided for education, jobs, and home ownership, enabling most families to live comfortably on one income. Reversing the century's steady decline in the birth rate, couples married younger and in greater numbers than at any other time.

In earlier eras, the family had fulfilled a broad array of economic, educational, social, and religious functions intertwined with the larger community. Relationships were valued for a variety of contributions to the collective family unit. The modern nuclear family household, fitting the resurgent ethos of the rugged individual, was designed to be self-reliant within the borders of its white picket fence. It became a rigid, closed system, isolated from extended kin and community connections—relational sources of resilience and adaptability. It also lost the flexibility and diversity that had enabled households to expand or reconfigure according to need. Structural fragility also resulted from changing expectations for marriage, based on the premises of voluntary commitment, intimacy, and companionship. Yet nostalgia for the stability, security, and prosperity of those times is understandable.

Periods of major social and economic turmoil are tremendously disruptive of family life. In the late 19th century, industrialization and urbanization brought smaller families, increased divorce rates, less connection to extended kin and community networks, more child abuse and neglect, and squalid slum conditions. We are currently in the midst of another stressful transformation to a postindustrial, technologically based economy. Family patterns have been altered by a host of interconnected factors: growing cultural diversity; economic restructuring; a widening gap between rich and poor; the aging of our society; and movements for equality and social justice for women, gay men and lesbians, and people of color.

With all these changes, the idealized 1950s model of the white, middle-class, intact nuclear family, headed by a breadwinner father and supported by a homemaker mother, is currently found in only 3% of households (Coontz, 1997). In its place, a diverse reshaping of contemporary family life, termed the "postmodern family," encompasses a hodgepodge of multiple, evolving family cultures and structures: working mothers and two-earner households; divorced, single-parent, and remarried families; and domestic partners, both gay and straight. Marriage and birth rates have both declined.

Dual-earner families are now the norm, accounting for two-thirds of all two-parent households (Barnett & Rivers, 1996). Two paychecks are needed in most families to maintain even a modest standard of living (Piotrkowski & Hughes, 1993). Traditional gender role divisions are no longer typical, as women's career aspirations, divorce, and economic pressures have brought nearly 70% of all mothers into the workforce. By choice, and even more by necessity, most mothers (both married and single) are currently in the workforce—nearly 75% of mothers of school-age children, and over 60% of mothers of preschool children.

More people are now living on their own, as the number of single adults has nearly doubled over the past two decades. At the same time, many more young adults live with their parents than a decade ago, either "sitting on the launching pad" or returning home for financial reasons. Those who marry are postponing it longer. At the same time, the number of unmarried couples living together has risen dramatically. Nearly half of all adults live in a cohabiting relationship at some time in their lives, although most go on to marry.

Single parents (either unwed or divorced) have become increasingly common; nearly half of all children, and over 60% of poor minority children, are expected to live for at least part of their childhoods in one-parent households. Single mothers head 25% of all households (up from 5% in 1960); in African American families, the percentage has increased to about 50%. The rise in unwed teen pregnancy appears to have begun declining recently. Yet the problem remains serious, with studies documenting the high risk of "children having children" for long-term poverty, poor-quality parenting, and a cluster of health and psychosocial problems (Chase-Lansdale & Brooks-Gunn, 1991).

Divorce rates, after climbing rapidly, are fluctuating at just under 50%. Since over 70% of divorced individuals go on to remarry, remarried families are soon expected to be the most common family form (Visher & Visher, 1996). Families formed through adoption have also been on the rise, for single parents as well as for couples (Anderson, Piantanida, & Anderson, 1993).

Although family structures are changing dramatically, people still view committed relationships as one of the most important sources of happiness, and 90% legally marry at least once by the age of 50. Most will marry more than once in their lives. The social movement for gay and lesbian rights has brought increasing visibility and advocacy for the normalization and legalization of same-sex domestic partners (Laird, 1993; Laird & Green, 1996). People want to share their lives with someone and seek an intimate relationship that provides comfort, romantic and sexual gratification, and friendship with a lifelong partner.

Yet our language and preconceptions about "the normal family" can pathologize or distort family relationship patterns. The label "latchkey child" implies maternal neglect when parents must work. The term "single-parent family" can blind us to the important role of a noncustodial parent (Walsh, 1991). A stepparent or adoptive parent is viewed as inherently deficient when framed as not the "real" or "natural" parent. One judge denied a parental rights request by a lesbian who had shared parenting for her partner's biological child, on the grounds that it would be too confusing for a child to have two mothers. Similar preconceptions often disenfranchise stepparents and adoptive parents. However, gains are being made in redefining the family. In one landmark court decision supporting gay parental rights, the judge concluded:

"It is the totality of the relationship, as evidenced by the dedication, caring, and self-sacrifice of the parties which should, in the final analysis, control the definition of family" (quoted in Stacey, 1990, p. 4). We need to be mindful that families in the distant past and in most other cultures have had multiple, varied structures, and that family processes matter more than family form for effective functioning.

CHANGING GENDER ROLES AND RELATIONS

If we view recent structural changes in the family as part of a historical continuum, the changing status of women emerges as the major dynamic from the end of the Victorian era to the present. Over the centuries (and still today in many cultures), marriage was viewed in functional terms: Matches were made by families on the basis of economic and social position, and wives and children were the property of their husbands and fathers. The family patriarch held authority over the women and children, controlling all major decisions and resources. For a husband to be certain of his (male) heirs, the honor of the family required the absolute fidelity of the wife and the chastity of marriageable daughters (Walsh, 1985). These values have often been enforced in Arab societies, for instance, through the veiling and cloistering of women in the household. In some African cultures the genital mutilation of young girls ensures that sex will never be a pleasurable temptation. In many patriarchal societies, polygamy has been considered the normal family arrangement. The husband, his wives, and their many children often live together in one household, and a man's social status is enhanced with each wife, whose status in turn increases with the birth of each son.

Although families had many more children in the past, women invested relatively less time in parenting; they contributed to the shared family economy in varied ways, from weaving to bookkeeping. Fathers, older children, extended kin, and neighbors all participated actively in child rearing. The integration of family and work life allowed for intensive sharing of labor among all family members. Industrialization and urbanization brought a redefinition of gender roles and functions. Family work and "productive" paid work became segregated into separate gendered spheres of home and workplace (Bernard, 1982). Domesticity became glorified as women were assigned to the exclusive role of custodian of the hearth, nurturer of the young, and caretakers of the old. Particularly in North American and British societies, the maternal role came to be reified to such an extent that mothers have been regarded as the primary, essential, and irreplaceable caregivers for the healthy development of children, and have been blamed for all child and family problems (Braverman, 1989). Yet women's unpaid domestic work was devalued and rendered invisible, with total dependency on the financial support of male breadwinners. When necessity brought women into the workforce, their wages and job status were lower than men's, and they remained bound to their primary family obligations—a dual disparity that persists. The belief that women's full-time homemaking/parenting role was essential for the well-being of all family members furthered the myth that any outside work was harmful, undermining their husbands' esteem as breadwinners and endangering their children's healthy development.

The breadwinner–homemaker model was highly adaptive to the demands of the industrial economy. However, the rigid gender roles, the subordination of wives to their husbands, and the peripheral position of fathers demanded by the workplace were not healthy for either the functioning of the family or the well-being of its members. The loss of community further isolated men and women from companionship and support. Role expectations for women to keep the family functional came at great personal cost, with a disproportionate burden in caring for others while denying their own needs and identities (McGoldrick, Anderson, & Walsh, 1989). For men, the work ethic and job schedules diminished involvement with their families. One critic wrote: "Each suburban family is somehow a broken home, consisting of a father who appears as an overnight guest, [and] a put-upon housewife with too much to do" (Skolnick, 1991, p. 60).

The belief that "proper gender roles" are essential for healthy family functioning and child development persisted in sociological conceptualizations of the normal American family. Based on Talcott Parsons' observations of white, middle-class, suburban U.S. families in the 1950s (Parsons & Bales, 1955), a leap was made from description of typical patterns in a particular time and place to prescription of those norms as universal standards. In that view, the nuclear family structure provided for a healthy complementarity in the division of roles into male "instrumental" leadership and female "socioemotional" support. Authorities in the fields of psychiatry and child development adhered to this family model, and to its corollary that the failure of a family to uphold proper gender roles would damage children and could even contribute to schizophrenia (Lidz, 1963).

The first wave of feminism in the 1960s came in reaction to the exploitive and stultifying effects of the modern family model, with its separate and unequal spheres for men and women. With reproductive choice and family planning, women turned to the work sphere, seeking the personal growth and status denied them in the traditional homemaker role. The "Superwoman syndrome" soon emerged as women sought to "have it all" by combining jobs and child rearing, but they soon found that they were adding a "second shift" (Hochschild, 1989), since most men have not made reciprocal changes toward equal sharing of family responsibilities. Numerous studies have found that employed women continue to carry nearly 80% of household and child care obligations (Hochschild, 1997). Although many men are doing substantially more than their own fathers did, it remains far less than their wives' share of the burden (Lamb, 1997). Accordingly, the second wave of the women's movement has made family politics central, in efforts to redefine and rebalance gender role relations so that men and women can both seek personal fulfillment, be gainfully employed, and share in the responsibilities and joys of family life (McGoldrick et al., 1989). Recent men's movements have also called for more active involvement in parenting by fathers, along with a reconnection with the fathers they barely knew. Although some advocate a return to the traditional patriarchal model, most men share with women the desire to forge a full and equal partnership in family life (Napier, 1988).

CULTURAL DIVERSITY AND SOCIOECONOMIC DISPARITY

One of the most important features of American families today is their increasing cultural diversity. Through immigration and earlier, higher birth rates in African American, Hispanic, and Asian families, people of color are expected to constitute over one-third of the U.S. population by the year 2000, and the proportion will continue to increase to over half in the coming decades (McGoldrick et al., 1996). Despite the myth of the melting pot, American families have always been diverse, because of the long U.S. tradition of immigration. Cultural pluralism can be seen as a source of strength that vitalizes our society. However, recent economic upheaval has aggravated racial discrimination and intolerance toward non-European immigrants and minorities, complicating adaptive challenges for those families.

Social scientists have too often generalized to all families on the basis of white middle-class experience. With structural changes in the economy over recent decades, however, the broad middle class has been shrinking, and the gap between the rich and poor has widened. The financial prospects of most young families today are lower than those of their parents, with a decline of over 30% in median income and more families living below the poverty line (Rubin, 1994). As noted earlier, most families require two incomes to support even a modest standard of living, health care expenses, and their children's education. Many are struggling anxiously through uncertain times as businesses downsize and breadwinners are let go after years of loyal service. As the economy has shifted from industrial manufacturing to services and computer-based technology, working-class and poor families with the least education, job skills, and employment opportunities have been hit hardest.

Declining economic conditions and job dislocation have had a devastating impact on many families' stability and well-being, fueling substance abuse, family conflict and violence, marital dissolution, homelessness, and an increase in poor single-parent households. Social and economic disempowerment has also contributed to the high rate of unwed teenage parenting. The failure of young inner-city black men to marry and to assume financial responsibility for children they have fathered has been linked in large part to their bleak employment prospects, reinforced by racism (Wilson, 1987, 1996).

Harry Aponte (1994) stresses that the emotional and relational problems of poor minority families must be understood within their socioeconomic and political contexts:

> The poor are dependent on and vulnerable to the overreaching power of society. They cannot insulate themselves from society's ills. They cannot buy their children private schooling when their public school fails. They cannot buy into an upscale neighborhood when their housing project becomes too dangerous. When society stumbles, its poorest citizens are tossed about and often crushed. (p. 8)

The economic and social conditions of women and children have worsened disproportionately (Barnett & Rivers, 1996; McGoldrick et al., 1989). Gender inequities persist in the workplace. The earnings gap between men and women, although improving somewhat over the past decade (due in part to a drop in male earnings), still leaves women currently earning under 75 cents to each dollar earned by men. Most single and divorced women rear children with little or no financial support from fathers. Even full-time employment doesn't sustain some above the poverty line. The number of children in poverty has increased 42% since 1970. Currently, nearly one in four children lives in abject poverty. Their life chances are worsened by persistent conditions of discrimination, neighborhood decay, poor schools, crime, violence, and lack of opportunity.

Such immense structural disparities perpetuate a vast chasm between the rich and the poor, increasing the vulnerability of the growing numbers of families "living on the faultline" (Rubin, 1994). It is crucial for our society to move beyond the rhetoric of "family values" to make structural changes that will support and sustain the vitality of families (Schorr, 1988).

EXTENDED AND MORE VARIED
FAMILY LIFE CYCLE COURSE

The aging of societies and families worldwide will pose major challenges in coming decades. Increased life expectancy, from an average of 47 years in 1900 to over 75 at present, has enabled more long-lasting marital and intergenerational relations, with four- and five-generation families increasingly common (Walsh, 1998b). Yet, with aging, serious and chronic illnesses also pose family caregiving challenges (see Chapter 8). By 2020, one-quarter of the U.S. population will be over 65. With fewer young people to support the growing number of elders, threats to Social Security and health care benefits are likely to fuel growing insecurity and intergenerational tensions.

The importance of sibling relationships often increases over the life span (Bank, 1977; Sandmeier, 1994). The centenarian Delany sisters, born into a Southern African American family, lived together throughout their lives, crediting their remarkable resilience to their strong relationship. When Dr. Bessie Delany (who died recently at the age of 103) was asked how she accounted for her sister's and her own longevity, she quipped, "Honey, we never married; we never had husbands to worry us to death!" As for mortality, she added, "I haven't been afraid to live, and I won't be afraid to die" (Delany & Delany with Hearth, 1993, p. 4).

Ironically, the current high divorce rate is due in part to the expectation that, unlike couples in the past, present-day couples have another 20–40 years to live after launching children. It is difficult for one relationship to meet the changing developmental needs of both partners over so many years. Margaret Mead (1972) noted the changing relationship priorities: In youth, romance and passion are paramount in choosing a partner; in rearing children, relationship satisfaction is linked more to the sharing of family joys and responsibilities; in later life, needs for companionship and mutual caregiving predominate. In view of these shifts, Mead recommended time-limited, renegotiable contracts and suggested that perhaps serial monogamy best fits the challenges over a lengthened life course. Although her vision has struck many as undermining the family, today's families are increasingly living out this pattern. Despite the high divorce rate, most people remain optimistic; they long for a romantic, committed relationship, and so they keep trying. Two or three marriages in a (long) lifetime, along with periods of cohabitation and single living, are likely to become increasingly common. This means that most adults and their children will move in and out of a variety of family structures. We will need to learn how to buffer these transitions and how to live successfully in complex arrangements.

Our view of the family must also be extended to the full and varied course of the expanded life cycle, to a wider range of normative (typical) developmental phases and transitions fitting the diverse preferences and challenges that make each family unique. Some women and men become first-time parents at the age when others become grandparents. Some who remarry have children younger than their own grandchildren. Adults who are single (Anderson & Stewart, 1994) and couples without children forge a variety of intimate relationships and significant kin and friendship bonds—for example, the close-knit networks of gays and lesbians, termed "families of choice" (Weston, 1991).

New technologies facilitating conception, and others prolonging life and the dying process, pose unprecedented family challenges. Tragically, in impoverished communities, the lack of adequate health care and the number of early deaths through neighborhood violence, drug abuse, and AIDS drastically foreshorten the life cycle for the poor. Research suggests a connection between an immediate present orientation, early pregnancies, and this bleak future outlook (Burton, 1990).

FAMILIES FACING THE FUTURE: THE IMPORTANCE OF RESILIENCE

The families of today and tomorrow are thus characterized by growing diversity in structure, gender, sexual orientation, culture, class, and life cycle patterns. Debates about the future of the family have touched a vulnerable core of anxiety about contemporary life in the postmodern era (Gergen, 1989). Families are struggling with actual and symbolic losses as they alter family arrangements and as their world changes around them. Many feel adrift on their own fragile life rafts in a turbulent sea (Lifton, 1993). Myths of the ideal family compound the sense of deficiency and failure for families in transition. There is a widespread sense of disruption and confusion about the very structure and meaning of family relationships—about what is "normal" (i.e., typical and expectable) in family life and how to construct "healthy" (i.e., optimally functioning) families. Disoriented and uncertain, many struggle to hold onto familiar patterns and yet question idealized family models from the past that don't fit their current situation, needs, and challenges.

Yet most families today are showing remarkable resilience, making the best of their situations and inventing new models of human connectedness. These "brave new families," as sociologist Judith Stacey (1990) has termed them, are creatively reworking family life in a variety of household and kinship arrangements. In what Stacey calls "recombinant family life," people draw on a wide array of resources, fashioning them into new gender and relationship strategies to cope with new challenges. In her ethnographic study of working-class families, she found men and women sharing housework and child care, unmarried working women choosing to have children on their own, strong extended family connections sustained across serial marriages, and long-time close friends claiming kinship. She also found same-sex couples exchanging marital vows and sharing child-rearing commitments, as gay and lesbian individuals more openly seek intimacy, community, and spirituality outside mainstream institutional forms. Stacey was particularly impressed by creative initiatives to reshape the experience of divorce from a painful, bitter schism and loss of resources into the formation of a viable kin network, involving new partners and former mates, multiple sets of children, stepkin, and friends into households and support systems collaborating to survive and flourish. It is ironic that such families are termed "nontraditional." Their flexibility, diversity, and community recall the resilience found in the varied households and loosely knit clans of the past.

Because today's world is marked by breathtaking change and fragmentation, our lives can seem utterly unpredictable; there are few absolutes. The loss of bearings can be experienced as overwhelming and alarming. Yet rather than collapsing under these pressures and threats, as Robert Lifton (1993) contends, we humans are surprisingly resilient. Lifton compares our predicament and our responses to those of the Greek god Proteus: Just as Proteus was able to change shape in response to crisis, we create new psychological, social, and familial configurations, exploring new options and transforming our lives many times over the life course. Similarly, Mary Catherine Bateson (1994) contends that adaptation "comes out of encounters with novelty that may seem chaotic" (p. 8). An intense multiplicity of vision, enhancing insight and creativity, is necessary today as families confront tumultuous change. Although we can never be fully prepared for the demands of the moment, Bateson argues that we can be strengthened to meet uncertainty:

> The quality of improvisation characterizes more and more lives today, lived in uncertainty, full of the inklings of alternatives. In a rapidly changing and interdependent world, single models are less likely to be viable and plans more likely to go awry. The effort to combine multiple models risks the disasters of conflict and runaway misunderstanding, but the effort to adhere blindly to some traditional model for a life risks disaster not only for the person who follows it but for the entire system in which he or she is embedded, indeed for all other living systems with which that life is linked. (1994, p. 8)

If we knew the future of a particular family, therapists and other helping professionals might be able to prepare that family with all the necessary skills and attitudes. But as family sociologists have concluded, it is doubtful that such stability or certainty has ever existed (Skolnick, 1991). Instead, ambiguity is the essence of life; it cannot be eliminated. We must help families to find coherence within complexity. In Bateson's apt metaphor, "We are called to join in a dance whose steps must be learned along the way. Even in uncertainty we are responsible for our steps" (1994, p. 10).

Kenneth Gergen (1989) observes that when we become aware of the multiplicity in diverse human experience, we begin to see that each ethnic community, political group, and economic class has its own limited, partial perspective and frames the world in its own terms. Gergen states,

> In the postmodern world we may lose the safe and sure claims to truth, objectivity, and authority; and the idea of self as the center of meaning. Yet we may gain something we have scarcely known in Western culture: the reality, the centrality and the fundamental necessity of relatedness.

Amid the swirling confusions and upheavals, we can help families to prevail by carving out aspects of life that can be controlled and mastered. In the process of small victories, families build competence and confidence. At the same time, as Bateson (1994) urges, families must be encouraged to carry on the process of learning throughout the life cycle in all they do—"like a mother balancing her child on her hip as she goes about her work with the other hand and uses it to open the doors of the unknown" (p. 9). The ability to combine multiple roles and to face new challenges can be learned. Encouraging such vision and skills is one of the core elements of a family resilience approach to practice.

CLINICAL IMPLICATIONS

Exploring Families' Notions of Normality and Their Own Identity

We have become increasingly aware that our views of normality and health are socially constructed (Walsh, 1993). The cultural ideals that are still pervasive in defining the "normal" family influence the standards by which families are judged—and judge themselves—to be healthy and successful. Families that do not conform are viewed as pathological and are stigmatized, making their adaptations more difficult.

Americans place a good deal of emphasis on being "normal" and "healthy." In these uncertain times, families increasingly worry about their own normality and judge themselves as deficient if they do not fit the socially desirable standard. In my research experience with nonclinical families, I found that many wanted confirmation that they were, indeed, normal. Other families declined to participate, fearing that under scrutiny they would be found abnormal. Their reluctance gave me perspective on what is commonly labeled as "resistance" in clinical practice. I believe that families often fail to come for help because they fear being judged dysfunctional and deficient. Too often this concern is misconstrued by clinicians as a further sign of pathology.

Those of us who are helping professionals also need to be aware of the implicit assumptions about family normality, health, and dysfunction we bring to our work from our own world views, based in our cultural standards, personal experience, and clinical theories (Walsh, 1993). Through these filtered lenses, we and our clients together co-construct the pathologies we "discover" in families, and set therapeutic goals tied to beliefs about healthy functioning. This makes it imperative to examine our own views of family normality and to explore those brought by our clients to the therapeutic encounter. These beliefs commingle to influence how we define and explain problem situations, feelings of success or failure, and therapeutic objectives.

It is important to explore each family's own identity and its notions of normality. In doing so, we might ask such questions as these: How do members view their own family, and how do they believe others see them? How do they compare their actual family situation to perceived cultural ideals? Beliefs that they fall short fuel feelings of failure and misguided efforts to fit inappropriate standards. For instance, the common belief that stepfamilies are inherently deficient often leads them to emulate intact nuclear families— sealing their borders, cutting off ties with noncustodial parents, and feeling they have failed when they don't immediately blend in the image of *The Brady Bunch*. (Of course, there were no ex-spouses or "out-laws" in that TV model, and a full-time housekeeper helped to smooth daily life.) As Carl Whitaker observed, the very attempts to fit the social mold of a normal family are often sources of problems and deep pain.

As researchers are finding, families with a variety of configurations can be functional. It is not the family form, but rather family processes and relationship quality, that matter most for hardiness. Many different arrangements are potentially workable, and none is inherently healthy or pathological.

Different family forms (e.g., an intact family, a single-parent family, or a remarried family) face different challenges, have different structural constraints, and possess different resources for functioning. Two-earner families must organize their households and family lives quite differently from the traditional breadwinner/homemaker model.

Defining and Assessing Families

At the outset of any family evaluation, it is important to gain a holistic view of the family system and its community linkages. This includes all members of current households, the extended family system, and key relationships that are (or have been) significant in the functioning of the family and its individual members. We must look beyond the boundary of the household in considering significant family relationships, particularly with the increased numbers of single-parent and remarried families and of individuals living on their own. A genogram (McGoldrick & Gerson, 1985) is essential as a systemic diagram, enabling both clinicians and family members to visualize the network of relationships in each family system. While the genogram is often thought of as a tool in exploring past family-of-origin patterns, it also has immense value in describing the current configuration of the family system; demarcating living arrangements in various households; noting patterns of alliance, conflict, and cutoff; and identifying existing and potential resources in extended kin and social networks.

Because family structures have been changing so dramatically, it is important to explore who family members include in defining their own family: who is significant and what the meanings of various roles and relationships are. Legal and blood definitions of "family" and social norms of the idealized nuclear family may constrain clients from disclosing important relationships. If a mother is not legally married, she may not mention a live-in boyfriend; however, it may be important to include him in couple or family sessions, in order to clarify his position and his potential to assume a supportive role for the mother and her children. A gay man reluctant to disclose his partnership with his lover may need encouragement to include this vital relationship in the therapeutic conversation. Clients who presume that "family" is equated with "household" may not mention other kin who are or could become important resources in their lives. The potential contribution of a noncustodial parent may be overlooked if focusing on a single-parent household renders him (or her) invisible or if the primary parent has written the ex-spouse off as hopeless. An elderly woman living on her own may say that she has no family, perhaps meaning that her husband has died or that her children live far away with little contact. A genogram may reveal a nearby nephew who could become a valuable resource.

Even pets, often neglected in family assessments, prove to be vital supports in resilience. Studies have found that pet owners enjoy better health, and that simply stroking a dog can lower heart rate and blood pressure—in both the person and the dog! Our dog was a mainstay for my daughter through the disruptive transitions of remarriage and our move into a new community. Targa is featured prominently on the multigenerational genogram she constructed for her stepgrandfather's 90th birthday.

A coevolutionary developmental perspective is needed to track significant events and transitions in families. A family timeline, accompanying the genogram, is extremely helpful in noting the confluence of events and symptoms of distress. Children in foster care may shift residences many times, for instance, and such shifts may both follow and precipitate distress. Because separation, divorce, and remarriage are evolving processes over time, we need to inquire about previous relationships and family units, the timing and nature of transitions, and future anticipated changes, in order to understand a problem in family developmental context. In particular, recent or impending changes in membership or household composition should be noted, as these changes may precipitate a crisis related to presenting problems. Focusing only on the present family household can result in tunnel vision, as the following example illustrates:

> A father, a single parent with custody of his son and daughter, sought help with his daughter's stormy behavior. In presenting the case for supervision, the therapist diagrammed the family structure as follows:

> The therapist had assessed the problem as a triangle in which a coalition between the father and his parentified son excluded the daughter, who then sought attention through misbehavior. Interventions had focused on rebalancing this triangle, with no progress. Outside the household and the frame of assessment and intervention, however, were critical relationship complications in this system (as illustrated in this revised diagram):

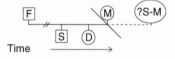

> Since a bitter custody battle 3 years earlier, the mother had been cut off from contact with the children; she had been condemned as "unfit" by the father because of an affair. The father had then plunged into a serious relationship with a woman who was now pressuring him to get married. The daughter was angry at having been being turned against her

mother by her father, saddened by her loss, and resentful of the new "replacement" mom in the wings. For his part, the father held unexpressed fears of remarriage, rooted in painful issues from his former marriage. These triangles and losses needed to be dealt with. In particular, ways needed to be found for the children to regain contact with their mother, with the father's support, before proceeding to consider remarriage and the complications of new stepparenting relationships.

It is worth reiterating that clinicians should be careful not to confuse a family's form or interactional style with its level of functioning. The idealized intact nuclear family structure with traditional gender roles often subtly underlies therapists' views of families and what should change, just as it can influence a family's self-appraisal. We must make clear to families that we do not assume that varying family arrangements are inherently pathological or the likely causes of any presenting problems. For instance, the school problems of a boy growing up in a single-parent family should not be presumed to be due to the absence of a father in the house. Key issues are whether the boy feels abandoned or cared for by those who are important in his life, and how positive bonds both within and beyond the household can be strengthened. Families of diverse structural arrangements all have the potential for healthy family functioning.

Helping Families Meet the Challenges of Change

All families have values. Some values maintain continuity with the past, in terms of commitment and personal responsibility; others may differ sharply, such as rejection of the patriarchal model. From a long-range perspective, concerns over the diversity of lifestyles are overshadowed by more serious problems, such as the aging of our population and the isolation of the elderly; the economic strain on families; and the cultural transmission of violence, sexism, and racism. Women and men must join forces to press for creative strategies to rebalance work and family commitments. In defining individual and family well-being, quality-of-life issues are at the fore, including a desire for more community involvement, spiritual meaning, social justice, and a concern for the environment. As the norm of the modern nuclear family has given way to a multiplicity of family arrangements, our challenge is to create social and economic policies and clinical approaches to support the new family realities (Harway, 1996; Pipher, 1997; Stacey, 1996).

Although many families today are confused and troubled, many more are showing remarkable resilience. Despite family instability and a larger context of economic and social uncertainties, most people are committed to forming and being part of a family. The change has come in the definition of "family," which has broadened to encompass a wide spectrum of relationship options. If we see this transition as an opportunity to experiment with new approaches to family life—to enlarge the repertoire of family patterns—our families and society can experience new growth and transformation to greater individual and family well-being. Attempts to forge new family arrangements are often met with tremendous institutional resistance; however, potentially viable models for families of the future are emerging through the creative strategies of ordinary families.

Crisis and challenge are part of the human condition. The concept of family resilience affirms the potential for survival and growth in all families, and offers a valuable framework for strength-oriented approaches to practice. Just as families face diverse challenges, there are many pathways to family resilience. Clinicians equipped with an understanding of key processes can mobilize untapped resources in distressed families, to help them cope more effectively with life crises and emerge strengthened. Chapters 3–5 describe and illustrate these keys to resilience.

P·A·R·T I·I

Key Family Processes in Resilience

C·H·A·P·T·E·R   3

Belief Systems:
The Heart and Soul of Resilience

Deep in my heart I do believe
We shall overcome someday!
—MARTIN LUTHER KING, JR.

Belief systems are at the core of all family functioning and are powerful forces in resilience. We cope with crisis and adversity by making meaning of our experience: linking it to our social world, to our cultural and religious beliefs, to our multigenerational past, and to our hopes and dreams for the future. How families view their problems and their options can make all the difference between coping and mastery or dysfunction and despair. This chapter draws on research and practice knowledge to identify key beliefs that facilitate resilience in families facing serious life challenges.

In the empirically based Western world, it is often said that "seeing is believing." Native Americans would say, "It may have to be believed to be seen." Beliefs are the lenses through which we view the world as we move through life, influencing what we see or do not see and what we make of our perceptions (Wright, Watson, & Bell, 1996). Beliefs are at the very heart of who we are and how we understand and make sense of our experience. As Sarah Taggart (1994) suggests, our core beliefs, whether secular or sacred, anchor us "in the dizzying vastness of the great unknown we call reality" (p. 20). In this way, beliefs come to define our reality.

Belief systems broadly encompass values, convictions, attitudes, biases, and assumptions, which coalesce to form a set of basic premises that trigger emotional responses, inform decisions, and guide actions. Facilitative beliefs increase options for problem resolution, healing, and growth, whereas constraining beliefs perpetuate problems and restrict options (Wright et al., 1996). Affirming beliefs that we are valued can help us to rally in times of crisis.

Believing that our own needs are "selfish" and "bad" can lead to selfless caregiving or relentless accommodation, leaving us depleted, guilty, or resentful. Beliefs and actions are interdependent: Our beliefs can facilitate or constrain our actions, and our actions and their consequences can reinforce or alter our beliefs. Some beliefs are more useful than others, depending on our predicament. Some are also more acceptable or preferred within a particular culture or context.

This chapter begins by describing the ways in which shared belief systems develop and evolve in families over time, and the importance of storytelling and narrative coherence. Key beliefs that facilitate family resilience are then identified and discussed. The importance of therapists' own beliefs in regard to treatment versus healing is also addressed.

HOW SHARED BELIEFS DEVELOP AND EVOLVE

Our beliefs are socially constructed, evolving in a continuous process through transactions with significant others and the larger world (Anderson & Goolishian, 1988; Gergen, 1989; Hoffman, 1990). We all exist in many domains of reality that we bring forth to explain our experiences. Beliefs join people together, as Wright et al. (1996) note:

> People experience commonalities not only because they have experienced similar events, but also because they construe and interpret the implications of events in a similar way. Through living together and being together we influence each other's beliefs. We develop our identities within our families, professions, and communities by the belief systems that we share and do not share with others. We live our lives only slightly aware, and sometimes not at all, of our beliefs and the effect they have on our own lives and the lives of others. (p. 23)

Families evolve shared beliefs, anchored in cultural values and influenced by their position and experiences in the social world over time (Dallos, 1991; Falicov, 1995; Hess & Handel, 1959; McGoldrick, Giordano, & Pearce, 1996). Certain beliefs about human nature are implicit in the behavior and relationships of all families (Kluckhohn, 1960). While sharing a congruent mythology, members of well-functioning families maintain openness to many differing viewpoints, lifestyles, and perceptions. Truth is seen as relative rather than absolute; this permits family members to approach reality as subjective and unique for each person and situation.

Family belief systems provide coherence and organize experience to enable family members to make sense of crisis situations. In his seminal research on family paradigms, David Reiss (1981) demonstrated that families construct shared beliefs about how the world operates and their own place in it. These paradigms influence how family members view and interpret events and behavior. They provide a meaningful orientation for understanding one another and for approaching new challenges. Shared beliefs develop and are reaffirmed and altered over the course of the family life cycle and across the multigenerational network of relationships. Because the family and social environment vary over time and for each individual, not all beliefs in a family will be shared (Bussell & Reiss, 1993). Different perspectives among siblings, for example, may arise out of nonshared experiences from their unique positions, influenced by genetic predisposition, birth order, gender, family roles, relationship dynamics, and the timing of critical events. Nevertheless, the dominant beliefs in a family system—and its culture—most strongly influence how the family, as a functional unit, will deal with adversity.

These shared beliefs shape family norms, expressed through patterned and predictable rules governing family life. Relationship rules, both explicit and implicit, provide expectations about roles, actions, and consequences that guide family life. Beginning in courtship, every couple makes a relational bargain, or "quid pro quo" (Jackson, 1977; Walsh, 1989)—a largely unspoken contract defining what the partners expect of each other and the relationship. In well-functioning families, relationship rules organize interaction and serve to maintain system integration by regulating members' behavior. Core beliefs are fundamental to family identity and coping strategies, expressed in such rules as "We never give up when the going gets rough," or "Men don't cry." Over time, mutual expectations need to be reappraised and rules altered in light of changing needs and constraints, such as when a father's disability disrupts assumptions about his role as breadwinner.

Family rituals store and convey each family's identity and beliefs in the celebration of holidays, rites of passage (e.g., weddings, bar/bat mitzvahs, graduations, and funerals), family traditions (e.g., anniversaries, reunions), and routine family interactions (e.g., dinnertime) (Wolin & Bennett, 1984). Rituals also facilitate life cycle transitions and transformations of beliefs. Rituals are encouraged in family therapy to mark important milestones, restore continuities with a family's heritage, create new patterns, and foster healing from trauma and loss (Imber-Black, Roberts, & Whiting, 1988).

The deep social and cultural roots of our beliefs often make it difficult to step outside our own context to notice and comment on them. My experiences while living and working in Morocco as a Peace Corps volunteer, and later serving as a consultant, not only immersed me in a culture quite different from my own; they also brought new perspectives on my social world upon reentry. I began to notice and question patterns of family organization and gender roles that I had always taken for granted as normal and ideal. As Mary Catherine Bateson has observed, "Seen from a contrasting point of view or seen suddenly through the eyes of an outsider, one's own familiar patterns can become accessible to choice and criticism" (1994, p. 31).

ORGANIZING OUR BELIEF SYSTEMS: STORYTELLING AND NARRATIVE COHERENCE

Meanings and beliefs are expressed in the narratives we construct together to make sense of our world and our position in it. Storytelling has served in every time and place to transmit cultural and family beliefs that guide personal expectations and actions. For centuries, Moroccans have gathered around storytellers in the lively marketplace of Marrakech, the J'maa el F'na, to hear tales of life and love, of tragic plights and comic relief, of human foibles and heroism. These stories are often dramatically acted out in costume and mime, with the perils and triumphs accentuated by Berber drumming. Like storytelling and theatre in cultures the world over, they offer personal mores, family values, and adaptive strategies for mastering life's challenges.

Cultural changes, disrupting traditional modes of understanding the self and others, generate heightened concern for coherence and integrity in life stories (Geertz, 1986). In today's technological societies, culture stories are transmitted through the mass media and the Internet, in images that both portray and saturate family life. Hollywood films and television drama powerfully shape and reflect the values and concerns of our times: what it means to be a man or woman; to be a family, a father, or a mother; to be successful or to fail. These images reach around the world, even to remote villages, where they are often strangely incongruent with local life. I've sat bemused with Moroccan Berber villagers (many of whom live without water or electricity), gathered around the TV (via satellite) in the local cafe, fascinated by tales of *The Brady Bunch* and *Beverly Hills 90210*. Not surprisingly, cultural anthropologists are finding multiple identities in the life narratives of young Moroccans (Walsh, 1985), much as youths elsewhere who are challenged by shifting norms and incongruities in our rapidly changing world.

Joan Laird (1989) notes that through storying we come to know ourselves, and we build coherent identities to make sense of the larger social context and our connectedness to it. Likewise, Susan Griffin (1993) asserts that all of us have a deep need to be connected to the larger society and to our own history. She contends that all history is a part of us, such that when stories are told and secrets revealed—whether about our own family members or about tragic events long ago or far away—our lives are made clearer to us.

Our need for enduring values and traditions, for stability and continuity, can be seen in the multigenerational transmission of myths and legends. Stories and rituals that preserve links to a family's cultural heritage are especially valuable for recent immigrant families, whose members can too easily lose their sense of identity, community, and pride in pressures for assimilation to the dominant culture (Falicov, 1998). In a course I teach, Loss, Recovery, and Resilience, I ask students to interview one another about their families' migration experiences, attending in particular to the traumas and losses they suffered and the sources of resilience that enabled them to survive, regenerate, and make their way in a new world. Recovering stories, when lost, can restore a vital sense of connection and meaning (see Chapter 10).

Stories have particular significance in response to crisis and adversity. In his memoirs of the Holocaust experience, Elie Wiesel (1995) attests to the importance of memory and storytelling: "Memory is a passion no less powerful or pervasive than love. . . . What does it mean to remember? It is to live in more than one world, to prevent the past from fading, and to call upon the future to illuminate it." Wiesel continues, "Survivors have only words, poor, ineffectual words, with which to defend the dead. So some of us weave these words into tales, stories, and pleas for memory and decency. It is all we can do, for the living, and for the dead."

Bertram Cohler (1991) has emphasized the importance of narrative coherence in making sense of disruptive events. We construct, organize, and synthesize our experiences. Adversity and the accompanying distress become tensions and organizing principles for a coherent life story and belief system (Bruner, 1986). Whether a natural catastrophe, a personal tragedy, or persistent hardship, adversity generates a crisis of meaning and a potential disruption of personal integration. This tension prompts the construction or reorganization of our life story and beliefs. Over time, we revise our stories of adversity and resilience to seek or maintain a sense of coherence and integrity. A major task of therapy involves the effort to reorganize a life story that presents past or ongoing misfortune as an impediment constraining the ability to move forward (Borden, 1992).

Psychotherapy offers a healing context for dialogue and storytelling. Arthur Kleinman (1988) has found that individuals and family members who have experienced serious illnesses benefit greatly from the opportunity to tell their stories of suffering. Yet there are cultural differences in how this may be seen as beneficial. For instance, counselors for Cambodian refugees who fled to the United States after widespread massacres in the 1970s found that many families told their stories of the terror and atrocities just once, and then preferred to go on with their lives and speak of it no more. The pathologizing context of a psychiatric setting also constrained their openness.

Stories and beliefs are essential elements in the process of change. Family therapists can help clients to recover important stories from the past that have become fragmented or lost in family processes of secrecy, denial, distortion, and relationship cutoff (Byng-Hall, 1995; Imber-Black, 1995; McGoldrick, 1995). Such stories often concern blame-, shame-, or guilt-laden incidents involving substance abuse; violence or sexual abuse; suicide; or accusations of unethical, scandalous, or illegal conduct. Narrative therapy approaches (Anderson & Goolishian, 1988; Freedman & Combs, 1996; White & Epston, 1990) view change as occurring when therapist and family collaborate in developing alternative meanings and new, more hopeful, affirming stories in place of problem-saturated narratives.

Key beliefs in family resilience can be organized into three areas, as outlined in Table 3.1. These beliefs involve the ability to make meaning of adver-

TABLE 3.1. Family Belief Systems: The Heart and Soul of Resilience

Making meaning of adversity
- Affiliative value: Resilience as relationally based
  - Crisis as shared challenge
  - Foundation of trust
- Family life cycle orientation
  - Normalizing, contextualizing adversity and distress
- Sense of coherence
  - Crisis as meaningful, comprehensible, manageable challenge
- Appraisal of crisis, distress, and recovery: Facilitative versus constraining
  - Causal and explanatory beliefs
  - Future expectations

Positive outlook
- Active initiative and perseverance
- Courage and en-*courage*-ment
- Sustaining hope, optimistic view; confidence in overcoming odds
- Focusing on strengths and potential
- Mastering the possible; accepting what can't be changed

Transcendence and spirituality
- Larger values, purpose
- Spirituality: Faith, communion, rituals
- Inspiration: Envisioning new possibilities
  - Creativity
  - Role models and (s)heroes
- Transformation: Learning and growth out of crisis
  - Reassessing, affirming, and altering life priorities
  - Commitment to help others; social responsibility

sity; a positive outlook, affirming strengths and possibilities; and transcendent beliefs for values and purpose, as well as solace and comfort.

MAKING MEANING OF ADVERSITY

The song "We Shall Overcome" became the clarion cry of the 1960s civil rights movement and has inspired hope and creative action in many parts of the world based in the belief that strength is best forged through collaboration. This simple yet profound phrase expresses the core conviction in relational resilience: In joining together, we strengthen our ability to overcome adversity.

Affiliative Value

The individualistic ethos underlying the myth of the rugged individual has left us out of touch with the communal and the interpersonal, contributing to the fragmentation and alienation so many individuals and families experience today. Like Dorothy in *The Wizard of Oz*, we find in life's journeys that there's no place like home. The poet Maya Angelou has remarked on this powerful yearning for "home": "The ache for home lives in all of us." But what is the meaning of "home" in our turbulent times, and how do we find our way home? Although the definition of the family is fluid and diverse, the foundations of a healthy family are the valuing of kinship and pride in family identity.

The idea of home also extends to a sense of community beyond the immediate family and intertwined in meaning and experience (Carter & McGoldrick, 1998; McGoldrick, 1995). "It is a powerful cultural fiction that we not only can, but must, make up our deepest beliefs in the isolation of our private selves" (Bellah et al., 1985). All concepts of the self and constructions of the world are fundamentally products of relationships, and it is through our interdependence that meaningful lives are best sustained. Just as Native Americans hold that something must be believed to be seen, Mary Catherine Bateson avows, "Community, like the sacred, is an idea that becomes reality because we believe in it" (1994, p. 42). We must then act on this belief, reaffirming it by putting it into practice.

This affiliative value was also found to be vital for optimal family functioning in the research by Beavers and his colleagues (Beavers & Hampson, 1990, 1993). Family members share a strong belief in the importance of family life. They share the conviction that people do not prosper in an interpersonal vacuum and that human needs are satisfied in relationships. Genuine caring proves effective even in families where parenting skills are more modest. An expectation of satisfaction from relationships, in turn, reinforces involvement and mutual investment.

Crisis as a Shared Challenge

Belying the myth of the rugged individual, meaningful kin and community connections are lifelines in times of distress. Investment in affiliation and collaboration increase our potential to surmount overwhelming challenges. Stinnett and DeFrain's (1985) research on strong families found that pulling together was one of the most important processes in weathering crises.

As we will see in Chapters 4 and 5, an affiliative value is expressed in a family's organizational connectedness and communication processes. For instance, a shared commitment to the marital vow "in sickness and in health" can bolster actions both to support optimal recovery and to sustain a relationship through an illness ordeal (Rolland, 1994). A relationship is strengthened when a crisis is viewed as a shared challenge, to be tackled together. One husband conveyed this relational view in recounting how he and his wife approached her diagnosis of breast cancer as partners. He realized not only that her life was at risk and that she needed his support, but also that their *relationship* was endangered by the illness and required their mutual support in facing the challenges ahead. In striking contrast, in the film *The Doctor*, a hotshot surgeon is thrown into a life crisis when he is diagnosed with cancer. His wife, realizing that something serious is wrong, asks in a caring, joining way, "What do we have?" He snaps back, " *We* don't have anything! *I* have cancer!" Framing it as his individual crisis, he shuts her out and, despairing, seeks comfort in an affair. Throughout the treatment ordeal that follows, he distances himself from her, refusing to let her into his emotional turmoil or to hear hers, and preventing them from comforting each other. He recovers, but the damage to the marriage is irreparable.

A Foundation of Trust

Families are best able to weather adversity when members have an abiding loyalty and faith in one another, rooted in a strong sense of trust (Beavers & Hampson, 1990). They share confidence that home is a safe and welcoming place and that they will always be there for one another. Here again, beliefs and actions are intertwined. Members are trustworthy; they can be counted on to stand by their word and stand by one another. Relationships are strengthened by actions toward trustworthiness, based on consideration of one another's welfare. Trust is essential for open communication, mutual understanding, and problem solving, as pioneer family therapists observed in troubled families. Ivan Boszormenyi-Nagy's (1987) concept of "merited trust" dovetails with Whitaker's view (Whitaker & Keith, 1981) of the importance of loyalty, accountability, and mutual commitment in creating a foundation of relational permanence, fostering a sense of group wholeness, and buffering periods of stress and disorganization. Boszormenyi-Nagy has emphasized the ethical dimension of family relationships in multigenerational legacies of parental accountability and filial loyalty, which guide members over the course of the life cycle.

Optimally, family attitudes encompass a positive view of humanity as essentially good, or at least as not malign in intent (Beavers & Hampson, 1990). Such underlying assumptions about people and reality enable families to relate with trust, without erecting stultifying interpersonal defenses. However, the ability to be trustful of the world and to view others as benign can be impaired by repeated experiences of discrimination, exploitation, or abuse. And yet family members must at least be able to assume benign intentions in their own important relationships. Mutuality is encouraged by the belief that other family members are struggling to do as well as they can under their particular circumstances and constraints, rather than that their actions are fundamentally hostile or destructive in intent. Confidence in one another's basic good will is essential to achieve closeness and collaboration, and to support trust, joy, and comfort in relating. In times of trouble, family members do best when they believe they can turn to one another as trusted partners and true kin.

A Family Life Cycle Orientation

Well-functioning families have an evolutionary sense of time and of becoming—a continual process of growth and change, progressing through the life cycle and over the generations. Strong transgenerational connections are experienced, with internal images brought up to date and modified as a guiding mythology evolves over time. Essentially, they have a family life cycle orientation (Beavers & Hampson, 1990), accepting the rhythms and flow of family life as children grow up and parents grow old and die. As children mature, they leave their families—not for isolated independence, but for other human relationships. Whatever their paths, they continue to value family and social connections across the life cycle.

Resilient families are better able to accept the passage of time and the need for change with new developmental challenges. Life cycle transitions, while disruptive, are also seen as milestones that can be an impetus for reevaluation of assumptions about the world and one's place in it. In this way, painful transitions can catalyze growth and transformation. In contrast, as

Betty Carter and Monica McGoldrick (1989) have observed, more dysfunctional families lack a dynamic sense of the passage of time and of continuities between past, present, and future. Symptoms of dysfunction commonly occur at times of disruptive transition. Family members may seem frozen in time. Some are terrified to move forward into the unknown. Many live only in the present moment, without a sense of past connection or future direction. Some become so focused on future goals that they are unable to live fully in the present. Others remain preoccupied with the past, holding on to old grievances, conflicts, or losses. Some attempt to escape the past through detachment from painful relationships and aspects of their history. Some reject their past by making reactive, oppositional choices in their lives; yet they often end up reenacting familiar scenarios.

Traumatic past experiences become encoded into family scripts that are often out of awareness, providing a blueprint for meaning and behavior when a family is facing a dilemma or crisis (Byng-Hall, 1995). Unresolved conflicts, secrets, and losses can reverberate underground, erupting in painful symptoms or destructive behavior, or enacted in family dramas at the next generation. Family myths can be either empowering or debilitating, depending both on their underlying themes and on their responsiveness to new circumstances. Clinicians who are trained to search for negative family-of-origin influences need to encourage clients to seek out positive multigenerational stories, (s)heroes, and legacies, which can inspire hope and courageous action in the face of adversity.

In working with all families, we should explore what "family" and "community" mean to them and seek possibilities for greater affiliation. Many hold vague idealized images disconnected from their actual lives. Others may have only scraps of torn and faded images of connections long ago or far away. For some, positive ties may be overshadowed by painful disappointment, conflict, or loss. Yet resilience and growth involve family members' coming to terms with their past, and integrating that meaningful understanding into their current lives and their future hopes and dreams. As Mary Catherine Bateson (1989) has observed, "Composing a life involves a continual reimagining of the future and reinterpretation of the past to give meaning to the present" (pp. 29–30).

The Shared Construction of Crisis Experiences

The meaning of adversity is filtered through family transactions. How families make sense of a crisis situation and endow it with meaning is most crucial for resilience (Antonovsky & Sourani, 1988; Patterson & Garwick, 1994). As Kagan (1984) found, for instance, families can have a positive mediating influence in children's adjustment to an emotionally stressful experience, such as a divorce, by sharing helpful perceptions and understanding of what is happening to them. The ability to clarify and give meaning to a precarious situation makes it easier to bear. It can also be transforming, bringing new vision and purpose to one's life.

The work of David Reiss (1981; Reiss & Oliveri, 1980) on family paradigms is especially relevant to family resilience, as noted earlier. An enduring set of beliefs, convictions, and assumptions about the social world is forged by pivotal family experiences. In turn, this family paradigm shapes and reinforces interactional patterns. This shared world view influences how a family approaches a stressful new situation and the meanings attached to anticipated life challenges. A critical event or disruptive transition can catalyze a major shift in a family belief system, with reverberations for both immediate reorganization and long-term adaptation.

Moreover, perceptions of a current event intersect with legacies of previous experience in the multigenerational system to forge the meaning each family makes of a challenge and its patterns of response (Carter & McGoldrick, 1998). Traumatic past experiences—particularly a similar situation or a crisis at the same nodal point in the life cycle a generation earlier—load meaning and apprehension onto the present situation, thereby complicating adjustment (Walsh, 1983). If a family was successful in mastering similar crises or transitions in the past, its members will approach a current situation with greater confidence. It is important to search for such successes in dealing with past adversity, which offer positive models that can be transposed to new situations.

The meaning of adversity also varies across cultures. Poverty, for instance, does not carry the same stigma in many places as it does in the United States. In Morocco, even the poorest families are not reluctant to discuss their economic situation. Although a regrettable hardship, poverty indicates only a lack of material goods at the present time and does not reflect negatively on personal character or family failings. It simply means that Allah has not smiled on this family, for reasons beyond human comprehension. Despite grim economic prospects, the belief is widespread that things are bound to change for the better, Allah willing (Rabinow, 1977).

Sense of Coherence

The concept of *sense of coherence* was developed by Aaron Antonovsky (1987) as a model for understanding the emergence of health (a "salutogenic" model, in contrast to a "pathogenic" one). It assumes that, given the stress-producing nature of the human environment, our "normal" state is disorder and chaos, rather than stability and homeostasis. The question then is, what factors promote stability and health in the face of disruption and change?

A sense of coherence is defined as a global orientation to life as comprehensible, manageable, and meaningful. A strong sense of coherence involves confidence in the ability to clarify the nature of problems so that they seem ordered, predictable, and explicable. Demands are believed to be manageable, mobilizing useful resources, including relational resources. Stressors are viewed as challenges that we are motivated to deal with successfully.

A sense of coherence has been found to contribute significantly to health, mental well-being, and quality of life, and to be far more influential than such individual traits as temperament or intelligence (Cederblad & Hansson, 1996). This concept taps into important elements missing in such concepts as *locus of control* and *mastery*, which focus more narrowly on self-reliance and specific coping strategies. Sense of coherence addresses meaningfulness, including existential feelings of social integration and purpose in life, as opposed to a sense of alienation, drifting, or stuckness. Recognizing that no single coping strategy is useful in dealing with diverse challenges, flexibility is encouraged in selecting strategies that may vary to fit the situation and culture.

Antonovsky and Sourani (1988) attempted to measure *family sense of coherence*, the perceived coherence of family life in coping with a specific crisis. They studied working-class married couples faced with the husband's disability and subsequent pileup of stresses. They found that a high sense of family coherence predicted better coping and adaptation, with greater satisfaction both within the family and in its fit with the community.

In our rapidly changing world, where meanings may seem arbitrary and ephemeral, we search for patterns in the midst of discontinuities, just as chaos theory finds patterning in seemingly random phenomena in the physical world (Gleick, 1987). In the psychosocial realm, we search for meaning in relation to shifting social contexts (Gergen, 1989). As we approach the new millennium, we are confronted with intrinsic uncertainties, and there is a renewed search for meaning and coherence. The rise of religious fundamentalism can be seen as a cultural reaction to this crisis and the difficulty in living with ambiguity (Bateson, 1994). We must seek coherence in the diversity and complexity of our actual experience. This sense of coherence fosters healthy adaptations to the unexpected or chance events that affect our lives and bring about transformations in family and social structures (Patterson & Garwick, 1994).

Appraisal of Crisis, Distress, and Recovery

Our appraisal of a stress event and of our resources to deal with the challenge strongly influences our response (Lazarus & Folkman, 1984). The same event may be perceived as irrelevant, benign, positive, burdensome, threatening, or harmful; it may be anticipated with pleasure or dread. Stressful life events are most distressing when we feel little control over them or when they pose a major threat to our present understanding of ourselves and the meaning of life (Cohler, 1987).

Whether an event is viewed as a problem and how distress is handled vary with different family and cultural norms. Epidemiologists find that at any given time, 75% of all people are "symptomatic," experiencing physical or psychological distress. Yet most don't seek treatment, instead defining their distress as part of normal life (Kleinman, 1988). A troubled family may not seek professional help or may attempt to deal with problems in other ways. Conversely, as mental health professionals are the first to avow, seeking help can be a sign of strength. In fact, studies have found that highly resilient people do reach out for help when needed, turning to kin, social, and religious support systems, as well as to professionals.

How family members define and frame a problem situation will influence how they attempt to deal with it. A family's general world view may not fit a particular challenge (Rolland, 1994). For instance, a family that believes that no effort should be spared until a solution is found may have difficulty accepting and living with a problem that can't be solved, such as an illness that cannot be cured.

Causal and Explanatory Beliefs

When adversity strikes, we attempt to make sense of how things have happened through causal and explanatory attributions (Kleinman, 1988; Kluckhohn, 1960). Some families hold a core belief that misfortune is a sign that they are sinful and deserve to suffer or be punished. Some blame others, or view themselves as victims in a dangerous and hostile world beyond their control. Many believe that adversity is simply a matter of bad luck. It's important to explore the family, cultural, and religious roots of such beliefs and their consequences.

Western culture emphasizes personal responsibility, in the belief that we are masters of our own fate. In U.S. society, we hold a curious split image of individual and family responsibility, crediting individuals for their success but blaming their families for any failures. Deficient parenting, by mothers in particular, is blamed for a wide range of individual and social problems (McGoldrick et al., 1989). Yet good parenting is rarely praised for contributing to individual or social well-being.

In many folk cultures, people turn to highly respected shamans or faith healers to confirm beliefs that they are not at fault for their problems (Wright et al., 1996). Blame for things that go wrong inside a family is externalized, as in beliefs that others who are envious, spiteful, or wish them harm may have brought about their plight. In cultures and religions based on fatalistic beliefs, adversity is ascribed to one's fate. Hindus may believe that misfortune is the result of bad karma, perhaps owing to one's conduct or circumstances in a previous life. In traditional Islamic societies, what happens in life, like poverty, is determined by Allah's will. A Moroccan friend once told me of his father's drinking and abandonment of the family, and of his mother's retreat into her own sorrows. When, from my American perspective, I was puzzled that he harbored no anger or blame toward them for his own life difficulties, he replied, "But you don't understand. I'll always be grateful to my parents: they gave me life."

In studying high-functioning, middle-class U.S. families, Beavers and his colleagues (Beavers & Hampson, 1990, 1993) have found that although they may never have heard of systems theory, they have what can best be described as a systemic orientation: They view causes and effects as recursive influences. For example, they see that attempts at autocratic control can trigger reactions of angry defiance, just as uncooperative defiance invites tyrannical control. Realizing mutual influences, family members avoid blaming, scapegoating, or typecasting as villains or victims. Moreover, they view behavior as resulting from many variables rather than from one "cause," and so they avoid linear causal assumptions. For instance, if a small child spills milk, many possible explanations are considered: The incident may have happened accidentally, and no motive should be attributed. There may be interpersonal meaning—for example, if the child wishes to provoke a parent. The child may be expressing upset unrelated to the family, or may be tired or anxious and therefore apt to make mistakes. Or the problem may be mechanical: The glass may be too large for small hands. High-functioning families consider many and multiple possibilities contributing to a problem, and their responses vary with the situation in a pragmatic fashion.

In contrast, Beavers and colleagues have found that poorly functioning families tend to adhere fanatically to one explanation, get locked into an idea of single causation, and are prone to blaming and scapegoating. The source of problems may be attributed to personal failings, with blame and guilt internalized; or else others may be held responsible, with blame externalized. Families whose members repeatedly blame one another tend to have more conflict and less solidarity than families who unite by attributing blame beyond their borders (Wright et al., 1996). However, a united front mobilized by the belief "Us against the world" can have a cost in social isolation, alienation, and mistrust.

In all family assessments, it is useful to explore patterns of problem explanation and attribution. Preoccupation with causal questions and accusations—"Why?" and "Who is at fault?"—invite blaming and scapegoating. Even in well-functioning families, parents (especially mothers) are particularly vulnerable to blame and guilt when something happens to a child, because of expectations of responsibility for their children's well-being. When adversity strikes, issues of blame, shame, and guilt can loom large, becoming as problematic as the crisis event.

> In one clinical case, Jean and Jerry were on the brink of divorce several months after their 3-year-old son had drowned in the lake behind their vacation cabin. Each blamed the other for not watching the boy, who waded into water to retrieve a ball and dropped from sight. They fought bitterly, faulting each other for negligence. It was crucial to explore and acknowledge each parent's own painful self-doubts and self-blame under the surface of their mutual attacks. Eventually, they both owned partial responsibility for the ambiguity in their communication about who was "on duty" at the time of the accident. Other contributing factors were also acknowledged, such as the rocky shoreline, which increased the risk of a fall. In shifting from blame to a fuller appreciation of many variables, Jean and Jerry became better able to share their sorrow, to consider what might be learned from the tragedy, and to begin a healing process together.

When people who are locked into a particular explanation of their experience are invited to reflect on their beliefs, they become freer to consider other possibilities. The following questions can be useful in guiding inquiry with families in crisis: How do family members make sense of the problem or crisis? How do they think it occurred? Do they fault themselves or anyone else? Do they believe it was accidental or intentional? Are family members preoccupied with blame, shame, or guilt? How do they agree or disagree in their views? What connections do they make to other adversities that have occurred in their lives and in their family's past history? How do cultural beliefs influence their views? Often this is the first time members have shared their private beliefs with one another. They may be surprised to learn that, deep down, each person blames himself or herself in some way, or that they've been fighting over assignment of blame in order to deflect unbearable pain, which can be more effectively eased through more empathic interaction.

Future Expectations and Fears

Beliefs about the future course of events concern personal agency or responsibility for a problem's maintenance, exacerbation, or change. Who or what is seen as making matters worse? Who could make things better? The locus of control may be seen as individual, familial, or extrafamilial. In a spiritual/fatalistic orientation, faith about what will happen may be placed in God.

Beavers and his colleagues have found that high-functioning families recognize that success in human endeavors depends, in part, on variables beyond their control; yet they share the conviction that with goals and purpose, they can make a difference in their own lives and those of others. They accept human limitations, believing that no one is completely helpless or all-powerful in any situation. Self-esteem comes from achieving relative competence, rather than absolute control, in dealing with a challenging situation. We can help families find ways that each member can contribute something helpful.

Our expectations, both conscious and out of awareness, are validated or disconfirmed in our daily living, especially through transactions with others. Our assumptions may lead us to take actions that fulfill our prophecies. Confidence in success encourages us to behave in ways that increase the likelihood of success (see below). Aaron Beck and colleagues (Beck, Rush, Shaw, Emery, 1987) have identified three self-defeating cognitive distortions, or types of faulty thinking, that increase human vulnerability: (1) minimizing or underestimating strengths; (2) magnifying or exaggerating the seriousness of each mistake; and (3) "catastrophizing," that is, expecting total disaster. These beliefs can be a major source of depression, not just a symptom.

Catastrophic fears are paralyzing assumptions that block constructive action and fuel self-defeating behavior. For instance, the catastrophic fear of loss, through rejection or abandonment, can lead us to behave in ways that bring about loss. Margo, a woman with breast cancer, who was terrified that her husband would no longer find her attractive and lovable after a radical mastectomy, withdrew from him. Fear of abandonment may also propel a partner to leave before being left. James, happily remarried after the death of his first wife to breast cancer, left his second wife abruptly within weeks of her diagnosis of breast cancer. She recovered; their relationship did not. The realization that there is no love without loss—that loss is inevitable in any relationship—can be a facilitating belief, enabling us to love more fully and to appreciate the time we do have together.

POSITIVE OUTLOOK IN OVERCOMING ADVERSITY

A positive outlook has been found to be vitally important for resilience. Perseverance; courage and en-*courage*-ment; hope and optimism; and active mastery are essential in forging the strength needed to withstand and rebound from adversity. Those who are resilient are able to view a crisis or a setback as a challenge. They approach it in an active way, invested in mastering the challenge and they emerge stronger for having done so.

Perseverance

Perseverance—the ability to "struggle well" and persist in the face of overwhelming adversity—is a key element in resilience. What may be taken for rigidity or stubbornness may also be seen as tenacity, a strong determination to persevere. At times, this requires bouncing back from failure to try and try again until we succeed. As Lillian Rubin (1996) put it, "We must be able to fall down seven times and get up eight." At times, we must make the best of a grim situation and stand firm, holding on with resolve.

The endurance and survival of harrowing life experiences can themselves be a source of pride. In studying resilience in African American men born into poverty and racism in rural Mississippi, Franklin (in Butler, 1997) was struck by their sheer capacity to survive to the age of 70 in those harsh circumstances. Elie Wiesel (1995) has written of the dehumanizing effects of the concentration camps where 6 million Jews, along with other "undesirables" such as gypsies and homosexuals, were annhilated by the Nazis. As one survivor attested, to survive Auschwitz while remaining a human being is itself a kind of heroism.

In Memory's Kitchen (DeSilva, 1996) is a poignant collection of recipes, poems, and stories written by the women starving in the ghetto and concentration camp at Terezin in Czechoslovakia. In an effort to endure the hunger, cold, and terror at the camp, the women met secretly to share and gather together their memories of the family life to which they might never return. They believed that they needed imagination and a link to their traditions to survive and preserve their identity and heritage. Their way of coping was to think of wonderful food—to transport themselves back into their kitchens and dining rooms, filled with joyous gatherings, loving husbands, lively children. The recipes evoked memories of feasts and celebrations, such as the blue plum strudel served at Rosh Hashanah, the Jewish New Year, and "Mrs. Pachter's *Gesundheit Kuchen,*" "good health" cakes traditionally taken to the mothers of newborn babies. Their remembrances were written on scraps of paper, stitched together by hand, and hidden to be retrieved after the war as a legacy of their lives. Although the women did not survive the camp, their endurance and their collected memories attest to the survival of the spirit.

Courage and En-*courage*-ment

Personal courage and the en-*courage*-ment of family, friends, and community are intertwined. As they did for the women of Terezin, encouraging and supportive relationships can build and sustain courage, especially in the face of overwhelming odds. In the gay community, the strong social networks have been vital linkages in sustaining the courage of persons dealing with AIDS over time (Weston, 1991).

The extraordinary courage shown by an ordinary person can also have profound meaning and inspiration for others, encouraging them to be bold. Rosa Parks is well remembered as the African American woman whose refusal to sit in the back of the bus became a defining moment at the start of the civil rights movement. Her courage shaped the spirit of the times. As Goethe wrote: "What people call the spirit of the times is mostly their own spirit in which the times mirror themselves."

The courage shown in the everyday life of ordinary families too often goes unnoticed. In the Cabrini Green housing projects in Chicago, parents and their children must pass through gang- and drug-infested corridors and courtyards daily to go to work and school; returning at night from a late shift is always hazardous (Kotlowitz, 1991). In a study of the family impact of neighborhood violence, interviews with mothers revealed enormous courage in steeling themselves each morning to get their families through another harrowing day, and trying, against all odds, to get ahead so that their children could have a better life.

Sustaining Hope

"What oxygen is to the lungs, such is hope to the meaning of life" (Brunner, 1984, p. 9). Sustaining hope in the face of overwhelming odds enables us to carry on our best efforts. The word "hope," originating in Old English, has found its way through many languages, with a similar connotation: "to leap with expectation." Hope combines an internal decision—a leap of faith—with an external event we strongly desire and expect to happen.

Hope is essential in repairing troubled relationships. Too often, partners give up on a marriage when they have lost hope that change can occur. Research-based couple interventions find that even in the most seemingly hopeless relationships, "reservoirs of hope" do exist and can be identified and strengthened (Markman & Notarius, 1994; Markman, Renick, Stanley, & Floyd, 1992).

Hope is a future-oriented belief; no matter how bleak the present, we can envision a better future. Hope for a better life for their children keeps parents in impoverished communities from being defeated by their immediate circumstances. The words of Martin Luther King inspire this hope: "We must accept finite disappointment but we must never lose infinite hope."

Learned Optimism

Although the "power of positive thinking" has become a cliche, considerable research evidence documents the strong effects of an optimistic orientation, particularly in coping with stress and crisis. High-functioning families have also been found to hold a more optimistic rather than a pessimistic view of life (Beavers & Hampson, 1990).

The concept of *learned optimism*, introduced by Martin Seligman (1990), has relevance for fostering family resilience. Seligman's earlier studies on "learned helplessness" found that people can be conditioned to become helpless and to give up on trying to solve problems, particularly when rewards and punishments are unpredictable or random, regardless of their behavior. When people learn that their actions are futile and that nothing they do matters, they no longer initiate action and become passive, dependent, and hopeless. Qualities of permanence, pervasiveness, and personalization contribute to learned helplessness in such beliefs as "Things like this always happen to me." There is evidence that depression and pessimism are mutually reinforcing and can deplete the immune system, impair physical health, and even hasten death, as with despairing elderly patients in nursing homes.

Interestingly, Seligman's own family experience heightened his interest in beliefs and explanatory styles. When he was 13, his father was paralyzed by a series of strokes that left him "physically and emotionally helpless." It was a foundation-shaking event that first depressed Seligman, but then lit a fire in him to do something to overcome passivity. The question that intrigued him was: Why did it spark that fire and not render *him* helpless, too? He became convinced that the difference had to do with dogged determination, persistence, and competitiveness: "I don't lie down and die." Family therapists will find it interesting that Seligman shifted his research attention from learned helplessness to learned optimism when he reached the age that his father had been at his paralysis.

An encounter with Jonas Salk, at a conference on psychoneuroimmunology, also redirected Seligman's focus to preventive work: Salk told him that if he himself were a young scientist today, he would focus on *psychological* immunization, not simply biological. Seligman contends that if helplessness can be learned, then it can be unlearned by experiences of mastery, in which people come to believe that their efforts and actions can work. He has theorized that through a process of "immunization," early learning that responsiveness matters can prevent learned helplessness throughout life. Currently his research team is "vaccinating" 10- to 12-year-olds at risk for depression, through work with suburban children, inner-city youths, children and their parents, and teachers who train children in cognitive-behavioral techniques (Seligman, 1995). To date, findings show that children who learn such skills as disputing their negative thoughts and negotiating with peers show less depression than control children, with effects increasing over time. Such findings point to the importance of strengthening family communication skills (see Chapter 5).

Although not everyone can change in every way, Seligman is convinced that, unlike IQ, pessimism can be altered. Although research suggests that pessimists may see the world most clearly, he believes that we must be able to use pessimism's keen sense of reality when needed, but without dwelling in its dark shadows. Yet a cheerful mindset is not sufficient; conditions must offer predictable and achievable rewards. Positive thinking is reinforced by successful experiences and a nurturing context.

Beliefs about Success and Failure

People offer a variety of explanations for their success or failure in a challenging situation. Such attributions are directly related to self-esteem (Brooks, 1994). In our mastery-oriented culture, researchers have found that resilient children with high self-esteem perceive success as largely due to their own efforts, resources, and abilities. They assume realistic ownership for their achievements and possess a sense of personal control over what happens in their lives. In contrast, children with low resilience more often believe that success and failure are matters of chance or luck, forces beyond their control. Such perceptions lower their confidence of future success.

Key beliefs about success and failure in resilient children have applications for family resilience. When mistakes or failure occur, highly resilient children view them as experiences from which to learn, rather than as occasions of defeat. They are more likely to attribute mistakes to factors they can change, such as insufficient effort or an unrealistic goal. In contrast, children with low resilience and self-esteem are prone to believe that their mistakes are due to their own deficits (e.g., "I'm just stupid") and that these deficiencies can't be modified. The senses of competence and control are intertwined.

Recent studies find striking gender differences in these beliefs, emerging in early adolescence (American Association of University Women, 1992). Boys tend to credit their own efforts for success but to attribute failure to bad luck. In contrast, girls tend to discount their abilities, seeing their successes as a matter of luck, and are more likely to fault themselves when things go wrong. These beliefs have been found to be reinforced through differential treatment by teachers (largely out of their awareness), such as greater attention and praise to boys. Such socialization processes contribute to declining confidence and self-esteem for girls, as well as lowered expectations for success.

Severe and persistent adverse conditions with forces largely beyond personal control, such as chronic poverty, breed helplessness and hopelessness. For poor minority youth, especially young African American men, both self-esteem and resilience erode when job opportunities and encouragement for success are lacking (Wilson, 1996). Future success becomes less likely as individuals and their families expect to fail and retreat from demands, or they resort to self-defeating coping strategies that worsen their situation.

Positive Illusions

In surveying epidemiological research, Shelley Taylor (1989) found that people who hold selective positive biases about stressful situations tend to do better than those who have a hard grasp of a reality that may be depressing, such as life-threatening illness. These "positive illusions" sustain hope in the face of crisis, enabling such individuals to carry on their best efforts to overcome the odds. Taylor also found that most people tend to see themselves as less vulnerable than others to a wide variety of risks. Among normal college students, individuals facing traumatic events, cancer and heart disease patients, and men at risk for AIDS, 85–90% of all subjects held such biases.

Taylor emphasizes that positive illusions are distinct from defensive denial or repression of distress, in that information about a stressful event or a threat is incorporated and its implications are absorbed. Whereas defense mechanisms become more exaggerated in response to anxiety and break down under extreme stress, positive illusions function as a buffer against extreme stress and promote strong mental health. They are associated with a wide variety of indices of adaptive coping, such as persistence at tasks, willingness to help others, and high functioning.

Such positive illusions are also common in couple and family relationships. Despite the current divorce rate of nearly 50%, few people believe that they will be among the divorce statistics. When researcher Blaine Fowers and colleagues (Fowers, Lyons, & Montel, 1996) asked married couples what they thought their chance of divorce was, the average response was only 10%. Over 75% of the couples did not even acknowledge divorce as a remote possibility. This led Fowers to look more closely at "marital illusions"—fantasies and unrealistic ideas people hold about marriage in general or about their partners in particular. He found that happy couples were more likely to form such illusions than unhappy couples, holding unrealistically rosy images of their relationships. They idealized their spouses, attributing more positive qualities to them than to anyone else and giving their partners more credit than themselves for the positive aspects of their marriage. Nevertheless, extremely unrealistic expectations that one can "have it all," or can meet all one's needs through marriage, placed an undue burden on the relationship and on the partner.

Resilience is not fostered by simply looking at "the sunny side" without acknowledging painful realities and giving voice to concerns. Each family's suffering is unique, and attempts to have persons "cheer up" or "count their blessings" can unintentionally trivialize their experience. Reassuring platitudes such as "It'll all work out," or "Life could be worse," though meant to offer comfort and solace, are usually felt to be unempathic and unhelpful when the pain and heartache experienced in the particular crisis situation are not heard and acknowledged.

Shared Confidence in Overcoming the Odds

Science is only now beginning to understand the chemistry of the will to live and dogged efforts to recover as fully as possible. Norman Cousins (1979) has written of his success in beating the odds when informed that he had a progressive and incurable collagen disease. Told to expect only months to live, he refused to accept the verdict. He was not in denial, because he was fully mindful of the seriousness of his condition. Yet deep down he believed he had a good chance to survive for much longer, and he relished the idea of bucking the odds. As Cousins observed, "I have learned never to underestimate the capacity of the human mind and body to regenerate—even when the prospects seem most wretched." The conviction that his own total involvement was necessary in achieving his aim was a major factor. Yet he didn't do it alone; he was selective in finding a physician with whom he could collaborate to fully mobilize all his resources in that endeavor.

Similarly, resilient families show unwavering confidence through an ordeal: "We always believed we would find a way out." This conviction and the relentless search for solutions fuel optimism and make family members active participants in the problem-solving process. Confidence in one another—a belief that each member will do his or her best—builds relational resilience as it reinforces individual efforts.

Finding Humor

Studies of resilience all find that humor is invaluable in coping with adversity. Cousins (1979) posited that if negative emotions can produce harmful chemical changes in the body, then positive emotions should have a therapeutic value. He attributed much of his own recovery from a life-threatening disease to his self-generated program, which included "laughter therapy"— watching old Marx Brothers films and *Candid Camera* vignettes, and being read selections from humorous books. Recent medical studies are documenting that humor can bolster our spirits and our immune systems in ways that encourage healing and recovery from serious illness.

For families as well, humor helps members cope with difficult situations, reduce tensions, and accept limitations. Humor can be particularly beneficial when it points out the incongruous aspects of a harrowing situation—the inconsistent, bizarre, silly, or illogical things that happen (Wuerffel, DeFrain, & Stinnett, 1990). In high-functioning families, members accept that people have the capacity to envision perfection and yet are destined to flounder, make mistakes, get scared, and need reassurance. This encourages both a sense of humor and an appreciation of paradox (Beavers & Hampson, 1993). As my mother, never at a loss for an aphorism, used to say, "Blessed are we who can laugh at ourselves, for we will never cease to be amused."

Mastering the Art of the Possible: Active Initiative and Acceptance

To be resilient, we need to take stock of our situation—our challenges, constraints, and resources—and then focus on making the most of our options. Both active mastery and acceptance are required. In her study of resilient adults, Higgins (1994) found that they took initiative in problem situations, accepted what couldn't be changed, and attempted to control and master what they could. In this way, resilient persons can be seen as masters of the art of the possible.

Remarkable mastery is often brought forth in the experience of immigration, which poses the challenges of loss and adaptation; strengths are forged through interweaving the old with the new for continuity and change. Immigrant women have often found food and cooking to be both a source of livelihood in the new land and a cherished link to the families and homelands they had to abandon. My grandmother Frimid came to Milwaukee with my grandfather from Budapest to escape pogroms against the Jews in the late 1880s. Forced to give up their previous lives, she used her cooking skills to start a catering business and raised geese in their backyard for *pâté de foie gras*, while her husband, who had been a Talmudic scholar, learned to become a shopkeeper. Drawing on her memories of life in Hungary, she found one year that the strange weather reminded her of a certain season in Hungary when the onion crops had failed. She withdrew all their savings from the bank and invested them in onions. Sure enough, the crop failed, and, having cornered the market, she became rich. Her picture on the front page of the newspaper was captioned, "Frimid: The Onion Queen." Family stories of her bold resilience have been a source of inspiration for me, as her namesake. (However, I have yet to realize any financial windfall!)

Beliefs concerning mastery and acceptance must be counterbalanced. Resilience requires acceptance of the limits of our power—appraising and acknowledging what we can influence and what we can't change, and then putting our best efforts into what is possible. A philosophical acceptance is most common among older people, and is an important source of wisdom with aging (Walsh, 1998b). Those of Eastern and Native American traditions are less focused on mastery and more attuned to living in harmony with nature. Control issues are more difficult for those of us with a European American mindset, who are very uncomfortable in situations where we don't feel in control. The practice of Western medicine provides an illusion of control over life and death. Seeking comfort in that illusion is one way to deal with our fear of mortality. But each time a patient dies or fails to get better, doctors—and family members—must confront the fact that this control is illusory. We live in an uncertain universe and can't "master" death. Still, we do have the ability to heal from traumatic experiences, even when we can't control or reverse them.

Moreover, mastery can be seen in terms of process. Family members may not be able to control the *outcome* of events, but they can make choices and find meaningful ways to participate actively in the *process* of unfolding events. They can be encouraged to carve out aspects they can influence. For instance, when death is imminent and no treatment options remain, family members can actively choose ways to participate in caregiving, the relief of suffering, and preparation for death. In such ways, they make the most of the time they have together and find comfort in loving one another well in the face of loss.

TRANSCENDENCE, SPIRITUALITY, AND TRANSFORMATION

Transcendent beliefs provide meaning and purpose beyond ourselves, our families, and our adversities (Beavers & Hampson, 1990). The need to find greater meaning in our lives is most commonly met through spiritual faith and cultural heritage. It may also be expressed through ideological views, such as deep philosophical, psychological, or political convictions (Wright et al., 1996). Transcendent beliefs offer clarity about our lives and solace in distress;

they render unexpected events less threatening and enable acceptance of situations that cannot be changed.

Values and Purpose: A Moral Compass

Understanding the connectedness of a life as a whole and in relation to others involves values, purpose, and meaning. Just as individuals survive and prosper best within significant relationships, families thrive best when connected to yet larger systems. A transcendent value system, whether conventional or unique, enables us to define our lives as meaningful and significant. To accept the inevitable risks and losses in loving and being close, families need a system of values and beliefs that transcends the limits of their experience and knowledge. This enables family members to view their particular reality, which may be painful, uncertain, and frightening, from a perspective that makes some sense of events and allows for hope. Without such perspectives, we are more vulnerable to hopelessness and despair.

In today's cynical social and political climate, holding ideals may seem naive, and yet values are needed more than ever in facing unprecedented challenges in our family and social world (Bellah et al., 1995; Doherty, 1996). In the public rhetoric on "family values," some argue that families fitting one mold have values while others don't. All families have values, however. Though some values vary with family diversity, many are held in common, such as parents' aspiring to a better life for themselves and their children. Persistent adversity may prevent families from fully living out their values. In work with families, it's important to explore their values and how they may have been strengthened or shaken by life crises. Family members can be encouraged to get in touch with their deepest values and best aspirations, and to commit themselves to live in ways that further the families and communities they envision in their heart of hearts.

In times of tragedy—whether the ravages of war, a terrorist bombing, or the brutal assault of a child—it requires strong idealistic beliefs to hold fast to core values and strive toward a better day. As family therapist Richard Chasin has observed, "Randomness takes the blue ribbon; evil takes the red; but from time to time justice shows" (personal communication, May 1994). Resilient individuals and families commonly emerge from shattering crises with a heightened moral compass and sense of purpose in their lives (Coles, 1997). His strong convictions and determination to achieve social justice enabled Nelson Mandela to withstand 27 years in prison; his vow to end apartheid was not only unshaken but further strengthened by his ordeal.

Families of homicide victims find strength by actively mobilizing their energies in seeking justice and find solace when justice is served. In banding together to support other families or prevent similar tragedies, their lives take on new purpose. In such ways, the development of an informed conscience often extends ethical concern, a commitment to action, and even a life course on behalf of others.

Spirituality

Many of our most fundamental beliefs are founded in religion and spirituality. Religions are organized belief systems, including shared and institutionalized moral values, beliefs about God, and involvement in a religious community (Wright et al., 1996). Religions provide consistent patterns for the living out of core beliefs, as well as congregational support in crises. Rituals and ceremonies offer participants a sense of collective self and, as Taggart (1994) so aptly puts it, "a place in the chaos of reality" (p. 32).

"Spirituality," an overarching construct, can be defined as "that which connects one to all there is" (Griffith & Griffith, 1998). Spirituality involves an active investment in internal values that bring a sense of meaning, inner wholeness, and connection with others. It may involve belief in an ultimate human condition or set of values toward which we strive; belief in a supreme power; or belief in a holistic oneness with the human community, nature, and the universe. It may also include numinous experiences, which are holy or mystical and difficult to explain in ordinary language and imagery. It invites an expansion of awareness, and with it personal responsibility for and beyond oneself, from local to universal concerns.

Spirituality can be experienced either within or outside formal religious structures. A discontinuity can exist between religious and spiritual domains in a person's life (Griffith & Griffith, 1998). Some may adhere to religious rituals and practices and yet not find spiritual meaning in them. Others may disavow formal religion, while finding and expressing spirituality in daily life. Congruence between religious and spiritual beliefs and practices yields a general sense of well-being and wholeness, while incongruence commonly induces shame or guilt.

Universally, the spirit is seen as our vital essence, the source of life and power. In many languages the word for "spirit" and "breath" are the same: Greek, *pneuma*; Hebrew, *reach*; Latin, *spiritus*; Sanskrit, *prana* (Weil, 1994). Yet spiritual beliefs and practices vary greatly across cultures. In Chinese culture, continuity of family relations is very important even after death (McGoldrick et al., 1991). Prayers may be said each day in front of a portrait of parents or grandparents placed prominently in the living room. It is believed that the spirits of the ancestors can be communicated with directly and, if honored appropriately, will confer their blessings and protect their progeny from harm.

Suffering invites us into the spiritual domain (Wright et al., 1996). Religion and spirituality offer comfort and meaning beyond comprehension in the face of adversity. Personal faith supports the belief that we can overcome our challenges. Yet, spiritual distress can impede coping and mastery and may foster an inability to invest life with meaning. Religious beliefs may in some cases become harmful if they are held too narrowly, rigidly, or punitively. One mother's self-destructive drinking was based in her belief that her child's death was God's punishment for not having baptized the child. A crisis may precipitate a questioning of long-held spiritual beliefs or may launch a quest for a new form or dimension of faith that can be sustaining. In the Bible, the book of Job is a story of resilience in which persistent adversity holds meaning beyond comprehension, and tests one's faith and endurance.

Many families in chronically impoverished, largely minority communities have lost faith. A pervasive sense of injustice, helplessness, and rage in being denied opportunity to achieve the American dream fuels cynicism about possibilities for a better life and loss of faith in the dominant belief system. In Harry Aponte's (1994) view, they suffer a deprivation of both "bread" and "spirit." At the core, these families suffer a poverty of despair, which robs them of their soul—of meaning, purpose, and hope. The Reverend Martin Luther King was and is a guiding spirit to many oppressed people through his abiding faith that social justice would prevail. Yet his was not a passive faith to wait for God's deliverance or for better times to come. Rather, it was a rallying call to collective action to bring about change, with an emphasis on personal responsibility and initiative.

Werner and Smith (1992) found that meaningfulness in terms of spiritual engagement was very important in long-term resilience. Faith can be even more sustaining than frequent participation in religious services or activities, which is also valuable. Medical studies suggest that faith, prayer, and spiritual rituals can actually strengthen health and healing by triggering emotions that influence the immune and cardiovascular systems (Dossey, 1993). In a study of elderly patients who had undergone open-heart surgery (Doka, 1998), those who were able to find some hope, solace, and comfort in their religious outlook had a survival rate three times higher than those who did not. What mattered most was drawing on the power of faith to give meaning to a precarious situation.

Spiritual connectedness and renewal can be found in communion with nature—in mountain vistas, a walk through the woods, a sunset, or the rhythm of waves on the shore. Many are attracted to gurus and places with high spiritual energy, such as cathedrals, healing waters, pilgrimages to Mecca or sacred shrines and temples. Beauty in many forms can have spiritual, healing effects. We can be inspired by great art, music, literature, or drama that communicates our common humanity. Music offers a powerful transcending experience in many cultures, from African American gospel singing, blues, and jazz to the ecstatic trance ceremonies of Gnawa nomadic tribes of the Sahara. As the Hopi Indians say, "To watch us dance is to hear our hearts speak."

For me, music has a deep spiritual resonance as well as a bond with both my mother and my daughter. When I was growing up, my mother was a concert pianist, a music teacher, and the organist at our Jewish temple. With an ecumenical command of the great hymns and religious music, she was also in demand to play for holidays, weddings, and funerals for congregations of various Christian denominations in our town. Music, whether secular or religious, was a transcendent experience for her—as it became for me, accompanying her on those many occasions, and inheriting her love of all forms of music, from classical to jazz. Although I don't quite share my teenage daughter's taste in alternative rock, I love her passion for music and her delight in hosting her own weekly music show on her high school radio station. When we are both stressed out, we stretch out together, close our eyes, and listen to Celtic and other inspiring world music.

The linchpins of resilience, faith, and intimacy are linked (Higgins, 1994). Faith is inherently relational; from early in life, when the most fundamental meanings about life are shaped within caregiving relationships, convictional faith is forged with others. Caring with and about others both sustains us and infuses our lives with meaning. Victor Frankl (1946/1984), in recounting his experiences in Nazi prison camps, came to the realization that salvation is found through love. As he visualized the image of his wife, a thought crossed his mind: " I didn't even know if she were still alive. I knew only one thing—which I have learned well by now: Love goes very far beyond the physical person of the beloved. It finds its deepest meaning in his spiritual being, his inner self."

Spirituality and religion have long been neglected in the mental health field; considered not the province of secular or scientific therapies, they have been regarded as matters best left to clergy or faith healers to address. Even with growing awareness of their profound influence, many are hesitant about approaching the spiritual dimension in psychotherapy (Prest & Keller, 1993; Walsh, 1999). The long tradition of separating psychotherapy from religion has marginalized and, in many cases, stigmatized spiritual beliefs, so that clients may only reveal the parts of their experience that fit normative expectations of what clinicians are concerned with. They may edit out the spiritual dimensions of their lives into seamless accounts that fit the dominant culture but render these beliefs and practices invisible. Griffith and Griffith (1998) urge therapists not simply to wait for clients to bring up spiritual matters, presuming them to be unimportant if not voiced. We clinicians may need to listen for what has not yet been expressed, and to show comfort and respect in exploring the spiritual domain as it is experienced. It is useful to draw out multiple stories and dimensions, deconstructing harmful aspects while encouraging new possibilities. For instance, some family members may hold an old childhood image of an all-powerful God as harsh and punitive, often connected to experiences of shame and helplessness when confronted by autocratic authority figures. We can invite stories of other spiritual experiences that have been positive, or even moments of inner peace, communion, and nurturance. These can be drawn upon and expanded.

As we expand our vision of psychotherapy as both a science and a healing art, we approach researcher Martin Seligman's belief that the soul—that which is deep within the personality—is the key to change, and that our change efforts must take the human spirit into account. Wright and her colleagues (1996) urge systems-oriented professionals to conceptualize persons as biopsychosocial–spiritual beings. To be most helpful to families, we must acknowledge that suffering, and often the injustice or senselessness of it, are spiritual concerns and that religion and spirituality can be powerful therapeutic resources for recovery, healing, and resilience.

Creative Inspiration

As Eleanor Roosevelt once said, "The future belongs to those who believe in the beauty of their dreams." Creativity is often born of adversity. Our imaginations can transport us beyond our crisis situation and can enable us to envision new possibilities and illuminate pathways out of our dilemmas. Resilient persons—and communities—often make the best of a tragic situation by finding something to salvage and seeing new possibilities in the midst of the wreckage. After a fire destroyed the city of Chicago in 1871, forward-looking community leaders gathered the world's greatest city planners and architects to rebuild it, thus making possible the transformation of the skyline and lakefront with innovative skyscrapers and vast public parks. We are all enriched when such creativity adds something valuable to culture and society (Csikszentmihalyi, 1996). Through their own creative processes, such writers as Ralph Ellison and Toni Morrison have drawn upon and transformed the brutalizing elements of the African American experience into art. Similarly, through music, the blues powerfully express and transcend the painful life conditions with which they deal.

Families must also be inventive to weather and rebound from adversity. A well-functioning family draws on a wide variety of inspirations to solve its problems, including past experience, family myths and stories, creative fantasy, and new and untried solutions. Bateson (1994) has underscored the need for an attitude of improvisation: "In trying to adapt, we may need to deviate from cherished values, behaving in ways we have barely glimpsed, seizing on fragmentary clues" (p. 8). During and after life-altering transitions, families often need to envision new models of human interaction.

Role Models and (S)Heroes

We can transcend the constraints of our own particular situations through the positive examples of others who model resilience and inspire our strength and success. Beyond the borders of our everyday world, we can be moved by the life stories of great men and women of courage and high attainment who have overcome adversity.

Children are often inspired to emulate famous athletes. "I want to be like Mike!" is chanted by children across boundaries of nation, race, class, and gender, who have found in Michael Jordan a hero who embodies many of the best qualities of resilience. Not resting on the laurels of his extraordinary talents in basketball, he works out many hours daily—honing his skills, pushing his limits, always striving for excellence, and developing new ways to compensate for injuries and aging. He maintains a tenacious will to win, to beat the odds, to persevere even when injured, and to rebound from failure and loss, which he views as challenges to try even harder. Although such an extraordinary person is commonly thought of simply as innately gifted, his many qualities of resilience were relationally based in his strong family upbringing (D. Jordan, 1996). His own heroes were his parents—his nurturant and spiritually devout mother, who instilled strong values, and his father, who was his mainstay and closest companion. In a life that seemed charmed, however, even Michael Jordan was not spared tragedy; his father was brutally murdered in 1994. In shock and grief, he left basketball, losing passion for the sport with the loss of his father. After turning to baseball (an earlier life connection with his father), he returned to basketball to lead a remarkable team in winning a fourth NBA title for the Chicago Bulls—on Father's Day. Hugging the trophy, he wept openly and dedicated the victory to the memory of his father. In many ways, Jordan broke the bounds of traditional gender codes for masculinity: by crediting the team effort that made this a truly collaborative victory, and by expressing his grief at his father's loss and his deep love for his family.

Parents can open windows to many realms and possibilities by reading together with their children from infancy. I grew up in a poor, working-class neighborhood, where most of my peers married and got factory jobs after high school. My own world and aspirations were enlarged through storytelling and reading. Some were constraining; such classic fables as "Cinderella" and "Snow White" were stifling in their gendered expectations that if I was sweet, compliant, and uncomplaining, I would be rescued by a prince and live happily everafter. However, reading the life stories of Jane Addams of Hull House and the scientist Marie Curie, I was inspired to imagine possibilities for my own life beyond the limitations of my immediate surroundings. Although I didn't consciously plan to follow those particular pathways, curiously enough, I later found myself drawn to social change and research. The book I remember most vividly from early childhood was *The Little Engine that Could*, which I now see as a wonderful story of resilience. When tempted to think of my own resilience as self-made, I need only remember that it was my parents who read that story to me at so many bedtimes.

With the complexities and ambiguities of life today, families need a variety of models who inspire a wide range of strategies for meeting life challenges. Yet, in seeking models, we often fail to see the many examples of heroism in our own families and communities. We attribute neglect to single mothers working out of the home when we need to appreciate the heroic feat of an undersupported parent who must juggle job, parenting, and household demands. Stories of uncommon courage and triumph over catastrophic events are valuable, but so too are stories of the remarkable strengths and vitality of ordinary families in weathering the storms of everyday life. In her winning school essay on the theme "A Woman I Most Admire," (*New York Times*, March 25, 1995) 11-year-old Amelia Chamberlain wrote about watching her mother leave for work one day:

> I watch from the house in wonder. How does she do it? How does she always remember to give me $3.60 for lunch money? How does she always remember to tell me that she loves me? How does she work all night and do errands all day? How does she raise me and my sisters on her own? She never gives up or says, "I can't go today." She never, ever, doesn't get up, no matter how little sleep she's gotten.

Amelia's story speaks to the courage and comebacks everyday people make every day—the heroic feats that don't get media fanfare as families make the best of the difficult lives they lead. For us as helping professionals, seeing the ways families draw on the capacity for resilience can inspire us to see and affirm the unrecognized strengths in every family we work with.

Transformation: Learning and Growth from Adversity

Resilience is promoted when hardship, tragedy, failure, or disappointment can also be seen as instructive and can serve as an impetus for change and growth. Resilient individuals believe that it's a waste of time and energy to be preoccupied with regret or bound up in retribution or nursing old wounds. Instead, they survey their experience and attempt to draw lessons from it that can be valuable in guiding their future course. In accepting what has happened and any persisting scars, they try to incorporate what they have learned into attempts to live better lives, and strive so that others can gain from their experience. A recent news story (*New York Times*, September 11, 1996) told of the life of James Coleman, Jr., a judge who was the first African American appointed to the New Jersey Supreme Court. The son of a sharecropper, he transcended early life trauma: "I've learned to use the hardships that I endured from that time to become my source of strength. I converted the energy and, to some extent, the anger that the system caused within me, into motivation" (pp. B1–B2). In turn, he dedicated his life to a career in justice based on fairness and what he believed to be right.

Learning from adversity, most resilient families believe that their trials have made them more than what they would have been otherwise. One couple nearly lost a son in a freak accident that shook the very foundation of the family. These parents share the belief that this crisis was like an epiphany: crystallizing a deeper appreciation of their family, a stronger sense of purpose in life, and a dedication to practice their values more fully. In the uncertainty and pain wrought by a life crisis, core beliefs come to the fore. As events are assimilated, they may come to be seen as a gift that opens a new phase of life or new opportunities.

THERAPISTS' BELIEFS: TREATMENT AND HEALING

The notion of healing is important in resilience. Distinct from curing, recovery, or problem resolution, healing is a natural process in response to injury or trauma. Sometimes people heal physically but don't heal mentally, emotionally, or spiritually; badly strained relationships may remain unhealed. Some may recover from an illness but may not regain the spirit to live and love fully. Yet we are able to heal psychosocially even when we do not heal physically, or when a traumatic event cannot be controlled. Similarly, resilience can be fostered even when problems cannot be solved or when they may recur. The literal meaning of healing is becoming whole—and, when necessary, adapting and compensating for losses of structure or function.

Treatment and healing are quite different concepts. Treatment is externally administered; healing comes from within the person, the family, and the community. In the West, scientific medicine has focused on identifying external agents of disease and developing technological weapons against them. Metaphors of war are prominent: "fighting" and "combating" illness; developing "aggressive" treatments to "destroy" disease. The "battle against" each new disease requires a new "weapon." An unbalanced focus on disease rather than health, and many patients' skewed clinical experience with serious and chronic illness, all contribute to pessimism (Weil, 1994). Even the word "remission" refers to a temporary abatement of disease processes that may recur.

In contrast, Eastern medicine is based on a different philosophy—a set of beliefs about healing processes and the importance of mind–body interactions. The healing system is a functional system, not an assemblage of structures. Chinese medicine, for example, explores ways to increase internal resilience as resistance to disease, so that whatever harmful influences people are exposed to, they can remain healthy. This belief in strengthening protective processes assumes that the body has a natural ability to heal and grow stronger. Mechanisms of diagnosis, self-repair, and regeneration exist in all of us and can be activated as the need arises. Knowledge about the healing system enables clinicians to enhance those processes at every level of biological organization, as the best hope for recovery when illness occurs. Interventions to promote these innate healing mechanisms are thought to be more effective than those that simply suppress symptoms (e.g., reducing a fever with aspirin).

In the field of family therapy, the treatment paradigms of medical and psychoanalytic models influenced early formulations of family pathology and strategies to reduce it. The more recent shift to strength-based approaches is predicated on the recognition and activation of a family's own healing resources (Minuchin, 1992). Yet powerful culturally based beliefs often lag behind new vision: Western combat metaphors still find their way into such innovative approaches as Michael White's "externalization of symptoms," framed in terms of battles to defeat negative forces (White & Epston, 1990).

Healing approaches to practice put faith in our clients' own strength to make themselves less vulnerable. If we believe that something can occur, its chances are greater than if we don't. Belief in drugs, miracle shrines, or healing rituals is clearly the basis of placebo responses that actually can be quite powerful (Weil, 1994). Resilience-based therapy inspires people to believe in their own possibilities for regeneration to facilitate healing and healthy growth. Therapeutic work best fosters healing when it is collaborative, activating a family's own resilience processes. Interventions aim to encourage the network of family relationships to become a healing environment for family members for the relief of suffering and renewal of life passages. This approach helps family members to shift their focus from problems and personalized blame to the healing of interpersonal wounds and striving to make things better. Families want to be healthy; as practitioners, we can strongly encourage their best efforts through genuine faith in each family's desire and potential for healing and resilience.

We must be cautious, however, not to attribute failures to overcome the odds or recover from adversity to insufficient positive beliefs, willpower, or spiritual purity. Some holistic health practitioners, emphasizing mental influences over physical states, have blamed patients or their families for not having had "good enough attitudes." To assume that families are responsible for their best efforts doesn't mean that they are at fault if they are not successful.

As we encourage families to alter constraining beliefs and author new stories of a better future, we must also make efforts to build a supportive social environment in which to bring their dreams to fruition. In middle age, Helen Keller (1929/1968) wrote:

> I had once believed that we were all masters of our fates—that we could mold our lives into any form we pleased. . . . I had overcome deafness and blindness and I supposed that anyone could come out victorious if he threw himself valiantly into life's struggle. But as I went more and more about the country. . . . I learned that the power to rise in the world is not within the reach of everyone.

For sustained commitment, an empowering belief system must be validated by experience and reinforced by larger social structures.

C·H·A·P·T·E·R 4

Organizational Processes: Family Shock Absorbers

The road to success is always under construction.
—ANONYMOUS

Families, in their diverse ways, must structure their lives to carry out essential tasks for the growth and well-being of their members. To deal effectively with crises and persistent adversity, families must mobilize their resources, buffer stress, and reorganize to fit changing conditions.

Family organizational patterns support the integration of the family unit (Watzlawick, Beavin, & Jackson, 1967; Minuchin, 1974). Such patterns define relationships and regulate behavior. They are maintained by external and internal norms, reinforced by cultural and family belief systems. Culturally normative rules influence many aspects of family organization, such as the generational hierarchy. Other patterns are based on mutual expectations in particular families, formed through explicit or implicit contracts that persist out of habit, mutual accommodation, and functional effectiveness. This chapter identifies the organizational elements in effective family functioning, highlighting key processes for relational resilience: flexibility, connectedness, and social and economic resources (see Table 4.1).

FLEXIBILITY

All families, whatever their form, need to develop a flexible yet stable structure for optimal functioning. Each family system maintains preferred orderly patterns, resisting change beyond a certain acceptable range. At the same time, a family must also be able to adapt to changing develop-

TABLE 4.1. Organizational Patterns: Family Shock Absorbers

Flexibility
- Counterbalancing stability and change:
    - Rebounding, reorganizing, adapting to fit challenges over time
    - Continuity, dependability through disruption

Connectedness
- Strength through mutual support, collaboration, and commitment
- Respect for individual needs, differences, and boundaries
- Strong leadership: Nurturing, protecting, and guiding children and vulnerable family members
    - Varied family forms: cooperative parenting/caregiving teams within/across households
    - Couple/coparent relationship: Equal partners
- Seeking reconnection, reconciliation of troubled relationships
    - Forgiving and remembering

Social and economic resources
- Mobilizing extended kin and social support; models and mentors
- Building vital community networks
- Building financial security; balancing work and family strains

mental and environmental demands. A dynamic balance between stability ("homeostasis") and change ("morphogenesis") maintains a stable family structure while also allowing for change in response to life challenges (Olson, McCubbin, et al., 1989; Olson, 1993; Beavers & Hampson, 1990, 1993).

Stability

To function well, a family requires the stability of predictable, consistent rules, roles, and patterns of interaction. Members need to know what is expected of them and what they can expect of one another. Reliability is crucial: family members can be depended on to follow through with commitments they've made.

Rituals and routines maintain a sense of continuity over time, linking past, present, and future through shared traditions and expectations. Routines of daily life, such as family dinner or bedtime stories, provide regular contact and order in what is increasingly a fragmented, hectic schedule for most families (Hochschild, 1997). In family assessment, it's very informative to ask what a typical day and week are like. Some families are too overloaded and fragmented even to have dinner together; parents may work on different shifts, with precious little time together at home. Seemingly small routines can make a big difference. Often children with school or behavior problems have no set bedtime, or bedtime is a nightly hassle, with overtired children becoming more wound up and exhausted parents' tempers likely to flare. Setting a reasonable bedtime is assisted by a nightly routine with pleasurable contact, such as reading, a bedside chat, and "tucking in." It also allows adults much-needed quiet time for respite at the end of a hectic day.

During times of crisis, disruption in daily routines compounds upset and confusion. When one single parent required long hospitalization, extended family members were encouraged to take turns moving in for periods of a week or so to stay with the children, who could sleep in their own beds, have their belongings at hand, and keep up daily routines and friendships, rather than experience further dislocation by moving in with relatives. When family life is reorganized, as it is with divorce, it is important for families to create new routines that also provide continuity of important bonds, such as Sunday brunch at Dad's house. Research on optimal adjustment of children after divorce shows that predictability and reliability of contact with a noncustodial parent are as important as the amount of contact (Walsh, 1991). Children are more likely to feel abandoned or uncared for when a parent drops in and out of their lives without clear expectations about the next visit, or when promises to call are vague and plans are repeatedly not kept.

Capacity for Change

Structural stability must be counterbalanced by the ability to adapt to changing circumstances and developmental imperatives over the course of the family life cycle, especially in response to crisis. Leading family therapists and researchers have all found that flexibility—the capacity to change when necessary—fosters high functioning in couples and families. As Virginia Satir (1988) observed, in healthy families the rules for members are flexible, human, appropriate, and alterable.

Similarly, studies find that factors predicting the long-term success of a couple relationship all involve the capacity for adaptability, flexibility, and change (Holtzworth-Munroe & Jacobson, 1991). Spouses must be able to evolve together and to cope with the multitude of challenges and external forces in their lives. Fewer couples would be wary of marriage, or would need to divorce and change partners to meet changing relationship needs, if they could forge relationships that are flexible enough to fit new challenges. We need to alter our rigid concept of marriage as a static institution. As the Hollywood film star Mae West once put it, "It's not that I'm opposed to the institution of marriage; I'm just not ready for an institution." Couple therapy can be especially helpful in recasting commitment in terms of dynamic processes, with the partners sharing power to mold and reshape the relationship over time (Walsh, 1989).

Counterbalancing Stability and Change

In David Olson's Circumplex Model of couple and family functioning (Olson, 1993; Olson, Russell, & Sprenkle, 1989), relationship systems function best with balanced (moderate) structure and flexibility. A moderately structured relationship has somewhat democratic leadership, with some negotiations including the children. Roles are stable, with some role sharing. Rules are firmly enforced, with few rule changes. A moderately flexible relationship has more egalitarian leadership, with a democratic approach to decision making. Negotiations are open and actively include the children. Roles may be shared, and change is fluid when necessary. Rules are age-appropriate and can be modified over time.

In contrast, families at dysfunctional extremes tend to be either overly rigid or chaotic, with too much or too little structure. At the chaotic extreme, disorganization prevails. Leadership is limited or erratic, with roles unclear and shifting. Decisions tend to be impulsive and not well considered. Parents swing between overindulgence and neglect. Family members have difficulty following through with plans and promises, and this sets up repeated disappointments in expectations. Similarly, limit setting and discipline may swing between extremes of underresponse and overly harsh crackdown. In rigid systems, one person tends to dominate through autocratic, highly controlling leadership. Most decisions are imposed, with limited negotiations. Roles are narrowly defined, and rules are inflexible. Under stress, families low in structure tend to become more chaotic and out of control, whereas rigid systems tend to become even more inflexible and their behavioral repertoire still more tightly constricted. As Satir (1988) observed, in rigid families rules become nonnegotiable and everlasting.

Family resilience requires the ability to counterbalance stability and change as family members go through crisis and challenge. Skiing provides a useful metaphor to visualize the dynamic balance needed (Walsh & Olson, 1989). Good skiers are able to maintain stability while shifting position fluidly to meet the changing demands of the terrain. Going down the mountainside, they maintain a stable but not rigid stance. When a skier stiffens up out of fear of losing control, the risks of falling and of serious injury are heightened.

My personal experience with skiing held valuable lessons for my practice as a therapist. As a novice, my catastrophic fear of speeding out of control and tumbling all the way to the bottom of the mountain led me once just to sit down at the top of a slope and refuse to budge from terra firma. Lessons with a pro not only enabled me to overcome my fear and enjoy skiing, but furnished useful clinical insights. A good ski instructor first teaches novices how to stop (control over runaway processes) and how to fall without getting hurt. Next, skiers learn how to maintain a dynamic balance of steadiness and flexibility, which requires a constant adjustment while moving forward through changing conditions. Although my internal cues signaling terror (e.g., my pounding heart) protested that I wasn't ready, my instructor calmly yet firmly encouraged me to try short runs on a gentle slope (behavior change preceding and facilitating internal change). He provided a secure mentoring relationship by demonstrating skills and going just ahead of me, assuring me that he would catch me (quite literally a "holding environment") if I went too fast and lost control. Each small success, along with his praise, increased my competence and confidence.

Applying this analogy to work with families helps me understand much of what is commonly labeled as "resistance" to change and how to work with it. Change is frightening largely because family members fear losing control of their lives in a runaway process that might leave them even worse off than they are in their present predicament. Fear of the unknown can outweigh current distress, which is painful yet familiar. Those who have been in crisis and have experienced a terrifying and overwhelming state of chaos quite understandably hold catastrophic expectations about change; they feel an acute sense of helplessness as they fear that events will spiral out of control yet again. This apprehension is especially intense for multicrisis families, as I will discuss in Chapter 9. Therapy may be particularly threatening, because its stated objective and methods promote change. Many therapists even think of themselves as change agents.

In understanding the importance of balancing stability and change, helping professionals can become more respectful about clients' hesitation to engage in a change process when they are in crisis or precarious situations. We can better appreciate their yearnings for less change and more stability, and can strive to achieve a flexible balance. Like the ski instructor, we can encourage a collaborative process in which we actively structure the therapy and contribute our expertise and support, yet help clients to feel in control of the therapy process. An initial priority is to help them learn how to prevent runaway change by building skills and confidence in small, manageable increments. We can also help them maintain continuities and build new structures as they undergo disruptive transitions and must reorganize (e.g., after the loss of a parent). In exploring what is needed and valued—what family members *don't* want to change or lose—we can then help them find ways to conserve those elements, or to transform them in more growth-enhancing ways. Tasks and directives are valuable in building new skills and confidence, as well as in learning how to fail (fall) safely, try again, and succeed.

These insights have particular relevance for helping families withstand and rebound from crisis. Families in crisis experience an immediate period of rapid disorganization, which is disorienting and chaotic. A fear of runaway change and a sense of being out of control are common at such times. It can be reassuring to normalize this experience, to slow down change processes, and to provide strong structure to contain reactions and support the ability to tolerate uncertainty as families gradually attain a new, more functional equilibrium.

Crisis events usually require a family to reorganize. With a major disruption or turning point in the family life cycle, such as divorce or remarriage, a basic shift of rules and roles (second-order change) may be needed. Traumatic events, such as significant losses, stress the family even further and require major adaptational shifts of family rules to ensure both the transformation and continuity of family life. For instance, a couple may have to flexibly alter traditional gender-based norms for a disabled husband to assume the role of homemaker as his wife becomes the primary breadwinner.

Rituals are valuable in marking important events and promoting both continuity and change. Celebrations of holidays, birthdays, rites of passage, weddings, anniversaries, and funeral rites are important in all cultures, although they have varied forms and symbolic meanings (Imber-Black et al., 1988). Whether secular or sacred, rituals and ceremonies offer transcendence and connection. They assist in facilitating life transitions as they strengthen family and community ties. Wedding rituals are as important in remarriage as in a first marriage, signifying the formation of a new family unit; involving children from previous marriages in the remarriage celebration fosters the process of integration. Ceremonies celebrating commitment vows are especially important for gay and lesbian couples, who are denied legal and formal religious sanction of their union. Finally, the renewal of vows can serve as a healing recommitment for spouses/partners who wish to repair a rupture in their relationship (see Chapter 10).

CONNECTEDNESS

A second central dimension of family organization involves *connectedness*. Olson (1993; Olson, Russell, & Sprenkle, 1989) has defined "cohesion" as the emotional bonding of family members with one another. In the assessment instruments developed by Olson's group, cohesion is assessed specifically in terms of such structural variables as boundaries and coalitions; time and space together versus apart; and involvement with friends, interests, and recreation. Families tend to do best when they balance closeness and commitment with tolerance for separateness and differences.

Beavers and Hampson (1990, 1993) describe similar processes in systems terms: "centripetal" and "centrifugal" tendencies. Families with a highly connected centripetal style orient their lives inward. Members seek satisfaction and connection primarily within the family, and children are slower to leave home. In centrifugal families, members turn more outside the family for satisfaction and often leave home earlier than the developmental norm.

In my work on resilience, I have come to prefer the term "connectedness" to describe the counterbalance of unity, mutual support, and collaboration with the separateness and autonomy of the individual. Family members can be highly connected and rally together in times of crisis as well as respect differences among members.

Balancing Unity and Separateness

For individuals *and* their families to surmount adversity, members need to believe that they can turn to one another, and at the same time that their own efforts, sense of competence, and self-worth will be nurtured and reinforced. In well-functioning families, members invest themselves in one another in their day-to-day involvement (Beavers & Hampson, 1990; Epstein et al., 1993). An optimally functioning family provides what psychoanalysts describe as a "holding environment" for its members: a context of security, trust, and nurturance to support individual growth and development (Scharff & Scharff, 1987). Family members take an active interest in what is important to each other, even though many interests may vary. They can respond empathically, without overidentifying or personalizing.

In times of trouble, family members do best when they can turn to one another for support and collaboration. As Stinnett and his colleagues (Stinnett & DeFrain, 1985; Stinnett et al., 1981) found, pulling together is one of the most important processes in weathering crises. Every member—even a small child, a disabled parent, or a frail grandparent—can have a part to play in easing family burdens or providing comfort, and each is helped by being included in some way. In assigning tasks or solving problems in family therapy, it's important to help the family find ways for every member to participate actively.

The comfort and security provided by warm, caring relationships is especially critical in withstanding catastrophic events such as wars, which induce social and personal uprooting, family disruption, separation and loss, mental and physical suffering, and vast social change. The security provided by families in war zones was found to be crucial in buffering such stresses as bombings, air raids, and the horrors of witnessing atrocities and violent death (Garmezy & Rutter, 1983). When evacuation is necessary, children fare best when they are able to stay together with other family members. In adoption and foster care, there is increasing recognition that siblings should be placed together if at all possible (Minuchin, Colapinto, & Minuchin, 1998).

In healthy families, individuals are able to be both differentiated and connected. In more independent yet supportive families, there may be considerable emotional separateness and time spent apart; yet members still share some time together, make some joint decisions, and support one another. In more connected families, emotional closeness and loyalty are stronger. Time spent together is highly valued, and many interests, activities, and friends are shared. However, mutuality is best achieved when individuals possess a clear sense of themselves.

Although family organizational styles vary considerably, extreme patterns of *enmeshment* and *disengagement* tend to be dysfunctional. An enmeshed pattern is characterized by diffuse boundaries, blurred differentiation, and strong pressure for togetherness, all of which interfere with autonomy and competence. Individual differences, privacy, and independence are seen as threats to group survival, and thus are sacrificed for the sake of unity and loyalty. Intolerance is shown for separation at normal developmental transitions. In times of crisis, enmeshed families may have a large network proffering support; however, they readily become overloaded and overreactive, and have difficulty managing stress. Pressures for consensus can interfere with problem solving.

In disengaged families, distance or rigid boundaries block communication, relatedness, and the mutually protective functions of the family. Family members feel cut off, with little caring or commitment. In a sense, the whole becomes less than the sum of its parts, as family members "do their own thing" with little involvement or synergy. Separate time, space, and interests predominate as individuals drift off on their own. Members are unable to turn to one another for the mutual support and problem solving that are so necessary in times of crisis. Instead, individuals are isolated from one another and left to fend for themselves, as in a cartoon captioned "The Dysfunctional Family Robinson," in which each family member is huddled alone on a separate little island.

Beavers and Hampson (1990, 1993) have found that extremely fused families tend to bind children and make it difficult for them to become independent. Internalizing disorders, such as anxiety and depression, are more likely to develop in these families. In contrast, in disengaged families, members drift off or are driven away. Children and adolescents are more likely to display externalizing problems, such as antisocial and aggressive behavior. Similarly, Stierlin (1974) described adolescent separation problems resulting from intense centripetal or centrifugal family pressures either to bind or to expel members.

Although such extremes are clearly not healthy, a family's functional *style* should not necessarily be equated with its *level* of functioning. Family and cultural norms vary widely in preferences for closeness and separateness. For instance, a highly cohesive family style may be both typical and functional in ethnic groups that value solidarity and community (McGoldrick et al., 1996). Such families live by the motto "All for one and one for all." They expect that individual needs will gladly be deferred to the common good.

Families must also shift their functional balance of connectedness and separateness to meet changing developmental needs as they move through the life cycle (Carter & McGoldrick, 1998; Olson, 1993). In families with small children, for instance, close nurturing and protective parent–child bonds are needed for the children's secure attachment and well-being (Bowlby, 1988). At adolescence, family organization typically shifts to lower cohesion and control, to accommodate emerging needs for increased freedom, independence, and autonomy (Combrinck-Graham, 1985). Pressures for change by one member can facilitate change in the system or meet with resistance, generating conflict or symptoms of distress.

In clinical practice, the terms "enmeshment" and "disengagement" have tended to be used too loosely, pathologizing patterns of high connectedness or separateness that may be normal (typical) and functional in different contexts (Green & Werner, 1996). In many ethnic groups, such as Middle Eastern and Latin American families, respect for elders and high concern and involvement in one another's lives may be mistakenly labeled as "enmeshment." In most such cases, "high cohesion" or "strong connection" would be a preferable term. The great emphasis placed on independence and self-reliance in the dominant U.S. culture can lead to faulty assumptions of dysfunction and setting of inappropriate therapeutic goals. A common related error is to presume that a family is pathologically enmeshed when high cohesion may be functional and even necessary in that family's life context, as when the family members must pull together to meet a crisis.

Joan Laird (1993) raises this concern in regard to the tendency to regard high cohesion in lesbian couples as "fusion," with implied pathology. Because women's socialization emphasizes closeness and dependence, a relationship between two women is more typically high in mutuality. In a study of lesbian couples, Zacks, Green, and Marrow (1988) used an assessment instrument based on Olson's circumplex model and found that partners indeed scored in the "enmeshed" extreme of cohesion—a pattern considered dysfunctional. Yet, for the women involved, this closeness was mutually satisfying and functional in fortifying their relationships within a homophobic social context.

Family Subsystems and Boundaries

Connectedness can be assessed more specifically in terms of proximity and hierarchy (Wood, 1985). Family boundaries—rules defining who participates how—function to clarify and reinforce roles and to protect the differentiation of the system (Minuchin, 1974). The *clarity* of boundaries and subsystems, particularly the boundaries between adult caregivers and children, is even more important than the particular composition of a family. Ambiguity in boundaries and roles complicates adaptation, as in families with a member missing in wartime, or those dealing with the progressive losses and confusional state of a member with Alzheimer's disease (Boss, Caron, Horbal, & Mortimer, 1990).

Although intrafamilial boundaries must be firm, the system must also be flexible enough for both autonomy and interdependence, which are needed for the psychosocial growth of members, for maintaining the integrity of the system, and for continuity and restructuring in response to stress.

Interpersonal Boundaries, Individual Differentiation, and Autonomy

Interpersonal boundaries define and separate family members, promoting individual identity and autonomous functioning. High-functioning families tend to maintain clear boundaries between members. A wife's needs are distinguished from her husband's. A teenager's privacy is respected. In more dysfunctional families, boundaries tend to be blurred and confused, with members intruding into others' personal space and privacy. Parents may be narcissistically involved, reflecting their own feelings and needs, or excessively involved, with difficulty in differentiating one person from another (Bowen, 1978). As one father explained in regard to hitting his son, "When I look at him, I see me; he's got all my bad habits, and I try to knock 'em out of him." In enmeshed families, there may be an unspoken rule against closing a door for privacy. A jealous, possessive husband may not tolerate his wife's going out with friends at night. An anorectic college student I worked with couldn't buy clothes unless Daddy took her shopping and had her try them on for his approval.

The development of well-differentiated identity and autonomy is important for competence. It requires respect for clear boundaries and an ability to accept differences. In high-functioning families, members take responsibility for their own thoughts, feelings, and actions. They respect the unique qualities and subjective views of others. In fact, the ability to tolerate and encourage separateness, differences, and autonomy fosters high intimacy (Whitaker & Keith, 1981). Autonomy should not be confused with low cohesion or disengagement (Beavers & Hampson, 1993), in which family members avoid contact or distance emotionally in an insecure, pseudoindependent stance.

North American and British cultures, viewing the rugged individual as the standard of healthy (male) maturity, have overemphasized the need to become independent *from* the family. Accordingly, traditional theories of healthy child development stressed the importance of separation and individuation processes. Closeness to and dependence on parents (especiallly mothers) were viewed as harmful to children—particularly to sons—hampering their ability to function successfully in the larger world (McGoldrick et al., 1989). Launching, or leaving home, has been regarded as the marker or proof of reaching adulthood successfully. However, economic conditions in recent years have brought many young adults back to the nest. Contrary to the myth of disconnection, research in adult development finds that most families maintain strong, *inter*dependent intergenerational relationships throughout life. Although most adult children and their parents prefer to live in separate households, they value proximity and contact—a pattern that has been aptly termed "intimacy at a distance" (Walsh, 1998b).

Contributions from feminist family therapists (e.g., McGoldrick et al., 1989; Weingarten, 1994) and from Stone Center theorists (Jordan, Kaplan, Miller, Stiver, & Surrey, 1991), who have advanced a relational model of human development, have challenged gender-based assumptions that promote disconnection. Whereas early family theorists emphasized boundaries and hierarchy—structural properties consonant with societal values for "healthy" male gender socialization—more recent family therapists have come to value relational connectedness for well-rounded human functioning and the ability to form and sustain collaborative and intimate relationships.

Generational Boundaries

Generational boundaries—the rules differentiating parents' and children's rights and obligations—maintain hierarchical organization in families. In well-functioning families, these boundaries too are clear and firm (Beavers & Hampson, 1993). Boundaries are established by parents or adult caregivers to reinforce leadership and authority and to deal effectively with such issues as nurturance and discipline. They also protect the exclusivity of a couple's relationship from intrusion by children or extended family. Three or even four generations may be actively involved in family functioning. A variety of arrangements can be workable if the social organization and generational hierarchy are clear. When parents and grandparents live together, intergenerational tensions commonly arise in regard to authority issues.

Generational boundaries may be breached by parentification of a child. Yet we should be careful not to presume dysfunction when children assume quasi-parental duties, especially in underresourced families. In single-parent and large families, it may be necessary and functional for older children to take considerable responsibility to assist with financial, housekeeping, and child care demands. In a family crisis (e.g., a disabling illness), a child may also be thrust into premature responsibilities, such as a caretaking role or a job to help out when a family is pinched financially. In healthier families, such role assignment is delegated with children assisting adults, who remain in charge. These responsibilities foster early competence and are not harmful, as long as the role burden is not excessive and other family members share tasks to the best of their ability. Boundary blurring becomes dysfunctional if parents abdicate leadership or turn to a child as an intimate mate or confidant, or if a child's own pursuits with schooling and peers are sacrificed.

Alliances and Teamwork

In well-functioning families, members form multiple and varied alliances around shared interests and concerns. In a two-parent family, a strong parental alliance with clear generational boundaries is important. Yet cultural preferences vary and should be explored in each case. For instance, in Latino families, the parent–child relationship may take precedence over the couple relationship as the dominant dyad (Falicov, 1995).

In family dysfunction, alliances and splits fluctuate erratically or rigidify. At times of crisis, intense upset can precipitate conflict, scapegoating, and cut-offs. For example, at their mother's death, two adult sisters fought over her jewelry and refused to speak to each other for many years, although they continued to live next door to each other. In triangulation (Bowen, 1978; Minuchin, 1974), two members (often a couple) draw in a third (typically a child) to deflect tension between them. The two may band together against, or in concern about, the third. The generational hierarchy becomes confused when a parent aligns with a child against the other parent (Haley, 1976). A child may be drawn in as a go-between for warring parents, or tugged in loyalty or power struggles. Distress increases when members become embedded in multiple triangles.

For resilience under stress, flexible alliances and teamwork are essential. Well-functioning families organize around individual strengths and interests. Many tasks are shared, while others are allocated. Progress is tracked with members held accountable for their part. Family members flexibly fill in for one another as need arises. It is important that no one is overburdened and others underfunctioning.

Shared Leadership: Nurturance, Protection, and Guidance

Parents are the architects of the family, laying the foundation for healthy family life in the structural arrangements, roles, and rules they construct. Today, family leadership is increasingly varied, from an intact two-parent family to single-parent and binuclear households, stepfamilies, and lesbian or gay partnerships. Families function best and children thrive when caregivers work collaboratively, with mutual accommodation to implement vital tasks. It is important for parents and other caregivers to be consistent in expectations and consequences for children. Caregiving arrangements that involve a grandparent or span separate households can function well as long as lines of authority and responsibility are clearly drawn and maintain mutual respect. With divorce and remarriage, children and their families do best when the adults are able to form cooperative parenting teams across households, involving both biological parents and stepparents (Ahrons, 1994; Whiteside, 1998). Families may need help for former spouses to put aside past grievances and for both old and new partners to overcome feelings of rivalry in order to work together for the sake of the children (see Chapter 10).

Strong leadership is crucial for the nurturance, protection, and guidance of children, as well as caring for elders and other vulnerable family members, especially in times of crisis. Leadership is also needed to provide basic resources (e.g., money, food, clothing, health care, and shelter) and to manage the many pressures and demands of everyday life (Epstein et al., 1993). In healthy families, leadership is clear; adults in charge do not abdicate their authority or responsibilities. At the same time, they are careful not to abuse or exploit their relative power over children, whose contributions influence decisions as their choices and responsibilities increase with developing maturity. Frustrating, self-defeating power struggles occur infrequently.

Families are critical learning contexts, created and responded to by all members. In well-functioning families, the exchange of benefits is far more frequent than punishments or mutual coercion (Patterson, Reid, Jones, & Conger, 1975). Parents/caregivers encourage children's success and reward adaptive behavior through attention, acknowledgment, and approval. They try not to reinforce maladaptive behavior. In less functional families, parents use more coercion and focus on misbehavior, failure, control, and punishment. Positive efforts and successes go unnoticed and unrewarded. Therapists can help families to affirm the positive behaviors and to encourage interests and talents. Since relationships involve exchanges over a wide range of possibilities, we can help distressed families find many opportunities for rewarding exchanges that enhance the relationship along with individual competence and self-esteem.

Families need effective methods of behavior control for keeping behavior within bounds so that transactions don't become dangerous or destructive. It's important to assess the rules and standards a family sets and the latitude allowed. Authoritative, flexible behavior control has been found to be the most effective style in middle-class families (Olson, 1993; Steinberg, Lamborn, Dornbusch, & Darling, 1992). Standards are reasonable, with opportunity for negotiation and change. Parents/caregivers are in accord when setting and enforcing rules. They are clear about what behavior is unacceptable, and intervene consistently when infractions occur. They make allowances when a situation calls for it, yet still maintain consistent expectations.

Rigid behavior control tends to be less functional. Standards are narrow, with minimal negotiation or variation across situations. Laissez-faire behavior control is also less effective, with few standards and total latitude allowed. Most dysfunctional is chaotic behavior control, with unpredictable and random shifts. Parents may let children run wild without rules or limits and then suddenly become rigid and punitive, so that children don't know what standards apply at any particular time or how much leeway is possible. Consequences for misbehavior fluctuate between no response and overly harsh punishment.

In highly disruptive crisis situations, very strong leadership is essential to restore order and direction in the midst of chaos. Moreover, as inner-city school teachers find, more authoritarian leadership is needed in classrooms and in families where community structures have broken down. Above all, caring discipline with firmness *and* warmth is most effective.

The resilience literature points to the vital importance of mentoring: guiding and inspiring children in positive directions. Yet, in the clinical field's focus on behavior control, we've given insufficient attention to the ways that parents, older siblings, extended family members, and community elders can all play a part in providing values, motivation, and active mentoring to children. This neglected dimension in clinical practice can be usefully approached by identifying and encouraging mentoring opportunities within the family network, supplemented by community resources.

Couple Relationships: Equal Partners

A couple functions best when each partner supports the better characteristics and creative aspects of the other in a mutual, equitable way. Family process research has emphasized the importance of role flexibility and balance to promote adult growth and development for both partners, with inequality contributing to distressed relationships and divorce.

Gender, like generation, is a basic structural axis in families (Goldner, 1988). Debates about gender roles and relations concern two distinct yet overlapping aspects of the gender gap: the *differences* between men and women, and their *differential* in power and privilege.

Gender Differences. The French phrase *"Vive la différence!"* expresses the view that men and women are essentially different in nature and that these differences provide a vital spark in couple relationships. Yet there is considerable evidence that although some differences are influenced by biologically based ("hard-wired") physical characteristics or predispositions, there is even broader overlap in individual traits, abilities, and preferences that have been culturally defined as "masculine" and "feminine" (Hare-Mustin, 1987). Most gender differences in family role expectations, relational styles, and constraints are largely shaped and reinforced through socialization from early childhood throughout adulthood to fit the values of the larger culture (McGoldrick et al., 1989). Studies on women's development find greater valuing of closeness and intimacy for relationship satisfaction (Jordan, 1992; Jordan et al., 1991). This gender gap is being bridged as men increasingly challenge constraining images of masculinity and seek greater emotional involvement in couple and family relationships.

Mothers, expected to preserve the well-being of all family members, typically play a key role in buffering families emotionally from the impact of crises. Regardless of the nature of the crisis or which family member is primarily affected, women (mothers, adult daughters, and daughters-in-law) tend to assume the lion's share of the myriad caregiving demands. In a traditional gender role split, women are likely to become overburdened, depleted, and unsupported, while men stand alone on the periphery, defined by their financial contributions. Helping women and men to explore ways to share burdens and appreciate each other's contributions can rebalance and strengthen all relationships.

Beavers and Hampson (1993) found that optimally functioning families show less gender stereotyping, both in couple relationships and in the raising of children. Although mothers typically do most child rearing, fathers tend to take more family responsibility than those in less functional families. In clinical practice, it is useful to explore and deconstruct gendered assumptions such as these: "Housework is women's work," "Women are naturally more nurturant," "Men are better with money," or "It's not manly to cry." Labeling human qualities as either "masculine" or "feminine" casts them as "proper" and "natural" for only one sex. We are all capable of a wide range of human functioning, and our resilience as individuals, couples, and families is strengthened as we expand and develop our full potential.

Power Differential. The balance of power is a fundamental issue in all couple relationships. In high-functioning families, partners are best able to work out strong egalitarian leadership in overt power and authority (Beavers & Hampson, 1990). Power is experienced through close, loving relationships, not through coercion. Control is expressed through self-control rather than control over others. Midrange and more dysfunctional families show more skewed power differentials, and wives, typically in a "one-down" position, are more likely to report being overburdened and depressed. The greater the power imbalance, with one partner maintaining a domineering stance over the other, the more dysfunctional and unsatisfying the relationship.

Issues of power sharing and equity are also important in same-sex couple relationships (Laird & Green, 1996). Lesbians, who have been reared according to feminine standards for collaboration and accommodation to the needs of others, may find it easier to share power and privilege. Gay men may have more difficulty with these issues, because male socialization fosters competitive strivings based on self-interests and power over others.

The balance of power is an issue distinct from whether a couple's organizational arrangement is complementary, with different role functions that fit together, or symmetrical, with similar and overlapping role functions. In principle, a couple's pattern can be complementary, without a dominant–subordinate dynamic. However, this is only possible if both partners' contributions are equally valued and neither one carries disproportionate burden or privilege. Couples are more prone to power imbalances in traditional family structures, reflecting the dominant–subordinate positions of men and women in the larger society and the different status of paid work versus unpaid housework and child care. When it is financially feasible to do so, many couples decide that it best fits their personal preferences and family needs for one partner to be the primary "insider" and the other the primary "outsider." Choice is important, and the partners must be attentive to culture, job, and family dynamics, which readily skew power and privilege over time (Walsh, 1989).

Dual-earner couples, today's norm, have more symmetrical relationships and face different challenges (Schwartz, 1994). When both partners hold jobs and share child care and housework, a division of labor needs to be worked out based on their particular situation, with demands, skills, preferences, and fairness taken into account. Bombarded by multiple, conflicting job and family pressures and by changes in role expectations, dual earners need to establish a very clear structure and yet to be highly flexible to shift gears and cover for each other as needs arise. Partners also need to deal with competitive conflict over the relative value of their contributions or competence in parenting.

Increasingly, both men and women are seeking to base family relations on a personal and shared vision of a more complete life. Yet most relationships are still skewed, as most employed wives continue to shoulder a disproportionate share of household, child, elder care responsibilities, and their coordination. Most men are more involved than their fathers were on the homefront, but most still carry far less household responsibility than their wives. With tremendous institutional resistance, it will be a continuing challenge in the decade ahead to counter rigid policies that devalue homemaking and caregiving, and that deny men and women full and equal partnership in family life (Edelman, 1992).

Reciprocity is essential for an equal partnership. Couple research supports the observations of Carl Whitaker (Whitaker & Keith, 1981) that a good relationship requires continuous balancing in terms of partners' interests and responsiveness. Mutual trust—and trustworthiness—are needed, so that each partner carries a fair share of responsibilities and enjoys equal privileges over the long term. In traditional marriage, the wife is expected to defer her needs to those of her husband—for instance, to pack up and move unquestioningly for his job advancement. In egalitarian and dual-career marriages, mutual accommodation and long-term reciprocity are crucial for relationship balance. This give-and-take is based on trustworthiness and follow-through—mutual assurance that each member's needs will be honored and that the exchange will balance out over time.

Addressing Gender and Power in Family Therapy. Family therapists have become aware that a therapeutic stance of neutrality and adherence to the tenet of circular influence tacitly reinforce cultural biases and ignore actual gender-based power differences in families. Ethically, we must challenge both overt and covert beliefs and practices that perpetuate abuses of power, particularly violence toward and sexual assault of women and children. We should also be mindful not to blame mothers reflexively for individual and family problems, to pathologize the traditional gender role caretaking responsibility as enmeshment and overinvolvement, or to fault working mothers for neglect. Concern for men's gender role expectations and experiences is also coming to the fore (Meth & Passick, 1990); researchers are exploring how the male model of rationality, control, competition, power, and instrumental success in the workplace has constrained men's family involvement, intimacy, and emotional expressiveness.

Women are more likely to seek professional help, to acknowledge distress, and to assume responsibility when problems arise in the family. We therapists need to work harder to engage men in couple and family therapy, because many men still view vulnerability and therapy as signs of weakness and inadequacy. Many men only overcome their reluctance to come for couple therapy when the loss of their partners or children is threatened. A partner in a one-down position (usually a woman) often feels that she has no power in a relationship other than to leave it. When a power skew is challenged, the initial defensive reactions of the more powerful partner need to be dealt with (e.g., fear of a reversal in the partners' one-up/one-down status, or fear that if the more dependent partner becomes more autonomous, she will leave). We therapists can encourage men's desire for and active involvement in change by tapping into their concerns about the treadmill of job performance, their role as breadwinners, and competitive power struggles that take a toll in estrangement from partners and children. We can help couples to transcend traditional gendered constraints and to develop creative new patterns that better fit and balance their needs. We can notice and explore gender role differences in order to bring assumptions and biases into greater awareness for discussion and change. For instance, we might ask such questions as this about skewed arrangements: "Since both of you work full-time, how was it decided that one of you would do all the cooking and housework?" We can explore stereotyped child-rearing patterns, or preferential treatment of sons over daughters. We can invite families to deconstruct the subtle yet powerful messages and constraining stereotypes that are played out in actual family life, and are observed and even reinforced by children. For instance, my husband and I share the belief that marriage should be an equal partnership. Yet, despite our best intentions, the old double standard creeps in. Our daughter once burst into my home office in the midst of my work to ask me to chauffeur her immediately to the mall. When I suggested that she ask my husband in the next room, she replied, "Oh, no! He's busy!" Whenever I jump up in response, I reinforce this unequal expectation.

We can actively encourage fathers to become more directly involved in child care, elder care, and housework, as well as in the coordination of home/ family demands. Often they must overcome feelings of incompetence, which may be reinforced by their wives' criticism that they aren't doing it "right." When women express ignorance and incompetence in regard to traditionally male domains, such as finances or "handyman" tasks, we can encourage them to gain new knowledge and skills. Tasks and directives are useful in this respect—for instance, having a father take charge of all housework and parenting responsibilities for a week without help (or criticism) from the mother. Many structural patterns operate on "automatic pilot." It can be an eye-opener for a dual-earner couple to review the management of a typical week in family life. We can then help the partners to renegotiate a better balance. It's also important to notice and change language patterns, such as speaking of men's "helping out" at home, which continues to imply that housework is really their wives' job. Women also perpetuate gender role assumptions, often unthinkingly. Once, when my husband and I both attended a conference and brought our daughter, someone asked where my husband was and I instantly replied, "He's babysitting." I would never have said that for my time spent with our child. Change is not a smooth process: we first need to notice what needs change, then catch ourselves when we repeat old patterns, and increasingly catch ourselves *before* repeating them, until new patterns become more ingrained.

Finally, we therapists need to be sensitive to ethnic or religious values that regard fathers as the heads of families. Core patriarchal values of authority and respect for men are embedded in many traditional cultures, as they are in some recent fundamentalist men's movements. This becomes a thorny ethical dilemma for therapists. It is crucial to assess whether presenting problems (e.g., a wife's depression) are connected to disrespectful and demeaning treatment, and to be especially alert to signs of physical abuse. Our values for social justice require recognition that subordination of women is essentially harmful and violates their human rights to dignity and equality (White & Epston, 1990). Families are strongest when both partners/parents share equally in authority and respect. Increased attention to sexism in larger social systems is needed, as we help men and women to build relational resilience by redressing their power differentials, sharing more fully in parenting, and expanding options for themselves and their children.

SOCIAL AND ECONOMIC RESOURCES

Mobilizing Extended Kin and Community Resources

In Bali, there is a wonderful tradition: All villagers participate in some way in the construction of every house in the village. By contributing a part of themselves, they all support the firm foundation of the community. Similarly, in rural areas, neighboring farmers pitch in to help one another in planting and harvesting crops. When families are open and generous, assisting others in need, they in turn, can count on neighbors and friends in times of adversity.

In our era of social fragmentation and self-reliance, we need to help families build these vital networks for resilience.

Founding family therapists (e.g., Satir, 1988; Whitaker & Keith, 1981) viewed well-functioning families as open systems with clear yet permeable boundaries, much like a living cell (Beavers & Hampson, 1993), with enough strength and integrity for highly involved interaction within its borders, yet permeable enough to allow a satisfying interchange with the outside world. In an optimally functioning family, members are actively involved in the world, relate to it with optimism and hope, and bring varied interests back into the family from their encounters.

Extended kin and social networks provide both practical assistance and vital community connection. They provide information, concrete services, support, companionship, and respite. They also promote a sense of security and solidarity. Community activities and religious affiliation also foster individual and family well-being—for example, through regular participation in church suppers, seniors' clubs, and parent–teacher associations. Emerging research suggests that there is something life-protective in belonging to a group and having regular social activity of any kind. This is particularly important for seniors in combating isolation and depression (Walsh, 1998b).

After my mother's death, with no family members nearby, my father's increased involvement in his men's organization brought him meaningful activities and structured social gatherings for many years. When he retired, living modestly on his Social Security check, he devoted his full time and energies to volunteer work, going to the staff office every day to assist in fundraising events on behalf of hospitals for children with disabilities. (My father had been disabled himself as a child.) As my esteem rose for my father, so too did my recognition of the value in such organizations as his, which I had earlier derided as "men marching in parades in funny hats." When my father died, all his lodge brothers, in their hats and full regalia, turned out for his funeral and gave him a glorious sendoff.

Linkages with the social world are vitally important for family resilience in crisis. Stinnett and colleagues (Stinnett & Defrain, 1985; Stinnett et al., 1981) found that strong families have the strength to admit they have difficulties and need help. When they can't solve problems on their own, they are more likely to turn to extended family, friends, neighbors, community services, and/or therapy/counseling. Conversely, family isolation and lack of social support contribute to dysfunction under stress. Recent research has documented what clinicians have long known: It is not simply the size of the network or the frequency of contacts that makes a difference; the degree to which contacts are helpful depends on the quality of the relationships. Since most people come for help when they are in crisis, assessment of social networks should identify conflicts and cutoffs that might be repaired. We clinicians need to search for hidden resources and to foster potential new connections. We also need to inform ourselves of community resources to facilitate linkages.

Extended kin networks in African American and other ethnic families have been misinterpreted by some as "disorganized" when they don't conform to the norm of the nuclear family household. We need to recognize the strength and resilience that are generated through these traditional kinship resources, particularly for poor single parents (Burton, 1990; Chase-Lansdale & Brooks-Gunn, 1991). Such values and flexibility have been vital in helping members of such families to survive the ravages of poverty, racism, and inner-city violence (Boyd-Franklin, 1993).

Because natural kin and community ties have become frayed for so many in our times, creative new connections that fit current family challenges often need to be established. For instance, many communities are turning to elderly persons who lack family contact and meaningful activities to provide needed assistance in understaffed child care centers. Both the youngsters and the elders reap tremendous benefits from this involvement. The children love the special "grandparenting" attention through such pleasurable and growth-enhancing activities as storytelling, games, and skill building. Older persons, who are too often undervalued and marginalized, feel energized, productive, and valued in contributing their knowledge, wisdom, and care. Particularly for elders who haven't enjoyed grandchildren of their own, this involvement provides a new and enriching opportunity late in life (Walsh, 1998b).

Multifamily groups are serving as valuable networks for distressed families—for example, by linking undersupported single parents or families coping with the strains of a serious illness. The Internet is also fast becoming a source of information and networking, such as for families seeking information about the special needs of a family member. Such support can be crucial in managing crises or prolonged stress.

Within both family and community, it's important to pursue many options in seeking out models and mentors. In cases where a parent is unavailable or unable to provide a positive influence, other mentoring relationships can be cultivated in the extended kin and community network. In inner-city neighborhoods, where positive mentoring relationships are desperately needed, Big Brothers/Big Sisters programs are demonstrating powerful results in preventive efforts with children at risk: Involved youths are less likely to join gangs or to take alcohol or drugs, and show higher school performance. The key in such a relationship is spending time together: engaging in chores and productive responsibilities, as well as fun activities, with a caring, positive role model, someone to look up to, learn from, and become close with. We also need to expand the narrow dyadic view of the relational base of resilience, and not expect one caregiver or mentor to meet all needs. When children are raised in a thick network of caring relations in family and community, the possibilities for nurturance and mentoring are many and varied. The African adage "It takes a village to raise a child" (Rodham Clinton, 1996) rings true more than ever today.

Enhancing Financial Security and Achieving a Family–Work Balance

To strengthen family functioning, families and clinicians alike need to take financial resources into account and to examine the structural supports and balances linking family and work systems (Piotrkowski & Hughes, 1993). In today's highly stressful life, two-earner and single-parent households experience tremendous role strain with the pressures of multiple, conflicting job and child care demands and inadequate supports (Hochschild, 1997). Parents are too harried and pressed to attend to their couple and individual needs. One working mother and father described their lives as being "like two speeding trains pausing briefly at the station to refuel and racing on." Although most women have become breadwinners, they do not yet equal men in status and compensation. Families face a real dilemma: If one parent (usually the mother) works less, income drops; but if both parents work full-time, time and energy for child and elder care are drained. The situation for single parents is even worse. The film *Kramer vs. Kramer* was hailed for showing that a father could develop into a fine parent on his own; however, it should be noted that he was fired from his job in doing so, because parental demands weren't tolerated by his employer. If families are to thrive, the workplace must be restructured to help workers achieve a better balance in their lives. These aims require a shift to a more equitable society, where family and community life is valued as much as paid work, and where men and women have equal opportunity and encouragement to achieve in both spheres.

The British child care authority Penelope Leach (1994) notes the paradox that after spending millions of dollars and developing the most advanced medical science to bring children into the world, U.S. society fails to support the essential conditions for families to raise children for healthy development. In a 1994 survey of 250,000 working women by the U.S. Department of Labor, the leading issues of concern to these women were the constant difficulty of balancing job and family obligations and the lack of affordable, high-quality child care. Many overburdened parents manage to keep their families and children functional only at a high cost to their own well-being; too many overloaded families break down as strains leave them more vulnerable to conflict and dissolution (Hochschild, 1997).

We can look to other nations' examples in developing new models to sustain family resilience. Although virtually all industrialized countries have been experiencing recent social and economic upheaval, disruptions else-where are cushioned by social policies that safeguard family well-being, child and elder care, and expanding roles for men and women. Throughout Europe, family policy is part of general economic policy, and governments provide a range of supports for families across income groups and without stigma attached. In Scandinavian countries, family life and child welfare are considered crucial to the well-being of society. Scandinavian policies and practices actively support a balance between family life and paid work for both men and women. These policies and practices are based on two assumptions: (1) that men and women are equally responsible for the financial support, daily care, and well-being of their children; and (2) that involvement in parenthood should not disadvantage people in job security, earnings, or advancement. Parental leave and a variety of child care arrangements are guaranteed *child* entitlements.

With mothers, fathers, and other caregivers in the workforce today, and with diversity in family structures and resources, U.S. families require a national commitment to affordable, high-quality child and elder care, universal health care, and more flexible job structures and schedules, in order to support healthy family functioning and the well-being of all members. Employers need to develop innovative options—including job sharing, a shorter work week, and home-based employment—to meet the child-rearing needs of both fathers and mothers, and to fit the abilities and constraints of older people who want or need to keep working through their later years. The whole concept of the Western family has to be expanded so as to legitimize and optimize the varied experiences of most families. Some countries, such as Britain, are ahead of the United States in legislation that recognizes family diversity and ensures that parental responsibility for a child's well-being always outweighs parental rights over a child (Leach, 1994).

We must beware of the myth of family self-reliance that has grown out of society's individualistic strain. The major problems of families today largely reflect difficulties in adaptation to the social and economic upheavals of recent decades and the unresponsiveness of larger community and societal institutions. These structural problems make it difficult for families to sustain mutual support and control over their lives. Skolnick (1991) advises that we put our efforts into supporting and protecting the family as

a place of enduring bonds and fragile relationships, of the deepest love and the most intractable conflicts, of the most intense passions and the routine tedium of everyday life. It is a shelter from the workings of a harsh economy, and it is battered by forces beyond its control.

In clinical work, family assessment and interventions must not be limited to the interior of the family, but must also attend to the family's interface with other systems and resources. We need to grapple with economic differences and the impact of poverty and disempowerment on families and their members—particularly on women, children, the elderly, and people of color. The change in women's work status adds pressure to women's demands for more egalitarian marriages. Greater financial independence, and less stigma in being unmarried or divorced, lessen the pressure to marry or to remain in an unsatisfying or abusive relationship.

Betty Carter (1996) urges clinicians to break through our reluctance to ask clients about their income and financial situation, and particularly about major shifts. For instance, over 20% of married women in the workforce earn more than their husbands. For many couples, relationship skew and strain are generated by the wife's job advancement or attainment of a higher income than her husband's; such events can stir culturally based insecurities and shame in the husband about his adequacy as a breadwinner. Marital tension and risk of divorce are heightened by difficulties in negotiating changing role relations and power dynamics. A single parent may need coaching to help negotiate a pay raise or a change in job schedule. Children may exhibit symptoms that reflect family concerns; for example, a son's school failure often coincides with his father's job loss.

> In one family assessment interview, Bill and Alice presented a tirade of complaints about their son's failing grades and stealing of Alice's savings from under their mattress. In exploring recent stresses, I learned that Bill had recently lost his second job, severely straining the family's finances, jeopardizing their home ownership, and fueling marital tensions. Feeling deficient as a provider, Bill was at a loss as to how else he could be a "good" husband and father. We examined expectations about what a "good father" meant for family members, and how their Italian American cultural beliefs equated "good father" with "successful breadwinner." We explored qualities and achievements other than a paycheck for which family members valued the father. Bill hadn't realized before how much he meant to them and how many ways he could contribute to raising his children well.

With major shifts in the economy, companies have displaced workers at all income levels and life stages. Those with the least education and skills are hardest hit, and their families are seriously affected. Rates of alcohol and drug use increase, along with marital and family conflict. Family support is crucial for displaced workers to regain confidence and build new areas of competence. A model family support group project developed by our Chicago Center for Family Health in partnership with a job transition program in Chicago (Operation Able) offers a psychoeducational approach to support and strengthen families strained by a breadwinner's job loss. In some cases, it involves the sudden loss of a white-collar job in middle age; for most, it involves the loss of low-skill jobs when a plant closes. The transition can run a roller-coaster course over months and even years; other placements are often only temporary and/or at a lower income. Weekly groups for 6–8 weeks provide orientation, support, and problem solving, with monthly sessions following to bolster confidence and family resilience over the long haul. In turn, families are better able to support the displaced worker's efforts.

There is no question that many families are in crisis today; yet this crisis reflects not merely problems *in* families, but scarce resources and a pileup of other social problems that burden families, especially those living in conditions of poverty and urban decay. The daily trauma of inner-city violence threatens even the healthiest families and their children with serious dysfunctional consequences (Garbarino, 1997). Harry Aponte (1994) has spoken out on the serious effects of the loss of community on family life, especially for the growing number of poor. In his view, the United States has become a society of stress, isolation, and distrust. Aponte believes that this societal fragmentation has made us a vulnerable people, and that because of it we lead the world in every category of violence, including murder, rape, and robbery. The poor "have all the personal and family problems everyone else has, along with the complications of a personal, family, and community (ecosystem) constitution weakened by chronic social and econmic problems" (p. 9). Teen pregnancy, single-parent families, divorce, alcoholism, and violence are not limited to the poor, of course; however, Aponte sees the poor as our "canary in the mines," warning us of our unsafe environment. Because the same conditions that are wounding the poor are also hurting everyone else in this country, finding a cure for America's poor may also heal the rest of society.

THERAPISTS' VIEWS
OF FAMILY ORGANIZATIONAL PROCESSES

No family form or style is inherently healthy or dysfunctional. Each family develops its own structure and preferences for certain transactional patterns. Whether those organizational processes are functional depends largely on their *fit* with family challenges in relation to developmental and social contexts. We need to extend our attention beyond the household to significant relational networks: All individuals are members of families, whether living under the same roof, within a community, or scattered at a great distance. The myth of the isolated nuclear family, intact and self-sufficient within the boundary of the white picket fence, should not blind us to the intimate and powerful connections among kin living apart. We need to recognize the significance of intimate partnerships and friendship networks, and to do whatever we can to rebuild our communities. The strength and support such networks provide to members confronted by adversity, such as AIDS (Walker, 1991; Landau-Stanton, 1993), is a model of community that too many families in the dominant culture have lost and can be inspired by.

For immigrant families in transition between two cultures, family processes that may have been functional in their country of origin may not enable them to adapt in their new culture (Falicov, 1998; Landau-Stanton, 1986). Such families may become caught between two social worlds, with tugs in incompatible directions. Here especially, we must assess the fit of individuals, couples, families, and their sociocultural context in any evaluation of health or dysfunction. Yet our objective should not be defined simply as helping them to "fit into" their new world; we need also to help families preserve valuable linkages with their cultural heritage.

Leading clinicians, as well as researchers, have noted the importance of key organizational patterns for healthy family functioning. Structural–strategic family therapists, led by Minuchin (1974) and Haley (1976), considered a strong generational hierarchy and clear lines of parental authority to be essential for optimal functioning. Bowen (1978) emphasized the importance of differentiation of self in relationships. Whitaker described the healthy family primarily as maintaining an integrated whole, characterized by appropriate separation of parent and child generations and by flexibility in power distribution, rules, and role structure (Whitaker & Keith, 1981). Above all, Minuchin (1974) urged us to view the family as a social system in transformation. With this orientation, many more families in distress can be seen and treated as average families in transitional situations, suffering the pains of accommodation to new circumstances.

Family and social networks are natural "shock absorbers" in times of crisis, as an anecdote from the career of Carl Whitaker vividly illustrates. Whitaker once presented a videotape of an interview with a "healthy family" at a meeting of the American Psychiatric Association. Many in the audience challenged him, pointing out a host of pathologies they detected. Labeling the father an "obsessive–compulsive personality," they viewed him as rigid and peripheral to the family, absorbed in his work. Whitaker rose to their challenge: He met with the family once a year over the next 5 years and then returned to the conference to present his findings. All family members were still functioning well. Most remarkable, for Whitaker, were their responses to crises that had occurred, as they do in all families. When the maternal grandmother became critically ill, for example, the mother turned her attention to providing the needed care, while the father made more time for the family. Rallying to respond to the crisis, he showed unexpected role flexibility in taking over household responsibilities and child care during those difficult months, and was able to comfort and support his wife and children through the illness and death of the beloved grandmother. As Whitaker noted, this family summoned its resources and showed its greatest strengths when challenged by crisis. We therapists need to share Whitaker's conviction that even in seriously distressed families, such resources can be brought forth to strengthen family resilience.

C·H·A·P·T·E·R 5

Communication Processes: Facilitating Family Functioning

> The important thing is being capable
> of emotions, but to experience only
> one's own would be a sorry limitation.
> —ANDRÉ GIDE, *JOURNALS*

Everyone would agree that good communication is vital to family functioning. However, expectations for "good communication" tend to be vague and utopian; cultural norms vary considerably. Family members also differ in their perceptions and priorities about communication. Parental desire for open communication may be viewed by adolescents as prying and intrusive. "Good communication" to the parents may mean that they want their teenagers to heed their advice and tell them where they're going, while teens wish their parents would listen more to *their* opinions and stop telling them what to do.

In recent decades, the challenges posed by high-pressured dual-earner family life, changing gender roles, postdivorce coparenting, and remarriage have made good communication ever more complex and difficult to achieve. In a sudden crisis or under prolonged stress, communication is likely to break down—at the very times when it is most essential for family resilience.

Communication can be defined broadly as the exchange of information, both socioemotional and practical/instrumental problem solving (Epstein et al., 1993). Every communication has two functions: (1) a "content" aspect, conveying factual information, opinions, or feelings; and (2) a "relationship" aspect that defines the nature of the relationship. The statement "Take your medicine" is a command with the expectation of compliance, and it implies a hierarchical differentiation of status or authority, as between parent and child. All verbal and nonverbal behavior, including silence—or spitting out the medicine—conveys messages, in this case, "I don't like it!" (an opinion) and "I won't obey you!" (a relationship statement). In every communication, either directly or indirectly, participants affirm or challenge the nature of their relationship.

A growing body of research on couple and family interaction has shed light on the most important elements in healthy communication. Olson (1993), for instance, has identified a number of specific skills in good communication, including speaking and listening skills, self-disclosure, clarity, continuity tracking, respect, and regard. Speaking skills include speaking for oneself and not for others. Listening skills include empathy and attentive listening. Self-disclosure involves sharing feelings about oneself and the relationship.

Because communication facilitates all family functioning, intervention efforts to strengthen family resilience focus on increasing family members' abilities to express and respond to needs and concerns, and to negotiate system change to meet new demands at crisis points. Three important aspects of communication are crucial keys for family resilience: clarity, open emotional expression, and collaborative problem solving (see Table 5.1).

CLARITY

Clear, Direct, Consistent Messages and Actions

A number of studies have found that communication clarity is essential for effective family functioning (Beavers & Hampson, 1993; Epstein et al., 1993; Olson, 1993). Satir (1988) also observed that, even allowing for cultural differences, communication in healthy families is direct, clear, specific, and hon-

---

TABLE 5.1. Communication Processes: Facilitating Family Functioning

Clarity
- Clear, consistent messages (words and actions)
- Clarification of ambiguous information: Truth seeking/truth speaking

Open emotional expression
- Sharing wide range of feelings (joy and pain; hopes and fears)
- Mutual empathy; tolerance for differences
- Responsibility for own feelings, behavior; avoiding blaming
- Pleasurable interactions; humor

Collaborative problem solving
- Identifying problems, stressors, options, and constraints
- Creative brainstorming; resourcefulness
- Shared decision making: Negotiation, fairness, reciprocity
- Conflict resolution
- Focusing on goals; taking concrete steps
- Building on success; learning from failure
- Proactive stance: Preventing problems; averting crises; preparing for future challenges

---

est. In short, family members say what they mean and mean what they say. Most communication is fairly straightforward, with messages conveyed to the person(s) for whom they are intended, rather than deflected onto other family members or transmitted through them. Verbal and behavioral messages are consistent and congruent. There is shared understanding; even with interruptions, members can pick up the thread and resume discussions over a period of time with effective results. Contextual clarity is also important in distinguishing reality from fantasy, facts from opinions, and serious intent from humor. The clarity of family rules is as important as the rules themselves, since they organize interaction, set behavioral expectations, and define relationships (Minuchin, 1974).

When communication is vague, distorted, or left unresolved, it breeds confusion and misunderstanding, as members operate on faulty assumptions or make attempts at "mind reading." It is especially crucial to be clear about the definition of relationships—what each member expects and thinks of the others, and what their transactions mean. For instance, it's important for a single mother to clarify what she means in calling the oldest son the "man of the house" after the father has left. Persistent ambiguity in messages about role expectations and blurred boundaries can foster depression and block mastery of challenging situations, such as caregiving for a family member with dementia (Boss, 1991; Boss et al., 1990). Communication unclarity can also adversely affect the course of serious physical and mental illnesses by increasing anxiety and confusion (see Chapter 8).

Clarification of the Crisis Situation

In times of crisis, it is helpful to clarify the stressful situation as much as possible. Often different family members have different understandings of events, based on bits and pieces of information or hearsay, and have filled in the blanks with their best hopes or worst fears. Shared understanding and acknowledgment of the prognosis of a life-threatening illness, the likelihood of an impending divorce, or the facts about a suicide are important for coping and adaptation. When family members have received limited or conflicting information—for instance, about a potentially serious medical condition or the fate of a missing child—they can be encouraged to gather more information, to request family meetings with medical professionals, to search through public records, or to press for official investigations to gain clarification. As we have seen in Chapter 3, family members do best when they can make meaning of what has happened, clarify what they can anticipate ahead of time, and determine how best to deal with it. Crisis experiences become more comprehensible and manageable when information and perceptions are shared, and when the meanings of events and their implications for family members' lives are discussed openly and fully.

When family members try to protect one another from painful or threatening information through silence, secrecy, or distortion, such communication blocks create barriers to understanding, informed decision making, and authentic relating (see below). Most members are usually aware of unspoken tensions in the family. Evan Imber-Black (1995) likens such a situation to having an elephant in the room—a huge beast in their midst that can't be talked about. Sometimes family members postpone any discussion until they feel certain of facts or a dreaded outcome, avoiding conversations altogether. It is usually more reassuring for them to share what information they can and to acknowledge the uncertainties they are dealing with. We can be helpful by coaching parents on ways to share potentially upsetting news with children—an adoption, a parent's alcoholism—and by advising them not to assume that if their children haven't asked, they aren't concerned. Truth telling is a vital process in coping with crisis and in healing from trauma, as we will see in Chapter 10.

OPEN EMOTIONAL SHARING

The recent interest in emotional intelligence, or "EQ" (Goleman, 1995), indicates increasing recognition of the importance of open emotional expression for successful coping and adaptation in life. Such abilities are developed in family interaction and can be encouraged in couple and family therapy.

Empathic Sharing of Emotions

In well-functioning families, an affiliative orientation can be seen and heard in behavior, voice tone, verbal content, and communicative patterns. Transactions are notable for a warm, cheerfully optimistic tone, with joy and comfort in relating. Members are able to show and tolerate a wide range of feelings—from tenderness, love, hope, gratitude, consolation, happiness, and joy, to such troubled feelings as anger, fear, sadness, and disappointment. Moderately well-functioning families may show occasional constriction in expressing feelings, or one member may under- or overrespond, but this doesn't disrupt family functioning.

A climate of mutual trust—a cornerstone of affiliative orientation (see Chapter 3)—encourages and is reinforced by the open, honest sharing of emotions in a well-functioning family. While messages are spontaneous, they are conveyed in a considerate way that respects the feelings, needs, and differences of others. There is strikingly little blame, personal attack, or scape-goating within the family (Beavers & Hampson, 1990). With an acceptance of uncertainty, ambivalence, and disagreement, members risk little in being known and open. Family members show interest in what each has to say and an expectation of being understood. Yet Gottman (1994) has found that active listening is not sufficient in and of itself—for instance, if a spouse simply verbalizes understanding of a partner's distress ("I feel your pain") without accompanying behavioral change to address concerns. When a family member is upset or expresses unmet needs, others best demonstrate empathic concern by responding in both word and deed.

In poorly functioning families, a climate of fear and mistrust is perpetuated through criticism, placating, blame, and scapegoating (Satir, 1988). Emotional expression becomes highly reactive, attacking, and critical (Bowen, 1978; Walsh & Anderson, 1988). Conflict can escalate out of control. A vicious cycle can ensue, for instance, when a parent responds to a son's misbehavior with threats to send him away, increasing his anxiety and provocative behavior, which then push parents beyond their tolerance and result in his expulsion.

Previous experiences of violence or traumatic separation in the nuclear family, in past couple relationships, or in families of origin can generate catastrophic fears. Such fears can lead to unspoken family rules to avoid all conflict. Unfortunately, this protective strategy heightens risks that unresolved tensions will build up and explode in violence or family breakup. In couple relationships, destructive cycles of criticism and stonewalling, generating contempt and despair, have been found to have a cascade effect: They lead over time to further withdrawal, loss of hope of repairing the relationship, and marital dissolution (Gottman, 1993, 1994).

Communication may be closed and secretive to avoid sharing painful feelings. Often this is done with good intentions of protecting children or other vulnerable family members, but its effects can be disastrous. For example, Mark, a man in his 40s, didn't tell his aging parents he was terminally ill until a week before he died; as a result, they had no time to anticipate and prepare emotionally for the loss of their only child. His death was so shattering that it triggered a heart attack in his father.

When parents are upset but try to spare their children from worry by not acknowledging their own feelings or by putting on a cheerful facade, children pick up the mixed messages. When parents don't explain the source of their distress (e.g., a precarious job situation or the death of a close friend), children are likely to blame themselves for being bad or unlovable. They may feel pressure to make up for parents' pain and suffering, or they may act on their best behavior so as not to burden them further. When children's own feelings and needs become submerged and unvoiced, they often erupt in symptoms of distress or problem behavior. Yet a crisis can also jolt family members into the need to deal with unexpressed feelings and unmet needs. An adolescent's drug overdose or a wife's threat of divorce can be the impetus for important conversations and changes to take place.

When families don't function well, ambivalent feelings are often not acknowledged or owned. Instead, they may become split between two partners or siblings, or two branches of a family. For example, members may have differing opinions on whether to terminate life support for a critically ill family matriarch, and they may become increasingly polarized as they argue intensely over the matter. After a tragedy, one sibling may carry all the sadness in a family while another becomes a clown to cheer up others. Enmeshed families may try to suppress mixed emotions or deny negative feelings and behaviors, while playing up the positive ones, presenting a false united front, or pseudomutuality. In more disengaged families, individuals may be strong in expressing negative or angry feelings, but wary of praise or affectionate messages. Family sessions can be invaluable in all these situations, helping members to get in touch with their own mixed feelings and to hear and accept the various feelings of others.

Open communication is especially important in dealing with a prolonged ordeal. One couple reflected on the importance of sharing their feelings through their son's cancer diagnosis, subsequent treatments, remission, and uncertain long-term prognosis. The husband said that his greatest lesson had been not to be afraid of fear; he had learned that bottling up his fears only increased them, but that expressing them openly eased his mind and brought the couple closer. Such expression is particularly crucial when family members are most likely to avoid contact and block communication to protect one another—and themselves—from painful feelings or memories of traumatic incidents. The unspeakable may go underground, becoming expressed in emotional or physical symptoms, or surfacing in other relationships or life contexts. In *The Body Speaks*, Griffith and Griffith (1994) present vivid case studies of psychosomatic distress occurring when important communication is blocked.

Loving Tolerance for Differences and Negative Emotions

As families move through various phases in adaptation to a crisis or prolonged challenge, such as a serious illness or loss, their communication processes will shift along with emerging priorities. Different feelings will surface at different times and be expressed in varied ways for every family member; loving tolerance and mutual support will be required, even when feelings are out of sync. For instance, a parent's anger at the murder of a child may be erupting just when other family members are ready to move on with life. Open communication does not mean "letting it all hang out," or constantly talking about the suffering experienced or a dreaded future catastrophe. It's essential that the reality of a crisis situation be acknowledged and that members turn to one another for meaning making, support, and reorganization of their lives; yet, over time, family members also need respite from focus on their ordeal. What's crucial is that communication not be blocked, so that members can feel free as needs arise to voice what is on their minds and in their hearts.

The innovative idea of "emotion coaching" emerged from a study of how parent–child interaction influences child development, recently completed by John Gottman (1998). He focused on how parents help their children cope with emotions. When parents are aware of their own emotions, they are better able to assist their children with feelings of anger and sadness. Acting as "emotion coaches," they treat feelings as healthy and worthy of attention. When parents do not deal with their own emotions, they may try to protect their children (and themselves) from negative feelings and shift to positive feelings as quickly as possible. Gottman found that emotion coaching helps children on many levels. For one, it helps them to regulate their physiological arousal. Also, if children receive emotion coaching from both parents, they show better peer relationships, do better academically, have fewer behavioral problems and physical illnesses, and are less violent and aggressive than those who receive no such coaching. Coaching was even found to buffer children from failing parental marriages.

Couple Communication and Intimacy

Epstein and his colleagues (1993) remarked that the most important finding in their research on family functioning three decades ago still holds true: The emotional health of children in a family is affected by the emotional relationship between their parents. When the couple relationship is warm and supportive, so that each partner feels loved, admired, and valued, children are more likely to be healthy and happy. This positive relationship between spouses did not depend on both individuals' being emotionally healthy, although this was obviously most beneficial.

In well-functioning families, adult needs for intimacy and sexual expression are understood and largely met. Intimacy for couples is fostered by relatively equal power. As Beavers (1986) notes, when couples toss aside struggles for power and control, they can experience deeper intimacy. The sharing of innermost selves is fostered in the presence of trust and the absence of fear.

Both partners can discuss their needs and differences, can show their own enjoyment, and can take pleasure in satisfying the other. Nonsexual physical contact, such as touching and hugging, is soothing and reinforces closeness. It is noteworthy that partners can find satisfaction in such intimacy with little or no sexual activity (Epstein et al., 1993). This is often the case, for instance, when one partner has a chronic physical condition that interferes with sexual functioning (Rolland, 1994).

With different gender socialization, women more often feel that their male partners don't talk about their relationship or share feelings enough, or that they aren't listening. Men, in contrast, tend to wish that their female partners would stop bugging them all the time. When a husband and wife seek help for "communication problems," for the wife this may be a complaint that her husband doesn't show enough affection, while for the husband it more likely means that the couple's sex life is disappointing. Psycholinguists have found that women and men communicate in largely different languages (Tannen, 1994). Women seek to build rapport by emphasizing connection and understanding, whereas men tend to stress reporting of facts and instrumental problem solving. Women are socialized to define themselves within a relationship, while men are reared to define themselves through individuation and separation *from* a relationship. Not surprisingly, this leads to differences in comfort with intimacy and dependence. In times of crisis, men who are uncomfortable with vulnerability tend to distance emotionally from their partners and to sexualize their needs for closeness, comfort, and support.

Sexual intimacy is bound up with other aspects of a couple's relationship. Dual-earner parents report that they are often too exhausted to enjoy sex and rarely have leisure time to nurture their relationship. At times of major family transitions, unexpressed feelings and needs centering around significant family decisions can have a negative impact on a couple's intimacy, as in the following case:

When Sheila and Carl came for therapy, they hadn't had sex since the birth of their third child, 4 years earlier. Carl had lost all desire for sex and withdrew whenever his wife expressed interest. Consulting a sex therapist, who explored the "mechanics" and tried to "jump-start" their love life, only made things worse. In exploring their relationship, Sheila complained that Carl never expressed his feelings; she stated that she always had to try to read his mind to figure out what he wanted, and that he was just like his father, who hid behind a newspaper whenever his wife tried to talk to him. Brought up in a Scandinavian family, Carl was unaccustomed to voicing his feelings and needs. To normalize and contextualize what was presented as his deficiency, I joked with them about the story of the Scandinavian man who loved his wife so much he almost told her.

As tensions eased through our conversations, Carl acknowledged that he had not wanted to have a third child because he felt burned out by their high-pressured dual-career lives. As their two sons approached adolescence, he had been going through a midlife shift, wanting to cut back on his heavy workload and enjoy life more with Sheila. She had wanted the baby so much that he hadn't wanted to say no, so he said nothing. When pregnancy didn't occur for many months, they underwent lengthy fertility procedures, and sex became a mechanical ordeal detached from pleasure. After the baby was born, Carl became increasingly distant. Looking back, he realized that he had been resentful of this intrusion in their lives and the additional financial burden they would have to carry for another 20 years. Sheila, who had secretly blamed herself for not being sexually desirable, was relieved to learn that her attractiveness wasn't the problem, and apologized for pressing to have another child. Carl owned that it hadn't been fair for him to blame her, since he had never really told her how he felt about any of it. Their marriage, which had been on the brink of divorce when they sought help, was now on the road to recovery, as more open communication processes increased mutual understanding and deepened their intimacy.

Fostering of Positive Interactions

Open expression of positive feelings is vital to counterbalance negative interactions. Relationships can tolerate considerable conflict as long as it is offset by much more positive communication, through expressions of love, appreciation, respect, and pleasurable interaction (Markman & Notarius, 1994). This underscores how important it is for therapists to go beyond the reduction of negative transactions, such as criticism and blaming, to active encouragement of positive interactions. When a chronically conflictual couple is helped to reduce tensions, the partners may experience a deadened sense of the relationship, reflecting the emptiness felt when they are unsure how to relate or move on from lingering anger. In the aftermath of a shattering experience, family members may feel numbed; chronic stress may lead to "battle fatigue." It can be helpful to revive pleasures that were once shared and to envision new possibilities for satisfying connection. I don't immediately recommend a candlelight dinner to partners who, in their discomfort, may slide back into lingering pain or conflicts. Instead, couples or families can be encouraged to plan activities together that give them a pleasurable shared focus,

such as a film or a sports event; that provide an opportunity for collaboration, such as a family softball game; or that offer a spiritually renewing experience, such as attending church or getting out in nature, to transcend their
immediate distress and draw strength for coping.

Mrs. Lamm and her four children were being seen in a therapy that was
stuck in their shared depression. They came for help after 12-year-old
Jeffrey attempted suicide by drinking some cleaning solvent. Family
therapy focused on their depression and anger at the father, who had
"disappeared" 3 months earlier without any word, leaving his family
uncertain of his whereabouts or whether he would return. The father,
who had a serious drinking problem, had drifted off several times in the
past, each time showing up a few weeks later as if nothing had happened.
This time it seemed that he might never come back. The more family
members talked about their helplessness and hopelessness, the more
weighted down the therapy became. The therapist, like the family, was
unsure where they were headed. The therapy seemed to be in limbo,
waiting for the return of the wayward father.

   Invited in as a consultant, I asked the mother and children how
things had changed with the father absent, and listened for a while to
their dilemma. I noted that they seemed to have lost the life of the family when the father wasn't around. Although his leaving and possible
return might be beyond their control, they could, if they pulled together,
regain the liveliness in their family. I asked what they enjoyed doing
together. They reported that the most fun they had ever had was going
fishing. I asked whether they might plan to go fishing one day soon,
possibly over the coming weekend. They nodded, but they all seemed
to be waiting for someone to make it happen. The mother was too depleted to take it all on her shoulders. I asked each child what he or she
might do to help make it possible. One child said he could clean off the
fishing poles in the basement; another said he could dig for worms;
the two others agreed to make sandwiches and pack a picnic lunch. The
mother brightened and offered to drive them to a favorite fishing spot
on Saturday morning. She and the children became animated in discussing the plans. I asked whether they could think of anything that might
keep them from going, in order to help them anticipate possible obstacles
(such as bad weather or a child's misbehavior) and reduce the risk of
disappointment by planning an alternative "rain date." Since the father's
unpredictability in his comings and goings was so problematic in this
family, it was especially important for expectations and plans to be clearly

communicated; for each member to take responsibility for his or her own part; and for all to agree that they would count on one another to follow through. The family arrived at the next session with spirits revived. After this, the Lamms were better able to take active initiative in other steps toward coming to terms with the ambiguous loss of the father and moving forward with life.

Shared humor can also be a vital source of family strength through crisis and hardship. Humor can help family members to detoxify threatening situations, facilitate conversation, express feelings of warmth and affection, lessen anxiety, and point out mistakes. It can reduce tensions, put members at ease, help them cope with a stressful situation, and restore a positive outlook. Humor can ease a direct confrontation, melt a defensive reaction, and lighten heavy burdens. Sharing a life story with both humor and pathos can have profound impact.

Family therapy pioneers were great believers that when therapists are able to appreciate both the grim and the absurd, therapy becomes more human, full of painful emotions as well as laughter. Whitaker stressed the importance of family humor and playfulness for creative fantasy and experimental process (Whitaker & Keith, 1981). However, humor can be destructive when used to express anger, cruelty, or contempt through biting sarcasm, or when used derisively to demean or make fun of others. In crisis-ridden families, humor may be lost altogether as family members become overwhelmed and depressed by the persistence of problems. Encouraging caring humor—members' laughing *with* one another—can revitalize families in distress.

COLLABORATIVE PROBLEM SOLVING

Effective problem-solving processes are essential for family functioning, especially in dealing with sudden crises or persistent challenges. Well-functioning families are *not* characterized by the absence of problems, although good fortune certainly makes life easier (Beavers & Hampson, 1990). What distinguishes resilient families is their ability to manage conflict well. This requires tolerance for open disagreement and skills for problem resolution.

Families need to develop effective strategies for managing, if not resolving, normal problems in daily living, as well as crises that arise. The practical and emotional aspects of a crisis situation are mutually interactive. When family functioning is disrupted by basic instrumental problems (e.g., the loss of a job and income), the ability to deal with emotional needs is also strained.

Likewise, a source of emotional distress, such as a threatened breakup of a marriage, can adversely affect school and job performance. A negative emotional tone between family members—anger, frustration, discouragement, or defeat—can block them from dealing successfully with serious or persistent problems. Both practical and emotional tasks of a major transition must be addressed. In divorce, for instance, a family must make decisions about household reorganization, financial support, custody, and visitation, as well as deal with the emotional resolution of grief and other complicated feelings such as anger, hurt, betrayal, or abandonment associated with losses (Walsh, 1991; Walsh et al., 1995). In cases where family members are constrained by traditional gender-based expectations for men to handle all instrumental problem solving and for women to be responsible for emotional expression and caregiving, fuller participation and sharing in these processes can be encouraged.

Based on the work of Epstein et al. (1993), several steps in effective problem-solving processes can be identified. Family members first need to recognize a problem and to communicate about it with those involved and those who might be potential resources. Collaborative brainstorming enables them to weigh and consider possible options, resources, and constraints, and decide on a plan. They then need to initiate and carry out action, monitor efforts, and evaluate their success. Well-functioning families manage to resolve most problems efficiently; communication, decision making, and action flow reasonably smoothly. Reviewing results permits them to fine-tune or revise their efforts as needed.

Identifying Problems and Related Stressors

When help is sought for a presenting problem—a wife's depression, a husband's drinking, a child's misbehavior—family systems therapists are careful to explore other recent or ongoing stressors in family life that may be reverberating throughout the system. A child or adolescent's behavior is often a barometer of family feelings and provides ample opportunities to draw fire from parents, thus deflecting concern from other painful or seemingly irresolvable family crises that require attention and assistance.

> Mrs. Wolff requested therapy for her 15-year-old son, Paul, stating that she feared that he "needed to be institutionalized" because his behavior was out of control. He had become surly and defiant in recent months, and she felt increasingly angry and helpless in dealing with him. The family assessment interview revealed that 8 months earlier, the maternal grandmother, with deteriorating Parkinson's disease, had moved in

with the family. Mrs. Wolff became tearful in describing her mounting difficulties in caring for her mother at home. She had had difficulty sleeping since finding her mother one morning on the floor, where she had fallen during the night. Alarmed by her mother's progressive loss of motor control, she felt helpless to prevent a potentially fatal accident.

When asked whether the family had considered placing her mother in an elder care facility, Mrs. Wolff replied that "institutionalization" was out of the question and had not even been discussed, since her father, on his deathbed a year earlier, had asked her to promise that she would always take care of her mother. Feeling alone in her dilemma, she deflected her conflicted feelings and sense of helplessness into struggles with her son. In a vicious cycle, the harder she tried to control him, the more defiantly out of control he became.

It's always important to explore how the response of a spouse or other family member may be contributing to the dilemma, and to encourage the potential resource their relationship can provide in meeting the challenges.

Mr. Wolff had increasingly withdrawn into his work over recent months, avoiding contact with his family. The therapist explored the strain of caregiving challenges on family relationships and asked Mr. Wolff what blocked his ability to offer more support. He choked up as he described how the current situation was reviving his feelings of guilt: When his own mother had become terminally ill, he had left all caretaking responsibilities to his sisters. He secretly blamed his own inattention for her rapid decline. Seeing his wife care for her mother rekindled his own felt deficiency and his sadness at his mother's death—uncomfortable feelings that he pushed away by distancing from contact.

Creative Brainstorming

When problems are identified, it's important to involve family members in creative brainstorming. In well-functioning families, parents act as coordinators—bringing out others' ideas, voicing their own, and encouraging choice wherever possible. Family members speak up, and the contributions of all members, from eldest to youngest, are respected as valuable (Beavers & Hampson, 1993).

It's important to understand obstacles to problem solving and ways they can be overcome. Family members are encouraged to discuss both resources and constraints, and to consider a range of options, weighing the costs and benefits for all family members. Openness to trying new solutions to meet new challenges is a hallmark of well-functioning, adaptive families. This flexible and inventive approach builds resourcefulness.

Intervention efforts with the Wolff family focused on resolving both practical and emotional aspects of the family's problems. Joining with Mrs. Wolff's desire to provide the best care for her mother, the therapist suggested that there might be other ways to accomplish this aim besides doing it all on her own. She encouraged the parents' collaborative brainstorming and information gathering to consider a range of home-based services and placement options for "Nanna."

Mr. Wolff's involvement, which brought needed support to his wife, was framed also as an opportunity for him to share more fully in caregiving arrangements, as he wished he had done for his own mother. The therapist provided a caring context for this emotion-laden problem solving, exploring each partner's conflicted feelings and encouraging mutual empathy. A family session explored the son's mixed feelings as well—his love for Nanna and sadness at her decline, along with his guilt for wishing that he hadn't had to give up his room to her. Normalizing and contextualizing the many feelings of family members as natural and common in their stressful situation were helpful in reducing blame, shame, and guilt. The therapist affirmed the family's honesty and caring intentions.

It was noted that perhaps the most important family member was missing from their problem-solving efforts—Nanna herself. Mr. and Mrs. Wolff were encouraged to include the grandmother in the planning for her care by having conversations with her at home and asking for her input to our next session. They were surprised to learn that she was acutely aware of the caregiving complications, but that she had been constrained from talking about them because she felt like such a burden. She came to feel more valued when her feelings and preferences were considered in making plans.

Shared Decision Making: Negotiation, Compromise, and Reciprocity

In Higgins's (1994) research on resilient individuals, she was struck by their ability to "love well" in long-term relationships. They established and maintained relationships marked by a high degree of reciprocity and concern for others as well as themselves. They made consistent and generally successful attempts to recognize the needs of others and to differentiate them from their own. They developed and actively participated in relationships that could withstand conflict, disappointment, anger, and frustration when the needs of either partner were not met. Such difficulties were actively and successfully negotiated throughout the relationship over time.

Family researchers have found negotiation processes to be crucial for optimal couple and family functioning across a broad diversity of families (Beavers & Hampson, 1990). In problem solving, the process of negotiation can be as important as the outcome. Family members' input is sought on major decisions. When therapists assess interactional processes, it's crucial for them to observe and clarify how important decisions are reached.

> Anna requested individual therapy for her depression, which had been triggered by the decision to move to another part of the country so that her husband, Bob, could take a better job. Because the crisis involved the marital situation, I asked the couple to come in together initially, to assess the problem jointly and determine how to be most helpful. When both were asked how the decision to move was made, Bob replied, "I told her I had this great job offer that I told them I'd probably take; what do you think about it?" Confronted with a decision all but made by Bob, Anna agreed because it was good for him, without considering her feelings and needs. After they had made all arrangements, she became acutely depressed about leaving her family, friends, and community. Bob was angry at her for burdening him with her sadness and regrets, wanting her to pull her own weight with the difficult practical demands of the transition. They both initially suggested that she should have a few individual counseling sessions "to adjust" to the move.
>
> I recommended that couple sessions and individual sessions with both partners be combined. The partners were strongly encouraged to revisit the decision-making process and to reconsider the options, costs, and benefits more collaboratively. They came to realize that both held mixed feelings about the move, but that Bob had expressed only the positive side, while Anna carried all the negative side. As their positions had polarized, their relationship became increasingly strained. The process of communication was as important as the final decision. Anna needed to participate actively in the decision making and to have her feelings heard and her preferences weighed in the balance. Had she met with a therapist individually to "adjust" to the move, she would most likely have carried resentment along with her accommodation.

Negotiation involves airing and accepting differences and working toward shared goals. Striving for an equal partnership and working out the complex demands of dual-career family life put a premium on negotiating , which requires comfort and skill in open communication and conflict resolution. To be successful negotiators, all family members need to learn how to talk and listen with compassion and understanding. They need to avoid and interrupt negative cycles of criticism, blame, and withdrawal—the attacks and defensiveness that corrode relationships. Those who are able to sustain happy relationships learn how to repair conversations that go badly and how to soothe each other when hurt or upset. One person might say, "This isn't working; let's try talking about this again," or "Let's both cool down and try to resolve our differences more calmly when we can hear each other." Such nurturing, monitoring, and support strengthen relationships as problems are resolved.

Quite often, negotiation and compromise are hindered by struggles over power and control. Battles over the relationship aspect of communication keep substantive issues from being addressed and resolved. Family members view compromise and accommodation in terms of winning versus losing, or having power over others versus being controlled or "one-down." Positions become rigid and nonnegotiable when compromise is felt to be "giving in" to the other. Dysfunctional relationships tend to have a skewed deference–dominance balance, with the overaccommodating individual becoming increasingly resentful over time. A lack of trust in reciprocity breeds short-term "tit-for-tat" exchanges, or a withholding on one person's part until the other "evens the score" between them. Lack of nurturing and supportiveness contribute to resentment. Outside stress, such as job or financial strain, heightens tensions and conflict.

Differences in gender socialization and power strongly influence negotiation processes and outcome. In situations such as divorce mediation, professionals need to be alert to skews in power, influence, and financial resources when negotiations aren't conducted on a level playing field (Walsh et al., 1995). Moreover, men and women typically enter into negotiation with different basic premises. Men are encouraged to argue their positions as forcefully and convincingly as they can, with the aim of winning—meeting their own needs as fully as possible. Women, reared traditionally to put the needs of others before their own, tend to defer and accommodate. It can be helpful in therapy to frame this dilemma in terms of these differing premises.

As Anna and Bob began to address their dilemma, Anna observed, "Somehow I always seem to defer to him. Maybe it's just my problem." I noted that this happens quite commonly between men and women because of the different ways we're raised and different rules we learn about negotiation. We explored how this might be happening in their situation: "Let me see if I understand your positions. It seems that for you, Bob, good negotiation means making the strongest case on your own behalf and pushing to win your case. Is that so?" Bob nodded, "That's true; sure." "And for you, Anna, good negotiation means consideration of Bob's needs and compromise of your own." Anna nodded, adding, "And since I never play by his rules and he never plays by mine, things always end up his way." I commented that it seemed to operate like "the subtle pull of gravity." Bob agreed, saying, "Right. It's like the norm is in my head. It's real comfortable." Anna added, "And you end up getting your way."

Such skewed communication patterns and power dynamics may be stable and remain unnoticed until a major life transition and accommodation trigger a relationship crisis, as in this case. Bringing the gender differences and power differential into awareness without blame helped the couple to work toward more balanced rules for negotiation, so that Anna could assert her needs more effectively and Bob could be more considerate and mutually accommodating. Expectations need to be periodically reexamined and renegotiated. Increasing reciprocity can greatly strengthen relationships.

Conflict Resolution

Negotiations concerning major life decisions do not necessarily proceed smoothly, and may involve intense conflict, pain, and anger. But in a well-functioning family these are experienced as transient disruptions that do not result in long-term despair, perceptions of failure, or family dissolution. Tolerance for conflict allows for overt disagreement and acknowledgment of differences, with resolution through agreement, compromise, or new framing of the problem. Resilient couple and family relationships require effective conflict resolution without a sacrifice of empathy. Mixed feelings are accepted as a part of life and of all relationships. Families handle them by acknowledging both (or many) sides of a dilemma and acting *on balance*—for instance, to serve the greater good of the family or the best interests of the children over the long run.

The best predictor of marital success is not the absence of conflict, but its management: how differences, as they are bound to arise, are handled and resolved. Conflict avoidance is dysfunctional over time, heightening the risk for later marital dissatisfaction and divorce. Most marriages end within the first 5–7 years, with the greatest difficulties occurring in the first 2–5 years as unresolved conflicts pile up and resentments grow.

To understand these corrosive interactions, John Gottman (1994) observed couples in early marriage (Time 1) and again 4 years later (Time 2).

Spouses who were likely to separate or divorce by Time 2 were already unhappy and separating emotionally at Time 1. Both were more defensive, making excuses and denying responsibility more than spouses with a successful marital course. "Yes, but" statements were frequent, and partners could muster only miserable, forced smiles. The researchers could predict with 90% accuracy which couples would be separated by Time 2, based on a vicious cycle in handling conflict. This cycle involved the husband's stonewalling and withdrawing as a listener, and the wife's expressions of criticism and contempt. The first stage began with marital conflict in which the husband became very physiologically aroused and stonewalled his wife, then eventually withdrew from the conflict. Over time he became overwhelmed by his wife's emotions and avoidant of any conflict with her. The husband's stonewalling was very aversive and physiologically arousing for his wife. In response, she tried initially to reengage him but was unsuccessful and was put off. This led to her emotional detachment and withdrawal, with expressions of criticism and disgust. Their lives became increasingly separate and parallel, as some wives have described: like two train tracks that never touched. As both withdrew and became defensive, the relationship was well on its way to separation and divorce.

Gender differences were found. "Hot" marital interaction led to significantly more aversive physiological arousal and stonewalling by men than by women. Stonewalling predicted a man's loneliness, and also a deterioration in his health, over the 4 years of the study. An interesting finding was that men who did housework were far less overwhelmed by their wives' emotions, less conflict-avoidant, physiologically calmer, and healthier over time. The researchers considered the possibility that there is some hidden benefit in doing housework! However, the significant variable probably has to do with more egalitarian relationships and fewer traditional masculine concerns about issues of competition, control, and vulnerability.

Left out of this grim picture is the pathway by which marriages can improve over time. As noted above, intense conflict by itself is not destructive of a relationship if it is offset by positive emotional expression, particularly by affection, humor, positive problem solving, agreement, assent, empathy, and active nondefensive listening. Gottman's research found that the ratio of positive to negative interactions needed to exceed 10:1 for a marriage to be on a trajectory of increasing satisfaction!

The most important lesson to be learned from marriages that failed is that even if conflicts are upsetting at the time, they can be necessary and beneficial to a relationship in the long run. In contrast, if partners are only agreeable and compliant or withdraw from conflict, the relationship is at high risk for deterioration over time.

Effective conflict management requires open disagreement with good communication skills for resolution. It's important to learn how to confront without being abrasive. In both conflict-avoidant and high-conflict couples, therapeutic interventions need to increase skills for handling conflict in order to stop the corrosive process that leads to disintegration of the relationship. To help partners manage negative emotions and respond compassionately to each other, Markman et al. (1992) developed the Prevention and Relationship Enhancement Program (PREP), which teaches couples how to fight constructively. Such approaches provide ground rules for handling conflict, which include the following: Difficult issues must be controlled; partners may mutually call "time out" whenever needed; escalating conflicts need to be slowed down; arguments should be kept constructive; withdrawal should be avoided; and involvement must be maintained. Partners can be coached to accomplish these aims. Couple therapy builds relational resilience by providing a safe context where partners can become more tolerant of differences and more skillful in managing and resolving conflict, so that both partners' needs are heard and met. The building of communication skills empowers a couple to "fight for the relationship."

Focusing on Achievable Goals; Taking Concrete Steps

For successful family functioning and resilience in overcoming adversity, the powerful belief in active mastery must be put into practice, both in daily problem solving and in meeting major life challenges. The Chicago Bulls coach, Phil Jackson, attributes much of superstar Michael Jordan's continuing success not only to his talent, but also to "an awareness level that allows him to apply whatever degree of intensity he thinks is required to win a game: "He has a concept in his mind's eye about how to approach each challenge. In the course of a game he visualizes what he wants to happen, and then he makes it happen" (quoted in Simon, 1997, p. 62). This ability was not inborn, but relationally based. In raising their five children, the Jordan parents emphasized the need to focus on goals in order to achieve them (D. Jordan, 1996). No matter what their objectives were as they were growing up, they were encouraged to focus intently and not to be distracted from efforts to attain them. This ability was also honed through the coaching style of Phil Jackson, who has written,

> In basketball—as in life—true joy comes from being fully present in each and every moment, not just when things are going your way. Of course, it's no accident that things are more likely to go your way when you stop worrying about whether you're going to win or lose and focus your full attention on what's happening *right this moment*. (Jackson with Delehanty, 1995)

This total involvement in immediate actions toward the pursuit of goals is remarkably like the experience of "flow" observed by Csikszentmihalyi (1996) in highly creative and successful people who find great satisfaction in their achievements—as much in the process as in the outcome.

Moreover, for a family, as for a team, success is fostered by collaboration. As Coach Jackson emphasizes:

> Winning has to do with a connectedness that's going on between people, an alertness and awareness that happens because there is positive energy in the community. And it doesn't matter whether the business is baking or producing a first-rate product or whether it's basketball. It has nothing to do with dominance or competition, although competition is such a part of our society. It has to do with the inner process that's going on in an organization that's producing positive vibration. . . . And so people like to come to work. They like to do what they're doing. They enjoy the fellowship and the community and the end results turn out to be good work. (Quoted in Simon, 1997, p. 63)

Building on Success; Learning from Failure

With each small shared success, family members' confidence and competence grow exponentially, enabling them to meet larger challenges. The acceptance of mistakes allows family members to fail without being attacked or defined as inadequate. Accountable for their own part when something has gone wrong, they learn not to repeat mistakes that might have contributed to a problem situation. Indeed, failed experiences can become instructive as family members recalibrate efforts or try a new tack to solve problems. As Albert Einstein remarked, "Anyone who has not experienced failure has not known success."

Taking a Proactive Stance: Preventing Problems, Averting Crises

When a potential problem looms on the horizon, members of well-functioning families face it fairly quickly, discuss it in a clear and open way, and address both practical and emotional aspects. In this proactive way, a crisis can be averted. Few unresolved problems lie dormant to pile up over time or complicate attempts to deal with major disruptions that arise. In facing new problems, family members excel in their ability to give and accept directions, organize themselves, elicit input from one another, negotiate differences, and reach closure coherently and effectively (Beavers & Hampson, 1990, 1993). Not all problems can be solved; in such cases, resilient family members find aspects of the situation for choice and action.

   Families can falter at various steps in a problem-solving process. Individuals may be constrained from sharing their feelings and opinions. If they are not accustomed to expressing themselves or being heard, they may not even be in touch with their own feelings and needs. As noted earlier, members may avoid bringing up a problem or a difference of opinion if they fear that conflict will escalate out of control and lead to violence or family breakup. It can be helpful for a clinician to reassure family members by pointing out that all relationships are bound to have disagreements, and that research finds that couples and families do best when they can voice their differences and work constructively to resolve them.

   Couples can be proactive in the earliest phases of their relationship, assessing their own areas of strength and vulnerability. Relationships at risk for breakdown can be identified even before marriage. PREPARE, a self-report inventory for premarital couples (Olson, Fournier, & Druckman, 1986), has been found to predict with 80–85% accuracy which couples will be happily married and which will be unhappy, separated, or divorced within 3 years of marriage. The inventory can identify areas of vulnerability for early intervention, in addition to encouraging more careful consideration of marital plans. Olson's group has found the strongest predictors of discord to be poor communication and conflict resolution, fueling unrealistic expectations and disappointment. Researchers could not discriminate those who would actually divorce from those who would stay unhappily married; this result supports clinical observations of the complexity of this decision, including religious convictions and consideration of children's well-being.

THERAPEUTIC APPROACHES
TO STRENGTHENING COMMUNICATION

Approaches from Various Models of Family Therapy

All approaches to couple and family therapy seek to repair and strengthen communication and problem-solving processes (Walsh, 1993). Systems-oriented therapists help couples and families share painful feelings and unexpressed needs more openly and directly, building relational empathy for one another as they solve problems (e.g., Paul & Grosser, 1991). In the Bowen (1978) approach, individuals are encouraged to take an "I position" in transactions, through clear statements asserting their own feelings, needs, and opinions. They are coached to manage their emotional reactivity to the words and actions of others. Complaints about others are reframed to express one's own needs for change, just as active initiative is encouraged to change one's own part in problem situations.

Structural–strategic approaches view well-functioning families as highly flexible in using a large repertoire of behaviors to cope with problems, in contrast to distressed families, which demonstrate a paucity of alternatives. The presenting symptom is seen as a communicative act in a repeated sequence of behaviors among family members, occurring when they are locked into an unworkable family pattern and cannot see a better way of handling it. Therapy focuses on problem resolution by altering interactional feedback loops that maintain symptoms. The therapeutic task is to formulate, or recast, the problem in solvable terms.

The Mental Research Institute's model (Weakland, Fisch, Watzlawick, & Bodin, 1974) brought attention to how families attempt to handle or resolve normal problems in living. All families confront problems; however, misguided attempts to solve them may make things worse. More recent solution-focused and narrative approaches (Anderson & Goolishian, 1988; de Shazer, 1985; Freedman & Combs, 1996; White & Epston, 1990) refocus attention from problems and the patterns that maintain them to solutions and the processes that can enable them. Therapists search for exceptions to problematic interactions and solutions that have worked in the past in other situations and might work now and in the future. In narrative approaches, the therapeutic conversation and the process of "restorying" a problematic experience are emphasized, with the aims of enlarging the story to include aspects that have been marginalized or left out, and envisioning new possibilities. Solution-focused therapists believe that complicated problems do not necessarily require complicated solutions. The risk here lies in not addressing the complex web of experience and reciprocal influences inherent in the social context of a problem.

Behavioral approaches to couple and family therapy emphasize the importance of family rules and communication processes. Building communication skills—particularly clear, direct expression of feelings and opinions, negotiation, and problem solving—is considered key to promoting more functional family processes. Therapists focus straightforwardly on the interactional behaviors and conditions under which social behavior is learned, influenced, and changed. Problem definition and intervention goals are specified in concrete and observable behavioral terms, with the aim of educating and guiding family members in a straightforward way to learn more effective modes of dealing with each other, as in Markman's (Markman et al., 1992) approach described above. The importance of positive rewards for desired behavior is stressed. Families are helped to change the interpersonal consequences of behavior, from overreliance on coercive control to more positive acknowledgment and approval of desired behavior.

The therapeutic relationship has stood out as a common denominator in research on the effectiveness of various approaches to psychotherapy over the years. This relationship is based in open communication and a trusting climate that fosters the ability to get in touch with and express a wide range of ideas, feelings, and opinions. Recent narrative approaches emphasize the healing power in therapeutic conversations. Empathic listening, genuine interest, and respectful curiosity by the therapist encourage family members to tell their stories and consider new perspectives on their troubling situations.

As therapists have come to work more collaboratively with clients, we have also become more human in our interactions. We consider disclosing aspects of our own life experiences when we believe it will be helpful to our clients, such as a story that establishes human connections, or one to be learned from. We need to be aware of our own feelings that are evoked by our clients and their life crises, and should strive always to respond in ways that meet their needs rather than our own. In becoming more compassionate to the suffering of others, we need to be comfortable with the strong emotions that may be stirred in us. When pain and suffering are expressed, tears may come to my eyes. It can be helpful for family members to see that in human encounters there is no shame in expressing vulnerable feelings or need to keep them locked away under control. At the same time, if messages are conveyed in hurtful ways to others or conflict threatens to spiral out of control, it is our responsibility as therapists to interrupt negative transactions and try to help family members find more constructive ways to express their needs or pain.

As family process research has documented, clarity of communication, open emotional expression, and collaborative problem solving are vital elements in family resilience. Regardless of the specific problem that brings a family into therapy, it is crucial to strengthen communication processes to relieve family pain and enhance family resourcefulness. In accord with the key beliefs for success described in Chapter 3, it is important to help families set realistic, achievable objectives in line with their larger vision; take concrete steps and build on small successes; learn from experience and mistakes; experiment with innovations; prepare for anticipated challenges; and above all else, expect the unexpected.

Teamwork for Competence, Confidence, and Success

Valuable lessons for successful family life and family therapy can come from observing how good sports coaches achieve team success by promoting teamwork along with individual confidence and skill in every member. As readers may have guessed, I live in Chicago and am an avid Bulls fan. I've been struck by the the many key processes of relational resilience demonstrated by the team. The extraordinary talents of their star player did not at first bring a championship, as the team was jokingly referred to as "Michael Jordan and the Jordanaires." When teamwork was developed by their Zen-inspired coach, Phil Jackson (see Jackson with Delehanty, 1995), each player was valued for his unique contribution and their collaborative plays and rebounds soon made them the most effective team in basketball history. Jordan as captain brought strong leadership yet shared the spotlight, giving up shots to enable teammates to score, and crediting successes to team efforts. Losses and errors were owned, and lessons were learned from them, inspiring greater motivation and effort to bounce back stronger. (Dennis Rodman deserves a resilience award for his phenomenal rebounds after missed shots!)

An extraordinary team isn't necessary for family members and helping professionals to apply these principles in raising resilient children and building stronger families and communities. My own family is fortunate to live in a town that values sports experiences for both boys and girls from the early years. Because research has found a decline in girls' self-esteem in preadolescent years, we supported our daughter's interest in team sports, which can be an important training ground for developing confidence, competence, and success. Most of the coaches—all fathers, mothers, and older siblings of players—bring out the best in players through skill building and continual feedback, praising their efforts and growing abilities. Teammates and parents on the sidelines join in with "Give it your best! Go for it! You can do it!" Losses and errors are viewed as part of the skill-building process. A disappointing strikeout also brings encouragement: "Good swing! Next time a little quicker and you'll connect." Although teams are competitive and winning is highly desirable, there is also an emphasis on building team spirit. The players invent rhymes and cheers to rally teammates and offer consolation in defeat. Even small successes and progress are celebrated at game's end. Season-end picnics include praise for accomplishments and humor at times when "we sucked!" Imaginative awards appreciate each player's contribution to the team, the leadership of coaches, and the supportive role of families.

In contrast, a coach one season had a rather negative, fiercely competitive style. His feedback to players reinforced a sense of failure and intrinsic incompetence: "Oh, no, not again!" "How could you have made such a dumb play?" "How many times have I told you *not* to . . . ?" The team fell apart and the girls, becoming tearful, sullen, and uncooperative, lost confidence and made increasing errors. With several girls on the verge of dropping out, the parents formed a support network and worked with the coaches to take a positive, strength-oriented approach.

Much like the critical coach, families can become caught up in a vicious cycle of negativity, focused on one or more members' deficiencies. What can be learned that can be applied to interventions to strengthen family processes?

First is the importance of encouraging a family environment that increases possibilities for success. Just as negative interactions can have a destructive cascading effect, small successes build on one another in a ripple effect, increasing family members' confidence to master more difficult challenges. Experiences of success in one arena of life lead to self-efficacy, enabling enhanced coping with other life crises (Rutter, 1985).

Second, it is crucial to attribute successes to family members, so they come to believe that their efforts and collaboration can make a difference. When we are successful as coaches, or therapists, the victory goes to the "team." Third, it is helpful to reinforce the belief that mistakes and failure not only are acceptable, but are also to be expected as a normal part of family life, especially under stressful conditions. Moreover, they provide valuable ways of learning. Foremost is the need to convey mutual caring and genuine confidence in family members' abilities to master challenges through *encourage*-ing communication.

C·H·A·P·T·E·R   6

Practice Principles
and Guidelines

The horizon leans forward
offering you space
to place new steps of change.
—MAYA ANGELOU

A family resilience approach extends strength-based practice by fostering family capacities to master adversity. This chapter first highlights key processes in family resilience to inform clinical assessment and intervention. Next, core practice principles are presented for reducing risk and vulnerability and strengthening resilience in distressed couples and families. Recommendations are then offered for more responsive family-centered service delivery and prevention efforts. Finally, I address the resilience needed by helping professionals to meet the demands of our challenging work and the profound changes occurring in our practice environment.

KEY PROCESSES IN RESILIENCE: A FRAMEWORK
FOR ASSESSMENT AND INTERVENTION

"No single thread" distinguishes healthy from dysfunctional families, as Lewis, Beavers, Gossett, and Phillips (1976) observed in their pioneering study. Clinical formulations that reduce the richness of family interaction to simplistic labels, such as "an enmeshed family," "an alcoholic family," or a "codependent relationship," stereotype and pathologize families. Instead, we must attend to the many strands that are intertwined in family functioning, and assess strengths and vulnerabilities on multiple system dimensions.

Our growing knowledge of processes in well-functioning families can inform clinical efforts to draw out, enlarge, and reinforce family resources. In Chapters 3–5, major research findings and clinical insights have been integrated into three domains of family functioning—belief systems, organizational patterns, and communication processes—to provide a useful framework for identifying family strengths and vulnerabilities. This framework is not intended to be followed in a linear fashion in conducting assessment interviews. Rather, it can serve as a useful map to orient us to attend to the many elements in family functioning and bring coherence to intervention planning. It can help us target key processes for strengthening family resilience as presenting problems are resolved.

Families most often come for help in crisis. When they are overwhelmed and their presenting problems skew attention toward deficits, a resilience-based framework offers a positive and pragmatic focus for intervention; it can generate optimism in the therapeutic process while grounding changes in specific, reachable objectives. While I am aware of my own subjectivity in mapping a territory we all inhabit, and of the risk of oversimplification, I still believe we can distill a set of key processes in family resilience to guide family assessment and interventions. Table 6.1 summarizes these processes from the discussion in previous chapters.

These keys to resilience are mutually interactive and synergistic. For example, connectedness finds expression in an affiliative orientation, organizational cohesion, as well as open emotional sharing and collaborative problem solving. A core belief that problems can be mastered both furthers and is reinforced by successful problem-solving strategies. A counterbalance of processes is also important, as in the fluid balance between stability and flexibility required for both continuity and change.

Various approaches to family therapy have emphasized processes in different domains. For instance, the structural model attends primarily to organizational patterns; behavioral approaches address communication processes; and narrative approaches focus on altering meaning systems. In practice, however, most therapists are attentive to processes across the three domains. Professionals of all theoretical orientations can usefully draw out and strengthen these key processes for resilience.

An ecological–developmental perspective—assessing functioning in both social and temporal contexts—is easier to maintain in theory than in practice. The concept of family resilience offers a flexible view, allowing us to identify basic elements in effective family functioning (as described in Chapters 3–5) while also taking family diversity into account, as well as the varied strengths needed to meet the demands of particular challenges over time (as illustrated in Chapters 7–9). It is crucial to assess each family's strengths and

TABLE 6.1. Key Processes in Family Resilience

Belief Systems

Making meaning of adversity
- Affiliative value: Resilience as relationally based
- Family life cycle orientation: Normalizing, contextualizing adversity and distress
- Sense of coherence: Crisis as meaningful, comprehensible, manageable challenge
- Appraisal of crisis, distress, and recovery: Facilitative versus constraining beliefs

Positive outlook
- Active initiative and perseverance
- Courage and en-*courage*-ment
- Sustaining hope, optimistic view; confidence in overcoming odds
- Focusing on strengths and potential
- Mastering the possible; accepting what can't be changed

Transcendence and spirituality
- Larger values, purpose
- Spirituality: Faith, communion, rituals
- Inspiration: Envisioning new possibilities; creativity; heroes
- Transformation: Learning and growth from adversity

Organizational Patterns

Flexibility
- Capacity to change: Rebounding, reorganizing, adapting to fit challenges over time
- Counterbalancing by stability: Continuity, dependability through disruption

Connectedness
- Mutual support, collaboration, and commitment
- Respect for individual needs, differences, and boundaries
- Strong leadership: Nurturing, protecting, guiding children and vulnerable members
  - Varied family forms: Cooperative parenting/caregiving teams
  - Couple/coparent relationship: Equal partners
- Seeking reconnection, reconciliation of troubled relationships

Social and economic resources
- Mobilizing extended kin and social support; community networks
- Building financial security; balancing work and family strains

Communication Processes

Clarity
- Clear, consistent messages (words and actions)
- Clarification of ambiguous situation: Truth seeking/truth speaking

Open emotional expression
- Sharing range of feelings (joy and pain; hopes and fears)
- Mutual empathy; tolerance for differences
- Responsibility for own feelings, behavior; avoiding blaming
- Pleasurable interactions; humor

Collaborative problem solving
- Creative brainstorming; resourcefulness
- Shared decision making: Negotiation, fairness, reciprocity
- Conflict resolution
- Focusing on goals; taking concrete steps; building on success; learning from failure
- Proactive stance: Preventing problems, crises; preparing for future challenges

vulnerabilities in relation to each family's particular socioeconomic situation and developmental priorities. We must always be mindful that key processes may be organized and expressed in varied ways, depending on diverse cultural values and family structures. For example, open emotional expression varies with different ethnic norms. Patterns of leadership, roles, and boundaries that may work best for an intact family may differ from those needed for a single-parent household with extended family involvement, or for a stepfamily spanning two or more households. The 10 key processes in resilience can be applied to diverse situations and through varied pathways to reach objectives consonant with family aims.

A family resilience approach requires an evolving view of family challenges and responses over time, rather than a cross-sectional view at one point in time. If we are to help families meet the demands of different phases of adaptation, we need to help them draw upon the various strengths needed to approach an impending crisis, to adjust in the immediate aftermath, and to reorganize their lives over the long term. Recurrent or persistent stresses pose different psychosocial challenges over time: Some families must repeatedly shift gears over a roller-coaster course, while others must deal with a progressively worsening situation. These challenges interact with emerging priorities in both individual and family life cycle passages. A holistic assessment of each family aims to clarify what the members' challenges and resources are, where they are coming from, and where they are headed.

CORE PRINCIPLES FOR STRENGTHENING
RELATIONAL RESILIENCE

A family resilience approach has much in common with many competence-based family therapy approaches: emphasizing a collaborative process and seeking to identify and build on strengths and resources. Yet whereas some approaches are acontextual, building basic competencies for day-to-day functioning or focused narrowly on resolving a specific presenting problem, a resilience approach links each family's processes with its unique challenges in order to enhance coping and mastery.

A basic premise guiding this systems-based approach is that serious crises have an impact on the whole family, and that, in turn, family coping processes influence the recovery and resilience of all members and the family as a unit (Langsley & Kaplan, 1968, Pittman, 1987). How a family confronts and manages a disruptive experience, buffers stress, effectively reorganizes, and reinvests in life pursuits will influence adaptation for all members. Interventions aim to build family resources to deal more effectively with stresses and rebound strengthened, both individually and as a relational system. Fostering the family's ability to master its immediate crisis situation also increases its capacity to meet future challenges.

To promote resilience in vulnerable children and families, Rutter (1987) has identified four general protective mechanisms that can be strengthened through interventions. Applying his schema to family systems, we can specify the ways in which key processes in family resilience can be mobilized:

1. Decreasing risk factors:

   • Anticipating and preparing for threatening circumstances
   • Reducing exposure or overload of stress
   • Providing information; altering catastrophic beliefs

2. Reducing negative chain reactions that heighten risk for sustained impact and further crises:

   • Buffering stress effects; cushioning impact, overcoming obstacles
   • Altering maladaptive coping strategies
   • Withstanding aftershocks, prolonged strains; rebounding from setbacks

3. Strengthening protective family processes and reducing vulnerabilities:

   • Enhancing family strengths; increasing opportunities and abilities for success
   • Mobilizing and shoring up resources toward recovery and mastery
   • Rebuilding, reorganizing, and reorienting in aftermath
   • Anticipating, preparing for both likely and unforeseen new challenges

4. Bolstering family and individual esteem and efficacy through successful problem mastery

   • Gaining competence, confidence, and connectedness through collaborative efforts
   • Managing challenge processes over time for sustained competence under duress

Clinicians should inquire routinely about recent and threatened change events, the family's approach, and their impact on family functioning, noting complications that pose a risk for immediate or long-term dysfunction. Therapeutic efforts should be attuned to each family's challenges and potential resources that can be mobilized to meet them. We can help families assess their crisis situation and identify ways to reduce risk factors, rendering challenges less threatening and more manageable. For instance, parents and other caregivers can be helped to provide leadership, guidance, nurturance, and protection in the face of disruption or loss. In anticipation of a crisis, through its midst, and in its aftermath, our aim is to strengthen key interactional processes to foster coping, recovery, and resilience, enabling the family and its members to integrate their experience and move forward in life.

Tracking Stressors and Coping/Adaptation Processes over Time

In all clinical assessment, a timeline is useful to track presenting symptoms in relation to past, ongoing, and threatened stress events, their meanings, and family coping strategies. Families don't simply react to stressful life events; their approach to potential stressors can either buffer or intensify their impact. Did members notice clouds looming on the horizon? Can they discuss them and mobilize resources to head off a crisis? Strains can be compounded by catastrophic fears and maladaptive coping processes, which can contribute to individual distress and/or family breakdown. Often family members and professionals become so focused on symptoms that they may not connect them to other crisis situations and stresses on the system, as in the following case:

> Over the past month, Jimmy, age 12, had stolen money twice at school to buy candy, had begun to skip classes, and had dropped to failing grades. School authorities presumed that the family, like many in their inner-city neighborhood, was either uncaring or unstable when no one responded to notes sent home. When a family counselor visited the home to assess the situation, she learned that Jimmy and his four siblings lived with their grandmother—their legal guardian since their mother's sudden death 4 years earlier. The grandmother had been hospitalized recently with a serious liver disease; although she was now at home, she required kidney dialysis several times a week. Jimmy, who had been very close to his mother, was now extremely anxious that he might also lose his grandmother. Moreover, all were aware that the burden of responsibility for five children added risk. In this close-knit, caring family, the children took turns staying home from school to care for their grandmother, with their aunt helping out. No one talked about the grandmother's condition, about the threat of another loss and dislocation for all the children, or about what arrangements would be made for their

care in the event of her further disability or death. As Jimmy said, "It was all just too scary to talk about."

In terms of Rutter's (1987) model, several steps were required in helping Jimmy and the entire family with their crisis situation. Most immediately, the counselor needed to decrease the risk factors, reduce negative chain reactions, and shore up resources for both the grandmother's care and the children's care. The grandmother's husband, who had never been involved in his stepgrandchildren's care, was encouraged to take a more active role with them to relieve the burden on his wife. The children's father, who had been out of contact since their mother's death because of a long-standing conflict with the grandmother, was encouraged to put old grievances aside and to become more involved in raising his children. He surprised everyone by rallying to this challenge; he had longed for more contact with his children, but had held back until called upon in this crisis. The aunt's efforts were affirmed and supported. Additional resources were found in an after-school tutoring program for Jimmy, currently the most vulnerable child. As the immediate stress was reduced, with family members managing more effectively and benefiting from new and strengthened relationships, attention could then be directed to addressing the family's future concerns (especially options for the children's future care) and to dealing with past unresolved loss issues from the mother's death.

This case illustrates how resilience-based intervention taps into the three domains of family functioning: meaning and mastery of the crisis; reorganization of family structural patterns; and development of effective communication and problem-solving strategies. Most serious life crises aren't limited to a single moment in time, but involve a complex set of changing conditions with a past history and a future course (Rutter, 1987). Thus, efforts to strengthen resilience must attend to coping and adaptation processes over time.

We need to pay particular attention to the cumulative impact of a pileup of stressors, as in the following case:

Mike and Maggie, on the verge of divorce, were seen for a marital evaluation. The couple's conflicts had escalated over the past 3 years, with increasing volatility and recent violence. When they first sought help, Mike was encouraged to move out for his wife's safety and to attend a group for men who batter. Maggie was referred to a women's group, where she was encouraged to leave the marriage, even though no couple assessment or intervention had yet been attempted. The couple had four young children, and they requested couple therapy to see whether they could salvage their marriage and keep their family intact. Although the violence was now under control, the therapist's focus on interrupting their repetitive cycles of bickering seemed unhelpful.

Called in as a consultant, I tracked the recent evolution of the family, finding that the onset and escalation of violence had coincided with a pileup of traumatic events, beginning with the sudden death of Mike's father, with whom he'd always had a stormy relationship. Next his brother had died of lung cancer, just as Maggie's mother, who had been a mainstay to her, began to deteriorate with Alzheimer's disease. With the local economy faltering, Mike's small business failed just as Maggie discovered she was pregnant again, and they feared losing their mortgage. Shortly thereafter, Mike lost control while driving and wrecked the family car, with the entire family barely escaping serious injury.

Mike had never mentioned this traumatic chain of events in his men's group, which focused on behavior control. He couldn't recall ever letting out his feelings to anyone, including Maggie, who had turned to her sisters for support. She noted that this was the first time they had ever talked openly about all that had happened, or had put it all together. After each event they had just tried to keep on going, although they were reeling under the series of shockwaves and the pressures of attending to the needs of four young children, as well as worries about their precarious finances. In Mike's words, he felt "assaulted"—bombarded from all sides by events beyond his control. Once they reviewed and took stock of these events, they were able to make meaning of the strain on their relationship, their frayed emotions, and Mike's assaultive outbursts. It was crucial that in normalizing and contextualizing the distress, the therapist not normalize violence as an acceptable response. Work on communication skills was important to prevent a recurrence of violence; yet that focus alone was insufficient without attending to the crucible in which the violence had flared up. When Mike and Maggie were encouraged in couple therapy to share their feelings and to comfort each other, they were able to pull together to recover emotionally from their losses and rebound to meet their family challenges.

As in the cases above, assessment involves a series of questions to assess both risk and protective factors. A genogram and timeline are enormously useful in noting the following:

- Recent—and threatened—stress events and their meaning
- Pileup of stressors
- Loading from past experiences: Success or complications with similar stressors
- Family coping processes and potential resources

Making Meaning of Crisis Experiences

It is crucial to explore the meanings a crisis holds for a family, and to be careful not to make assumptions based on our own experience or concerns. Questions such as "What stood out for you?"—about both the situation and the family's response to it—acknowledge the unique experience of each family and the subjective views of various members on what is most meaningful, troubling, or remarkable (Wright et al., 1996). It's especially important to coach families to help children and vulnerable members make sense of a crisis or threat, and to provide reassurance that they will be cared for. Family members' well-being is improved when they understand more fully what's happening, what their options are, and what the implications are for each person and for the family as a whole. Resilience is fostered as we help them gain a sense of coherence, rendering their crisis experience more comprehensible, manageable, and meaningful.

Clarifying Ambiguity

There is a common human need for information to make sense of a critical incident and understand how it happened. It is important to clarify family members' understanding of a crisis event: what they have been told by whom, and what they believe deep down. Often family members hold quite different assumptions and beliefs. In one family, heated conflict erupted over the mother's well-being. She had been diagnosed with lupus, but little information had been given to her or the family about her prognosis or management of the chronic condition. Some family members worried that she was working too hard and that it would kill her; others thought she was doing too little and playing on everyone's sympathies. Amid all the bickering, she finally took to her bed—fearful and unsure about what to do, and feeling unsupported by her family.

Helping family members to gain information eases their anxieties and helps them cope and adapt. We can encourage them to actively pursue and share information, and can coach them on locating reliable sources (medical or public records, news articles, etc.). With a signed release, therapists can contact medical professionals to assist families in sorting out complicated or conflicting information about illnesses or disabilities, and can encourage doctors to convene a family consultation to clarify the situation and offer management guidelines. We can also encourage clients to seek information to bring greater clarity and closure to past traumatic experiences, as in the following case:

> Dennis was having recurrent nightmares about the death of his brother Al 10 years earlier in a car crash. He now worried constantly about the safety of his own son—named after Al—and imagined every sort of traffic accident. The circumstances of Al's death were ambiguous; his parents had arranged a closed-casket funeral, and afterward no one in his family had wanted to talk about it. As we worked together, I encouraged Dennis to locate a friend of his brother's who had been in the car and had survived the accident. He had to track him down in another part of the country, but managed to reach him within a few weeks. The friend was open and informative: Their buddy driving the car had been drinking and swerved out of control, striking a tree. Al had died instantly of a skull fracture. It brought some solace for Dennis to learn that his brother had not lain helpless in pain before dying. Having a clearer comprehension of the accident helped Dennis gain greater closure. It also reduced his global anxiety that "anything could happen at any time" to his son. Drawing a lesson from the incident, he took more realistic precautions himself, and he taught his son never to mix drinking and driving.

Helping Families Live with Uncertainty

In many cases, we need to help families to live with uncertainty. For some, the future course and outcome of a life-threatening situation (e.g., a serious illness) cannot be predicted or controlled. For others, we must help them clarify what they can about past events and find a way to live with persisting ambiguity and the possibility that they may never achieve full clarification. Families often have difficulty going on with their lives when they're unable to gain tangible evidence to clarify the cause of a tragedy. In the 1996 crash of a TWA flight off the coast of New York, family members were tormented by the slowness in recovering remains and by the persistent questions about the cause of the crash. Many families found some solace in holding a memorial service at the edge of the waters where the plane went down. They also forged resilience by banding together to advocate for more information and renewed efforts to determine the cause. Families of the victims of a 1988 Pan American crash at Lockerbie, Scotland, found their pain revived by this incident—as one father described it, "like a scab torn off a deep wound." Yet many of those families found the strength to come forward and offer support to the TWA crash survivors, and this furthered their own long-term recovery as well.

In many instances, family members may be helped to come to terms with a tragedy beyond their comprehension and control by drawing on their spiritual resources to make meaning and find comfort and solace through their faith. Exploring spiritual beliefs and practices should become part of all efforts to help families overcome adversity.

Seizing Opportunities in the Midst of Crisis

As therapists and families work to solve presenting problems, we can seize opportunities for personal and relational growth out of the crisis that brings them for help. We can help clients cast their crisis situation in a new light. As the saying goes, "It's not what you look at, it's what you see." When facing a crisis, it's helpful to look back to past family experiences with adversity, for lessons that can be drawn about both helpful and unhelpful approaches. In the aftermath of a crisis, we can help family members explore what can be learned from their situation. There may be important lessons about risk and vulnerability, or the about need to anticipate pitfalls and take more precaution in the future. In building resilience, we help families strive to integrate the fullness of their crisis experience.

Often something valuable is gained from a crisis that might not have been learned or obtained otherwise. Adversity may bring a startling recognition of the importance of relationships that had been taken for granted or written off. A crisis can lead family members to question, review, and redirect their lives. A disruptive family relocation can also be a milestone for taking time out to reassess life and relationship priorities, or to affirm and strengthen commitments. A woman devastated by the loss of her husband, around whom she had oriented her life, may find that her initial sense of emptiness leads her to develop new talents and a stronger sense of self. We can open these pathways to growth.

Bolstering my conviction that resilience can be brought forth in any family, my research and practice show that even the crisis of an emotional breakdown of a family member can jolt the family into awareness of needed changes, as members rise to the challenge. In the following case, a son's crisis was precipitated by the "loading" of his father's past trauma at the same age.

While on a summer trip in Europe, 18-year-old Martin Stein had a psychotic episode and was brought home and hospitalized. After a very constrained family interview, his mother asked to meet with me individually. She told of the father's past Holocaust experience as a Jewish refugee from Poland. At the age of 18, he had watched as Nazis shot his brother in the head and took his parents away to their deaths. He survived his own concentration camp experience, came to the United States, and became a physician. On their first date, seeing the camp numbers on his arm, she asked him about his experience. He was so visibly shaken that she never again asked. His past was never mentioned as their children were growing up, even though the tattooed numbers were a visible reminder. An implicit rule, serving to protect him, rendered the unbearable memories and emotions unspeakable. Then, for Martin's 18th birthday, his father's gift was a trip to Europe. Martin went off, but wrote home revealing that he was unable to enjoy himself, because he was aware that terrible things had happened to his father there. The parents didn't reply. Martin attempted to go to Auschwitz, but broke down en route, becoming incoherent and delusional.

This crisis was a turning point. The Stein family taught me that resilience can emerge even in families that have been rigidly governed by long-standing rules that become dysfunctional over time. Therapists can help to mobilize new strengths at whatever point they encounter a family. What had been unspeakable had gone underground and became expressed in the birthday present when Martin reached the same age his father had been when he experienced his traumatic losses. Family members were commended for their long-standing loyalty to their father and their wish to spare him pain. At the same time, it was agreed that their silence was no longer needed, since the father was not as vulnerable as he had been years earlier. The "gift" was framed as an opportunity to open up communication and to reintegrate old cutoffs. My follow-up with the family a year later found that the parents had made a trip to the father's family home in Poland, which was immensely healing for him and deepened the couple's relationship. Martin was doing well in college, and (coincidentally) was majoring in communications.

Normalizing Family Distress

A normalizing orientation heightens our appreciation of each family's unique set of experiences and beliefs, as well as its commonalities with other families in similar life circumstances. Strained relationships or breakdown in family processes may be understandable and expectable under the stressful circumstances the family is undergoing.

Depathologizing and Contextualizing the Problem Situation

Shortly after our family moved into a new house and community, our dog, Targa, began to misbehave. Previously house-trained, she now soiled our best rugs; more seriously, she jumped on hapless visitors at the front door. Nothing we tried helped. When she knocked one poor soul backward down the stairs, we realized we needed help and called a highly recommended pet behavior therapist. Of course, when he came to the front door, Targa approached him docilely, tail wagging. She behaved perfectly in response to his every command. Finally, the therapist looked at us intently and stated, "Well, I don't think the problem is your *dog* . . ." (We knew he meant *we* were the problem.) He then asked me to go into the kitchen and call Targa to come to me. She didn't budge. (Problem enactment!) I felt terrible; it must all be my fault. The therapist asked whether we ever punished her severely, and we immediately assured him we hadn't. Later, my husband confessed that he had once whacked Targa with a newspaper after she had ruined his parents' rug. It was his turn to feel guilty. Fortunately, our friends helped us regain a contextual perspective, reminding us that the living transition was as disorienting and stressful for our dog as it was for us. And I realized that the only time I would call her into the kitchen was to lock her in there when we went out and left her alone in the house. No wonder she wouldn't come there when called. Her behavior was now understandable—a natural response when viewed in context. Making meaning of the experience and reducing self-blame helped enormously as we resolved the problem over the following weeks.

This microevent in our lives brought only small distress in comparison to the serious problems confronting families when they seek help, but there are some important parallels. Parents initially feel deficient when they have a problem they are unable to resolve. Often they are referred for family therapy because they are told (or it is implied) that the family is the real problem. Then the symptomatic family member responds wonderfully to the therapist/expert and only displays the problem behavior in family transactions. The therapist's immediate success reinforces parental feelings of deficiency. They may leave the session feeling worse than when they arrived. Often blame and shame lead them not to return; they may then be written off as dysfunctional and resistant.

As noted in Chapter 2, ordinary families worry a good deal about their own normality. In a culture that readily pathologizes families and touts the virtues of self-reliance, family members are likely to approach therapy feeling abnormal for having a problem and deficient for not solving it on their own. Such beliefs are compounded by the confusing changes and pressures in family life today and by the lack of relevant models for effective functioning. Furthermore, referrals for family therapy are often based on the faulty presumption that the family is the "real" problem and cause of any individual distress, or that such distress must serve a function for them.

A fundamental tenet of strength-based approaches to family therapy is that most families do not seek suffering or intend harm to their members. Most parents want desperately to do the best for their children, but may need help finding viable solutions to their distress. It is crucial to explore any blaming and stigmatizing experiences families may have had in contacts with other mental health professionals, schools, or courts. Such families expect therapists to judge them negatively and may mistake a silent or neutral stance for confirmation of this view. Clinicians should explore each family's beliefs about its own normality or deficiency and the models and myths they hold as ideal. And we need to disengage assumptions of pathology from the rationale for participation in therapy and make it explicit that every family member is an essential resource in problem solving.

The aim of normalizing is to depathologize and contextualize family distress. It is not intended to reduce all problems and families to a common denominator, and it should not trivialize a family's unique experience or suffering. We must be careful neither to oversimplify the complexity of family life nor to err by normalizing truly destructive family patterns. Violence and sexual abuse should never be normalized as acceptable, even though they are all too common. Likewise, respect for diversity is not the same as "anything goes" when family processes are destructive to any member. Family therapists have moved beyond the myth of therapeutic neutrality to sort out serious ethical questions and therapeutic responsibility.

Using Respectful Language and Constructs

Effective intervention requires learning the language and perspective of each family, in order to see problems through its members' eyes—to understand the values and expectations that influence their approach to handling the problem or their inability to change. Narrative therapists have heightened our awareness of the power of words: They may reflect pessimism and foster blame, shame, guilt, and failure; or they can express hope, pride, and confidence about ability and potential.

Increasingly, if families' costs for therapeutic services are to be even partially covered by third-party payment, an individual member must be labeled with a psychiatric diagnosis fitting categories in the DSM-IV. Family therapists prefer to conceptualize problems in terms of interactional processes. Systemic descriptions focused toward solutions open up more possibilities for change. Yet we still must avoid demeaning language and pejorative assumptions about dysfunctional families. Because the very language of therapy can pathologize a family, even unwittingly, we must take great care in choosing our words and in framing questions and responses that are respectful of families.

Reframing and Relabeling

Through such techniques as reframing and relabeling, a problem situation can be redefined in order to cast it in a new light and to shift a family's rigid view or response. In the early days of family therapy, techniques such as positive connotation were used by strategic therapists as clever tactics to outwit families (Anderson, 1986; Nichols & Schwartz, 1995). However, reframing can help to alter a destructive or blaming process, overcome impasses to change, and generate hope. Problems can be depathologized when viewed as normative, expectable, transitional stresses. Symptomatic behavior can be viewed as a survival strategy—an attempt to live with an unbearable situation or to prevent a feared outcome. We may note the helpful, albeit misguided, intentions of caring members trying to help one another.

Reframing distress contextually helps clients view themselves, their problems, and their strengths in a more positive and hopeful light. A problem presented as "inside" an individual, such as a character trait, may be redefined behaviorally in an interactional context. For example, a label of "histrionic personality" may be recast in terms of a wife's futile attempt to get attention from her unresponsive husband. In a vicious cycle, the more she complains, the more he withdraws; the more he distances, the more upset she becomes. In such reformulation of a set, new solutions can become apparent (Weakland et al., 1974).

Narrative "restorying" and Michael White's technique of "externalizing" problems serve as means through language and perspective to reframe problem situations—to present them in more empowering terms that facilitate problem resolution. In externalization (White & Epston, 1990), the therapist recasts a problem (often a child's problem) as an external force that is responsible for wreaking havoc in family members' lives. The therapist's goal is to align with the child and family as partners who together will defeat this negative force, leaving the child and family feeling victorious. Clinicians must be careful, however, not to rely too heavily on reframing techniques. We need to keep in mind that an attitude adjustment may not be enough to surmount overwhelming obstacles; knowledge, skills, and opportunities to succeed are also required.

Identifying, Affirming, and Building Family Strengths

All competence-based approaches are, at their core, about bringing out the best in people (Waters & Lawrence, 1993). A stance that sees and appreciates their best helps them to do their best. We can affirm strengths by finding something worthy to commend about each family member. Although no family is strong in every area, all families possess strengths and resources. Amid very real limitations, we can foster resilience by noticing members' assets and potentials, and by finding ways to nurture and praise their positive intentions, efforts, and achievements. They may have the sense that they are drowning in an ocean of inadequacy, but everyone has "islands of competence" that are, or could be, sources of pride and accomplishment (Brooks, 1994).

Crediting Positive Intentions

Resilience-based therapeutic work helps family members to develop in ways that bring forth their deepest desires for mastery and belonging. I prefer to err on the side of assuming that members' intentions are positive, or at least benign, even when their actions may be ineffective or hurtful. For example, we can affirm a father's desire to be a better parent, aligning with his healthier core to help him gain control over his explosive temper. The assumption of a positive intent behind or alongside problematic behavior helps family members to become less defensive and more open, and to strive for their best.

Praising Efforts and Achievements

It's important to see families as struggling as well as they can with very difficult situations. Although disagreeing with an adolescent's mishandling of a risky situation, for instance, we might credit his astute observations of the predicament he faced and ask how he might draw on those insights if he faced another danger. It's important to note small, concrete examples of caring efforts and actions, such as making it to a session despite a snowstorm. In every session, alongside problem solving, we can make sure to ask how new endeavors are going (e.g., a teen parent's job training program) and to applaud progress. Every family member has some talent or special interest to express; we can let them know we care about their lives and pursuits beyond their problems. The praise offered must be genuine, however. Empty praise will only ring hollow.

   Wherever possible, we can try to shift a vicious cycle to a virtuous cycle. For example, even though a teen mother at times loses control or lashes out at a child, I may share my observation of other signs that she loves the child and has the capacity to be nurturing. I may praise the parenting skills and bonds I observe in a session, such as tenderness in cradling her infant, and point out how responsive the baby is to her loving care. She may initially respond with disbelief ("I am? She is? Really?") and then caress the child, who then breaks into a smile. So often family members comment that coming to sessions has helped them realize they're really not as bad off as they thought.

We can honor the relational base of resilience as we celebrate individual success. I once gave a long-stemmed rose to a single mother on the occasion of her daughter's graduation from college, to honor her important contribution to her child's success. Another time, I took a photo of beaming immigrant parents and their son, holding up his GED certificate. At the end of therapy, I gave the parents and son each a copy of the photo in a small frame, so that they could always keep in mind—in good and bad times—the son's hard-won achievement and the parents' pride and love.

Drawing Out Hidden Resources and Lost Competence

When families are in distress, their view beccomes problem-saturated. They most often seek help when they have reached an impasse, their coping and problem-solving efforts are exhausted, and they feel overwhelmed and inadequate. Their abilities to solve their own problems may be hidden, inaccessible, or forgotten. Family members benefit from therapeutic conversations that bring into awareness untapped resources or strengths to which they have become blinded. We can help them to regain lost competence and to recognize loving concern that may be overshadowed by their current distress. Solution-focused and narrative therapists search for *exceptions* to a problem situation—positive interactions or abilities shown at other times or in other parts of their lives that can be drawn upon now (Freedman & Combs, 1996). For instance, asking spouses about their ways of findng pleasure together before their troubles arose can help to rekindle lost intimacy or bring to the foreground positive aspects of their lives that may have been trampled on by persistent adversity.

Finding Strengths in the Midst of Adversity

Even more valuable than finding positive exceptions *apart from* presenting problems, a family resilience approach emphasizes the importance of finding strengths *in the midst of* adversity. For example, we might commend family members' tenacity in struggling to overcome a financial setback or their courage in rebuilding their lives after a shattering loss.

Adversity can bring out the best in family members. Yet, in distress, they may not notice these strengths. By highlighting them, we help them to recognize their own resources; in doing so, we increase their confidence that these strengths can be accessed if future need arises. As we support their efforts to manage a crisis well, family members often discover resources they never knew they had and forge new areas of competence. A husband may develop new tenderness in caring for his wife after her serious accident. A father who may have been uninvolved with his children can learn new parenting skills and achieve closer ties when forced to manage on his own as a single parent. Whereas a solution-focused therapist might target a search for strengths on better times, a therapist taking a resilience approach hones in on the worst of times, striving for meaning making and mastery.

> Ray and Barbara sought help for intense conflict in the seventh month of her second pregnancy. The therapist's attempts to refocus on happier times and future visions for the new baby fell flat. As a consultant, I explored the meaning of this pregnancy. I learned that Ray and Barbara had lost their first child shortly after birth and now were fearful that the worst would happen again. They tried to push that experience out of their minds and avoided talking about it. Yet they were quite anxious and found themselves arguing over plans for the baby's room. I first asked them to share their stories of the first pregnancy—from their initial hopes and dreams, their preparations, and the anticipatory joy of family and friends, to the unexpected, shattering loss on what should have been their happiest day. The tears came anew as they recounted the details of the birth, the hushed voices of the medical staff in the delivery room, and their utter devastation in learning that the baby was anencephalic and would not survive. Afterward, each partner had gone over those events and images separately, but they had never looked back together or shared their pain. Well-meaning friends told them to put it behind them and move on—a faulty approach to resilience. Now Ray and Barbara found themselves hesitant to share feelings or invest in plans for the child soon to arrive.
>
> Acknowledging their sorrow, I shared with them my admiration for their courage in trying again to have a child. We then turned to the immediate future challenges: I asked them which parts loomed as most difficult and how each might best support the other in areas of vulnerability through the weeks still ahead before the birth. We also discussed how they might communicate their wishes and needs to friends and family members, who in their anxiety either distanced or hovered nervously around them, uncertain of how to be helpful.

Ray and Barbara's contacts with health care professionals were also explored. Much of their anxiety came from ambiguous statements from their doctors that "there was nothing to worry about" this time. They were encouraged to gain fuller comprehension from a genetic counselor. Because they feared that in their high anxiety they might not ask all the questions on their minds, or might not clearly hear and understand the responses, I suggested that they write down their questions in advance and meet with the counselor together; they also decided to take a tape recorder. It was clarified that the new baby's fetal development was normal and that future children were at no higher risk because of the past event. In more fully sharing and integrating their past crisis with their current concerns, Ray and Barbara were able to approach the impending birth with new perspective and investment.

Building Empathic Connections with and between Family Members

Often therapists find it hard to be empathic with a family member who has been neglectful or is abrasive. Yet such empathy is key to a working alliance. For instance, a mother's hard edge might be seen in terms of the feistiness she developed in order to keep her family afloat through tough times and her ex-partner's bouts of drinking. We can identify with her hard struggle as a single parent and applaud the fact that, given the obstacles she faces, she's managing much better than she's given credit for.

We can also help family members gain greater compassion for one another through asking them to share their life stories, the traumatic experiences and pain they have suffered, and the resilience they have shown in weathering those ordeals. A mother who is resented for overprotecting her children can be seen in a new light—as wishing to spare them the harm that she herself endured in childhood sexual abuse. The confusion of a father who is at a loss in dealing with a teenager is clarified when he describes how his own father wasn't there for him; we can be empathic with the challenge of inventing good parenting without a good model. Viewing current dilemmas in the light of life experience can make them more understandable, and flawed individuals can be seen as more human, struggling as best they know how.

Stavros brought his 17-year-old only son, Stavros, Jr., for therapy to "straighten him out." An immigrant, Stavros was furious that his son had left their church, was hanging around with "no-good" friends, and was on the verge of school dropout. Steve (as the son preferred to be called) sat respectfully quiet in the session, yet defended his friends and was obstinate that he didn't care about school or religion. Steve felt constantly pressured by his father to succeed academically and go to college to get a good job. He looked down on his father's work history of low pay and long hours, and felt badgered to make up for the father's "failure" in life.

I asked Stavros whether he had ever shared his full life story and the difficulties of immigration. In a hushed voice, he revealed that he felt ashamed of his humble beginnings and poor English. Encouraged to tell his story, he described the brutal military regime that he had fled; he was forced to leave school at 17 with his brother to escape being drafted. Although he had excelled in school, he ended up working as a janitor and taking odd jobs in order to send money back to his aging parents. Like many immigrants, he realized that he would have to start from scratch and struggle for a living, but his determination was kept strong by his hope that his efforts would enable his children to have a better life. Things became even harder when Steve's mother died after a long illness, when the boy was 12. Spending nothing on himself, Stavros secretly put away a few dollars whenever he could for his son's college education. He was so proud to have such a smart son. How could Steve not care about his future?

Steve, although initially claiming lack of interest in his father's story, listened intently. His voice broke as he said he hadn't realized what his father had been up against, how much courage it had taken to do all he did, and how he had struggled for the sake of his parents and his son. Steve began to see his father not as a failure, but a hero. Moreover, he hadn't been aware of his father's pride in him; he had only felt his disapproval and disappointment. For his part, Steve needed his father to be more tolerant of his friends, activities, and beliefs, so different from the father's experiences and world view in the old country. Through their conversations over several sessions, Stavros was able to hear how Steve's differences weren't so much a rejection of his father as they were a way to find himself in another culture. Stavros reflected, sadly, that in demanding that Steve do everything *his* way, he had become no different from the military dictator he had fled. Father and son were helped to find a better balance. While coming of age, Steve still needed his father's encouragement and support in making his own choices for a good life. Cast in a new light, the very possibility of choice meant that Stavros had truly succeeded in his dream of a better life for his son. He had given him the gift of freedom.

In addressing Stavros's harsh and overbearing treatment of his son, it was crucial to learn (and to help his son to appreciate) how he came to that position, and to understand its protective function. I admired his concern for his son's future so that Steve would have a better opportunity for success in life. Reaching greater mutual understanding enabled him to be less controlling and more accepting of Steve's autonomous strivings. In turn, Steve became less likely to make bad choices for himself out of angry defiance. To foster family resilience in cases such as this one, it's essential to help members reach new understanding and esteem for one another.

Adopting a Positive, Future-Oriented Focus

The poet Audre Lorde reflected, "When I dare to be powerful—to use my strength in the service of my vision, then it becomes less and less important whether I am afraid." People coming for help are often stuck in a vision of their lives that is narrow and joyless, filled with adversity, suffering, and fear. Approaching clients about their hopes and dreams encourages them to imagine a more satisfying future and seek to achieve it (Penn, 1985).

Families should be encouraged to consider and prepare together for such later-life challenges as retirement, transitional living arrangements, and end-of-life decisions—discussions that are commonly avoided. Future-oriented questions can also open up new possibilities for later-life fulfillment. One son was concerned about how each of his parents would manage alone on the family farm if widowed, but he dreaded talking with them about their death. Finally, on a visit home, he got up his courage. First he asked his mother, tentatively, whether she had ever thought about what she might do if Dad were the first to go. She replied, "Sure; we've never talked about it, but I've thought about it for years. I'd sell the farm and move to Texas to be near our grandkids." Her husband scratched his head and replied, "Well, if that ain't the darndest thing! I've thought a lot about it too, and if your mother weren't here, *I'd* sell the farm and move to Texas!" This conversation led the couple to make plans to sell the farm, which had become increasingly burdensome, and move to Texas, where they enjoyed many happy years.

In work with distressed couples and families, a positive, future-oriented focus shifts the emphasis of therapy from "What went wrong?" to "What can be done for enhanced functioning and well-being?" Together, we and our clients can then envision possible options that fit each family situation, and optimistic yet realistic aims that are reachable through shared, constructive efforts. This involves imagination, a hopeful outlook, and initiative in taking actions toward desired goals. A future-oriented focus is valuable even when a current crisis reactivates past traumatic experiences, as in the following case:

Joanne and Ralph were seen in family consultation after their 22-year-old son, Joey, had a serious drug overdose on the eve of his wedding. Asked how she felt about her son's leaving home and getting married, Joanne noted that it was harder for her than it had been with the other children, but she didn't know why. Consulting on the case, I asked whether Joey had been named after her (he had), and asked about her own experience of leaving home and getting married. Joanne told of running off to marry her husband against her father's strong objections. She had been furious at his opposition, and he, in turn, had refused to speak with her again. He died 6 months later of a heart attack without the opportunity for reconciliation. At this point in her story, Joanne became tearful and said, "Somehow it feels the same now."

It was crucial to inquire beyond the obvious dyadic relationship between Joanne and her father to explore other system patterns that might also be fueling current difficulties. Joanne had been very close to her mother, who, once widowed, spent the rest of her life depressed and lonely. When I asked her whether she ever worried that history might repeat itself, Joanne admitted that she worried about her husband's health and his disregard of his overweight condition. In recent months he had complained of chest pains, but had refused to see a doctor. Joey's leaving aroused her fear that something terrible would happen to Ralph and she would end up like her mother.

With Joanne's catastrophic expectations and the lack of a model for later-life marriage (Ralph's mother had also been widowed), she and Ralph had never discussed any dreams or plans for their future together after launching their children. Brief couple therapy focused on exploring their future possibilities. Ralph had a medical workup and started to take better care of himself. They celebrated their son's wedding and impulsively took a "refresher honeymoon" on their own.

In helping a family move forward, it's important to make connections between the past, present, and future so that family members can understand current distress and integrate their experiences. They can't change the past, but we can help them learn from it to chart a better future course.

Refocusing from Complaints to Aims

Distressed couples and families can become caught up in a vicious cycle of negativity, focused on each other's deficiencies and constantly finding fault. Despite our inclinations to support the underdog and to interrupt scapegoating, therapists must be cautious not to adopt a critical stance toward a critical parent or spouse; this only reinforces cycles of blame and widens the sense of deficiency. Asking a parent, "Why are you so hard on your child?", or commenting to a wife, "It seems like you can't see anything good in your husband," only criticizes them for being critical. Instead, it's important to understand the stress, pain, and frustrations underlying such criticisms, and to help family members refocus from complaints (what's wrong) to positive aims (what can be done to make things better). What would improve an unbearable situation? How would a marriage need to change for the better for a spouse on the edge of divorce to reconsider? What would a more satisfying family life look like? What changes would they have to make to achieve it?

After hearing family members' complaints in an assessment interview, it's important to ask what they hope to *gain* through counseling. We shouldn't assume that the desired change is simply solving presenting problems or reducing distress. I'm frequently surprised, as I was in this case:

> In a family evaluation, the parents, Manny and Sylvia, presented a tirade of complaints about their son's troublesome behavior. After listening to their descriptions of frustrating, unsuccessful attempts to deal with the situation, I asked what they most hoped to gain in our work together, expecting to hear that the son should shape up. Instead, Manny replied, his voice choked up: "I'd like to learn how to show love to my kids." When I asked to hear more about that, Manny responded, "My dad had a temper—he only knew how to yell." I asked what that had been like for him as a kid, and noticed how attentive the children were, realizing that he had felt as bad as they did with him now. When asked what that experience had taught him, he said, "I don't know any other way, but I'd like to do better by my kids."

Here again, in linking past experience with present distress, a future vision can become a positive force to break destructive patterns and achieve healthier relationships.

Instilling Hope and Optimism

While being empathic with the suffering of our clients, we must also instill hope and optimism that they will triumph over their adversities. For example, I may say,

> "I understand that you're experiencing a lot of pain and conflict right now. I'm also convinced that you have many strengths as a family. I believe that beneath the pain and upset, you care deeply about one another. One

sign of that caring is that you all made an effort to come in and meet to solve your problems. I'm quite hopeful that if you will work together on these issues, you have strong potential to make things better. I'll be glad to work with you, to support your best efforts."

When clients have lost hope to pessimism, we might ask: "Has there ever been a time when you felt more hopeful about the situation? What was different then? Who was most helpful? How?" Conversations can explore what might be learned and applied to the present dilemma, as well as what they imagine could help them regain hope. What might their partner, parents, or others say or do that might reinvigorate them? Often one spouse or partner will turn to the other and say, "I just need you to hold me and tell me you love me. That will keep me going through this crisis." A family bear hug at the end of a session can bolster an overwhelmed parent. One of my students told a beleaguered family that he understood how it was hard for members to feel hopeful at that moment, but that he had enough hope for all of them and firmly believed that they would weather their crisis. He offered to lend them some of his hope to tide them over until their own hope was restored.

Encouraging Shared Efforts, Concrete Steps, and Perseverance

To foster family resilience, we need to create a therapeutic climate that maximizes the possibilities for members to be successful and to experience success as largely due to their shared efforts and abilities. These affirming beliefs and successful experiences generate realistic hope and optimism that through supporting one another, they can master their challenges. To accomplish this, we can encourage all members' responsibility and pride in their part in the process. We need to recognize efforts and offer to help in developing more effective joint strategies for coping and problem solving. As they become successful more of the time, they will come to believe that these shared efforts can make a difference, as in Seligman's "learned optimism" (see Chapter 3).

It's most important to help families initiate and follow through on concrete, achievable steps toward objectives, especially when challenges loom as overwhelming and goals seem remote. As my colleague Carol Anderson tells families trying to help a loved one make progress in the aftermath of a mental breakdown, "Yard by yard, it's just too hard; inch by inch, it's a cinch." Small successes can be sources of pride and accomplishment to build on, with increasing confidence and competence. Achieving success in one arena of life, such as productive school functioning, can lead to enhanced efficacy, enabling more successful coping in other areas.

Helping Families to Accept Human Limitations

The Navaho say that the way to tell that a rug has been made by human hands is by the presence of flaws. As helping professionals, we can cultivate acceptance of imperfections within families—as well as acceptance of our own limitations—by viewing flaws not as defects, but instead as part of being human. Our therapeutic approach should foster the belief that mistakes and failures are normal aspects of life, especially under stressful conditions. We can help family members to own errors and to view them as important experiences from which to learn, rather than as demoralizing defeats. It's also useful, in whatever ways possible, to attribute mistakes to factors that members can change (e.g., insufficient effort or an unrealistic goal) rather than to innate deficits that can't be modified. This is most challenging, yet essential, with families who have experienced many crises or chronic difficulties and have come to feel beaten down by repeated failure.

In our work with families in crisis, we must remember that resilience does not mean bouncing back instantaneously or always maintaining cheerful optimism and steady progress. Dealing with adversity may be a matter of taking three steps forward, two steps back. Family members are bound to have times when they "hit the wall" and need respite, when they take a wrong turn, or when they "bottom out" in despair. When family members experience setbacks, we need to hang in with them to encourage them to rebound and persist in their efforts.

Involving Families in Recovery from Individual Trauma

Even when a crisis strikes an individual and other family members are not directly touched by the event, a systemic approach considers how all are nonetheless affected by it and by the family response. Some may not currently be showing symptoms of distress, but may hold hidden concerns and be at heightened risk for later problems. A family resilience approach draws members together for mutual support and healing. All benefit from family interventions and become better resources for one another.

Heather, a 14-year-old girl, was raped by a 17-year-old football player at a party. Although she had individual counseling, she continued to be depressed many months after the event. Family sessions had not been held, out of a concern to protect her privacy; yet everyone in the family had heard something about the incident. Although no one talked openly about it, it preoccupied their thoughts. Heather read their silence as condemnation. She was convinced that they were all talking about her behind her back, just as her schoolmates were. She believed that they all saw her as a "slut"; that she had enjoyed the rape, or had even invited it; and that she was the one at fault and should never have gotten the popular senior into trouble by reporting it to the police. These beliefs led her to drop charges and withdraw from friends and family members, finally taking a handful of Valium in a suicide attempt.

With this secondary crisis, a family session was held. Heather's parents revealed genuine concern and felt terribly guilty that they had not been more supportive. Unsure what to say or do that would not further upset Heather, they had tried their best to be cheerful and go on as if everything were normal, leaving the therapy to the professional counselor. They believed Heather's account of the rape and in no way blamed her; rather, they blamed themselves for having let her go on the date. The family session also revealed that Heather's 17-year-old brother, Brian, had been doing poorly in school since the incident. He was upset with himself for not having warned Heather not to go out with the boy, a binge drinker who bragged about his conquests with girls. Heather's 12-year-old sister, Amy, just entering puberty, was also traumatized by the incident: She was terrified that she too was vulnerable to assault, and was unsure whether she could trust any boys. The family shutdown in communication had left her unable to voice her own fears.

The family therapist affirmed the courage they were showing now in being so honest and open in sharing their feelings about such a painful crisis. She normalized, as a common response, the parents' uncertainty about how to be helpful after the incident; she acknowledged their positive intentions to help Heather feel better by being upbeat, as well as the natural wish to move on as if it hadn't happened. Yet, she added, the family communication block had left all family members isolated with concerns they couldn't express. Heather was asked what it meant to hear the reactions of her family. She was moved to learn how much they cared about her, and surprised that her parents and brother had blamed not her but themselves. The therapist framed their self-criticism as understandable in the situation, since it stemmed from their concern for her well-being. The mother also felt badly that her focus on Heather and her efforts to be upbeat had kept her from realizing that Amy too might be upset. The therapist applauded them for taking important steps now to begin to deal with what had happened. She encouraged the parents to talk with each of their children over the coming weeks, to learn more about the meanings of the rape event for each and to help them gain a better perspective on it.

The parents were seen without the children for part of the next session, so that they could further explore their own feelings about the rape. The father said he had felt enraged at the boy, but, not being a "violent" man, he had contained his feelings and tried to put the incident behind them. The mother revealed that the rape had triggered her own memory of a sexual assault when she was a teen; at that time the term "date rape" did not exist, and she had told no one, secretly blaming herself for not having been able to fend off the unwanted advances. Her husband's response was compassionate, yet he was surprised that she had never told him before. She was tearful in describing the shame she had carried long after the incident. Her belief that he'd think less of her had constrained her from ever telling him. This conversation brought her to decide to tell Heather about her own experience, so as to encourage her not to carry shame and self-blame.

The parents were encouraged in their efforts to deal more directly with the range of feelings and responses experienced by their children, to comfort them, and to support each other as well. In following sessions, the whole family seemed more animated and much closer as they related their further discussions. The mother's conversation with Heather had brought a deeper mutual empathy, and redirected their focus toward making the perpetrator of the assault accountable for his behavior. The parents strongly urged Heather to follow through with legal charges against the rapist, and assured her that they would back her every step of the way.

The therapist asked the family members to consider what might be learned from the incident and its aftermath. They discussed practical steps they might take both individually and as a family, with parental leadership, to ensure greater security in potentially dangerous situations. They talked about realizing the importance of turning to one another to air concerns, dispel faulty assumptions, and gain support.

The therapist then asked whether their experience inspired them to consider taking any actions that might be helpful to others in prevention or recovery from sexual assault. In discussing this during the next week at home, Heather decided to act on an idea she'd had to start a hot line with classmates for kids in trouble. The parents encouraged her plan and got the support of school officials. Brian became active in organizing the service, signing up trusted friends to offer rides home for kids calling in who had suffered assault or feared a precarious situation. The parents organized a parents' association meeting at the school, where the family therapist and the school counselor were invited to offer information about rape, its impact on families, and the important role family members can play in recovery. She urged them to be aware that boys, as well as girls, are sexually assaulted, but are even less likely to come forward about it because of homophobic attitudes in our culture. Parents were encouraged to work with other parents more effectively to ensure that all social events were chaperoned and that no liquor or drugs were available. The family initiatives and networking generated by this crisis fostered a sense of empowerment and healing for Heather and her family, strengthening their bonds and sense of community.

Research on posttraumatic stress disorder—whether it follows war, catastrophic events, or situations of violence and sexual abuse—finds that everyone in the family experiences ripple effects or secondary trauma, even when the initial impact centers on one family member (Figley, 1989). Reciprocally, everyone in the family contributes to the course and outcome of the crisis situation. It's important to provide family members with opportunities to talk separately and together about their feelings and experience, and to build mutual empathy and support for repair and healing of trauma effects. A commitment to community activism can further strengthen family resilience and can benefit countless others.

RE-VISIONING SERVICES TO STRENGTHEN FAMILIES

Brief therapy approaches that focus too narrowly on problem solving may err in presuming that a family, once unblocked from a dysfunctional pattern, will be able to shift to and sustain healthier modes on its own. At the other extreme, growth-oriented approaches risk pushing clients toward unrealistic and unreachable ideals of couple satisfaction or family functioning. A family resilience approach strikes a balance between extremes, in being both pragmatic and growth-oriented. It is future-focused while understanding where families are coming from. This approach targets key family processes to strengthen family functioning and resourcefulness as presenting problems are solved. All human services can be re-visioned from a family resilience perspective.

Collaboration and Teamwork

A family resilience approach emphasizes the value of collaborative efforts in surmounting life challenges. In crisis, mutual support is most likely to break down as members hunker down in isolated, self-reliant modes of coping or in adversarial positions. When we encourage empathic communication and shared problem solving among family members, we strengthen relationships as problems are tackled together. Couple and family conjoint sessions implicitly set a collaborative context. More explicitly, we can invite clients to think of themselves as partners or teammates, who become more resourceful through joint efforts.

Collaboration is also essential between the family and helping professionals. Some clinical approaches have depicted therapy as an adversarial struggle, with therapeutic skills taught as powerful tactics to overcome family resistance and reduce family pathology. Implicit in such power-based approaches was a skewed relationship between the competent expert/helper/healer and the deficient or pathological family. Recognizing that successful interventions depend on family resources, more recent approaches to family therapy work in partnership with the family, building on existing and potential strengths.

In addition, helping professionals must work more collaboratively with one another on teams and across disciplines, both within and across systems, in order to overcome fragmented and unresponsive service delivery. Human services have tended to be problem-centered—narrowly focused on a symptomatic individual, or perhaps a partner, parent, or identified caregiver, while the family network (and other strains and potential resources) remains only a dim backdrop.

When services are designed to be family-centered, efforts can be better coordinated and proactive in helping all family members through concerted efforts (Ooms & Preister, 1988). Such an approach is advocated by the Collaborative Family Health Care Coalition, founded by Donald Bloch, which seeks to encourage patient–family–provider collaboration in the treatment of health problems and accompanying psychosocial challenges.

Multisystem, Community-Based Interventions

If families are to sustain themselves and meet their challenges successfully, they require environmental support. Family therapists have expanded the focus beyond the interior of the family, more to seek and build linkages between individuals, families, their social networks, and larger systems (Imber-Black, 1988). For instance, fostering a partnership between school professionals and families can make all the difference between children's risk of failure or dropout and their chances of resilience and success (Comer, 1997). A community-based family resource perspective is especially needed in work with multicrisis, vulnerable families. Interventions aimed at enhancing positive interactions, supporting coping efforts, and building extrafamilial resources work in concert to reduce stress, to enhance pride and competence, and to promote more effective functioning in these families (see Chapter 9).

Flexible Service Delivery

To be responsive and proactive to family challenges over time, our service delivery systems must be more flexibly organized. This poses a dilemma for managed care: Adaptation can't happen all at once in four to six sessions. Yet this doesn't mean that we must swing to the other extreme of vague, open-ended contracts with unlimited therapeutic horizons. One of my colleagues worried that attending to adaptations over time would mean that once a couple or family is seen for help, members remain in treatment for life. Part of the problem lies in the concept of "treatment." A resilience-based approach more closely fits the model of preventive family medicine and the concept of "healing." When we think of our physical health, we don't think of ourselves as patients in perpetual medical treatment, even though we see our physicians both in crisis and for periodic checkups, and develop a relationship with them over time.

We need to re-vision the traditional therapeutic contract and the rigid schedule of weekly sessions until termination, so that interventions can fit varied challenges and adaptive processes. Therapy can be focused on building a family's strengths to meet immediate psychosocial demands of a major transition or crisis situation and can prepare for the anticipated course ahead. For example, when a couple is seen around a divorce, it is helpful to approach separation, custody, and visitation options in a planful way (Walsh et al., 1995). We can be proactive by helping parents to anticipate transitional distress and complications that commonly occur over time, (e.g., changes in residence, a remarriage, or decisions about a child's education or religious affiliation). It is also helpful to provide information on postdecree mediation or other appropriate services to address postdivorce challenges, if and when they arise.

The family systems–illness model developed by Rolland (1994; see Chapter 8, this volume) has potential value as a useful framework for intervention to promote family coping and resilience with a range of adversities. Family challenges and intervention priorities will vary, depending on the crisis patterning: *onset* (acute vs. gradual), *course* (brief vs. recurrent vs. constant vs. progressively worsening), *outcome*, degree of *incapacitation*, and *uncertainty* about its trajectory. Stressors are approached as ongoing processes with landmarks, transitions, and changing demands. Each phase in the unfolding of events poses developmental tasks that may require different strengths from a family. A brief crisis requires immediate mobilization of resources; however, after the initial period of disequilibrium, a family may be able to reorganize and resume accustomed patterns in living. With permanent change or persistent adversity, the family must grieve the loss of its precrisis identity and alter familiar patterns, as well as hopes and dreams, to accommodate a new set of circumstances. This framework can guide consultations and periodic family "psychosocial checkups" to strengthen the family's capacity to manage stress-related crises or sustained efforts over the long haul.

Just as families need more cohesion to pool resources in times of crisis, more intensive professional help is needed at such times. Likewise, just as families can shift balance to more separateness in stable periods, family functioning can be sustained with more intermittent therapeutic contact during plateaus of adaptation. During the initial crisis phase (which may last from a few weeks to several months), sessions can be held weekly, or more frequently if the situation is urgent. Family members can be seen separately and in different combinations—for instance, a suicidal adolescent can be seen both privately and with the family. Over time, progress can be sustained by meeting at less frequent intervals (e.g., biweekly or monthly). More intensive, focused sessions can be held at predictable stress points, such as the first anniversary of a child's death; preferably such sessions should be scheduled in advance to prevent a crisis from developing. Help can also be available as needed when unexpected problems or new disruptions occur.

Systems-Oriented Approaches: Many Pathways to Resilience

Just as there are many pathways to healthy family functioning, our view of family therapy must be expanded from the traditional treatment paradigm to a variety of systems-based approaches to strengthen and support families. Family therapists frequently combine individual and conjoint sessions in their therapeutic work, as noted above. In the course of couple or family therapy, meeting with individual members can allow the clinician to get a fuller picture, particularly when communication is guarded or volatile. Careful planning, timing, and focus are important, with attention to issues of confidntiality and triangulation.

Psychoeducational models (Anderson, Reiss, & Hogarty, 1986; McFarlane, 1991), family support programs (Kagan & Weissbourd, 1994), marital and family enrichment (Guerney, 1991), and family consultation (Wynne, McDaniel, & Weber, 1986) have considerable potential for providing needed information, skills, and support to families in crisis and to those coping with serious and persistent disorders. Workshops and programs in problem solving and communication skills training are being designed to stabilize and strengthen families; divorce prevention programs for high-risk couples are one example. We need to develop a range of such programs in natural community settings for family-focused prevention and early intervention services.

Multifamily groups, providing psychoeducation and a support network, are particularly well suited to promoting family resilience. Such groups have broad potential to provide useful information, coping strategies, and social support for families facing situations that range from serious illness (see Chapter 8) to a breadwinner's job dislocation, or a perinatal bereavement. Pertinent research on family functioning can inform interventions and can be shared with family members, who are hungry for information to clarify ambiguities and for guidelines to manage stressful situations. Strengths are developed through contact with other families dealing with similar challenges. As families come to realize that some problems are common and expectable, they learn from a variety of experiences as they forge their own solutions. Families respond positively to the depathologized framing of their distress as a family challenge and to the definition of group objectives in terms of strengthening family resilience.

Prevention: From Reaction to Proaction

In emerging priorities for mental health and health care, resources must be shifted from more costly treatment to less costly prevention services. Most programs addressing the adversities facing children and families are reactive, focused on salvaging victims from the wreckage. It makes more sense to offer proactive, wellness-based services—to educate and bolster those at risk *before* problems become entrenched and multiply. The case for preventive services, such as family support or family life education, is strengthened by mounting evidence that programs providing information, resources, and opportunities for skill and knowledge development, in an ongoing rather than a crisis-triggered manner, are both effective and cost-effective (Coohey & Marsh, 1995).

Resilience-building family intervention can serve as a psychosocial inoculation, to boost immunity or hardiness in facing adversity. By strengthening resilience in families before crises develop, we decrease their risk and vulnerability, fortify their capacities to cope with stress, and increase their abilities to face new challenges. Preventive actions may attempt to lower risk by modifying environmental conditions or circumstances; to shore up vulnerability, buffer stress, and develop crisis prevention skills by strengthening family interaction processes; and to mobilize supportive resources by building kin and community networks.

Preventive interventions may be offered before, during, or after the development of a problem situation. Primary prevention and family life education are strategies for creating support and empowerment for individuals and families at risk (Harris, 1996). For instance, Chicago-based programs such as Family Focus and Ounce of Prevention work with new teen parents to foster healthy parent–child relationships and early child development, and to support the parents' own educational, job, and social functioning. As family thera-pists and other professionals concerned about family well-being, we can offer our knowledge and encouragement of health-promoting strategies through community consultations and public speaking.

Secondary prevention consists of early intervention, as in an early phase of crisis or initial adjustment to a stressful transition. Tertiary prevention consists of actions taken later in the course of persistent problems to prevent further recurrence or exacerbation. For instance, psychoeducational ap-proaches with chronic mental illness help patients and families manage stress to enhance coping, increase functioning, and reduce the risk of relapse and rehospitalization (Anderson et al., 1986).

From a resilience standpoint, *all* therapeutic efforts can be preventive if we help distressed families develop strengths to avert future crises. The treatment of a knee injury (an experience I can relate to) offers a useful anal-ogy. Physical therapy not only aids in recovery, but also strengthens the resil-ience of muscles in the vulnerable area so that future injury can be prevented. Many brief crisis intervention approaches are helpful for short-term recov-ery, but unless family resilience is strengthened future crises are likely to overwhelm a vulnerable family, requiring further rounds of crisis interven-tion in revolving-door emergency treatment.

It has always puzzled me why family-centered mental health services are not offered on the preventive, cost-effective model of family medicine or dentistry. From early childhood, we are taught how to brush our teeth and prevent cavities. Dentists schedule routine checkups, rather than waiting for problems to develop and become serious. Every 6 months a card in the mail reminds me to come for my checkup. I don't want to go, and I'm tempted to let it slide if I'm not in pain, but a follow-up phone call (outreach) gets me in. I'm always glad when nothing's wrong, and I get a free toothbrush to keep me brushing. When there is a problem, I'm relieved that it's been taken care of early, and it's usually smaller and easier to fix. If we could implement such a model for psychosocial care, a great deal of tragedy and suffering could be prevented.

Premarital counseling and multicouple workshops are becoming more widespread, often under the auspices of religious groups (e.g., the Catholic Church conducts Marriage Encounter weekends). Often premarital coun-seling is informed by inventories designed to assess relationship strengths and target trouble spots that predict higher risk of later marital difficulties or di-vorce. The PREPARE and ENRICH assessment tools (Fowers & Olson, 1989) have been found to have broad relevance and reliability with couples in cultures as diverse as African American, Latino, and Japanese (Olson, 1993). David Olson has joked that, as sequels to PREPARE, an assessment for couples considering divorce could be called DESPAIR, and another for couples considering remarriage might be named BEWARE.

Increasingly, schools, religious organizations, and community centers are offering psychoeducational programs on early pregnancy prevention and the challenges of parenting, in order to reach teens before pregnancy occurs. Increased outreach effort is particularly needed to raise young men's awareness and expectations of responsibility for preventing unwed pregnancies and for taking an active role in parenting any children they father. Psychoeducational groups are especially valuable in helping young parents to begin child rearing on a solid footing. Faculty at our Chicago Center for Family Health have developed a community-based psychoeducational program called Parents as Partners, to focus on the challenges and rewards of shared parenting of infants and young children. Because the transition to parenthood is especially fraught with conflicts between job and parenting demands for dual-earner couples, such groups provide a setting for bringing some balance and order to the chaos frequently experienced.

In sum, resilience-based services foster family empowerment as they bring forth shared hope, develop new and renewed areas of competence, and build mutual support. From this perspective, it is not enough to solve a presenting problem; in fostering resilience, we enable families to meet new challenges more effectively. Every intervention is thus also a preventive measure.

STRENGTHENING THERAPIST RESILIENCE

Engagement with Clients and Colleagues

Family therapists have shifted from emphasizing pragmatic strategies and tactics for change to recognizing the essential importance of the human element in the therapeutic relationship. For clients to be open and receptive to change, helping professionals must be genuinely interested in their life stories and concerned about their well-being. We must be understanding of their predicament, must empathize with their pain, and must encourage their best strivings. We need to be comfortable in bringing ourselves fully into the therapeutic conversation, modeling and teaching by example in our therapeutic transactions, and sharing (as appropriate) what we've learned from our own human experiences with adversity.

"Courageous engagement" of therapist and clients—a wonderfully apt phrase offered by Waters and Lawrence (1993)—is at the heart of competence-based work and collaborative efforts to build resilience. We, as therapists, as well as our clients, need courage to question and challenge constraining myths; to support attempts to move from a helpless, victimized position; and to en-*courage* our clients to go after what they really want. It requires courage to expect more and take risks for better relationships and life goals. When we work from this perspective, our clients are better able to take steps toward positive change and to live with greater ease in situations that are unchangeable.

Our own resilience as therapists is also relationally based, fostered through collaboraton with colleagues, supportive work systems, and satisfying personal relationships. As caseloads increase in numbers and complexity while staff resources are cut back, the risk of professional burnout is heightened. I encourage students and therapists to create supportive professional networks and to seek out learning experiences at each phase and transition in their careers. Postgraduate family therapy training centers can offer a revitalizing professional home, nurturing contact and growth through participation in workshops, courses, and case consultation groups. Collaborative consultation teams are ideal for building comraderie, competence, and confidence. Ongoing group experiences provide mentoring relationships, collegial support, and revitalization along with skill enhancement. A monthly peer consultation group can sustain professional growth and connectedness.

In practice settings where teams are not feasible, a "buddy system" can readily be formed. Trusted colleagues can serve as mutual resources and consultants when clients are in crisis or a professional is undersupported and discouraged. My close colleagues and I continue to turn to one another, and we always find our spirits renewed and our creative energy rekindled as a result.

One time a colleague asked me to observe a session with a client after he had nearly fallen asleep in the last session. He was upset that he was becoming bored and irritated with his client, Gloria, a middle-aged mother whose husband had recently left her. As I watched, I could see the two of them go into a near-trance induction that paralyzed the therapy. Intending to show empathy for her plight, my colleague sat quietly nodding in concern as she went on and on about her sad situation, recounting everything bad that always happened to her. As his thoughts drifted and he looked away, Gloria increased the intensity of her drama to reengage him, which only irritated him more. This relational mantra repeated itself week after week.

As my colleague and I reflected together on the situation, it became apparent that by concentrating so intently on Gloria's sorrowful story, he was unwittingly reinforcing her passive, victimized position and her belief that others could only care about her if she evoked their sympathy. For change to occur, he needed to show genuine interest in Gloria as a lovable person who deserved and could achieve a better life for herself and her children. As the focus of the therapeutic conversation shifted to noticing and affirming her strengths, she came alive, and he had no difficulty sustaining his investment in helping her rebound from the devastation of the divorce. A resilience-promoting therapeutic relationship seeks to repair the damage from traumatic experience, to expand the client's vision of what is possible, and to support actions and relational resources in pursuit of those dreams.

Waters and Lawrence (1993) encourage therapists to see our clients' struggles and confrontations as the mythic "hero's journey"—a view consonant with the resilience approach. They note Joseph Campbell's observation that the heroes of myths are all on a quest against the odds to slay a dragon or other foe, as in the Biblical story of David versus Goliath. The hero comes to participate in life courageously and decently, in the way of nature—not in the way of personal rancor, disappointment, or revenge. When we take such a view of our clients, we can more easily appreciate the positive, competent aspects of their life journeys and our own efforts. Waters and Lawrence state:

> In our work, this goal of a courageous engagement with life guides us more than a desire to avoid the "negative" aspects of symptoms. In therapy, our clients are the heroes attempting to "slay their dragons," but if we lose sight of that and become preoccupied with their dysfunction, victimization, or handicap, we are less helpful to them. We must see that at their core is their desire for mastery and belonging. They become heroes when they—and we—have the courage to struggle against those obstacles and transform the possibilities of life. (1993, p. 58)

Balance in Our Professional and Personal Lives

Therapists are also challenged to achieve a healthy balance in our professional and personal lives. The risk of "compassion fatigue" (Figley, 1995), and the potential for spillover of painful and threatening issues (in both directions), come with the territory of our chosen work. The professional and the personal each hold meanings for the success of the other, if we are able to apply them wisely and keep aware of our clients' and our own values and situations, our commonalities and differences. The safe boundaries and hierarchies of more traditional psychotherapy can become blurred in more collaborative therapeutic relationships. But the gains are worth the challenge. If we keep in mind that resilience does not mean invulnerability, we become more human and compassionate in our helping relationships and more fully engaged with our families, friends, and community.

A week before the 1989 annual meeting of the American Association for Marriage and Family Therapy was scheduled to be held in San Francisco, a devastating earthquake struck the Bay Area. I was among several professionals contacted to weigh decisions about whether to go ahead with the meeting and, if so, how to address the trauma and its aftermath. City officials urged us to proceed with the meeting, in order to demonstrate our confidence that normal life could be resumed. We arrived to find streets and stores deserted, with the Bay Bridge and parts of major highways in wreckage. With the leadership of trauma expert Charles Figley, we facilitated an open forum for Bay Area professionals to offer a context for discussion of their experience, although we were unsure how many might attend or what issues might come up.

As the large room overflowed, we formed a very large circle. Some were community workers, called in to assist families whose homes and neighborhoods had been destroyed. Many others were therapists doing their best to help their clients deal with the terrifying experience and disruption in their lives. As participants began to speak, bottled-up emotions surfaced. Many were enraged that the poorest of families, many migrant workers, were suffering the most and receiving the least attention from authorities and the media. Many helpers and healers were themselves traumatized by the experience and struggling to restore a semblance of order and security in their own family lives as they were called upon to help others. The comfortable boundaries between therapists and clients were shattered by the earthquake, as all were affected. The situation remained precarious as aftershocks occurred. It was helpful for these therapists to realize that resilience doesn't mean invulnerability. In sharing their own vulnerability and rebuilding their own homes alongside those of their clients, their human bonds deepened. The forum sparked other supportive networks for airing personal and professional concerns and for reenergizing efforts on behalf of client communities.

The Changing U.S. Health Care Context: Mastering Professional Challenges

An "earthquake" is currently jolting the very bedrock of our professional field of practice. Our own resilience as helping professionals is essential as we face new challenges in meeting the needs of increasingly diverse families in the midst of upheaval and uncertainty in our ability to provide those services. Within the coming decade, most Americans will receive their health care through managed care arrangements, which will affect all segments of human service delivery, both public and private. As the health and mental health care

systems undergo major overhauls in the shift to managed care, family therapists and other helping professionals are expected to work in very different
environments, with a cost-conscious, bottom-line orientation. The argument
for managed care has been based in part on criticism of therapies that become endless quests for vaguely defined, value-laden visions of health. At the
other extreme, however, are "quick-fix" approaches as the corporate profit
incentive takes precedence over provision of appropriate services. New jar-
gon (e.g., "capitation"), additional paperwork, reduced professional fees, and
reimbursement plans are being used to promote and rationalize cost cutting.
Practitioners may be paid no more for a full-hour family session than they
are for a 10-minute medication refill or a pat on the back. To obtain reimbursement or gain authorization for more than a few sessions, therapists are
pressured to overpathologize their clients by insistence on a diagnosis of severe and chronic psychiatric disorder. Client confidentiality is violated by
record-keeping practices. The severe financial disincentives for practitioners,
the restricted access to services, and the stigmatizing of clients undermine
our core principles as helping professionals and must be fought courageously
to ensure high-quality care to the families we are committed to serve.

Despite these daunting challenges and transformations in our field, I am
convinced that systems-based, family-centered services will continue to be
in demand, because of the broad range of problems to which our approach
can successfully be applied and the cost-effectiveness of helping all family
members through interventions that strengthen the family as a functional unit.
Recognizing the potential in relational resilience, helping professionals of all
disciplines must put aside our rivalries and band together in collaborative
efforts to overcome barriers that threaten our common mission to promote
healthy individual and family functioning. We must become more articulate
and vocal about the importance of family services and family-centered care,
and we must marshal research evidence in support of our expertise and effectiveness. The keys to resilience for our clients are also keys to our own
professional resilience.

Mending the Social Fabric

Systems-oriented professionals, I believe, have an ethical responsibility to direct our energies beyond our office walls and toward repair of the social fragmentation that heightens the risk for family breakdown. It would be uncon-
scionable to help families withstand the onslaught of social and economic
pressures in their lives without making every effort to eradicate destructive
social forces. The resilience of the field of family therapy is also strengthened

when we actively invest in larger system change and social movements—when we lend our expertise to help mend the frayed social fabric. Systemic changes are needed to address larger institutional and cultural influences that breed poverty and discrimination and that severely strain families. Collaborative professional and family advocacy can strengthen efforts to overcome these barriers and promote family-centered policies that enable families to thrive.

Family Resilience
through Crisis
and Challenge

C·H·A·P·T·E·R   7

Loss, Recovery, and Resilience

In accepting death, we discover life.
—BUDDHIST TENET

The tragic killing of Ennis Cosby, as he changed a tire at the side of the road, evoked a compassionate response around the world. The loss of the only son of Bill Cosby, an American father figure who transcends racial and class barriers, underscores the vulnerability of all families to human tragedy beyond their control. Coming to terms with death and loss is the most difficult challenge a family must confront.

From a family systems perspective, loss can be viewed as a transactional process involving those who die with their survivors in a shared life cycle, recognizing both the finality of death and the continuity of life. Such a perspective also considers the impact of the death of a family member on the family as a functional unit, with immediate and long-term reverberations for every member and all other relationships. A family resilience approach fosters the ability to face death and dying, to come to terms with loss, and to move forward with life individually and collaboratively, strengthened as a family unit.

This chapter first looks at death and loss in sociohistorical context. It then presents a framework for systemic assessment and intervention to ease the dying process and foster resilience in the face of loss. A developmental perspective considers loss processes over time and across the family life cycle. Major family adaptational challenges in loss are then described, with attention to key interactional processes—belief systems, organizational patterns, and communication processes—that can be interwoven to promote recovery and resilience. Critical variables are identified that can place individuals and families facing loss at heightened risk for immediate or long-term dysfunction. Guidelines are offered for dealing effectively with complicated situations.

DEATH AND LOSS IN SOCIOHISTORICAL CONTEXT

Throughout history and in every culture, mourning beliefs and rituals have facilitated both the integration of death and the transformations of survivors (Walsh & McGoldrick, 1991). Each culture, in its own ways, offers assistance to the dying and to the community of survivors who must move forward with life.

Times of profound loss may feel unique, as if nothing like this had ever happened before in history. We can't know exactly how anyone will respond. Yet, as Mary Catherine Bateson (1994) has observed, the bereaved are part of a cultural drama that asserts basic ideas about the nature of life and death and the human heart: "Individual responses follow cultural patterns, each experience offering analogies for others" (p. 19).

Some cultures rehearse for grief and loss, while others deny or minimize them, as in mainstream U.S. culture. Some societies organize their recognitions of bereavement to support the expression of grief, while others are oriented around efforts to help the bereaved quickly regain control and forget. Bateson (1994) has noted, for instance, that "Filipinos are fortunate in having a worldview which allows them to face the inescapable fact of death, including it in the rhythm of life and a continuing understanding of God's mercy." In contrast, "Americans treat grief almost like a disease, embarrassing and possibly infectious" (p. 20). To avoid breaking down, some impose a rigid self-control, fitting with the cultural expectation that grief should be minimized. Whereas loss is an occasion for family and community cohesion in most cultures, Americans worry about "intruding" on the grief of others and are wary about facing their own mortality and loss. After the initial mourning period, the phone stops ringing; visitors and invitations come with decreasing frequency. It is not uncommon for bereaved persons to see, out of the corner of an eye, friends or neighbors turning away or crossing a street to avoid the discomfort of contact.

A growing body of research finds that individual mourning responses vary widely within U.S. society (Wortman & Silver, 1989). Yet, in whatever different forms and circumstances they occur, mourning processes promote healing. Although there is considerable diversity in individual, familial, and cultural modes of dealing with death and loss, family processes are crucial influences in healthy or dysfunctional adaptation to loss.

The socially constructed myths of the normal family reinforce the denial of death (Walsh, 1993). However, contrary to the idyllic image of the traditional family as intact, stable, and secure, families across the ages have had to cope with the precariousness of life and the disruptions wrought by death. As is still true in impoverished communities throughout the world, death in earlier eras struck young and old alike, with high rates of mortality for infants, children, and women in childbirth. Until medical advances in the 20th century, life expectancy in the United States was under 50 years—a period now considered midlife. Parental death often disrupted family units, shifting members into varied and complex networks of full, half-, and step-relationships in vast extended kinship systems.

Before the advent of hospital and institutional care, people died at home, where all family members, including children, were involved in the preparation and immediacy of death. Modern technological society has fueled the tendency to deny death and to distance from grief processes, making adaptation to loss all the more difficult. In contrast to traditional cultures, contemporary society lacks cultural supports to assist families in integrating the fact of death with ongoing life (Becker, 1973; Mitford, 1963/1978). Geographical distances and emotional estrangement separate family members at times of death and dying. Medical advances have complicated the process by removing death from everyday reality, while at the same time confronting families with unprecedented decisions to prolong or end life.

As the 20th century comes to an end, we are being jolted into a heightened recognition of the importance of facing death and loss. The worldwide AIDS epidemic has forced greater attention to death and dying. Also, the approach of middle age for the baby boom generation has prompted a shift in public consciousness from a preoccupation with youth to the realities of aging and mortality. Families are beginning to reclaim the dying process through such directives as living wills and more meaningful memorial rites.

Amid the social and economic upheaval of recent decades, families are dealing with multiple losses, disruptions, and uncertainties. This chapter focuses on loss through death; yet the family challenges and processes described here have broad applicability to other experiences involving loss, recovery, and resilience (see also Chapter 8). In helping families to deal with their losses, we enable them to transform and enhance their relationships as they forge new strengths to face future life challenges.

LOSS IN SYSTEMIC PERSPECTIVE

By and large, the mental health field has failed to appreciate the impact of loss on the family as an interactional system. Clinical attention to bereavement has focused on individual mourning processes and attended narrowly to grief reactions in the loss of a significant dyadic relationship. Two decades ago, when Monica McGoldrick and I first attempted to publish our findings on the high concurrence of grandparent death with the birth of offspring hospitalized for serious emotional problems in young adulthood, skeptical reviewers in psychiatry thought it absurd to imagine that individuals could be affected by the death of a grandparent they never knew (Walsh, 1978). A systemic perspective is required to appreciate the chain of influences that reverberates throughout the family network of relationships with any significant loss. Family processes mediate the immediate and long-term effects of a death for partners, parents, children, siblings, and extended family. Legacies of loss find expression in continuing patterns of interaction and mutual influence among the survivors and across the generations. The pain of death touches all survivors' relationships with others, some of whom may never even have known the person who died.

Epidemiological studies have found that the death of a family member increases vulnerability to premature illness and death for surviving family members (see Walsh & McGoldrick, 1991), especially for a widowed spouse and for parents who have recently lost a child. Furthermore, family developmental crises have been linked to the appearance of symptoms in a family member. In view of the profound connections among members of a family, it is not surprising that adjustment to loss by death is considered more difficult than any other life change.

Although family systems theory introduced a new paradigm for understanding family relationships, few in the field of family therapy approached the subject of loss, reflecting the cultural aversion to facing and talking about death. As Murray Bowen (1978) noted, "Chief among all taboo subjects is death. A high percentage of people die alone, locked into their own thoughts, which they cannot communicate to others" (p. 80). Bowen saw at least two processes in operation: "One is the intrapsychic process in self, which always involves some denial of death. The other is the closed relationship system: People cannot communicate the thoughts they do have, lest they upset the family or other."

Bowen advanced our understanding of the loss experience as profoundly influenced by and, in turn, influencing family processes. He described the disruptive impact of death or threatened loss on a family's functional equilibrium. Bowen viewed the intensity of the emotional reaction as governed by the integration in the family at the time of the loss and by the significance of the lost member. The emotional shock wave may reverberate throughout an entire family system immediately or long after a traumatic loss or threatened loss. It is not directly related to the usual grief or mourning reactions of people close to the one who died. Rather, it operates on an underground network of emotional interdependence of family members. As Bowen observed, "The emotional dependence is denied, the serious events appear to be unrelated, the family attempts to camouflage any connectedness between the events, and there is a vigorous emotional denial reaction, when anyone attempts to relate the events to each other" (1991, p. 83). Bowen maintained that knowledge of the shock wave provides valuable information for therapy; without it the sequence of events may be treated as unrelated. Therefore, it is essential to assess the family system, the functional position of the dying or deceased member, and the family's overall level of adaptation, in order to understand the meaning and context of presenting symptoms and to help the family in a healing process.

Another family therapy pioneer, Norman Paul, commented on the reluctance of therapists, as well as clients, to confront the topic of death. He noted the paradox that although a constant shadow of death exists in all lives, all are entertaining notions of their own immortality. Paul and Grosser (1991) found that however intense the aversion to facing death and grief, their force will find expression nonetheless. Grief at the loss of a parent, spouse, child, sibling, or other important family member, when unrecognized and unattended, may precipitate strong and harmful reactions in other relationships— from marital distancing and dissolution to precipitous replacement, extramarital affairs, and even incest. He cautioned that a clinician's own aversion to death and grief may hamper our ability to inquire about loss issues, notice patterns, and treat a systemic problem as grief-related; the result is often an unhelpful focus on secondary problems. Paul has advocated an active therapeutic approach to confront hidden losses, foster awareness of relational connections, and encourage mutual empathy in conjoint couple and family therapy.

In the early development of the field of family therapy, attention to observable here-and-now interactional patterns blinded many to the relevance of past or threatened losses that were out of view. Therapists following more recent postmodern approaches may not grasp the significance of loss events that are minimized or unmentioned in a client's life story. Without inquiry and exploration, traumatic losses may remain disconnected, ambiguous, or distorted.

> Joe came to therapy to stop his drinking and extramarital affair because he feared he was on the verge of destroying everything important to him. Most of all he feared losing his son, Adam, age 8, if his wife divorced him. When doing a genogram, the therapist noted that his only brother, also named Adam, had died at the age of 8. Yet Joe insisted that this was "no big deal" and had nothing to do with his current destructive behavior and catastrophic fear of loss. It was crucial for the therapist to urge him to explore possible connections, instead of simply accepting his initial denial of meaning.

Loss is a powerful nodal experience that shakes the foundation of family life and leaves no member unaffected. It is more than a discrete event; from a systemic view, it can be seen to involve many processes over time—from the threat and approach of death, through its immediate aftermath, and on into long-term implications. Individual distress stems not only from grief, but also from changes in the realignment of the family emotional field. The meaning of a particular loss event and responses to it are shaped by family belief systems, which in turn are altered by all loss experiences. Loss also modifies the family structure, often requiring major reorganization of the family system.

A death in the family involves multiple losses: the loss of the person, the loss of roles and relationships, the loss of the intact family unit, and the loss of hopes and dreams for all that might have been. If we are to understand the significance of loss processes, we must attend to the past as well as the present and future. Each loss ties in with all other losses and yet is unique in its meaning. We need to be attuned to both process and content, and to explore both the factual circumstances of a death and the meanings it holds for a particular family in its social and developmental contexts. The family life cycle model of Carter and McGoldrick (1998) offers a framework for taking into account the reciprocal influences of several generations as they move forward over time and as they approach and respond to loss (see also McGoldrick & Walsh, 1998).

FAMILY ADAPTATIONAL CHALLENGES IN LOSS

The ability to accept loss is at the heart of all skills in healthy family systems. Beavers and his colleagues (1990) found that in high-functioning families, the ability to accept change and loss is closely linked to the acceptance of the idea of one's own death. By using the human capacity for symbolism, defining ourselves as part of a meaningful whole, our own death and that of our loved ones can be faced more openly and courageously. In families showing the most maladaptive patterns in dealing with inevitable losses, members tend to cling together in fantasy and denial to blur reality and to insist on timelessness and the perpetuation of never-broken bonds. Adaptation to loss involves an interweaving of the three major domains of family resilience processes—belief systems, communication processes, and organizational processes.

Research on loss has found wide diversity in the timing and intensity of normal grief responses (Wortman & Silver, 1989). Because the bereavement experience is so variable, it is more useful to think of facets of grief, rather than sequential stages (Weil, 1994). Shock and denial are often the first reactions ("No, this can't be happening"). Although denial can become mal-adaptive if it persists, it is a natural anesthetic and may be very useful as an initial mechanism, permitting a basic level of functioning when the full impact of grief would be devastating. Anger and rage may follow ("How could this happen to me?"), often giving way to wishful fantasy or bargaining ("If only I become a more loving child, Daddy will live"), which yields to depression and feeling that one can't go on ("Life is not worth living"). Various facets may alternate and may be reexperienced, particularly at nodal events and family gatherings. Although painful and disruptive, grieving, in its many forms, is a healing process.

Adaptation does not mean resolution, in the sense of some complete, "once-and-for-all" getting over it. Nor does resilience in the face of loss mean simply putting it behind you, cutting off from the emotional experience, and moving on. Mourning and adaptation have no fixed timetable, and significant or traumatic losses may never be fully resolved. Coming to terms with loss involves finding ways to make meaning of the loss experience, put it in perspective, and move ahead with life. The multiple meanings of any death are transformed throughout the life cycle, as they are integrated into individual and family identity and with subsequent life experiences, including other losses.

Both research and clinical experience suggest that there are crucial family adaptational challenges in loss, which, if not dealt with, leave family members vulnerable to dysfunction and heighten the risk of family conflict and dissolution. When these challenges are dealt with adequately, they tend to promote both immediate and long-term adaptation for family members and to strengthen the family as a functional unit. The first involves sharing the experience of death, dying, and loss. The second concerns family reorganization and reinvestment in other relationships and life pursuits.

Sharing the Experience of Death, Dying, and Loss

Open communication processes are essential for sharing the experience of death, dying, and loss. Shared acknowledgment of the reality of death and dying is the first priority. All family members, in their own ways, must confront the reality of a death in the family. Bowen (1978) drew our attention to the importance of direct contact with the dying, and in particular to the inclusion of children and other vulnerable family members. He urged visits to the dying person whenever possible. Well-intentioned attempts to protect vulnerable members from the potential upset of exposure to death isolate them from the shared experience and risk impeding their grief process. As he noted, they can be harmed more by the anxiety of survivors than by exposure to death.

Although individuals, families, and cultures vary in the degree to which direct expression of feelings is valued or functional, research on well-functioning families finds that clear, open communication facilitates family adaptation and strengthens the family as a supportive network for its members. A climate of trust, empathic responses, and tolerance for diverse reactions are especially crucial in facing death and loss. Acknowledgment of loss is further facilitated by clear information about the facts and circumstances of a death or dying process.

Inability to accept the reality of death can lead a family member to avoid contact with the rest of the family or to become angry with others who are moving forward in the grief process. Long-standing sibling conflicts and cutoffs can often be traced back to the bedside of a dying parent. By contrast, when death and dying are faced courageously with loved ones, relationships can be deeply enriched. At the death of her partner after a debilitating illness, Bonnie was sad but also at peace:

> "The simple fact is, Jennie's body stopped. There was no unfinished business between us. I had carried a lot of fear about death. Jennie showed me how to feel more alive and more open, even in her last days. She accepted that she was dying, even though she didn't want to go. Acceptance didn't mean feeling jolly or that she liked the situation, just that this was the truth at the moment."

Facing Threatened Death and Loss

In the case of life-threatening situations such as serious illness, acknowledgment of the possibility of loss may begin tentatively, with the diagnosis of a high-risk condition. When family members don't know what to say or do, or wish to spare one another pain, they tend to say nothing and avoid contact. Uncertainty about a prognosis leaves families up in the air and even more cautious about sharing concerns about death and loss. The wish to deny or minimize the experience can shut down communication altogether (Rosen, 1998). The unspeakable may go underground to surface in other contexts or in symptomatic behavior, as in the following case:

> An expert in child sexual abuse consulted me about a case that puzzled her. A mother had brought in her 5-year-old son, Nicky; she was concerned that he might have been molested at preschool, because she kept finding him fondling himself. The therapist's evaluation revealed no indication of sexual abuse. I suggested the possibility that Nicky might be expressing anxiety about other concerns, and advised her to meet with

the parents and explore other stresses in the family. The mother, again coming alone, revealed that 8 months earlier the father had been found to have stomach cancer, and had undergone surgery to remove his stomach (and, reportedly, all the cancer).

It was important to understand how the family had coped with that life-threatening crisis and its aftermath. The mother said that on the day of his discharge from the hospital, her husband had insisted that he felt fine and that he wanted to go on with life as normal, putting the incident behind them without further mention. To respect his wishes, she never brought it up. When asked how this sudden, life-threatening experience had affected her, she burst into tears, saying that it had shaken her sense of security. She had tried to push her fears of loss out of her mind until the past month, when something suspicious was noticed in her husband's checkup, raising new uncertainty about his prognosis. The parents hadn't told the children and assumed they were OK, since they never asked questions about their father's health. After a pause she added, "Now that you mention it, every night when we say grace before dinner, Nicky adds, 'And please, God, take care of Daddy's stomach.'"

In times of crisis or threatened loss, it is urgent for family members to open up blocked lines of communication. It may be useful to meet with a patient or family members individually or in different combinations, working toward a whole-family session. In the situation above, I recommended meeting first with the parents to help them share their feelings and fears. A resilience-based approach was useful to normalize their reactions as common in such situations, and to help them develop more effective coping strategies for mutual support in dealing with the challenges and uncertainties that lay ahead. Coaching enabled the parents to plan how best to share information with their children, help them to express concerns, and provide comfort and support.

Despite a family's discomfort in opening communication about death and loss, it is imperative that veils of secrecy be lifted, particularly if any family member is showing symptoms of distress. I try to help the family to find ways to talk about the unspeakable—the threat of loss and the many other concerns—and to talk about it with children in age-appropriate ways that neither overburden nor overprotect them.

Framing events, such as receiving a diagnosis, cast meaning about a serious illness and how to deal with it (Rolland, 1994). Health care professionals need to be aware of their metacommunication: They may unwittingly contribute to blocked communication and isolation among family members by telling the patient or another family member separately about a life-threatening prognosis, leading them to presume that it is unwise to talk openly about it together. With an uncertain prognosis, I recommend beginning by helping families to face the *possibility* of loss, then the *probability* of it, and finally the *certainty* of impending loss, when life saving efforts are futile. The timing of these shifts depends on each situation over the course of the life-threatening condition.

Epidemiological research points to the importance of maintaining hope in the face of uncertainty with a life-threatening condition (Taylor, 1989; see Chapter 3, this volume). Patients and their families are better able to rally when they hold "positive illusions," or selective biases toward an optimistic view that they can "beat" a potentially fatal illness. Unlike denial, which can foster self-destructive behavior or acting as if there is no risk, this optimistic view is a conscious choice based on full recognition of the actual situation, and it is supported by steps to maximize the likelihood of a positive outcome. For instance, hearing that there is only a 20% odds of recovery, a patient and family may decide to put all their energies on the positive side, hoping and striving to be in that 20%. In beginning to help families face the *possibility* of death and loss, it is important not to rob them of their hope, as long as death remains uncertain.

It is useful to ask families what information they have received about the prognosis, and what each member believes about the future course, exploring their best hopes and worst fears. Often, these beliefs will be split among family members, with some quite hopeful while others expect the worst. Polarized views can generate strong conflict, particularly if decisions must be made about whether to pursue or forgo further treatment options. I find I often have to help families obtain clearer information about the medical prognosis, treatment options, and management issues, which are often not presented by physicians in a helpful way.

Family communication may be blocked by the superstitious belief that talking about death may cause it to happen. Often family members fear that if they bring up the possibility of death, the patient or others may think that they want the person to die. This concern is especially strong when a relationship has been troubled or prolonged caregiving has been burdensome, and there is a guilty wish for the relief that death would bring. It is helpful to explore such beliefs and feelings, normalizing and contextualizing them as common and understandable in the family's situation.

It is useful to discuss the dilemmas posed by uncertainty, and to help members tolerate different views among them. I find it helpful to ask such questions as these: "What is it like for you to live with such uncertainty?" "While we all hope for the best, *what if* the worst were to happen?" "What if a medical crisis were to end life suddenly and unexpectedly? What would be the hardest part?" "What regrets might you have later about things left unsaid, unasked, undone?" "Without giving up hope, how might you prepare for the possibility of loss?" "What might you want to say or do with and for one another?"

When death is highly probable, and preferably before it is imminent, I strongly urge families to confront that reality and take advantage of whatever time they may have left together. (See Chapter 10 for approaches to healing reconciliations in troubled or estranged relationships.) Drafting advance directives and living wills in consultation with loved ones is an important way to take charge and to collaborate in important decision making. Discussions may concern not only life-and-death issues, but also pain control and palliative care—ways to keep terminally ill persons comfortable and comforted as death approaches. Hospice care, particularly at home, benefits all involved in the dying process. It is also valuable to plan funeral or memorial rites together and to discuss wills and legacies, so that the wishes of the dying can be directly communicated, potential conflicts of interest can be averted, and the burdens and misunderstandings of survivors can be lessened.

When the patient and family members realize that time is not unlimited, they can reap benefits in shifting priorities and concentrating on making the most of each day, rather than postponing or putting aside important things. Acknowledging the precariousness of life and the possibility of loss can heighten appreciation of loved ones, especially when relationships have been taken for granted or blocked by petty grievances. Indeed, couples and families often report that coming closer through threatened loss was their most precious time together, regardless of the outcome.

Our Western beliefs in mastery and control over our destiny make it difficult to accept death and dying, which are often experienced in terms of powerlessness, loss of control, and failure. Buddhism teaches that "in accepting death, we discover life" (see Walsh, in press). In doing so, we live more fully and with greater awareness of our choices to make the most of our life situation. Americans are "doers," invested in goal-oriented action, achievement, and problem solving. Many avoid contact when they believe there is nothing they can *do* to stop death. We are uncomfortable simply *being with* loved ones who are dying. When my father was terminally ill, I found visits with him difficult. A consummate "doer," I kept trying to think of errands I could run for him or things I could do to make him more comfortable. As I calmed my own anxieties, I became better able simply to be present—sitting at his bedside, quietly keeping him company, stroking his arm, taking his hand. I still have precious memories of those long days spent together: at times chuckling over *I Love Lucy* reruns, at other times gazing peacefully out the window at the large flowering mimosa tree as the sunlight streamed through it each day from dawn through dusk.

Rituals to Mark the Loss of a Life and a Loved One

Funeral rituals and visits to the grave serve a vital function in providing direct confrontation with the reality of death and the opportunity to pay last respects, to share grief, and to receive comfort in the supportive network of the community of survivors (Imber-Black et al., 1988). Family members should be encouraged to plan a meaningful service and burial or cremation— involving the dying person if possible, so that his or her wishes are taken into acount. It is most memorable when important loved ones take part in the service, offering stories that remember and celebrate the life passage and many-faceted personhood and relationships of the deceased. In one especially moving service, a father's son and daughter from his second marriage recounted both poignant and humorous stories of their everyday interactions. Then his son from a previous marriage came forward; saying he was never comfortable with words, he played a stirring song on the flute that he had composed in memory of his father.

In the Jewish tradition, as in many others, it is considered even more important to attend a funeral than a wedding, because it both honors a life and marks its loss. Key processes in resilience are movingly expressed in the Jewish mourners' Kaddish, chanted together by loved ones gathered at shiva after the burial:

> At times, the pain of separation seems more than we can bear; but love and understanding can help us pass through the darkness toward the light.
>
> And in truth, grief is a great teacher, when it sends us back to serve and bless the living. . . .
>
> Thus, even when they are gone, the departed are with us, moving us to live as, in their higher moments, they themselves wished to live.
>
> We remember them now; they live in our hearts; they are an abiding blessing. (Central Conference of American Rabbis, 1992)

Families should be encouraged to plan meaningful rites together, to press reluctant members to attend, and to encourage loved ones to take part in some way. Sometimes family members avoid a funeral and visits to the cemetery, wishing to hold onto a loved one or to avoid the pain of loss by not confronting the reality of death. Yet, paradoxically, the meaning of the life and the relationship can be appreciated more fully when the loss is marked. It is never too late to hold a memorial service, to lay a headstone at a grave, to hold a ceremony to scatter ashes, or to plant a tree in memory of a loved one. Drawing family members together on an anniversary or at a holiday gathering to remember one who has died can be a profoundly healing and connecting experience; it keeps the memory of the deceased alive as it sustains relational resilience among survivors. On the 20th anniversary of my mother's death, I wanted to find a meaningful way to celebrate her life with my husband and daughter, who had never known her. My mother's deep love of music brought to mind the carillon bells of the Rockefeller Chapel on my campus at the University of Chicago. I arranged for a simple concert in her memory, and we climbed to the top of the bell tower and looked out into the night sky as the bells pealed harmoniously.

The Aftermath of Loss

Open communication is vital for family resilience over the entire course of the loss process, but especially in the transitional turmoil of the immediate aftermath. When we take into account the many fluctuating and often conflicting responses of all members in a family system, we can appreciate the diversity and complexity of any family mourning process. Families are likely to experience a range of feelings, depending on the unique meaning of the relationship and its loss for each member and the implications of the death for the family unit. The mourning process also involves shared narrative attempts to put the loss into some meaningful perspective that fits coherently into the rest of a family's life experience and belief system. This requires dealing with the ongoing negative implications of the loss, including the loss of dreams for the future.

As a family experiences a loss, members are going to be touched in different ways and to show a wide range of reactions, depending on such variables as their age and individual coping styles, the state of their relationships, and different positions in the family. Children's reactions to death will depend on their stage of cognitive development, on the way adults deal with them around the death, and on the degree of caretaking they have lost.

Empathy is needed for one another's positions and an ability to respond caringly. Tolerance for different responses and timing is important. Strong emotions may surface at different moments, including complicated and mixed feelings of anger, disappointment, helplessness, relief, guilt, and abandonment, which are present to some extent in most family relationships. In dominant U.S. culture, the expression of intense emotions tends to generate discomfort and distancing in others. Moreover, the loss of control experienced in sharing such overwhelming feelings can frighten family members, leading them to block all communication about the loss experience to protect one another and themselves.

If a family is unable to tolerate certain feelings, a member who directly expresses the unacceptable may be scapegoated or extruded. Unbearable or unacceptable feelings may be delegated and expressed in a fragmented fashion by various family members. One may carry all the anger for the family, while another is in touch only with sadness; one may show only relief, while another is numb. The shock and pain of a traumatic loss can shatter family cohesion, leaving members isolated and unsupported in their grief, as in the following case:

> Mrs. Ramirez sought help for her 11-year-old daughter Teresa's school problems, which had worsened in recent weeks. In order to understand "Why now?", the therapist explored recent events in the family. The oldest son, Raul, age 18, had been caught in the crossfire of a gang-related shooting. The shot that killed him had also shattered the family unit. The father withdrew, drinking heavily to ease his pain. Miguel, the next eldest son, carried the family rage into the streets, seeking revenge for the senseless killing. Two other middle children showed no reaction, keeping quietly out of the way. Mrs. Ramirez, alone in her grief, deflected her attention to Teresa's school problems.
>
> Family sessions over the following 10 weeks provided a context for shared griefwork. Family members were encouraged to share their feelings openly and to comfort one another. It was especially important to involve the "well" siblings, who had been holding in their own pain so as not to upset or burden their parents further. The therapist helped the parents to obtain legal counsel, to gain the necessary information to navigate the court system, and to plan and carry out concerted actions, with Miguel's assistance, to seek justice for the murder. They were also helped to sort through Raul's posessions, each family member choosing something as a keepsake—his jacket, a favorite shirt, his prized guitar. They dreaded Raul's impending birthday. The therapist encouraged them to think of something they might do together to remember him. The family decided to go to church—for the first time, in a long time, all together—and to light candles in his memory. The therapist also suggested that they invite grandparents, aunts, uncles, and cousins to join them there. This led them afterward to spend the whole evening together, telling old family stories, as Miguel strummed Raul's guitar.
>
> Such processes repaired the family's fragmentation, promoting a more cohesive network for mutual support and healing. On follow-up, Teresa's school problems and the father's drinking had subsided. The experience of pulling together to deal with their loss had strengthened their resilience, helping them to cope better with other problems in their lives.

Reorganization of the Family System and Reinvestment in Other Relationships/Life Pursuits

The death of a family member leaves a hole in the fabric of family life. It disrupts established patterns of interaction. The process of family recovery involves a realignment of relationships and redistribution of role functions needed to compensate for the loss, buffer transitional stresses, and carry on with family life. As in the following case, children can be harmed even more by their family's inability to provide structure, stability, and protective caregiving than by a loss itself.

> Marie, a woman in her 50s, sought help for depression after the sudden death of her younger brother, Jim, who had been her mainstay in life. When she was 7 years old, her mother had died of cancer. Marie vividly recalled that as relatives came and left on the night of the death, she put on her best dress and sat on the edge of her bed in her room, holding her brother's hand, waiting to be called to say their good-byes. No one came for them, nor were they taken to the funeral. In the chaotic upheaval that followed, she and her brother were separated for a time, sent to stay with various relatives. When she returned home, her bereft father, isolated in his grief, would come into her bed late at night, turning to her sexually for comfort and contact. Continued uncertainty about where she and Jim would live perpetuated their anxiety and sense of abandonment. Finally, her father's remarriage brought stability and an end to her secret ordeal.

As this case reveals, families sometimes fall apart after an unbearable loss, and adults are unable to nurture and protect children. Preoccupied by their own loss, they may breach generational boundaries, using children inappropriately to meet their own needs. We should keep in mind that sibling bonds can be vital resources for resilience, especially in such cases. Such a bond had been a lifeline over the years between Marie and Jim; his sudden death not only was devastating in itself, but reactivated her childhood trauma.

Family roles and responsibilities may interfere with mourning. A father's role as chief financial provider may reinforce his tendency to block emotional expression to keep in control and function at work. Commonly, in single-parent families, children and well-intentioned relatives collude to keep a bereaved mother strong because everyone depends on her. When parental grieving is blocked, emotions may explode in conflict, and children are more likely to become symptomatic. It is important to help overburdened family members structure the time and space they need for their own grieving, and to rally the contributions of others to provide the respite needed for healing.

Promoting cohesion and flexible reorganization in the family system is crucial to restabilization and resilience. Some families may take flight from losses by moving precipitously out of their homes and communities, which adds further dislocation and loss of social support. Some seek immediate replacement for their losses, through affairs, sudden marriages, or pregnancies. These replacement relationships are complicated by the unmourned losses. It is important to help such families pace their reorganization and reinvestment.

By contrast, the upheaval experienced in the immediate aftermath of a loss leads other families to hold on rigidly to old patterns that are no longer functional, in order to minimize the sense of loss and disruption in family life. Later, the formation of other attachments and commitments may be blocked by fear of another loss. Overidealization of the deceased or a sense of disloyalty may also contribute to reluctance to accept a new member who is seen as replacing the deceased, particularly when the loss has not been integrated.

The process of mourning is quite variable, often lasting much longer than people expect. Each new season, holiday, and anniversary is likely to reevoke the loss. Family therapy with loss requires the same ingenuity and flexibility that families themselves need to respond to various members and subsystems as their issues come to the fore. As changes occur in one part of a system, changes in other parts will be generated. Decisions to meet with an individual, couple, or family unit at various points are guided by a systemic view of the loss process.

FACTORS IN FAMILY RISK AND RESILIENCE

The impact of a death is influenced by a number of variables in the loss situation and the family processes surrounding it (Walsh & McGoldrick, 1991). It is important for clinicians to be aware of patterns that tend to complicate family adaptation and pose higher risk of dysfunction. Whether the therapeutic aim is to work preventively at the time of a loss, or to understand and repair long-term complications, these risk factors should always be carefully evaluated and attended to in interventions to promote healing and resilience.

Nature of the Loss

The manner of death poses varied challenges for surviving family members and needs to be explored in any clinical assessment.

Sudden versus Lingering Death

Sudden deaths or deaths following protracted illness are especially stressful for families and require different coping processes. When a person dies unexpectedly, family members lack time to anticipate and prepare for the loss, to deal with unfinished business, or in many cases even to say their goodbyes. Clinicians need to explore and help family members with painful regrets and guilt over what they wish they had done differently, had they known that loss was imminent.

When the dying process has been prolonged, family caregiving and financial resources are likely to be depleted, with the needs of other members put on hold. Relief at ending patient suffering and family strain is likely to be guilt-laden. Moreover, families are increasingly faced with the dilemma over whether and how long to maintain life support efforts, at great expense, to sustain a family member who may be in a vegetative state with virtually no hope of recovery. The fundamental questions of when life ends and who should determine that end have generated controversies concerning medical ethics, religious beliefs, patient/family rights, and the possibility of criminal prosecution. Families can be torn apart by opposing views of different members or coalitions. Clinicians can help family members to prepare and discuss living wills, to share feelings openly about such complicated situations, and to come to terms with any decisions taken. Moreover, such decisions should be reviewed, and revisions flexibly considered over time, or as health conditions change, since people commonly change their minds over the course of an illness when faced with a dreaded situation.

Ambiguous Loss

Ambiguity surrounding a loss interferes with adaptation, often producing depression in family members (Boss, 1991). A loved one may be physically absent but psychologically present—for example, when a solidier is declared missing in action. The uncertainty about whether a missing family member is dead or alive can be agonizing for a family. In the case of a missing child, a family may become consumed by efforts to maintain hope while fearing the worst, and by desperate searches and attempts to get information to confirm the child's fate.

In other situations of ambiguous loss, as in the case of Alzheimer's disease, family members may be physically present but no longer their former selves, or unable to recognize loved ones (Boss, 1991). It is crucial to help family members deal with the progressive loss of mental functioning and important aspects of their relationship without extruding the person as if he or she were already dead. At the same time, with prolonged strain over many years, it is important to validate the needs of a spouse or adult children to go on with their own lives while providing care.

Violent Death

The impact of a violent death can be devastating, especially for loved ones who have witnessed it or have narrowly escaped themselves. Body mutilation or the inability to retrieve a body complicates family mourning processes. After the loss of a family member in a major disaster, such as a bombing incident or a plane crash, survivors commonly report their inability to begin mourning until the body, or personal effects belonging to their loved one, is recovered and the death becomes physically real. The senseless tragedy in the loss of innocent lives is especially hard to bear, particularly if it is the result of negligence, as in drunk driving. The killing and loss of lives in war may haunt survivors and affect their family relationships for years to come in posttraumatic stress disorder (Figley, 1989).

U.S. culture and mass media depictions promote violent solutions to conflict. Lethal firearms have contributed to an alarming increase in homicides and accidental shootings, particularly of children by other youths. Although we most fear random violence, murders committed by relatives and acquaintances are all too common. Clinicians should be especially vigilant when couple conflict escalates into violence, and should take murderous threats quite seriously, especially when women attempt to leave abusive relationships. Families of murder victims are in need of ongoing support and advocacy, because all too frequently they experience further trauma and strain in lengthy, convoluted legal processes and all-consuming efforts to seek justice for the crime. They may only be able to go on with their lives if and when they feel that justice has been served. Many find strength and new purpose in joining with others to prevent similar tragedies from happening.

Families and their communities may show extraordinary resilience in pulling together in the wake of a natural disaster (Figley, 1989) or a major tragedy, such as the 1995 Oklahoma City bombing incident. However, an entire community can be traumatized by persistent violence and an ever-present threat of recurrence. For poor families in blighted inner-city neighborhoods, daily life is much like living in a war zone (Garbarino, 1997). Neighborhood-based programs such as Take Back the Streets build family and community resilience, as they combat violent crime by bringing residents, police, and social agencies together to work collaboratively and build a sense of pride and empowerment. In some programs, mothers serve as monitors in local schools to help ensure the safety of students. In others, both younger and older men form mentoring relationships with gang members and preteen recruits, in efforts to stem the tide of violence and encourage school and job pursuits toward a better life.

Suicide

Suicides are among the most anguishing deaths for families to come to terms with, particularly when they are impulsive, seemingly senseless, or apparently intended to hurt or punish loved ones. The recent rise in adolescent suicide attempts and death symbolism demands attention; both peer drug (or binge drinking) cultures and larger social forces reinforce a sense of alienation and romanticize self-destructive behavior. Clinicians also need to be alert to family influences, such as threatened abandonment or sexual abuse, that may pose a heightened risk of suicide. Current life-threatening family situations can trigger catastrophic fears of loss and self-destructive behavior.

When a suicide has occurred, clinicians need to help family members with the anger and guilt that can pervade their relationships, particularly when they are blamed or blame themselves for the death. The social stigma of suicide also contributes to family shame and coverup of the circumstances. Such secrecy distorts family communication and can isolate a family from social support, generating its own destructive legacy. Clinicians should routinely note family histories of suicide or other traumatic losses that may predict future suicide risk, particularly at an anniversary, birthday, or holiday time.

> Daniel, age 13, and his family were at a loss to explain his recent suicide attempt and made no mention of an older deceased brother. Family assessment revealed that Daniel had been born shortly before the death of an elder son at the age of 13. Daniel grew up attempting to take the place of the brother he had never known, in order to relieve his parents' sadness. The father, who could not recall the date or events surrounding the death, wished to remember his first son "as if he were still alive." Daniel cultivated his appearance to resemble photos of his brother. When he had reached the age of his brother's death, and his growth spurt at puberty was changing him from the way he was "supposed" to look, he attempted suicide to join his brother in heaven. Family therapy focused on enabling Daniel and his parents to relinquish his surrogate position so that he could move forward in his own development.

The importance of a careful evaluation for depression cannot be overemphasized. Where indicated, psychotropic medication can rapidly help to improve a bleak outlook, to allow a person to assess life constraints and options from a clearer perspective, and to restore hope and energy to reengage in life. In many cases, finding ways to reduce physical suffering or social isolation is also important in helping a person regain the desire to live. Although a therapist or loved ones cannot always prevent a suicide, the risk can be lowered by opening communication, mobilizing the support of family and friends, and exploring the meaning of past or ongoing trauma. Helping a depressed family member to integrate painful experiences and to envision a meaningful future beyond disappointments or losses is vital in strengthening both individual and family resilience.

> Mick, a construction worker left permanently disabled and wheelchairbound by the collapse of a building, began to drink heavily; one night Peg, his wife, found him passed out on the floor, with his hunting gun ready to be fired. In individual and conjoint sessions, we explored the multiple losses he had suddenly experienced: his family role as breadwinner, his "tough guy" image, and the active life he had always expected to live. Realizing that he was loved, valued, and needed by his wife and children not for his paycheck, but for himself, was most crucial to his inner healing and resilience, recharging his will to go on living. With his family's encouragement, Mick found new ways to be productive and active. He eventually set up a home-based small business and began to coach his son's soccer team.

Euthanasia and assisted suicide—the personal options for taking control over the dying process and the timing and manner of death—are fast becoming hotly debated public policy issues as societies are aging and medical interventions prolong the lives of increasing numbers of persons with chronic, painful, and deteriorating illnesses. In such situations, the wish to die with dignity, by controlling or hastening the end of one's own life and suffering, poses excruciating ethical, legal, and spiritual dilemmas for patients, their families, and health care professionals. Therapists can help to open conversations to explore options and their meaning. It is also useful to broaden focus from the identified patient to consider what end-of-life decisions a spouse or other adult family member would want for themselves.

Family and Social Network

A family's belief systems, organizational processes, and communication processes are all crucial mediating variables in adaptation to loss. The general level of family functioning and the state of family relationships prior to and following the loss should be carefully evaluated with attention given to the extended family and social network. Particular note should be taken of the following variables.

Belief Systems

Clinicians are only beginning to appreciate the power of belief systems in families facing death and attempting to heal the pain of loss. Beliefs about death and the meanings surrounding a loss are rooted in multigenerational family legacies, in ethnic and spiritual beliefs, and in the dominant society's values and practices. A strong orientation toward mastery can hinder acceptance when death and loss cannot be controlled. Family members may despair when, despite their best efforts, optimism, or medical care, they cannot conquer death or bring back a loved one. Active participation in caregiving, decision making, and meaningful rituals can foster healing. The ability to draw on spiritual beliefs provides meaning, solace, and comfort and can promote acceptance.

Clinicians need to be especially attuned to beliefs that foster blame, shame, and guilt surrounding a death (Rolland, 1994). Such causal attributions are especially strong in situations of traumatic death where the cause is uncertain and questions of responsibility or negligence arise. Commonly family members hold a secret belief that they themselves or others could have, or should have, done something to prevent a death. It is important to help members share such concerns and come to terms with the extent of their responsibility and limits of control in the situation.

Connectedness

Adaptation to loss is facilitated by family cohesion for mutual support, balanced with tolerance of and respect for different responses to loss by various family members. Extreme family patterns of enmeshment or disengagement pose complications. At the enmeshed extreme, families may demand a united front and regard as disloyal and threatening any individual differences, which then must be submerged or distorted. For instance, they may collude in denying the contribution of alcohol or smoking to a death and may be intolerant of dissent. Some family members may seek an undifferentiated replacement for the loss in another relationship and may have difficulty with subsequent separations, holding on at normal developmental transitions. At the disengaged extreme, family members tend to avoid the pain of loss with distancing and emotional cutoffs. In family fragmentation, members are left to fend for themselves, isolated in their grief.

As clinicians encourage family members to come together around a loss, we also need to balance togetherness with tolerance for different responses within families. The expectations that individuals may have different coping styles, may be out of phase with one other, and may have unique experiences in the meaning of a lost relationship need to be normalized.

Extended Family, Social, and Economic Resources

The family loss experience is buffered by the availability of kin and social networks to draw upon as resources. These are especially crucial in widowhood. Our cultural emphasis on self-reliance often constrains survivors from asking others for help. Relatives and close friends often want to be helpful, but may not know how to. Asking others to spend a few hours with children can offer much-needed respite for bereaved parents, as it lets children (who may be feeling quite vulnerable) experience a network of caregiving. When long-standing conflicts, cutoffs, or social stigma have left families isolated from friends and relations, clinicians working with loss can be helpful in promoting healing reconciliations. A lack of community connections also makes loss more difficult to bear; clinicians can encourage outreach and involvement in potentially supportive networks, such as religious, social, and neighborhood groups. It is also important to inquire about the draining of finances by costly, protracted medical care, and about the loss of economic resources with a death.

Flexibility

Family structure (in particular, rules, roles, and boundaries) needs to be flexible, yet clear, for reorganization after loss. At the chaotic extreme, a disorganized family will have difficulty maintaining enough leadership, stability, and continuity to manage the transitional upheaval. An overly rigid family is likely to resist modifying set patterns to make the necessary accommodations to loss. Family members can be encouraged to turn to others they trust to share roles and responsibilities, particularly in the immediate wake of a loss.

It is helpful to inquire about what changed and what did not change with a death, and to sort out what to hold onto and what to let go of, both immediately and over time. It is useful to normalize the desire to maintain familiar patterns in the wake of loss, understanding the need for continuity and stability in the midst of overwhelming loss and disruption. It is also important to clarify apparent resistance to change (e.g., keeping a room untouched) as an effort to hold onto the web of connections to the loved one who died.

Prior Role Functioning

The more important a person was in family life and the more central in family functioning, the greater the loss. The death of a parent with small children (Worden, 1996) is generally far more devastating than the loss of an elderly grandparent who has become more peripheral to family functioning. The loss of a leader or caregiver will be sorely felt. The death of an only child, the only son or daughter, or the last of a generation leaves a particular void. Families risk dysfunction if, at one extreme, they seek to avoid the pain of loss by denying the significance of an important family member, such as the matriarch, or by seeking instant replacement, such as a new mother for young children. At the other extreme, they can become immobilized if they are unable to reallocate role functions or form new attachments.

Relationships at the Time of Death

Family relationships are bound to have occasional conflict, mixed feelings, or shifting alliances. When conflict has been intense and persistent, where ambivalence is strong, or when relationships have been cut off altogether, the mourning process is more likely to be complicated, with fallout for other relationships. In therapy, the coaching process can be useful to address either immediate or long-term complications of a loss (Walsh & McGoldrick, 1991). The death of a troubled or absent parent is difficult; an adult child may have long grieved for a parent he or she never had. The greatest sadness can come from knowing that what might have been can never be. One woman was hospitalized at age 70 with depression, following the death of her 94-year-old father. She had vied unsuccessfully with her younger sister throughout her life for her father's favor. On his deathbed, he called for her sister. Even in later life, what pained her most in his death was the loss of future possibility that she might one day win his approval.

When death is anticipated, as in life-threatening illnesses, therapists should make every effort to help patients and their families to reconnect and to repair strained relationships before the opportunity is lost (see Chapter 10). Often this requires overcoming hesitance to stir up painful emotions or to dredge up old conflicts for fear that negative confrontations will increase vulnerability and the risk of death. Family therapists need to be sensitive to these fears, to interrupt destructive interactional spirals, and to help family members share feelings constructively with the aim of healing pained relationships, forging new connections, and building mutual support. A conjoint family life review (Walsh, 1998b) can foster transformation by helping members to share different perspectives, to place hurts and disappointments in the context of the family's life cycle challenges, to recover caring aspects of relationships, and to update and renew relationships that have been frozen in past conflict.

Open Communication versus Secrecy

When a family confronts a loss, open communication facilitates the processes of recovery and reorganization, as described above. Secrecy and myths distort communication about the loss experience and contribute to symptomatic behavior. This is most likely to happen in situations where acknowledgment of factual circumstances or of certain feelings, thoughts, or memories is prohibited by family loyalties or social taboos. The coverup of an alcohol-related accident, a drug overdose, or a suicide is common and carries its own painful legacy for survivors in further blocked communication, cutoffs, and self-destructive behavior, often fueled by a vague, pervasive depression, guilt, or shame. It is important to promote a family climate of mutual trust and support, so that members can face the true circumstances of a death and come to terms with it.

Societal Context of Loss

Homophobic societal attitudes compound the pain of loss in gay and lesbian relationships (Laird, 1993; Laird & Green, 1996). The death of a partner may be mourned in isolation when the relationship has been kept secret or has met with disapproval by the family or community. Because gay men and lesbians lack the legal standing of marriage, survivor benefits and the ability to maintain relationships with a partner's biological children are in jeopardy.

The AIDS crisis has generated tremendous fear and stigma. Many (including some clinicians) distance from persons with HIV/AIDS, impairing family and social support, as well as the delivery of critical health care. Distinctions are too often drawn between "innocent victims," such as children born with AIDS, and those who are condemned for having "brought it on themselves" through homosexuality or drug use. Helping professionals can work to reduce social stigma and unfounded fears of contagion, so that death from AIDS is not made even more painful and isolating for all.

The AIDS epidemic has been all the more devastating in the gay community—and, increasingly, for men, women, and children in poor inner-city neighborhoods—because of the multiple losses and anticipated losses experienced in relationship networks. As new treatments are changing the outlook for those with AIDS from a certain fatal prognosis to an uncertain course, new challenges are posed by the rigors and expense of treatments, and many must reorient lives that they had given up. For most, the new treatments remain inaccessible. Survivor guilt may contribute to self-destructive behaviors by partners. Yet, more often, remarkable resilience is fostered by strong couple bonds and social networks.

The impact for families of war-related deaths is also heavily influenced by social attitudes about the war involvement. Loss can be assuaged by a common sense of patriotism and heroism when a war is thought to be waged for a noble cause. However, intense conflict about a war seriously complicates family (and societal) adaptation, as was the case with the Vietnam War and its aftermath. Bitter legacies of unresolved political, ethnic, and religious conflict are passed down from generation to generation. We bear witness each day to the wrenching agony in many parts of the world—from Northern Ireland to Bosnia and Rwanda—where families and communities have been torn apart, each death leading to more killing. Yet the resilience of the human spirit emerges from seemingly endless cycles of violence in renewed efforts for peace through negotiatiated settlements that seek mutual understanding and compromise for the sake of future generations. Such efforts draw on many of the principles and skills therapists and mediators use to resolve conflict in families and communities.

Gender Constraints

Although most societies have been undergoing rapid social change, normative expectations for men and women in families are still strongly influenced by gender-based socialization and role constraints (McGoldrick et al., 1989). With a death in the family, mothers are particularly vulnerable to blame and guilt arising from expectations that they bear primary caretaking responsibility for the well-being of their husbands, children, and aging family members. Women have been reared to assume the major role in handling the social and emotional tasks of bereavement, from the expression of grief to caregiving for the terminally ill and surviving family members, including their husband's extended family. Now that most women combine job and family responsibilities, they are increasingly overburdened in times of loss. Men, who have been socialized to manage instrumental tasks, typically take charge of funeral, burial, financial, and property arrangements. They tend to be more emotionally constrained and peripheral around times of loss. Cultural sanctions against revealing vulnerability or dependence block emotional expressiveness and their ability to seek and give comfort. These constraints undoubtedly contribute to the high rates of serious illness and suicide for men after the death of a spouse.

Different responses of men and women to loss can increase marital strain, even for couples with previously strong and stable relationships. After the death of a child, fathers are more likely to withdraw, take refuge in their work, or turn to alcohol or an affair. Uncomfortable with their wives' expressions of grief, they may become angry or fear loss of control of their own feelings (framed in dominant U.S. culture as "breaking down" and "falling apart"). Women may perceive their husbands' emotional unavailability as abandonment when they need comfort most, thereby experiencing a double loss. When men are helped to become more expressive and involved in illness and death and in the family bereavement process, the quality of their marriages improves markedly (Walsh & McGoldrick, 1991).

These patterns have important implications for loss interventions. Individual approaches appear to have limited impact on recovery when marital relationship dynamics are not addressed as well. Most commonly women come for help—or are sent by their husbands—with depression or other symptoms of distress concerning loss, while their husbands appear to be well-functioning and deny need for help themselves.

Marlene was being seen in individual therapy for inconsolable grief, after her only child, 18-year-old Jimmy, had collapsed and died in her arms. Marlene and Matt, a working-class African American couple, had worked very hard to raise Jimmy well and were extremely proud that he had just earned a scholarship to college. Although Matt too had lost his only child, he refused therapy for himself, saying he was fine and didn't need any help. Yet he drove Marlene to each session and waited for her in the car. I suggested that the therapist invite him in as a helpful resource to his wife. When presented with clinic forms to sign, however, he balked; he did not want to fill out a symptom checklist or to be labeled as needing help. His stoic manner of maintaining control was a source of pride to him.

When men have difficulty acknowledging vulnerability and sorrow at a time of tragedy, their wives may then carry the emotions for both of them. Since their son's death, Matt found it difficult to be near his wife, because it aroused his fear of losing control and breaking down. He wanted the therapist to "fix" her and return her. However, individual therapy may fuel disappointment and resentment toward the unavailable partner, who is felt to be distant and insensitive (all the more so in contrast to an empathic therapist). Conjoint work can begin focus on the more ready spouse and move toward the more reluctant one. Not surprisingly, as Marlene's depression began to lift, Matt's deep pain surfaced—first as anger, then as sorrow. He was able to benefit from the therapy to facilitate his own grief process, and she was able to comfort him. A couple or family approach is essential, so that therapy does not foster individual resilience at the cost of marital and family breakdown. Conjoint work builds relational resilience, deepening bonds.

Interventions need to be aimed at decreasing the gender-based polarization so that both men and women can share in the full range of human experiences in bereavement. Encouraging empathy and support in couple and family sessions strengthens the ability to withstand and rebound from loss together.

Timing of Loss in the Family Life Cycle

The meaning and consequences of loss vary, depending on the particular phase of life cycle development a family is negotiating at the time of the death. The particular timing of a loss in the multigenerational family life cycle may place a family at higher risk for dysfunction (McGoldrick & Walsh, 1998). Factors that influence the impact of a loss include (1) untimeliness of the loss; (2) concurrence with other losses, major stresses, or life cycle changes; and (3) history of traumatic loss and unresolved mourning. In each situation, the nature of the death, the functional position of the person in the family, and the state of relationships will interact in crucial ways. A family life cycle perspective can enable clinicians to foster adaptation and resilience in ways that strengthen the whole family in future life passages.

Untimely Losses

Deaths that are premature or "off-time" in terms of chronological or social expectations, such as early widowhood, early parent loss, or death of a child, can be immensely more difficult to come to terms with (Neugarten, 1976). Untimely losses are complicated by the lack of social norms, models, or guidelines to assist in preparation and coping. Such a loss is experienced as unjust, ending a life and a relationship before their prime, robbing hopes and dreams for a future that can never be. Prolonged mourning, often lasting many years, is a common occurrence. Long-term survival guilt for spouses, siblings, and parents can block life satisfaction and achievements for years to come.

Early Parent Loss. Children who lose a parent may suffer profound short- and long-term consequences, including illness, depression, and other emotional disturbances in subsequent adult life (see McGoldrick & Walsh, 1998). They may later have difficulty in forming other intimate attachments, with catastrophic fears of separation and abandonment. A child's handling of parent loss depends largely on the emotional state of the surviving parent, as shown in Marie's case (see p. 187 above). Griefwork with the surviving parent and efforts to organize and strengthen the supportive role of the extended family can make all the difference in children's ability to cope and adapt. Children need help in making meaning of the loss experience appropriate to their developmental stage. Stabilizing their home situation, and providing clear reasurance that they will be well cared for and not abandoned, are essential. Children also show better adjustment when not separated from their siblings, since sibling bonds are a crucial resource in resilience.

An inspiring portrayal of family resilience is found in the film *Crooklyn*, by Spike Lee (1994). The film looks at life through the eyes of a 10-year-old daughter in an African American family struggling to get by financially and raise five children well in a blighted urban neighborhood. The parents' relationship is not without conflict and skew; the mother is the solid bedrock of the family, and the father is often inconsistent, underresponsible, and self-absorbed. Yet, when the mother is found to have terminal cancer, the father rises to meet the challenges, drawing on previously untapped resources within himself to provide strength, security, and comfort to their children. The daughter is brought to the hospital for time with her mother, who touchingly shares her love and her hopes and dreams for her. When the daughter, devastated by the death, angrily refuses to get dressed and attend the funeral ("What for? It's not going to bring her back!"), her father's tender empathy for her feelings along with authoritative firmness enables her to join family and friends to pay their last respects together. Her older brother, long her tormentor, moves over to sit beside her and hold hands, opening up a new bond. Heeding her mother's last request, she takes on new responsibility, keeping an eye out for her youngest brother. When weeks later she finally breaks down, frightened and sobbing, her father's arms encircle her as he encourages a conversation to help her express all her bottled-up emotions. She asks, "Will I get cancer too, like Momma?", and then admits her greatest fear: "You won't leave us too, will you? Or send me away?" The father's responses are thoughtful, honest, and reassuring. Seeking a way to make meaning and find some solace in her mother's death, she asks, "Momma was in a lot of pain, wasn't she?" "Yes, she was." "Then it's good that she's gone to a place where she's not suffering any more." "That's a real nice way to put it," he tenderly replies. As the film ends, it is clear that many challeges in surviving the loss are yet ahead, but a secure family foundation has been laid.

Child Loss. The death of a child, reversing the natural generational order, is also a devastating loss for a family (Rando, 1984). It is often said, "When your parent dies, you have lost your past. When your child dies, you have lost your future." The untimeliness and injustice in the death of a child can lead family members to the most profound questioning of the meaning of life. In addition, of all losses, it is hardest not to idealize a deceased child; this may complicate relationships with surviving siblings.

With the loss of a child, a parental marriage is at heightened risk for discord, distancing, and divorce, as discussed above. However, spouses who are able to support and sustain each other through the tragedy can forge even stronger relationships than before, underscoring the critical role of couple and family therapy in child loss. In the death of a child, it is also crucial not to neglect the impact on siblings, who may experience prolonged grieving or anniversary reactions for years afterward. A sibling's death is likely to be accompanied by an experienced loss of parents who are preoccupied with caretaking or grieving. Normal sibling rivalry may contribute to intense survival guilt that can block developmental strivings well into adulthood. Some parents turn to a sibling as a replacement, as in the case of Daniel (see above).

The impetus to have another child is very common and can bring solace. However, parents should be advised to allow themselves time to experience the loss so that the new relationship is not burdened by replacement needs or by attachment difficulties, as in the following case:

Bill and Jean were seen in couple therapy for conflict over their inability to name their baby, now almost a year old. The solution-focused therapy succeeded in two sessions in naming the child; however, Jean then became suicidal. It was learned that they had conceived this child only 3 months after the loss of a much-desired pregnancy, for which Jean blamed herself. Upon learning that her grandfather, who had abused her as a child, had died suddenly, she was overcome by a "crazy mix of emotions." She went out all night drinking and partying "to get away from it all," and suffered a miscarriage the next day. Urged by well-intentioned relatives to have another child "to get over it," she found herself unable to attach to the new baby. It only made matters worse when, pressed to name their daughter, Bill and Jean gave her the name that had been chosen for the other baby.

Careful evaluation is needed before intervening in a problem situation. Losses during pregnancy and perinatal deaths tend to be hidden and minimized. The impact of such loss experiences will depend greatly on spousal support and on religious or cultural beliefs about the meaning of stillbirth, infertility, miscarriage, or abortion.

Loss of a Partner. Early widowhood can be a shocking and isolating experience without emotional preparation or essential social supports. Other couples and peers at the same life stage commonly distance to avoid facing their own vulnerability. Here too, immediate replacement may lead to further complications.

> Doreen and Nick were seen in couple therapy because she felt their "semicommitted" relationship was "deadlocked" and wanted either to get married or to end it. Most nights Nick came for dinner; after her girls went to bed, he and Doreen would set up a cot next to her bed, where he spent the night, returning to his own apartment each morning. The therapist learned that 6 years earlier, within a few months of the sudden death of her husband, Doreen had accepted an offer by Nick, an old friend, to move with her children to his community to start a new life. Nick found her a job and an apartment next to his own. Because they had moved too quickly into this relationship, its status remained ambivalent. Doreen, devastated by the loss of her husband, had initially found support and consolation from Nick and the move a welcome escape; yet she became depressed, overweight, and unhappy in her job. Couple sessions revealed Nick's ongoing casual affairs with other women and his refusal ever to commit himself fully again since a bitter divorce and cutoff from his children. Doreen decided to end the relationship and move on with her life. With this loss, she found herself dreaming nightly of her deceased husband and was flooded with intense longings for him.

It is common for unresolved mourning from a past loss to surface at the breakup of a replacement relationship. Individual sessions are valuable at that time to attend to the delayed grief process; to review the earlier courtship, marriage and family life; and to explore the many meanings of the loss and subsequent life passages. Issues of loyalty and guilt are crucial to address.

Concurrence with Other Losses, Stresses, or Life Cycle Changes

The temporal coincidence of a loss with other losses, other major stress events, or developmental milestones may overload a family and pose incompatible tasks and demands. In family assessment, a genogram and timeline are particularly useful in tracking sequences and concurrence of nodal events over time in the multigenerational family field (McGoldrick & Gerson, 1985). Sketching a timeline can alert clinicians to concurrence of losses and stressful transitions and their relation to the timing of symptoms. Particular attention should be paid to the concurrence of death with the birth of a child, since the processes of mourning and parenting an infant are inherently conflictual. Moreover, as in the case of Daniel's family, a child born at the time of a significant loss may assume a special replacement function that can be the impetus for high achievement or dysfunction. Similarly, a precipitous marriage in the wake of loss is likely to confound the two relationships, interfering with bereavement and with investment in the new relationship in its own right. When stressful events pile up, mobilizing the support of family members is especially important.

Past Traumatic Loss and Unresolved Mourning

Some individuals and families are made hardier by past traumatic loss experiences, whereas others are left more vulnerable to subsequent losses that have not been dealt with by the family. Past losses can intersect with current life cycle passage in many ways, such as the separation issues and self-destructive behavior of substance abusers (Stanton, 1977). It is crucial to explore possible connections to earlier traumatic losses in the family system, particularly when issues of separation, attachment/commitment, or self-destructive behavior are presented in therapy. In cases of marital/couple breakdown, clinicians should be attentive to losses that coincided with the onset of relational problems and any that occurred at the start of the relationship (as in the case of Doreen, above). Any significant losses in the family that coincided with the birth of the symptom bearer should also be noted. The death of a grandparent within 2 years of the birth of a child can contribute to later emotional problems in the child—particularly at the time of separation and launching attempts in young adulthood, which disrupt the family equilibrium.

It is important to note transgenerational anniversary patterns, that is, when the occurrence of symptoms coincides with death or loss in past generations at the same point in the life cycle. Individuals may become preoccupied with their own or their spouses' mortality when they reach the same age or life transition point (e.g., retirement) at which a parent died. Many persons make abrupt career or relationship changes, or start new fitness regimens and feel they must "get through the year," while others may behave self-destructively. Unresolved family patterns, or scenarios, may also be replicated when a child reaches the same age or stage that a parent had reached at the time of a death or traumatic loss (Walsh, 1983). It is crucial to assess a risk of destructive behavior at such times. The more seriously dysfunctional a family, the more likely it is that such linkages are covert and disconnected. In one chilling case, a 15-year-old boy stabbed a man in an apparent episode of dissociation that the family ignored. Upon psychiatric referral after a third such stabbing, a family assessment revealed that the father, at the age of 15, had witnessed the brutal stabbing death of his own father.

In some cases, dissociation and denial may be functional and even essential for an individual to survive and master catastrophic trauma and loss; this was true, for example, during the Holocaust. However, the maintenance of such patterns over time may have dysfunctional consequences for other members of a family system, constricting relationships and risking serious fallout for the next generation.

An appreciation of the power of covert family scripts (Byng-Hall, 1995) and family legacies is important to an understanding of the transmission of such patterns in loss (McGoldrick, 1995). Anniversary reactions are most likely to occur when there has been a physical and emotional cutoff from the past and when family rules, often covert, prohibit open communication about past traumatic events. Interventions are aimed at making covert patterns overt and helping family members to come to terms with the past and differentiate present relationships, so that history need not repeat itself.

In order to help families with loss, therefore, family therapists must reappraise family history, replacing deterministic assumptions of causality with an evolutionary perspective. Like the social context, the temporal context provides a matrix of meanings in which all behavior is embedded. Although a family cannot change its past, changes in the present and future occur in relation to that past. Systemic change involves a transformation of that relationship.

HELPING FAMILIES HEAL AFTER LOSS: THERAPEUTIC GUIDELINES

Healing and resilience in the face of loss are not simply matters of individual bereavement, but also of family mourning processes. Of all human experiences, death poses the most painful and far-reaching adaptational challenges for families. A systemic framework for clinical assessment and intervention with loss is crucial to examining the reverberations of a death for all family members, their relationships, and the family as a functional unit.

An understanding of family adaptational challenges in loss and key interactional processes in recovery guides a family resilience approach in clinical practice. An awareness of critical factors in the nature of the loss, in the family and social context, and in the timing of loss in the family life cycle alerts us as clinicians to issues that require careful attention in any systemic assessment and intervention approach. Given the diversity of family forms, values, and life courses, we must be careful not to confuse common patterns with normative standards, or to assume that differences in family bereavement are necessarily pathological. Helping family members deal with a loss requires respect for their particular cultural heritage and encouragement to be proactive in determining how they will commemorate a death. Although it is generally better to foster openness about death, it is also crucial to respect members' pain and their timing in facing the emotional meaning of a loss.

Just as there are many pathways in the family mourning process, there are many ways for clinicians to approach loss systemically. Because all family members and their relationships are affected by a loss, individual, couple, and family sessions may need to be combined flexibly to fit varied adaptive challenges over time. By strengthening key relationships and the functioning of the family unit, a healing process can reverberate throughout the system, benefitting every member.

Although open communication and mutual support are emphasized, active processes in dealing with death and loss are also encouraged. The drawing up and discussion of wills, living wills, and directives by all adult family members (not only the most vulnerable ones) are advised. Planning and participating in meaningful memorial rites are also encouraged, as are visits to the grave—not only at the time of loss, but also on anniversaries, even years later. In cases where mourning has been blocked, it's helpful for clients to sort through and bring in old photos and memorabilia, which open up memories and trigger the flow of old and new stories. They can be encouraged to share stories and mementos with children, other family members, and friends, setting off a chain of positive mutual influences for recovery and new resilience.

Dying and healing are not incompatible. To die as a healed person means viewing one's life as complete and accepting the body's disintegration. Buddhist traditions prepare for healing into death. In many cultures and times, "the art of dying" has been a popular theme of discourse, and it might well be revived as families begin to reclaim the dying process. Bereaved families can find strength to surmount heartbreaking loss and go on in a meaningful life by bringing benefit to others from their own tragedy. Clinicians can help clients to find pride, dignity, and purpose in their darkest hours through altruistic actions such as organ donation, memorial contributions to medical research or scholarship funds, or taking the initiative in forming support groups for families of those with AIDS, or community coalitions to stop drunk driving or domestic violence.

As clinicians our own resilience is needed for work with loss. In turn, the profound nature of this work reaffirms our capacity to meet the most difficult therapeutic challenges. In creating a safe haven where family members can open up and share deep pain and intense emotions, we need strong support, encouragement, and perseverance to overcome the many fears and protective barriers of family members facing death and loss. We also need to be accepting of the limits of our control over life-and-death matters: Despite our rescue fantasies, we cannot stop death or bring back a loved one. Moreover, we must become comfortable with the stirring of our own emotions by a tragic death and loss. One man, who had worked hard in therapy to begin to forge a relationship with his distant and critical father, came back to see me in crisis. His father had suffered a serious stroke and lay in a coma in intensive care, with the prognosis uncertain. Tears came down my own cheeks as he cried openly, saying, "I can't bear to lose him when I only just found him."

Work with death and loss puts us in touch with our own vulnerabilities. There is no safe boundary between clients and therapists; we all must experience and come to terms with our own losses and mortality. Forming caring therapeutic bonds in the face of loss deepens our humanity and offers a model to clients of living and loving beyond loss. As Robert Lifton (1979) has said, "There is no love without loss." In accepting loss, we open ourselves to life and love.

It can be a profoundly moving experience for us as clinicians, as well as for family members, to collaborate in the creative transformations and deepening of relationships that occur in the healing process. And, in opening ourselves to loving connections, we are better able to face the challenges of loss. The play *Nomathemba* (Shange & Shabalala, 1995) recounts the value of relationships in the face of the many losses and dislocations accompanying the turbulent transitions in South Africa. As the group Ladysmith Black Mambazo chant, "Sorrow felt alone leaves a deep crater in the soul; sorrow shared yields new life."

C·H·A·P·T·E·R   8

Coping and Resilience in Chronic Illness and Family Caregiving

All the world is full of suffering; it is also full of overcoming it.
—HELEN KELLER, *Midstream: My Later Life*

Serious illness can be experienced as a wake-up call about life. It can heighten and alter our sense of priorities, which are too often lost in the helter-skelter demands of daily living. It can force us to make changes in our patterns of living, as well as our hopes and dreams. Serious physical or mental illnesses pose a myriad of challenges for couples and families, requiring considerable resilience for coping and adaptation. This chapter highlights salient issues for a family resilience approach to chronic illness and disability.

PRACTICING THE ART OF THE POSSIBLE: LESSONS FROM LIFE

Over the course of the life cycle, serious illness strikes all individuals and their families; therapists are not immune. Our own experiences with suffering from illness and with caregiving challenges can teach us many things about resilience and how it can be fostered in our work with families that must learn to live as well as possible with persistent conditions.

In 1985 I was hospitalized with meningitis on return home from a consultation in Morocco. I was informed of the diagnosis, but was given no information about what I might expect. The first few nights, the nurses woke me several times but never told me why, so I presumed that it was to make sure I was still alive. At the end of the week, I was informed that the crisis period was over, my EEG appeared normal, and I could go home and resume "normal activity." When I asked for guidelines, I was told only to avoid stress for a while. The next night, I hosted a dinner party for close friends; I thought that this was "normal activity"—celebratory and fun—not what I considered stressful. However, I collapsed before the end of the evening. At my follow-up appointment with the neurologist a few days later, I was angry. I asked for clearer guidelines: "How should I know what's too stressful?" I'll never forget his reply: "If you walk to the corner and need an ambulance to get home, then that was too much." This was not helpful. If I only found out *after* I required the ambulance, I had no guidelines to protect myself and avert a health crisis.

The year that followed was a long nightmare. I struggled to meet the demands of a flourishing career and of parenting an active 3-year-old child. I could pull myself out of bed to get my daughter off to nursery school and then teach a 3-hour seminar, only to collapse with piercing headaches, dizziness, and exhaustion for the rest of the day. I had no memory of what I had said in class. I tried to work on a draft of a book, only to have excruciating difficulty finding words and forming coherent sentences. My doctor was amiable but patronizing, each time telling me simply to "take it easy" and I'd soon feel better, as if I were exaggerating my difficulties for sympathy. I felt helpless and despairing. My resilient self was not bouncing back.

After a year of "taking it easy," I was still not much better. I consulted another neurologist, who performed further tests and found that I had suffered considerable neurological damage, particularly to the vestibular system; this accounted for my persistent symptoms. Although the news was more grim, this physician was more helpful and hopeful. His approach was closer to a healing and resilience philosophy than to the traditional treatment paradigm. Its central assumption (based on growing scientific evidence) was that the human brain has considerable plasticity; it is able to repair itself and modify its wiring to compensate for injury and loss, if we actively mobilize our resources for recovery. Working collaboratively, he took time to listen to my concerns and answer my questions, gave me informational brochures, drew diagrams of the brain injury, and helped me to comprehend my illness experience. Medication controlled the pain and dizziness. Convinced that the brain, like other body parts, needs exercise to function well ("use it or lose it"), this physician started me on a program of strengthening exercises to reduce my vulnerabilities and restore my mental energy and functioning. He encouraged me to persist in my teaching and writing efforts, but in a more planful, incremental way, which would allow me to regain my proficiency gradually. He helped me not to become discouraged when symptoms worsened at times of high stress, to anticipate such times in the future, and to restructure my life to buffer stress more effectively. Months later, much improved, I asked him how he and my first neurologist could have approached the same patient so differently. He laughed and said, "I've known Dr. X for years; we play tennis together. When he has an injury, he stops playing for a few months and takes it easy. When I have an injury, I get physical therapy and get back on the court as soon as possible. It's all in our world view."

Indeed it was. Looking back, I can see that the successful approach to my persistent condition embodied many of the key processes in resilience and was based in a collaborative therapeutic partnership. Unfortunately, one link was missing: inclusion of the family. Although I came through the worst of the ordeal personally strengthened, my marriage, already strained, didn't survive. Yet the many months of quiet contemplation enabled me to gain a new perspective on my life and to deepen the precious bond with my child. Over time, I had to come to grips with the long-term sequelae of the brain injury, accepting the challenges I would have to live with. I learned to practice the art of the possible.

THE ILLNESS EXPERIENCE: A SYSTEMIC PERSPECTIVE

A family resilience approach to serious illness is based in a systemic orientation; it involves language and concepts that humanize the challenges of illness and that encourage optimal functioning and relational well-being.

Bridging the Mind–Body Split

The development of an integrated biopsychosocial approach to both psychiatric and medical disorders requires a paradigmatic shift from the traditional Western view of mind and body as distinct and separate (Bateson, 1979). Although theories of a more intimate mind–body connection began with psychosomatic disorders, it has become increasingly evident that emotional distress contributes to a wide range of physical symptoms, lowers physiological immunity, and can hasten death (Griffith & Griffith, 1994). Likewise, serious physical illness and disability are often accompanied and exacerbated by anxiety, confusion, and depression, particularly among individuals lacking social support.

However, mental illnesses in particular continue to be stigmatized and treated differently in health care policy and practice, despite conclusive research findings that many of them have a biological base. The first impulse in managed care developments was to "carve out" mental illnesses, with suspicion of greater malingering and abuse of benefits. Strong efforts by the mental health professions and consumer lobbying groups are yielding some success in changing attitudes and policies toward parity, but we are far from over-coming old prejudices.

Toward a Biopsychosocial–Spiritual Orientation

Although the phrase "biopsychosocial" is in wide currency, it is not typically translated into practice. In most psychiatric settings, for example, biological approaches coexist with individually based psychoanalytic and cognitive-behavioral models. What is missing is the psychosocial bridge connecting in-dividuals with their families and environments.

Moreover, it is now well documented not only that physical illness has a significant impact on family functioning, but also that families can influence the physical health of their members (see Anderson, Kiecolt-Glaser, & Glaser, 1994; Campbell, 1986; Campbell & Patterson, 1995; Fisher, Ransom, & Terry, 1993; Steinglass & Horan, 1988). Key processes in family resilience may have important ramifications for physical hardiness and recovery from illness. For instance, since stress events have been linked to a range of health problems, efforts to strengthen family resilience might well contribute to enhanced biological functioning, such as bolstering physiological immune processes (Herbert & Cohen, 1993). Family support is also essential in compliance with treatment and medication regimens.

A family resilience approach, based in a systemic, biopsychosocial ori-entation toward illness causes and course, attends to family challenges, cop-ing efforts, and contributions to optimal functioning. Whether they are liv-ing with a serious "physical" illness (e.g., diabetes or multiple sclerosis) or with a persistent "mental" illness (e.g., schizophrenia or major depression), indi-viduals and their families need to forge resilience to weather crises and com-plications over the long-term course of a persistent condition.

Cultural traditions and spiritual beliefs must also be understood and integrated in a holistic approach. For instance, many traditional cultures have explained mental disturbances as forms of possession by spirits. When one Hmong family from Southeast Asia brought a young daughter to a Califor-nia hospital emergency room for treatment of a seizure, a cross-cultural cri-sis ensued (Fadiman, 1997). The family members wanted the daughter's dis-tress alleviated, but they didn't want to stop her seizures, which they regarded as sacred trance states signifying positive connection with the spirit world. As they put it, "The spirit catches you and you fall down." The well-intentioned medical staff gained a court-ordered removal of the girl from her parents in order to treat her seizures; however, this only heightened her distress and alienated the family, who refused all further treatment after her return home, resulting in the daughter's death. If the medical staff had tried to develop a collaborative relationship with this family and to understand its cultural beliefs, instead of taking an adversarial approach, the tragedy might well have been averted.

The "Illness Experience" in Families

As helping professionals, our approach to illness can either constrain or facilitate coping and adaptation (Wright et al., 1996). Our language matters in the way we speak of "a person with a disabling condition" rather than "a disabled person." Similarly, caregivers must be viewed as persons with human needs that must be understood and validated. In contrast to the biomedical term "disease," connoting pathology and contagion, the term "condition" refers more broadly to any physical or psychological impairment that interferes with the ability of individuals to function in their environment. With medical advances, increasing numbers of people are living longer with chronic conditions than ever before. For many, the term "chronic" conjures up pessimistic views of hopeless cases and institutionalization. Actually, chronic conditions vary in their course: Some may remain fairly stable; some progressively deteriorate; and others alternate between relatively stable periods and acute episodes requiring hospitalization or more intensive medical attention (Rolland, 1994). Prognosis may vary from a normal life span, to shortened life expectancy or unpredictable death, to fatal. Chronic conditions are rarely cured. Instead, they are managed as well as possible over time through individual and family efforts, with the support of health care systems and community resources (Kazak, 1989).

The term "illness experience" best captures the human experience of living with symptoms and suffering (Kleinman, 1988; Rolland, 1994; Wright et al., 1996). "Illness experience" refers to how impaired persons and members of their family and social network perceive, live with, and master the physical and psychosocial challenges of painful symptoms, disability, and treatments. With life-threatening conditions, it also includes the experience of carrying on with life in the face of an uncertain prognosis and anticipation of death and loss. For instance, therapeutic discussion of a woman's experience of breast cancer, mastectomy, and subsequent treatments of radiation and chemotherapy would broaden to explore how it affects her body image, her relationship with her husband, and her life priorities in the face of possible recurrence and death. In addition, what is the illness experience for the husband? How can the spouses shelter their relationship to weather the strains over time? How can parents approach their children's concerns about loss? How should they respond to a daughter's worries about the threat of cancer for herself? How are family, work, and social functioning affected? How can kin and social resources be mobilized? When illness strikes a family member, the entire family requires attention for the optimal coping and adaptation of all.

Family Systems Approaches to Health Care

Family-systems-based health care is a growing field of practice. The most recent family intervention models with serious illness are grounded in a stress–diathesis model, addressing the interactive influences of biological vulnerabililty and environmental stresses. Intervention is aimed at management of the illness, and the family is viewed as an indispensable ally in treatment. Reducing the family's stress and strengthening its protective functioning, along with improving the patient's functioning, are inseparable goals of intervention.

Meeting Varied Psychosocial Challenges over Time

The particular challenges of specific illnesses differ in many ways; yet there are also many commonalities, depending on psychosocial demands and the timing of an illness in the life of a family. The family systems–illness model developed by Rolland (1994) provides a useful framework for evaluation and intervention with families dealing with chronic illness and disability. To enable us to think systemically about the interface of any chronic disorder and the family, the model casts the illness in systemic terms according to its pattern of psychosocial demands over time. The unfolding of a chronic disorder is viewed in developmental context, involving the intertwining of three evolutionary threads: the illness, individual, and family life cycles. The model addresses three dimensions: (1) "psychosocial types" of illnesses; (2) major developmental phases in their course; and (3) key family system variables.

On the first dimension, illnesses can be grouped by key biological similarities and differences that pose distinct psychosocial demands for the individual and family. Illness patterning can vary in terms of onset (acute vs. gradual), course (progressive vs. constant vs relapsing), outcome (fatal vs. shortened life span or possible sudden death vs. no effect on longevity), incapacitation (none vs. mild vs. moderate vs. severe), and the level of uncertainty about the trajectory. Using these variables, we can describe any chronic biological disorder in terms of its "psychosocial type." Each type of condition poses a pattern of practical and emotional demands that can be thought about in relation to the style, strengths, and vulnerabilities of a family.

On a second dimension, the concept of time phases provides a way for clinicians to think longitudinally about chronic illness as an ongoing process with landmarks, transitions, and changing demands. The crisis, chronic, and terminal phases have salient psychosocial challenges, each requiring particular family strengths or changes. For instance, the crisis phase involves the initial period of socialization to chronic illness. Family developmental tasks include creating a meaning for the disorder that preserves a sense of mastery, grieving the loss of the preillness family identity, undergoing short-term crisis reorganization, and developing family flexibility in the face of uncertainty and possible threatened loss. Gradually, families must come to accept the persistence or permanence of the condition, learn to live with illness-related symptoms and treatments, and forge an ongoing relationship with professionals and institutional settings. In the chronic phase, families must also pace themselves to avoid burnout, manage relationship skews (as in caregiving), and juggle the competing needs and priorities of all family members. They must find ways to preserve or redefine individual and family developmental goals within the constraints of the illness, as well as to sustain intimacy in the face of threatened loss.

The psychosocial demands of any condition can be thought about in relation to each phase of the disorder. The key processes in family functioning, such as belief systems, organizational patterns, and communication processes, can be approached as they fit the evolving situation. This framework can guide periodic family consultations, or "psychosocial checkups," as salient issues and priorities surface and change over time. It also informs evaluation of general functioning and illness-specific family dynamics, such as the interface of the illness with individual and family development; the family's multigenerational history of coping with illness, loss, and other adversity; and the meaning of the illness to family members.

As therapists, we must be flexible in helping families to meet emerging challenges over the uncertain course of a serious, life-threatening illness, as the following case illustrates:

> I have worked with Kate at various phases and transitions over an 8-year course of breast cancer. She and her husband, Wayne, have shown remarkable courage and resilience through two recurrences, maintaining active initiative in searching out the best treatment options. I've coached them to listen and respond sensitively to their children's concerns as these have emerged, and to keep channels of communication open. Wayne has been unstintingly supportive of Kate and flexible in shifting his work schedule to be more available in parenting their three children during difficult periods. Kate decided to maintain her part-time clerical job, which she experienced as "an island of normality," taking her mind off her own condition as she tackled mountains of paperwork and enjoyed

socializing and light banter with other staff. She was open in informing colleagues of major changes in her condition, and took time off when needed; otherwise, however, she preferred not to discuss her illness at work, keeping a boundary to preserve non-illness-focused aspects of her life. She took vacations from therapy during periods of remission, wanting to "just smell the roses" during stable plateaus, but called proactively when new complications loomed on the horizon.

A year ago, when the cancer spread to her lower spine, Kate underwent an experimental bone marrow transplant, once again beating the odds and doing well over the past year. However, in the midst of her recovery, her mother, in her late 70s, was diagnosed with untreatable colon cancer, which progressed rapidly to death. A month later Kate called, concerned about Mollie, her 12-year-old daughter. She had found a letter that Mollie had written to a friend, saying that she was desperately unhappy and wanted to run away. We held a family session, where at first Mollie railed against her teachers, concluding that she wanted to go away to boarding school because "life sucks!" When I asked how the grandmother's recent death had affected family members, Mollie's eyes filled with tears. Her parents' receptiveness helped her to share her fear: "Grandma's death scared me so much. She died from cancer, and Mom has had cancer three times. I suddenly realized how easy it could be for Mom to die. Sometimes I have nightmares that the cancer hasn't all gone away. Then I just want to run away. If the cancer comes back again, maybe we won't be so lucky." Both parents held her, soothing her as she sobbed. Mollie's siblings were encouraged to share their feelings and concerns as well. I supported the parents' efforts to talk about the dilemmas in living with uncertainty and the wish they each had—that they could just make the cancer go away once and for all. Both parents reassured the children that Mom indeed was continuing to do well, and vowed to be honest with them if the situation changed. The discussion turned to ways they could make the most of family time together.

This case illustrates how even when parents handle an illness experience as well as possible at one crisis point, other crises will arise over time that require renewed—and new—conversations. Here, the death of the grandmother challenged the shared belief that the mother would continue to beat the odds: If the grandmother could die from cancer, then so could she. Also, as Mollie approached adolescence, she had greater comprehension of her mother's condition and all it would mean to lose her. The time had come in this family to talk more openly about that possibility. Coming to terms with an illness and its ramifications is never a once-and-for-all matter, but a process that must be worked on over time.

Putting the Illness in Its Place

Instead of framing a chronic illness in terms of an adversarial battle against a disease, it can be more helpful to recognize the influence of the condition, master the possible, accept what is beyond control, and come to terms with living with it. To do this successfully, families must find ways to "put the illness in its place" (Gonzalez et al., 1989). Setting boundaries as to when, where, and with whom illness concerns are discussed can be helpful, just as Kate, above, kept boundaries in her work life to preserve "an island of normality."

For a couple, a chronic condition can skew the relationship over time between the impaired partner and the caregiving spouse (Rolland, 1994). The persistent intrusion of an illness into all aspects of family life can fuel despair, as in the following case:

Mike and Delores, in their mid-40s, came for couple therapy as growing conflict threatened the survival of their marriage. In the first session, they argued over money, sex, and Mike's whereabouts on weekend nights. Neither partner mentioned that Delores had been suffering for many years from multiple sclerosis, even though her difficulty in walking with a cane was evident. When asked about her condition, both minimized it as "nothing new" and resumed fighting over petty grievances.

Separate individual sessions were held, to allow the therapist to hear more about the illness experience and to afford each partner the opportunity to express concerns more freely. Mike revealed that he was alternately depressed and furious at Delores because of her increasing disability and dependence. They had traditional breadwinner–homemaker roles in their marriage. As her illness progressed, she was less and less able to keep the house clean or to manage shopping and errands, and had lost all interest in sex. It bothered him to come home and find her "lying around" while he worked an exhausting construction job plus overtime to keep up with her medical bills. He harbored fantasies of leaving her, became irritated with her over small things, felt ashamed, and then drowned his frustration in bouts of heavy drinking at a neighborhood bar on weekends. As for Delores, the less she felt in control of her own body, the more controlling of Mike she became. She alternated between feeling irritated and resentful that he wasn't more attentive to her needs, and feeling guilty for being a burden on him.

It was important to reframe Delores and Mike's dilemma as not attributable to his failings or hers, but rather to the burdens imposed on their relationship by a progressively deteriorating illness. They were then better able to hear and comfort each other as they shared the ways in which each had been devastated by the illness and how it had ravaged their relationship, their financial security, and their hopes and dreams for the future. Strains also came from living with uncertainty about the long-term unfolding and extent of Delores's disability, as well as the possibility of her early death. Their marriage was strengthened as they banded together to reduce the intrusion of the illness in their lives and find better ways to live with it. Delores, realizing that Mike's night out with the boys was not an affair, encouraged him to go out when she couldn't; in turn, he agreed not to drink to excess. Feeling less trapped, he was kinder toward Delores and supported her need for outlets and visits with friends. They decided to set aside a little money each week toward a weekend trip for their upcoming anniversary.

When a chronic illness looms increasingly large in the life of a person and loved ones—imposing heavy physical, emotional, and financial burdens, and diminishing hopes and dreams for the future—it is crucial to help clients regain a view of each person and their relationship as defined by more than the illness. Couple therapy can help each partner gain empathy for the other's position, address such issues as guilt and blame, and rebalance their relationship to enable them to live and love as fully as possible.

Key Family Resilience Processes in Chronic Illness

The belief systems of the ill person, important family members, and health care professionals color the illness experience and all healing transactions (Rolland, 1994; Wright, Watson, & Bell, 1994). We need to work with causal explanations of how and why health problems occurred and persist, as well as beliefs about the role of helping professionals and the family in the treatment process and outcome. Rolland (1994) has described the constraining or facilitating influence that the hospital setting and standard procedures can have. For instance, he describes the impact of "framing events"—for example, when health professionals, by taking a spouse or a parent outside the patient's room to give news of an unfavorable diagnosis or prognosis, unwittingly convey the message that this information is best not shared with the patient, and perhaps not even with other family members. All family interaction is then constrained by the catastrophic fear that talking about the illness and its life-threatening possibilities will be harmful or even hasten death. By contrast, in sharing acknowledgment of the illness situation, family members can help one another make meaning of the experience and master the challenges they face.

Organizational patterns shift with various adaptational demands over the course of an illness. For instance, a father's heart attack generates a family crisis. Before the heart attack, a family with teenagers might be moderately flexible and separate—patterns appropriate to its life cycle stage. With a heart attack, the family may shift rapidly to extremes. Very high levels of cohesion occur as the illness crisis draws members together. Chaos is generated with the emotional upheaval and the need to alter many daily routines dramatically. Over the next several weeks, the family attempts to bring the chaos under control by reorganizing some of its routines. Six months later, family functioning may remain closer and more structured in response to the disability. Although all families change in response to a crisis, many need help in adjusting their roles, rules, and leadership to achieve a new balance that maximizes their resources and coping skills as the illness enters a more chronic, long-haul phase.

Open communication is also vital. One set of studies by Beavers and colleagues examined adaptation and competence in families with a child with mental retardation (Beavers, Hampson, Hulgus, & Beavers, 1986). Contrary to clinical lore that such families are permeated by a sense of chronic sorrow leading inevitably to family dysfunction, these studies found a wide range of responses. Families that were able to deal openly with their feelings adapted well. Members were able to express a wide range of feelings, including joy as well as sorrow and frustration; some even noted that the presence of a child with a disability might have contributed to their strong mutual support. In contrast, the most dysfunctional families revealed despair, which was reinforced by a strong taboo on expressing these feelings. Such studies illustrate the need for clinicians to facilitate open communication for optimal adaptation to illness and disability.

The value of group support for individuals facing similar challenges has been demonstrated. David Spiegel (1993), for instance, found that women diagnosed with metastatic cancer who participated in a weekly support group showed a much better adjustment and doubled their average survival time (from 19 to 37 months). Spiegel noted that, in contrast to the sort of "cheering up" commonly thought of as social support, the group did not discourage the expression of negative feelings; it actively encouraged open sharing of the full range of thoughts, beliefs, and emotions surrounding the members' experience.

THE GRAYING OF THE FAMILY: ILLNESS AND CAREGIVING CHALLENGES IN LATER LIFE

As societies are aging, the number of people with chronic conditions is increasing dramatically. Those impaired are living longer with disabilities than ever before (Walsh, 1998b). Even though most elders do maintain good health, loss of physical and mental functioning, chronic pain, and progressively degenerating conditions are common preoccupations. In the United States, health problems and their severity vary greatly (Baltes, 1996). Among seniors aged 65–84, arthritis, high blood pressure, and heart disease are most prevalent. Over age 85, the risk of cancer and the extent of other disabilities increase, together with intellectual, visual, and hearing impairment. Physical and mental deterioration may be exacerbated by depression and a sense of loss of control, reverberating with the anxiety of family members.

Family caregiving for seniors is a major concern. The increasing numbers of frail elderly over 85 pose growing demands for long-term care and financial coverage (Baltes, 1996). By 2020 there will be twice as many elderly (14 million) needing long-term care as there are today. In 1970 there were 21 "potential caregivers" (defined as people aged 50–64) for each person 85 or older; by 2030 there will be only 6 such potential caregivers, and this shortage will put a severe strain on intergenerational relations. As the average family size decreases, fewer children are available for caregiving and sibling support. With more people marrying and having children later, those at midlife—the so-called "sandwich generation"—are caring simultaneously for children and adolescents, as well as for aging parents, grandparents, and other relatives. Finances can be drained by college expenses for children just as medical expenses for elders increase. Adult children who are past retirement age, and facing their own declining health and resources, must assume responsibilities for growing numbers of infirm parents. The likelihood of being caregivers for one or more aging family members is rapidly increasing.

Growing numbers of elders with chronic conditions are receiving care at home, producing a crisis in caregiving (see Walsh, 1998b). Only 5% of the elderly are maintained in institutions; yet chronic health problems require increasing hospitalizations, medical costs, and home-based care for daily functioning. Family and friends are the front lines of support; nearly three-fourths of disabled persons over 65 rely exclusively on these informal caregivers. As the pool of caregivers dimishes, those giving care are badly strained by multiple pressures.

Women at midlife are especially burdened, as job demands are juxtaposed with expectations to maintain traditional responsibilities for homemaking, child rearing, and elder care. Caregiving responsibilities have been almost exclusively the domain of women, in their roles as daughters and daughters-in-law; three out of four primary caregivers are women. Their average age is 57, but 25% are aged 65–74, and 10% are over 75. As women have become fuller participants in the workforce, and their incomes have become essential in two-parent as well as single-parent families, rebalancing of work and family roles is needed. Yet few employers offer schedule flexibility or consider men as caregivers.

Prolonged caregiving takes a heavy toll. Eighty percent of caregivers provide help 7 days a week, averaging 4 hours daily. In addition to housekeeping, shopping, and meal preparation, two-thirds also assist with feeding, bathing, toileting, and dressing. The lack of useful management guidelines by most medical specialists adds to the confusion, frustration, and helplessness family members commonly experience. Some aspects of chronic illness among elders are especially disruptive for families, such as sleep disturbance, incontinence, delusional ideas, and aggressive behavior. One symptom and consequence of such family distress is elder abuse, which is most likely to occur in overwhelmed families that are stretched beyond their means and tolerance.

Alzheimer's Disease and Other Dementias

Among the most difficult illnesses for families to cope with are dementias— progressive brain disorders (Baltes, 1996). Alzheimer's disease, accounting for 60% of dementias, is one of the most devastating illnesses of our times. It affects 10% of persons over 65 and nearly half of those over 85. The disease is often not correctly diagnosed, with cognitive losses erroneously assumed to be a natural part of aging. The irreversible course of the disease can persist anywhere from a few years to 20 years or more, and the psychosocial and financial dilemmas it creates can become agonizing for families. Over time Alzheimer's disease strips away mental and physical capacities, resulting in gradual memory loss, disorientation, impaired judgment, and finally loss of control over bodily functions. Persons with Alzheimer's may repeatedly ask the same questions, forgetting earlier answers, or may prepare a meal and forget to serve it. They may easily get lost and forget how they got there or how to get home. With impaired memory and judgment, they may forget entirely about a boiling pot or a child under their care, or make disastrous financial decisions. It is most painful for loved ones when they are not even recognized or are confused with others, even those long deceased.

Since medical treatment of the illness is limited, a custodial bias has prevailed in its management. Individuals kept at home on low-dose or drug-free regimens do not show decrements as severe as do those in institutions, who tend to be highly medicated and isolated from familiar people and surroundings. Adult day care can partially relieve family burden. Family psychoeducation and support networks can provide relatives with help in meeting caregiving challenges, coping with stress, and dealing with confusion and memory lapses. Useful illness-related information and management guidelines reduce the risk of caregiver depression, particularly in cases with considerable ambiguity in the illness course (Boss, 1991). Family members can be helped in grieving for the loss of a loved one's family roles and relationships.

Common Issues in Caregiving for Aging Family Members

In approaching all serious illness in the elderly, clinicians and researchers need to expand the narrow focus on an individual caregiver—typically a wife, sister, daughter, or daughter-in-law—to encourage the involvement of all family members as a caregiving team. It is important for clinicians not to assume that family distress indicates a family causal role in deterioration of a chronic illness. Family intervention priorities should include (1) stress reduction; (2) information about the elderly person's medical condition, functional ability, limitations, and prognosis; (3) concrete guidelines for sustaining care, problem solving, and optimal functioning; and (4) linkages to supplementary services to support family efforts. To meet caregiving challenges, communities must support families through a range of services from day programs to assisted living, and through commitment to full participation of elders (including those with disabilities) in community life.

Issues of intergenerational dependence come to the fore as aging parents lose functioning and control over their bodies and their lives. Meeting the increasing needs of aging parents should not be seen as a parent–child "role reversal," as some imply. Even when adult children give financial, practical, and emotional support to aging parents, they do not become parents to their parents. It should be kept in mind that despite frail appearance or childlike functioning, an aged parent has had over 50 years of adult life and experience. Family therapists can open conversations about dependence-related issues with sensitivity and a realistic appraisal of strengths and limitations. An elderly father may be driving with seriously impaired vision, unwilling to admit the danger or give up his autonomy to be driven by others. Older parents often fail to tell their adult children that they are financially strapped because of the shame and stigma of economic dependence in our society. Adult children can be coached on ways to develop a filial role—taking responsibility for what they can appropriately do for aging parents, while recognizing their own constraints.

If an aging parent becomes overly dependent on adult children, who become overly responsible through anxiety or guilt, a vicious cycle may ensue: The more they do for the parent, the more helpless the parent may become, with escalating neediness, burden, and resentment. Siblings may go to opposite extremes in meeting filial responsibilities, as in the following case:

> Mrs. Zia, a 74-year-old widow, was hospitalized with multiple somatic problems and secondary symptoms of disorientation and confusion. She complained that her two sons, Tim and Roger, didn't care whether she lived or died. The sons reluctantly agreed to come in for a family inter-

view. On the phone Roger offered his belief that his mother's hospital-ization was merely a ploy for sympathy, to make him feel guilty for not being at her beck and call as Tim was. He said he had learned years ago that the best relationship with her was none at all. In contrast, Tim had become increasingly responsible for his mother, particularly since she had been widowed. Yet the more "helpful" he was, the more helpless she became in managing her own life. He felt drained by his mother's growing neediness.

The overresponsible son was coached to be more "helpful" by chal-lenging his mother to function maximally rather than doing everything for her. The underinvolved son was encouraged to join with his brother and to relieve him of some specific burdens. Both sons were helped to communicate their feelings and concerns directly with their mother and to be patient in listening to her. They were advised not to be put off if she initially resisted the changes. With anxiety in the system reduced and the two sons working together, Mrs. Zia's thinking and functioning im-proved markedly.

Caregiving challenges can be burdensome; yet they can also become opportunities for family members to heal strained relationships and begin to collaborate as a caregiving team. When conflict has been intense and persis-tent, when ambivalence is strong, or when family members have become es-tranged, caregiving for aging relatives is more likely to be complicated. Life-and-death decisions become more difficult, as in the following crisis situation:

Joellen, a 38-year-old single parent, was deeply conflicted when her fa-ther, hospitalized for long-term complications of chronic alcohol abuse, asked her to donate a kidney to save his life. She felt enraged to be asked to give up something so important when he had not been there for her as a father over the years. He had been a mean drunk, often absent and many times violent. She was also angry that he had brought on his dete-riorated condition by drinking and had refused to heed his family's re-peated pleas to stop. Furthermore, she was hesitant to give up a vital organ when she thought about caring for her children and their possible future needs. Yet, as a dutiful daughter and a compassionate woman, she also felt a sense of obligation and guilt: She did not want her father to die because she had denied him her kidney.

When I suggested that Joellen talk with her mother about her di-lemma, she learned that her father had also asked her siblings for the kidney donation. Because she was estranged from them, she feared that old rivalries would be stirred up as to who would be seen as the good, giving child or the bad, selfish ones. I encouraged Joellen to overcome her reluctance to meet with her siblings to grapple with the dilemma, and then to persevere when the meeting proved hard to schedule. When the siblings finally met, they were surprised to learn how torn each of them felt. Old rivalries shifted as they began to reach out to one another.

I suggested that they broaden their focus and begin to plan together how they might collaborate to share the many challenges likely to come up in caring for *both* of their aging parents. As they each envisioned taking a part of future responsibilities, the elder brother, who was healthy and had no plans for a family of his own, volunteered to donate a kidney for their father. The decision was also less conflictual for him, because he had experienced better times with the father in earlier years before the problem drinking. As the others offered to support him and agreed to contribute to their parents' future well-being in ways that fit their abilities and resources, the beginning of a new solidarity was forged.

Even when family contact has been severed, my experience has taught me never to give up on relationship possibilities before trying to reengage members. Without support, a family may have become overwhelmed and burned out by persistent stresses in coping with an illness, especially if the condition has been uncontrolled by medication or exacerbated by self-medicating alcohol or drug abuse. Recurrent crises can fuel helplessness and hopelessness; escalating conflict may become destructive. Yet the immediate relief of a cutoff is commonly overshadowed by family members' continual worry about the elderly person's well-being and their abiding sorrow or guilt that they could not (or did not) help their loved one.

Family members commonly distance out of sheer exhaustion and depleted resources. Siblings may distance from painful past experiences, failed rescue attempts, anger over destructive behavior, or the fear that they will be pulled into a bottomless pit of selfless caregiving. There may also be fears of contagion or concerns of heightened genetic risk: "If my mother got breast cancer, it could happen to me." Loss issues and survival guilt are common as well: "How can I be successful and enjoy life when my sister's life has been devastated by her illness?" "How can I continue to care for my partner with dementia, when he no longer recognizes me?" There may well be inner conflict over responsibility for being a loved one's keeper, with the sacrifices extracted by an illness. It's useful to question all-or-none assumptions of involvement: "I avoid all contact, because if I open the door an inch, I'll give over my life to endless caregiving." My work with many in this position—parents, siblings, and adult children of frail elderly—has heightened my appreciation of all they have struggled with. Our successful work in bridging new connections has strenghtened my conviction that it is rarely too late to repair and redefine frayed bonds (see Chapter 10).

Placement Decisions

The point at which failing health requires consideration of nursing-home placement is a crisis for the whole family. Placement is usually turned to only as a last resort—when family resources are stretched to the limit, and most often in later stages of mental or physical deterioration. Nevertheless, feelings of guilt and abandonment and notions about institutionalization can make a placement decision highly stressful for families, particularly for adult daughters, on whom the caretaking expectations typically concentrate. A case described earlier in this book—that of the Wolff family in Chapter 5—underscores the importance of inquiry about elderly family members even when problems are presented elsewhere in the system; such problems may express concerns related to the caretaking crisis. It is also crucial to attend to a spouse's distancing and lack of support (in the Wolffs' case, this was due to the husband's lingering guilt over having left the care of his dying mother to his sisters).

Family sessions can enable members to assess needs and resources, weigh the benefits and costs of options, and share their feelings and concerns before reaching a decision together. Often through discussion new solutions emerge that can support the elder's remaining in the community without undue burden on any member. Organizations such as the Visiting Nurses Association can provide homebound services and inform families of community backup resources. Respite for caregivers is crucial to their well-being. When placement is needed, we can help families see it as the most viable way to provide good care, and help them navigate the maze of options.

Dealing with terminal illness is perhaps the family's most painful challenge, often complicated by agonizing end-of-life decisions. The rising rate of suicide among the elderly involves a desire for dignity and control over their own dying process. It also may be a response to unmet needs for pain control and palliative care, and/or to worries about financial and emotional burden on loved ones. Clinicians need to work with families to reduce suffering and make the best arrangements to keep the seriously ill person comfortable and comforted, while balancing the needs of other family members.

FAMILY COPING WITH MENTAL ILLNESS

Conditions involving mental and emotional impairment can be extremely painful and difficult for individuals and their families to deal with. Clinical

approaches toward mental illness have been undergoing major transformations over recent decades. Accompanying the shift from a nature-versus-
nurture controversy to a biopsychosocial orientation has been a shift from
shunning families as pathogenic influences to involving them as valued resources and collaborators in the treatment process. The core principles that
guide a family resilience approach can reduce stress and maximize functioning for individuals with mental illness and their families.

A Biopsychosocial–Systems Orientation to Mental Illness

Historically, the field of mental health has swung back and forth between
polarized positions assuming either biological or social causality in schizophrenia and other chronic mental disorders (Walsh & Anderson, 1988). In the
first classification before the turn of the century, a biological base for schizophrenia (then known as dementia praecox) was posited. By the 1940s, psychoanalytic propositions held that the most serious and chronic mental disorders were rooted in the earliest mother–infant bonds. Others have argued
that schizophrenia is merely a myth or a metaphor, symptomatic of family or
social pathology and maintained to serve a function. Adherents to this view
oppose any labeling of illness, diagnosis, hospitalization, or medication, ar-
guing that they foster a stigmatizing "patient" identity and a chronic course
(Haley, 1980). At the other extreme, biological determinists have focused
narrowly on evidence for genetic and biochemical bases of mental illness and
on psychopharmacological interventions, failing to see any value of family
involvement in treatment. Despite ample evidence of the complicated, mutual influences between biological vulnerability and environmental stress factors in the course of major mental disorders, a biopsychosocial orientation
remains not well integrated into treatment approaches (Walsh & Anderson,
1988; Walsh, 1995b).

  I was fortunate to benefit from clinical training in the late 1960s on an
experimental psychiatric inpatient unit at Yale (Tompkins 1) based on the
philosophy of milieu therapy—a patient–staff community with combined
interventions, including psychotropic medication, individual, group, family, and multifamily group modalities. In the early 1970s, I coordinated the
family studies in a schizophrenia research program funded by the National
Institute of Mental Health and directed by Roy Grinker, Sr. Grinker was a
visionary psychiatrist who regarded a biopsychosocial–systems orientation
as fundamental to the study and treatment of schizophrenia, borderline disorders, and other serious mental conditions (Walsh, 1987b). These experiences put into practice a true interactionist perspective, recognizing the
importance of both nature *and* nurture, and attending to the recursive in-

fluences of the individual, the family, and larger social systems through their ongoing transactions over the course of an illness. My very first family therapy experience in 1968 clearly demonstrated the importance of this "both–and" position:

> I first met Emmy Lou at her admission to the psychiatric inpatient unit. She was a 48-year-old woman in a low-cut pink polka dot blouse, green plaid skirt, and silver spike heels, with a 1940s hairdo coming undone, bright fuchsia rouge, and off-center lipstick. She chattered in an animated yet disconnected way. Emmy Lou was hospitalized for the treatment of manic–depressive (bipolar) disorder, from which she had been suffering for over 20 years. Shortly after she and her husband, Walt, had fallen in love and married, she had her first manic episode while the couple was vacationing in Paris. She dressed up like an exotic dancer and went out alone into the streets, dancing all night before her distraught husband and the gendarmes found her beside the Seine River. Every spring, almost like clockwork, Emmy Lou had a manic episode; each time she painted her face, dressed in multihued, mismatched outfits, and went off on a wild spree.

Although we wish at times to live adventurously, a manic episode is painfully frantic and usually ends quite badly, with considerable suffering for the person and for loved ones, who must pick up the pieces after the mayhem subsides. Bank accounts may be depleted, or individuals may put themselves and others at risk of serious harm through poor judgment, impulsive actions, and grandiose schemes that go awry. Crashing depression may follow.

> Walt was a devoted husband who took an active role in raising their two children, by then teenagers. He took Emmy Lou to all the best treatment centers; stood by her through her recurrent breakdowns, hospitalizations, and brief recoveries; and kept hoping for a cure. Emmy Lou was admitted to our psychiatric unit for a trial of lithium, a newly experimental drug treatment at the time. Emmy Lou and her family were also referred for family therapy as part of the milieu approach. A first-year psychiatry resident and I eagerly began seeing our first family, and as Emmy Lou made an astounding recovery, we credited our skillful family therapy interventions for the great success (only jokingly, of course, as we admitted that lithium might have had some effect).

This family taught me an invaluable lesson. Even when a disorder is clearly biologically based and can be managed over time with psychotropic medication, the involvement of the family in treatment is crucial for patient and family adaptation. The family didn't *cause* her disorder, but they too suffered its disruptive impact. Moreover, the family members didn't *need* Emmy Lou to be ill; nor did her symptoms serve a function for them. Nevertheless, they had oriented family life around her disturbance over the years. Any recovery, though it is everyone's greatest wish, requires major readjustments for all family members and reorganization of the family unit. Although medication can reduce florid symptoms, all loved ones must reorient their relationships and patterns of living so that they can move forward with their lives.

> Patterns of family functioning, set in place over the years to compensate for Emmy Lou's illness, needed to be altered to make a place for a more functional wife and mother. Walt had increasingly taken over the household duties, and Emmy Lou's responsibilities had been reduced to feeding and walking the dog. Her competence and confidence needed to be restored, and the spousal/parental partnership needed to be rebalanced. Walt and the kids would have to shift their expectations of Emmy Lou. They were nervous and uncertain how to relate without the illness to define their roles. Discharge planning and reentry sessions with the family members enabled them to share their feelings about this major change in their lives, and to reorganize long-standing illness-centered patterns to fit their vision of healthy family life. We scheduled a follow-up family session for early spring, in anticipation of the time a recurrence would be expected. Each spring, family members hovered over Emmy Lou, vigilant for the first signs of another episode. The follow-up session offered an opportunity to discuss fears of a setback, to ensure that medication levels were adequate, to reaffirm confidence in Emmy Lou, and to sustain the family's gains.

To optimize the patient's functioning, reduce the risk of serious relapse, and prevent the need for rehospitalization, family members should be partners in treatment from the time of hospital admission through discharge, with planned follow-up and referral for outpatient sustaining care. The first few weeks and months following psychiatric hospitalization can be the most challenging. Lacking orientation and guidelines, the family may not know what to expect or how to proceed. Family members and medical professionals may share the unrealistic beliefs that "treatment" was accomplished by the professionals (and drugs) in the hospital and that "normal" life can be resumed with discharge. Following a "honeymoon" period of relative calm, tensions are likely to mount as problems resurface. Family members need to develop new communication skills and to reorganize interactional patterns, in order to reduce stress and support the optimal functioning of the recovering individual. With the drastic reductions in the length of hospital stays (is "drive-through" stabilization far off?), families need assistance with their heavy burden for long-term care (Lefley, 1996).

From Deficit-Based to Resource-Based Approaches to Therapy

A focus on deficits, reinforced by psychiatric nomenclature, exerts a powerful influence in clinical practice. Recent policies in managed care worsen the situation by demanding diagnosis and documentation of more severe pathology for therapy to be reimbursed beyond a few sessions. When those with recurrent emotional distress seek help, they often carry pathology-loaded baggage from previous treatment experience. A resource-based approach aims to transform this experience.

> Jessie and Ted, a recently married couple in their late 20s, sought help for Jessie's phobic anxiety, which prevented her from leaving their apartment without a panic attack. She was evaluated for psychotropic medication, which lowered the intensity of her anxiety; yet she remained alone in the apartment all day, becoming increasingly depressed and ruminating about the emptiness of her life and the hopelessness of her emotional problems. The couple had recently moved from the city where Jessie had grown up, so that Ted could take a new job. In the first few sessions, Jessie talked at great length about her "dysfunctional family," her mother's chronic alcoholism and depression, and her own recurrent episodes of panic, which had led to three psychiatric hospitalizations. She had spent the last 6 years in psychoanalysis, with sessions several times a week until their move. Now fearing she was coming "unglued" again, she was making crisis calls to her former therapist. Ted was attentive and caring toward Jessie, yet frightened by her agitated state and catastrophic fears.
>
> A deficit-oriented therapy might have continued to focus on past family damage and Jessie's resulting limitations and emotional fragility. A therapist might have felt sympathy for the "normal" spouse stuck with a damaged partner, or else might have assumed both partners in a marriage to be equally dysfunctional, and searched for underlying pathology in Ted as well. A resource-oriented family resilience approach identified and encouraged their strengths. Ted was solid, stable, and caring. His attraction to Jessie was understandable: She was a lovely woman, warm, affec-

tionate, attractive, and smart. Ted's fears from a past failed marriage also played a part. Recently divorced by a woman who had left him to pursue her career, he appreciated Jessie's devoted loyalty to him. However, he neither anticipated her suffering nor "needed" her helplessness.

As our sessions became dominated by Jessie's accounts of how her long history of emotional problems "explained" her current plight, I shifted focus to the recent transitional crisis in the life of the couple—the disruption wrought by their relocation. I asked how the decision had come about. The partners had shared their feelings, concluded that on balance it would be a good move, and arrived at the decision jointly. Still, there was a skew in the experience of the transition, generating more stress for the more vulnerable partner. The move furthered Ted's career advancement; his new job focused his attention; and his extended family lived nearby for support. Jessie, who wanted to assume a homemaker role and hoped to start a family soon, had lost her community network, her therapist, and a satisfying job. She felt isolated in long, empty days in their apartment in an unfamiliar city. The loss of structure and support fueled her anxiety and rumination, further eroding her confidence and future hopes and dreams.

Making meaning of the recent symptoms in the context of this major transition was pivotal to Jessie's adaptation and the couple's resilience. I expressed my conviction that a major relocation is stressful for a relationship as well as for individuals, and that by strengthening their resilience as a couple, they would both more likely make the best adjustment. To help them begin to form a new support network and to anchor them in their new community, I explored their interest in joining a church that fit their beliefs and lifestyle, encouraging them to make several visits. Within weeks they found a new "spiritual home" and a congregation of "kindred souls." Jessie met several women through the church who took her under their wing, helped her get oriented, recommended good neighborhood resources, and accompanied her on errands. These small concrete supports eased her insecurities and helped her gain a sense of mastery over the "foreign" environment. As her comfort increased, we talked about the library job she had left behind and her love and knowledge of books. Ted encouraged her to volunteer in the church's fund-raising sale of used books. Her success in that endeavor led to a volunteer position in the neighborhood library. That experience in turn led within a few months to a part-time job in a bookstore, a short bus ride away. With Ted's confidence in her, she overcame her "fear of becoming panicky" and excelled on the job, which she found to be a rewarding challenge.

It was vital to our work that Jessie stop defining herself as damaged, but rather broaden her identity as a likable and interesting person, with many positive attributes as well as vulnerabilities. It was also crucial that she experience therapy not as a place to nurse old wounds endlessly (as in her past therapy), but as a place to develop latent talents and abilities. Jessie came to look back on her prior therapy as an addiction: Over the years, her vulnerability and overdependence on her therapist had increased to the point that she doubted her ability to survive on her own when that contact ended.

Our therapy ended successfully after 5 months. Jessie's medication was tapered off gradually. A year later, I received a birth announcement with a very cute baby picture and a note of appreciation for helping Jessie and Ted launch their new life together. Yet life doesn't follow an orderly course. Six months later Jessie called in a panic: Ted's company had been bought out, and he might be downsized out of a job. Over several sessions, the couple considered possible options if a "worst-case scenario" required them to move again. The ax fell a few months later, but the couple was prepared and Jessie didn't panic. Ted had already begun a job search, which landed him a good position in a desirable community where Jessie planned to return to complete college. We met for a few sessions before the move, and I linked them to a trusted colleague in the new community if the need arose. Jessie's physician recommended that she resume her antianxiety medication if needed during the expectable turmoil of the move. We scheduled a follow-up phone contact, and they sent a card at holiday time expressing their pride at how smoothly the new transition had gone: With all they had learned from their previous move, they now considered themselves experts on relocation. Jessie even thought about writing an article on the subject.

From "Schizophrenogenic Mother" to Respectful Collaboration

Clinicians and investigators have long sought to understand and effectively treat the most debilitating mental disorders, but have too readily pathologized families and excluded them from involvement. For example, the concept of the "schizophrenogenic mother" blamed disturbances in the mother's character and parenting style for causing schizophrenia. A spate of impressionistic case studies—many conducted without any contact with the families—posited an array of characterological and parenting deficits in the supposed "schizophrenogenic mother," ranging from symbiotic overinvolvement, overprotectiveness, and intrusiveness to cold, harsh, rejecting attitudes.

In the late 1950s, schizophrenia research based on a family systems perspective shifted from a linear, deterministic view of maternal causality to attend to multiple, recursive transactions in the family network. Still, in the early development of the field of family therapy, the focus was primarily on dysfunctional family transactions implicated in the ongoing *maintenance* of symptoms of schizophrenia, if not their origins. The era of the "schizophrenogenic mother" was unfortunately followed by that of the "schizophrenic family."

In the 1970s, studies comparing young adults with schizophrenia and those with other severe emotional disorders found a wide range of family functioning (Anderson & Walsh, 1988). No single pattern distinguished families with a schizophrenic member. Moreover, with growing evidence of a biological base, it became clear that there is no one-to-one correlation between individual disorder and family pathology. Clinicians must be careful, therefore, not to label families by the diagnosis of a member's condition. There is no "schizophrenic family," any more than there is a "diabetic family."

More recently, as psychiatric research turned to biochemical processes, family studies shifted their focus from questions of origin to quesitons of influences in the future *course* of a chronic illness. For instance, high "expressed emotion" (i.e., critical comments and emotional overinvolvement) predicts later symptomatic relapse for vulnerable individuals with schizophrenia, major depression, and anorexia nervosa (Walsh & Anderson, 1988). By identifying such process elements, we can target family interventions toward lowering stress and risk of relapse as we strengthen both patient and family functioning.

Over the past decade, a fundamental shift has occurred toward respect and support of individuals and families coping with major mental illnesses. Yet greater availability of community supports and reduced stigma associated with mental illness are still needed for individual and family well-being. The deinstitutionalization movement, which began three decades ago, had the admirable aim of supporting mentally ill individuals in the community; however, it failed to follow through with funding for adequate outpatient services to sustain independent living. In psychiatry, policies of utilization review, treatment contracts, and managed care have further reduced hospital stays to "pit stops" for rapid stabilization. Psychotropic drug management, while controlling psychotic symptoms, has been insufficient in maintaining independent patient functioning. We see the failure of these policies in the tragic numbers of troubled persons living precariously from day to day in the streets. The expectation for families to assume the primary caregiving burden for patients over the chronic course of an illness, coupled with family dissatisfaction with traditional psychiatric approaches that blamed families and were unresponsive to their distress, have brought increased pressure from families themselves. Through advocacy groups such as the National Alliance for the Mentally Ill (NAMI), families have found their voice, articulating their needs for more supportive programs and community resources (Hatfield & Lefley, 1987).

Funding for family research, which has been almost exclusively problem-focused, should be redirected to identify and support the family resources needed to cope effectively with the difficult challenges of serious mental illnesses (National Institute of Mental Health, 1993). Research efforts should be conducted in partnership with families. Family advocacy groups such as NAMI might well become involved in such research, which would clearly benefit distressed families.

Collaborative Family Approaches

Research and practice developments with schizophrenia are informing family intervention with a range of serious and persistent mental illnesses. Success depends on mobilizing family and community resources through collaborative therapeutic relationships. Assessment and intervention are not aimed at searching for past causal factors, nor do they presume that an individual's disturbed behavior serves a function for the family. Family members are viewed as caring and vital resources for long-term adaptation in the community. As noted earlier for chronic illness in general, reducing stress and strengthening the supportive functioning of the family, along with improving the patient's functioning, are inseparable goals.

It is crucial for us as clinicians to explore and counter the stigmatizing experiences of families who have felt blamed for recurrent symptoms or failed treatment efforts. We must also not presume that current family distress is indicative of long-standing pathology or is the cause of an individual's symptoms. Much of the family distress evidenced at a hospitalization is fueled by the immediate crisis situation. A child, partner, or parent may have been suicidal, wandering the streets disoriented, or tormented by paranoid delusions. Recurrent episodes can devastate a family. The family may be coping as well as can be reasonably expected in the face of persistent challenges and depleted resources over time. Referral for family therapy should be disengaged from causal assumptions; rather, it should be based on the value of therapy in strengthening family resilience to manage the stressful challenges of living with persistent mental illness.

Combined treatment strategies have been found to be most effective with serious mental illnesses. Psychoeducational family therapy approaches combined with psychotropic medication have proved more effective than either intervention alone in preventing or delaying relapse in schizophrenia (Anderson et al., 1986; Goldstein & Kopeikin, 1981; Falloon, Boyd, & McGill, 1984; McFarlane, 1991). Long-term drug maintenance may be necessary to control the severity of symptoms and to prevent lengthy and repeated hospitalizations. The addition of patient involvement in a social skills group boosts social functioning and decreases social isolation.

Psychoeducational approaches provide information, management guidelines, and social support to family members in their role as caregivers over the course of the illness. The stress–diathesis model underlying these approaches is based on the assumption that a core biological vulnerability and environmental stresses interact negatively to produce disturbed thinking and behavior. The family is viewed as an indispensable ally in treatment. These approaches do much to correct the blaming causal attributions experienced by so many families of the mentally ill. A connecting phase establishes an alliance with families by attending in a noncritical manner to the family's needs and experiences, and to specific areas of stress in their lives. In the Anderson et al. (1986) model, a day-long survival skills workshop provides a group of families with information and management guidelines, followed by brief (2- to 3-month) family therapy focused on helping patients take concrete steps toward stable functioning in the community, and by long-term multifamily groups to sustain gains.

The basic principles of these psychoeducational approaches can be adapted to fit varied treatment settings and practice with a range of disorders. Brief, focused family consultation (Wynne et al., 1986) is similar in its responsiveness to the family members' stress as caregivers, and in the setting of concrete, realistic objectives in active collaboration with the family. Families that have been critical of more traditional treatment have responded positively to the development of these approaches.

HELPING FAMILIES LIVE WELL
WITH CHRONIC CONDITIONS: PRACTICE GUIDELINES

General Clinical Priorities

In the treatment of serious physical and mental conditions, it is vital to build family strengths, resources, and successful coping strategies. When common illness challenges are identified, and when problem-solving assistance is offered through predictably stressful periods over the long-term course, families are better able to plan how to handle stresses and to prevent or ameliorate future crises. Flexibility is needed in tailoring interventions and responding to different family members as needs arise. Clinical priorities should include the following:

1. Reducing the stressful impact of the illness on the family
2. Providing information about:

   • The illness/disability, treatment strategies, and likely course
   • Patient abilities, vulnerabilities, and potential
   • Importance of compliance with medication, treatment, or diet regimens, and (where applicable) with physical therapy/rehabilitation to reduce vulnerability and increase functioning
   • Expectable psychosocial challenges for the family

3. Offering practical guidelines through different phases of the illness for:

   • Ongoing stress reduction
   • Managing symptoms and complications of the condition
   • Problem solving and crisis prevention
   • Building strengths for optimal functioning and well-being
   • Respite and attention to other needs, family members, and life priorities

4. Providing links to services that can support the family's caregiving efforts and maintain patient functioning in the community, for example:

   • Home health care support
   • Day care, structured work programs, and social contact
   • Assisted living and group homes

Brief Therapies

Brief problem-solving family therapy, providing structured, focused interventions, is useful to many families challenged by a chronic illness. Improved functioning along with reduced stress and conflict can be achieved through pragmatic focus on concrete, realistic objectives that can be met over several months. Once a higher level of functioning has been reached, gains can be sustained and setbacks averted with monthly or periodic family therapy or multifamily group sessions.

We should be cautious not to assume (as some brief therapy approaches do) that the simple interruption of destructive patterns will enable families to find better solutions and ways of functioning on their own. Families confronting the demands of a serious and chronic illness are unsure whether they are doing too much or too little and how to navigate unfamiliar and challenging situations. Family members greatly value information, management guidelines, and help in setting realistic expectations. Perhaps the most neglected and important family issue is the need for respite—time out from illness and caregiving concerns for family members to meet their own and others' needs, replenish their energies, and revitalize their spirits.

Psychoeducational and Multifamily Group Approaches

The value of psychoeducational family approaches (based on the principles described above) has been shown in treatment studies of a range of serious mental and physical illnesses (Anderson et al., 1986; Gonzalez et al., 1989; Hatfield & Lefley, 1987; McFarlane, 1991). These family interventions have been found to prevent or delay relapse, to increase compliance with treatment regimens, to reduce family stress, and to improve both patient and family functioning. Multifamily therapy groups and self-help groups are especially useful for sustaining care and support over the long haul of a chronic illness. Professionally led multifamily groups, typically composed of four or more families or couples, focus on ways to manage situational stress, loss, and transition, while strengthening relationships and problem-solving abilities in the process. The group context provides a social support network and opportunities for family members to learn from one another's experiences, to gain perspective on their own crisis situation, and to reduce guilt and blame. The shared experience helps to reduce family isolation and stigma, especially with such illnesses as AIDS and schizophrenia.

Multifamily interventions may have a short-term or periodic structure, varying from a single day-long workshop (Falloon et al., 1984; Anderson et al., 1986) to weekly or monthly meetings. A psychoeducational multifamily workshop provides information about an illness, what to expect, and guidelines for coping and adaptation. Monthly meetings over a longer time span can sustain gains, avert crises and setbacks, and address new challenges, particularly in situations where ongoing or recurrent strain with chronic disorders is inevitable. They encourage families that may be isolated to establish support networks that extend well beyond the group sessions.

Crisis Intervention/Crisis Prevention

Crisis intervention should be available to families in times of acute distress, since most chronic disorders involve periodic exacerbation of symptoms. Therapists must be active and provide enough structure to help temporarily overwhelmed families to reorganize and gain control of threatening situations. Because individuals with mental impairment (e.g., major depression, schizophrenia, developmental disorders, or dementia) may lack motivation, use poor judgment, or fail to comply with medication, family collaboration is crucial to keep patients involved in treatment and to help families reduce stress to manageable proportions. Without such guidance, many patients and their families rebound from one crisis to the next; achieve few gains over time; and risk emotional exhaustion, serious conflict, and relationship cutoff.

Community-Based Sustaining Care

Families are our most valuable resources in treating serious and persistent illness. We must encourage collaboration, understand caregiving challenges, and support their best efforts. We can help family members find meaningful ways to contribute to the care of an impaired member, while also setting boundaries for their own well-being. Our clinical interventions can strengthen their resilience in coping with persistent stress and can deepen their bonds. Yet families cannot carry the burden alone.

Continuity of care and community-based management are critically important over the long-term course of serious illnesses. Because U.S. society lacks a coherent approach to caring for people with disabling chronic conditions, growing numbers live in deteriorating health and lack access to appropriate and affordable services (Walsh, 1998b). Families in poverty, especially minority families, are most vulnerable to environmental conditions that heighten the risk of serious illnesses, permanent disabilities, and early mortality, as well as caregiver strain. Diseases such as asthma, diabetes, high blood pressure, and heart disease are most prevalent among the poor. Without sustaining care and support for family caregiving, many individuals become isolated, their condition sadly deteriorated and their family ties frayed beyond repair.

We must re-vision chronic care, which at present is thought of narrowly in terms of medical services and nursing-home placement. A report commissioned by the Robert Wood Johnson Foundation (Institute for Health and Aging, 1996) takes a broader view to address chronic care challenges for the 21st century. The report envisions a system of care—a spectrum of integrated services, medical, personal, social, and rehabilitative—to assist people with chronic conditions in living fuller lives. Such a continuum of care is needed to ensure that persons receive the level and type of care appropriate to their condition and their changing needs over time, and to support independent living, optimal functioning, and well-being as long as possible.

Both family and community resilience can be nurtured if we, as helping professionals, reach out to persons with disabling conditions and their families, respect their dignity, and work to forge viable extended kin and social supports. In many cases, basic needs for human connection and productive functioning can be met through such programs as structured group living arrangements and sheltered workshops, tailored to the vulnerabilities and potential strengths of residents. The lesson to be drawn here is that our efforts to sustain resilience must be relationally based: We must shift from faulty expectations of self-reliance in *independent* living to programs that bolster functioning and spirit through *interdependent* living.

C·H·A·P·T·E·R 9

Strengthening Vulnerable Multicrisis Families

Many families, especially those in poor communities, are buffeted by frequent crises and persistent stresses that overwhelm their functioning. A family resilience approach is most needed and beneficial with families that have come to feel beaten down and defeated by repeated frustration and failure. This chapter offers a conceptual base and practice guidelines for strengthening highly vulnerable families—for supporting their best efforts to manage their stress-laden lives and overcome the odds of high-risk situations. In focusing on their potential, such families gain a sense of hope and confidence that they can rise above persistent adversity.

TOWARD A BETTER UNDERSTANDING OF HIGHLY VULNERABLE FAMILIES

Increasingly, in a range of practice settings and human service systems, we are seeing families that are chronically stressed by serious problems cutting across many dimensions of family life (Kaplan, 1986). More than one family member may be considered at risk, and two or more generations of a family may need assistance. Battered by internal and external pressures, such a family can become overloaded and destabilized. Couples are at high risk for conflict and breakup; single parents are depleted; and family members may suffer from ill health, serious emotional problems, substance abuse, violence, and sexual abuse. Recurrent crises and chronic distress carry over from year to year and from one generation to the next.

Historically, highly vulnerable families have been defined and categorized in terms of their deficits. The label of "severely dysfunctional family" reinforced the view that multiple problems are endemic to a pathological family type, seen as untreatable. Focus on the interior of the family and on faulty parenting contributed to blaming these families, without appreciating the precarious life conditions and overwhelming challenges that besiege them. Advocates of more recent strength-based approaches prefer such terms as "high-risk" and "multineed" families, as somewhat more positive than "multi-problem" families (Kaplan & Girard, 1994). Yet even these terms can carry such negative connotations as "too risky to live in (or work with)" and "excessively needy." Swadener and Lubeck (1995) prefer to think of children and families "at promise."

It is most important to see vulnerable families as being overloaded and undersupported; as having many past and ongoing challenges and unmet needs; and as being at high risk for future serious problems and breakdown. We need to view them not as "problem families," but as families struggling with many problems, which are largely beyond their control and often not of their own making. Crisis situations are often embedded in problems in the community and the larger society, which must be addressed. Crises may also be fueled by reactivation of past traumas, which need to be understood and integrated for greater resilience.

Family Challenges of Poverty and Discrimination

It is a cruel paradox that crisis may be the only constant in the lives of poor families. Because they live so close to the edge, each crisis—whether job loss, illness, or violence—threatens to plunge them into a financial and emotional abyss. Despite the recent upturn in the U.S. economy, the gap between the rich and the poor continues to widen. Poor families confront relentless stresses of unemployment, substandard housing, and inadequate nutrition and medical care. They are surrounded by neighborhood blight; crime, violence, and drugs undermine their efforts. Parents struggle to provide their children with the basic essentials of food, clothing, and shelter, and worry constantly about their safety. Life prospects are bleak, with limited education, job opportunities, and access to community resources. Temporary or part-time work without benefits makes it hard to break the cycle of poverty and despair. Such problems present mammoth challenges to even the healthiest families and the most seasoned therapists. In work with highly vulnerable families, the challenges may seem insurmountable.

Because of the combined psychological, social, and economic burdens of poverty and discrimination, poor minority children and families are even more at risk for multiple problems and crises due to forces beyond their control. Poor people are stereotyped and marginalized; people of color who are poor suffer doubly. The challenges for immigrant families are heightened still further by cultural differences and language barriers. Intertwined family and environmental stresses contribute to school difficulties for children and to high risks of school dropout, gang and criminal activity, and teen pregnancy— all of which worsen family strains.

Interventions to reduce family vulnerability are sure to fail if they do not address the environmental forces that pose an immediate threat to family survival. As Harry Aponte (1994) observes, the poor, tragically, have become our "canary in the mine"—their suffering a warning of the toxicity of our social environment. The plight of poor families challenges all of us to face this toxicity. We must direct our efforts to restore health not only to these families, but also to the community and the larger society.

Multigenerational Developmental Challenges

Family vulnerability is heightened by a pileup of stressors over time (Walsh, 1983). With a single, isolated crisis, a family must mobilize quickly but can then return to "normal" life. Multiple traumas, losses, and dislocations can overwhelm coping efforts. Recurrent crises repeatedly disrupt family life. The demands of many persistent challenges overload the system and drain resources. A family developmental perspective helps to contextualize family distress over the life course and across generations. Psychosocial demands change over time with the process of adaptation to each crisis and change, interacting with individual and family life cycle passages. To take just one example, the loss of a job or a marriage may also precipitate a change in residence, which triggers multiple dislocations for different family members, such as challenges for children in a new school with new peers in an unfamiliar neighborhood, as parents are preoccupied with redirecting their lives. Therapeutic response must be attuned to these varied and changing demands.

We can help families gain awareness of the heightened risk when stressors pile up, and of the need to reduce conflicting pressures or postpone further disruptive changes. When overstressed, family members are more likely to compound their difficulties through fatigue, diminished competence, or errors in judgment. For instance, within days of the fatal drug overdose of his oldest son, a father was pressing for the family to move far away. The therapist helped the parents to consider that a precipitous move would create more dislocation and might later be regretted, since it was motivated by the wish to take flight from the tragedy, without future direction, planning, or thoughts about the implications for the surviving children.

A systemic approach to family history, unlike a deterministic search for "the cause" or "the origin" of problems, yields understanding of the many intertwined influences on family processes over time and of the meaning and impact of stressful events for the family (McGoldrick & Walsh, 1983). For a multicrisis family, a genogram may be filled with incidents of trauma and loss. Research by Stanton (1977) and Coleman (1991) found that the self-destructive behavior of many addicts was connected to devastating losses of family members and friends, particularly through homicide, suicide, and abandonment. It is important for us as therapists to identify the most salient events in such a chain. We need not explore every incident in detail, but can attend to recurrent patterns and their legacies. It is crucial to understand how current symptoms and catastrophic fears are fueled by such experiences. For example, a man's fears of intimacy and loss are more understandable when we realize the many separations and abandonments he experienced in his family of origin. His drinking stirs his wife's catastrophic fears based in painful memories of her parents' marriage shattered by alcohol abuse. An understanding of where families are coming from can inform and empower members in the future directions they take.

STRENGTH-BASED, FAMILY-CENTERED SERVICES

Core Principles

Families presenting with multiple, complex, and severe problems, more than one symptom bearer, and recurrent crises make up a disproportionately large segment of human services caseloads. Tragically, they are most likely to be ill served and to fall between the cracks (Kaplan & Girard, 1994). Services have tended to be deficit-based, individually focused, fragmented, crisis-reactive, inaccessible, and defined by professionals for clients. There is an emerging consensus on a new model of family-centered services based on the following core principles (Ooms & Preister, 1988):

- Identifying and building on family strengths and resources that empower families
- Taking a family-centered approach to individual problems
- Providing flexible, holistic services
- Emphasizing prevention and early intervention
- Community-based and collaborative partnerships by professionals and families

From a Deficit-Based to a Resource-Based Model

Uri Bronfenbrenner (1979), a champion of families, has decried deficit-based public policies and services: To qualify for help, potential recipients must document their families' inadequacies many times over. Meager services are rationalized by preconceptions that vulnerable multicrisis families are hopelessly dysfunctional. Negative stereotypes of parents as destructive, hostile, and uncaring stigmatize overwhelmed families. Preconceptions of them as unreachable, unmotivated, and untreatable have darkened the horizons of our therapeutic work. The assumptions we make about families drive the questions we ask and our therapeutic expectations. Thick files of past problems and failed treatments create an adverse framework for any therapeutic contact. Too often professionals underestimate these families and their ability to understand and tackle their problems (Kaplan & Girard, 1994).

Yet these families often show remarkable strengths in the midst of adversity. Many are resilient in simply making it through each day in the face of unrelenting stress and hardship. Resourcefulness can be seen in the inventive ways they make the most of meager earnings. Most parents do care about their children and want a better life for them, although a myriad of difficulties may block their ability to act on these intentions. They often know what they need to change in their lives, if only we are able to value their input, listen well, and support their best efforts.

A resource-based perspective is especially useful in work with multicrisis families, empowering families to manage their stress-laden environments (Berg, 1997; Minuchin, Colapinto, & Minuchin, 1998) . When treatment is overly problem-focused, it grimly replicates the joyless experience of family life, where problems seem all-pervasive. Interventions that enhance positive interactions, support coping efforts, and build extrafamilial resources are more effective in reducing stress, enhancing pride and competence, and promoting more effective functioning.

From an Individually Based to a Family-Centered Approach

Human service systems, by and large, treat problems as individually based—for example, a teen's pregnancy or a youth's delinquency. With services compartmentalized and individuals categorized narrowly according to presenting symptoms, there is insufficient attention to the person as a whole or to the family and social context. Often agencies that in principle avow the importance of the family actually, in practice, only see the individual—or, at best, hold occasional sessions with a mother or primary caregiver. With very heavy caseloads and complicated family situations, workers may doubt whether there is any way to be helpful at all. When they lack training in effective family systems work, a failed experience may reinforce beliefs that multiproblem families are beyond repair and not worth investment.

One of my students, wanting to work with families during her field placement in the juvenile justice system, found that despite her agency's stated mission to work with incarcerated youths and their families, in practice no families were currently seen. Her supervisor explained that over the years agency staff had found it too difficult to try to get "such dysfunctional families motivated for treatment" and no longer "wasted their resources." Instead, they met individually with the youth offenders. Yet most youths return to live with their families on discharge—or run away from other placements to their families. Therefore, family involvement is essential to assist in making the transition back into the community, to support educational and job training pursuits, to reduce family stress, and to strengthen family functioning and support. Without work with families, these youths are highly vulnerable to being lured back into street gangs, which in their own ways offer an alternative to the family cohesion they yearn for. Amidst the destructive involvement with violence, crime, and drugs, gangs also offer youths the identity, leadership, loyalty, respect, mutual support, and protection that are so often lacking in their own families. When these elements are shored up in the family foundation, home can become an anchor for at-risk youths, strengthening their resilience.

Regardless of which member of a family seeks help or which agency is approached, we need to broaden the focus to the family network of relationships to explore potential contributions to solving problems. Maintaining a family focus doesn't always mean seeing the whole family together. It does involve holding a systemic view that recognizes the important connections of all family members, including those who are absent, such as previous foster parents; a parent who has died, is estranged, or is incarcerated; or members who simply refuse to participate in family meetings. A bedridden parent can receive tapes of sessions and can add comments to be played at the next session. Letters can be written to an absent father and discussed in therapy before being sent.

A family-centered approach is needed for service delivery across systems: child welfare, health care and mental health care, substance abuse treatment, and education. Family systems training is essential. Once we are able to view the family as an interlocking web of relationships and to identify the patterns that connect various members, their problems, and possible solutions, we can begin to make meaning of complicated situations and have a greater likelihood of success.

From Fragmented to Holistic Services

Social service systems often recreate and intensify family confusion in their disorganized way of handling problems. Many different workers and agencies are isolated and uncoordinated in their efforts, offering crisis-focused, individually oriented services in a piecemeal fashion. Too often, the needs and problems of children and families are divided into separate, rigid categories that fail to address interrelated problems and solutions. Persons are often sent from one agency to another in search of services. A family's initial frustration in dealing unsuccessfully with its problems may then be directed into anger at professionals and agencies, which makes matters worse.

Functional communication between agencies must be improved. Commonly, several agencies work sporadically with various family members; services are often duplicated or even conflict with one another. In the course of presentations to professionals in various communities, I've had the experience of hearing about a difficult case from a participant, only to have others, from other agencies, be startled to realize that they are working with other members of the same family. For example, in the Carver family, Tina, age 13, was seeing a school social worker for truancy and failing grades. Her brother Eddie, 14, was in counseling in a juvenile detention center after arrest for petty theft. Mrs. Carver was seeing a community mental health worker for recurrent depression. Mr. Carver was functioning marginally with an untreated drinking problem. His mother, living in the home, required extensive medical attention for chronic lupus, a painful, debilitating disorder.

As Ooms and Preister (1988) have remarked, given the barriers and problems that these families face, the miracle is that some family members do become adept at negotiating these system mazes to improve their lives. For effective services, a broad, comprehensive approach is required, viewing family members and needs as interrelated, requiring coordinated and integrated services and a pooling of resources. Services must be viewed holistically, tailored to each family's challenges, and provided in the context of community, ethnic, and religious affiliations.

From Crisis-Reactive to Prevention-Oriented Services

Community mental health services often operate on the triage principle, helping the "walking wounded," who have the best chances of recovery. Too often families with massive problems remain unattended to (Kaplan & Girard, 1994). Brief interventions or "magic bullet" approaches cannot address more entrenched, pervasive problems. A limited focus may not allow for the relationship building and intensive restructuring of family life that are needed for a family to consolidate and sustain gains. Complex family situations cannot and should not be oversimplified to meet managed care or agency requirements. For instance, an eight-session authorization commonly received may be used up in 2–3 weeks for adequate response to serious crises. Flexibility and responsiveness over time are required to attend to persistent problems and prevent future crises.

Regrettably, prevention has received little funding, although it is far more costly to treat a crisis after it occurs. As Kaplan and Girard (1994) note,

> Our shame is that we pay scant attention to children and their families and spend little money on them until it is absolutely necessary. To qualify for help, an individual or family is categorized, assigned a pathological label, and placed under the auspices of a federal or state agency. This experience is dehumanizing and stigmatizing; worse, the help often comes too late. As a society, we must undergo a philosophical shift. (p. 15)

By putting energy into families "up front," we increase their coping ability and prevent problem escalation and chronicity (Harris, 1996).

Community-Based Partnership

Services must be accessible and should be defined and led by the local community. Families and human service providers should work as partners in a collaborative problem-solving effort, with the family as the senior partner in defining its own needs, goals, support, and changes. Services should support and supplement family functioning rather than substitute for it.

Programs based on this family-oriented philosophy are increasingly being developed around the United States (see below). Such programs seek to create strength-focused family partnerships through home-based and neighborhood services and through a relational, multisystemic approach to strengthening children and their families. They combine approaches to alleviate individual symptoms (e.g., a child's school problems and a mother's depression) with family and larger systems interventions. Efforts are made in such programs to create a strong sense of community, and to overcome fear and mistrust through informal contact, program newsletters, and activities such as family and staff potluck dinners. The need to work flexibly in partnership with schools and communities is emphasized, as is the need to foster consumer (family) participation in setting priorities and seeking solutions. Head Start is a good example of a program designed to empower families (Kaplan & Girard, 1994). Family participation is encouraged in all aspects of the program. Parents are active collaborators in program decision making; they participate in activities as volunteers, observers, and paid support staff. Working closely with professional staff to learn how to help their own children, many parents have dramatically improved their own lives.

The Movement for Family-Based Services

In many parts of the country, there is a growing movement toward neighborhood- and home-based, family-centered services, assisted by organizations attempting to unify the effort, such as the National Association of Family-Based Services (Kaplan, 1986). Family-centered programs are founded on the belief that families are our best resource. Family support and preservation programs maintain that the best place for children is with their families as long as their safety is not compromised. Advocates urge social services to shift from the premise of replacing families to supporting and strengthening them. When placement is necessary, it must be reconceptualized as family-centered, so that residential and foster care are conceived in ways that support rather than sever family ties.

Family Support Programs: Prevention and Early Intervention

The family support movement has concentrated on prevention and early intervention (Children's Defense Fund, 1992; Dunst, 1995; Dunst, Trivette, & Deal, 1988; Family Resource Coalition, 1996; Harris, 1996; Kagan & Weissbourd, 1994). The ideal model is based on local *family resource centers* that are readily accessible and provide a range of information and services to support and strengthen families. Professionals and neighborhood paraprofessionals assist families with life cycle transitions. Most focus on providing education in parenting and support in raising young children, particularly for single teen mothers. They also link families with formal and informal services and support networks. Family support programs work with communities, school systems, hospitals, and corporations to pool efforts. They operate at the grassroots level and are consumer-oriented, neighborhood-based, and voluntary.

Family Preservation Programs

Despite the broad array of family-based models, all family preservation programs have a dual commitment: to protect children and to strengthen families. The aim, instead of child placement, is family empowerment. In traditional child welfare services, a worker with an overflowing caseload is put in the untenable position of responsibility for every child's safety. In a family preservation approach, the worker and family identify mutual areas of concern; there is a balance of accountability for any future neglect or abuse; and many family members are actively involved in meeting safety needs. Highly trained staff with low caseloads work with families in their homes to assess risks, reduce stress, and strengthen leadership, nurturance, and protection (Kaplan, 1986). Child safety is a chief concern. Not all families are candidates for family preservation; placement is necessary when children are at high risk of serious neglect or of physical or sexual abuse, and when families prove to be unworkable. Wherever possible, efforts are made for family reunification.

Many programs are modeled after the Homebuilders. Families are referred when a child is at imminent risk of out-of-home placement. Program goals are to prevent such placement through immediate home-based intervention to defuse the crisis, stabilize the family, and teach new problem-solving skills to avoid future crises. Intervention is intensive over 4–6 weeks: Therapists spend as much time as necessary with families and are on 24-hour call, often putting a year's worth of outpatient services into a month. Of note, therapists work with only two families at a time, spending up to 20 hours a week with each. Additional support is available as needed (Kaplan & Girard, 1994).

Future Directions

The field of family-based services includes a range of programs from prevention to treatment, but these efforts have generally not been well integrated. Family support programs, emphasizing early intervention, typically work with families over more than a year, unlike many family preservation programs, which are crisis-focused and offer brief, intensive treatment. There is tremendous potential for offering a continuum of services, from family support and psychoeducation through more intensive intervention and preservation programs. The National Resource Center for Family Support Programs and the National Association of Family-Based Services are encouraging such service integration.

A developmental, systemic perspective would greatly strengthen program efforts. Family support programs, because of their preventive focus and foundational linkages with the field of child development, have tended to focus on early mother–child relationships; only more recently have they expanded to involve the family caregiving network. A family life cycle orientation could guide program development from pregnancy and birth on through adolescence to later life, old age, and dying. Services could include preventive approaches, such as family life education, as well as more intensive help negotiating stressful crises and transitions. Families could use services on and off across the life cycle, as fitting their needs and circumstances.

The movement for family-based services has arisen separately from developments in the field of family therapy, with little cross-fertilization. Family therapists know little about the family support and preservation programs, and workers in those programs often lack training in systemic assessment and family intervention skills. Family support programs have been wary of family therapy from their outset, based largely on misperceptions that all family therapy, like traditional "treatment" models of psychotherapy, is deficit-focused and oriented to middle-class private-practice settings. From the earliest years of family therapy, such pioneers as Salvador Minuchin and his colleagues (Minuchin, Montalvo, Guerney, Rosman, & Schumer, 1967) developed innovative approaches to strengthen poor inner-city families. Ross Speck and Carolyn Attneave (1973) developed a network therapy approach for assisting families in crisis, assembling and activating a caring social network—kin, friends, and neighbors—to resolve overwhelming problems, rekindle hope, and build community connectedness. With the broader shift to strength-based collaborative approaches throughout the field of family therapy over the past 15 years, along with a growing commitment to multiple-level interventions to strengthen and support the most vulnerable families, the time has come for family therapists and family support advocates to join forces and to share our knowledge and experience. Greater collaboration will enable us all to be most effective in supporting families' efforts to strengthen their resilience.

ASSESSMENT AND INTERVENTION PRIORITIES

A family resilience approach is based on the conviction that even the most distressed families want to be healthy and have the potential for change and growth. That potential may be blocked by depleted resources or self-defeating survival strategies. Family members may not see other options in their situation. A strength-based reorientation begins in the first contacts with a family.

Information Gathering: Assessing Family Stress, Vulnerabilities, Strengths, and Potential

In my experience, many families are initially put off by past experience with judgmental, deficit-based evaluation. They may assume that even neutral questions seek causal, blame-placing explanations. It is important for us as helping professionals to be explicit about our intentions in gathering information: to understand family stresses, their meaning, and their impact, as well as family objectives and pathways for moving forward. We need to assess families within a positive framework, searching for resources as well as vulnerabilities and constraints, all in relation to the challenges they face.

Most often, a request or referral for help centers on an immediate crisis focused on one family member, such as a child's behavior problems. However, on first contact with the family, a number of problems often become evident and other family members may be in great pain. When we see that a son's vandalism, a father's disappearance, and a mother's depression are all connected, it's easier to focus on common concerns and aims. Some problems, such as child misbehavior, may be reactive to a crisis event. When the presenting problem is seen as a helpful warning signal, like the alarm of a smoke detector, it can alert the family to the need to attend to the crisis situation. Pulling together to tackle pressing concerns helps to calm down the entire system and instill hope that other problems can be mastered.

Information gathering lays the groundwork for therapist–family collaboration in identifying strengths and prioritizing areas of concern. What are all the significant family connections? In dealing with a crisis, how does the family attempt to buffer stresses? What patterns of interaction escalate anxiety and conflict, increasing vulnerability and risk of serious dysfunction? Which members can be instrumental in strengthening the family? What hidden resources might be drawn upon to manage stresses and overcome barriers to success? How can change in the core family unit have a positive ripple effect for all members? It can be very hard to gather information when a family is in perpetual crisis and members' attention is scattered. Rather than waiting for things to calm down, it's better to make some time in early sessions in order to understand underlying stresses and identify patterns that connect members' distress.

Genograms (McGoldrick & Gerson, 1985) are especially useful in diagramming very complex family systems—for instance, families where each child may have had a different father, or foster care has been involved. A therapist might draw a genogram interactively with a family, using Magic Markers and large sheets of paper. Children are often surprised and delighted to see how people are connected and where each one fits in the network of relationships. Seeing everyone on the same page is especially meaningful for fragmented families that have experienced many losses, cutoffs, and reconfigurations. Seeing the connections can also help a therapist to keep from getting overwhelmed, in the same way it helps a family.

Drawing a family timeline fosters a developmental perspective, as family members recall key nodal events and their disruptive impact. What organizational shifts occurred at what times, and how did a family recalibrate itself in the aftermath of traumatic events? In a multicrisis family, a timeline helps to order the jumble of stressful events and changes in family life over the years. For instance, family members can better comprehend a parent's withdrawal into alcohol abuse when this is placed in the context of a pileup of painful losses. Both the genogram and the timeline are valuable visual and concrete tools for assembling many disconnected fragments of experience into a fuller, more coherent family narrative.

When family life has been saturated with problems, it's essential that genograms and timelines also identify particular relationships and periods of time that offered islands of calm, connection, and hope in the midst of the turbulence. These positive experiences, often invisible when assessment and therapy are problem-focused, offer models and resources to be drawn upon and enlarged. A woman abused by her father may have had a very positive relationship with a grandfather or uncle, for example. Even if that person is no longer alive or available, identifying the qualities in the relationship can provide a template in forming new, healthier relationships.

Diagnostic assessment can be useful in identifying serious mental illness, determining the risk for destructive behavior, and evaluating the need for psychotropic medication. However, labels such as "borderline personality disorder," which locate the problem in a person's character structure, reinforce a sense of permanent damage and deficiency. It's more helpful and hopeful to identify behavioral/interactional patterns that can be changed. We should also be careful not to label a family by its members' problems (e.g., "an alcoholic family"). In a strength-based approach, therapists should put nothing in a case report that we would not feel comfortable sharing with family members (Kaplan & Girard, 1994). Encouraging clients to read and offer input in letters to agencies or the court respects them as active partners in therapy.

Key Family Resilience Processes: A Framework for Assessment and Intervention

The three-domain framework of key family resilience processes, presented in Chapters 3–5, was developed over many years training therapists for family work with many serious and persistent problems. It facilitated my own shift from labeling families as "severely dysfunctional" (Walsh & Olson, 1989) to identifying particular vulnerabilities and resources that can be strengthened. When both families and clinicians are flooded by a sea of confusion in the midst of crisis and chaos, the framework serves as a map to help us focus attention and sort out important information to guide intervention. I have found it especially valuable in keeping mindful to search for resources when a myriad of problems monopolizes attention. As information emerges helter- skelter in the course of interviews, it can then be mapped in a way that helps us to keep systemic and to identify key elements for intervention focus to strengthen family functioning.

Belief Systems

The experience of many recurrent crises can lead families to carry the foreboding belief that something bad is bound to happen. This expectation is highly disruptive, generating collective anxiety and skewing perceptions of ongoing experience and future possibilities. Overwhelmed by their predicament, family members may become resigned. Seeing no alternatives or solutions, they become pessimistic and defeated, which further erodes their self-esteem. All-or-none thinking is common, with difficulty in seeing shades of grey between extremes (e.g., winning vs. losing, good child vs. bad child, all-controlling vs. helpless).

Catastrophic fears and destructive behavior patterns are often grounded in multiple traumas and losses that permeate family history. With a brother in prison and a son recently killed in a drive-by shooting, one mother sadly observed, "You never know who will be with us or lost tomorrow." Many parents and children try to numb the recurrent pain, terror, and helplessness with alcohol or drugs, or by shutting off emotions and concern about others or themselves.

The continuities of past, present, and future in life cycle passages may become distorted. Past traumas may be alive in the present, reactivated by new experiences or through constant preoccupation, as if painful events of long ago happened only yesterday. In some cases, patterns of abuse, neglect, or abandonment may be repeated in current relationships, as if history is destined to repeat itself. In other cases, memories may be totally cut off (e.g., a wife may have no memory of her alcoholic father, who disappeared when she was 8). Generally, the more traumatic the experience, the more likely it is to be dissociated, with repercussions for all other relationships. It's important to notice connections that aren't made by the family, such as a son's drug overdose on the anniversary of his brother's drive-by murder.

Social scientist Linda Burton (1990), who has conducted extensive research on poor inner-city families, has found that the grim statistics of their life chances have fostered a foreshortened sense of the life cycle. With such a high proportion of young males killed through violence, lost to drugs, or in prison, youths have lost a sense of future, which contributes to a here-and-now focus and to the high rate of teen pregnancy. Men are lucky if they survive into adulthood; women are often grandmothers by their early 30s.

When families are buffeted by severe and persistent adverse conditions that are largely beyond their personal control, such as chronic poverty and racism, we need to help them counter a pervasive sense of helplessness and hopelessness. It is important not to give up on families that seem at first to resist our help. Listening to family members' prior experiences with helping professionals can shed light on their pessimism and mistrust: their many disappointments have led them to expect to fail (and to expect us to let them down). By conveying our belief in families' potential, we can help families to believe in themselves, and can thus foster pride, courage, perseverance, and hope for the future.

Families need not only to solve problems, but also to reach for purpose in life. By helping family members tap sources in family history, culture, and spirituality, we can help them connect with traditions, rituals, beliefs, and common meanings and goals of life. To the extent that religion plays a part in their lives, it can offer a vision beyond themselves to help them face life challenges. Indeed, spiritual resources can be a lifeline for family members, offering solace and faith in a better day while inspiring them with courage to do their best to overcome barriers to success. As families connect with their values, heritage, and dreams for the future, solutions to problems then emerge as their pride and dignity are enhanced.

Harry Aponte's (1994) work with poor minority inner-city families led him to recognize that they suffer a poverty of despair that robs them of spirit—of meaning, purpose, and hope. A pervasive sense of injustice, helplessness, and rage is rooted in being denied access to opportunity, power, and privilege in society. Aponte urges us as therapists not to limit our work to simplistic pragmatic solutions, or to neglect spiritual hunger by assuming that the poor are too downtrodden to care about meaning and purpose. In the midst of despair, there still survives a spirit of love, courage, and hope in poor communities, although it is often muted. Aponte believes that therapists can make a difference if we recognize the power of that spirit. In addition to more jobs, better schooling, and health care, we must work to cultivate a diversity of cultural values, social structures, and spiritual practices to foster meaning and purpose.

Belief in the sustaining power of a relationship can fortify individuals through adversity even when they are cut off from direct contact (e.g., during forced separation). In her novel *The Color Purple*, Alice Walker (1983) tells the life story of Celie, an African American woman who grew up in crushing poverty in the South, was sexually abused by her father, and then suffered chronic maltreatment by her husband. Throughout life's ordeals, Celie drew on her relationship with her sister for resilience. Although they were separated at adolescence, their nourishing connection was sustained over the years in imagination and in letters they were uncertain were ever received. They carried on daily conversations with each other in their heads. The meaning of their relationship was so profound that they continued to write letters over the years, despite the fact that none reached the other (Celie's husband secretly hid the letters) until they were discovered late in her life.

Organizational Patterns

Most highly distressed families seen in clinical practice and social service agencies are single-parent and reconstituted families. We must keep in mind that families of varied forms can function well. Still, in families with many problems and scarce resources, the losses and dislocations accompanying each change in family status and household membership can compound the confusion and difficulties in restabilizing and reorganizing. When pent-up pressures become intolerable, a parent may threaten to leave, or may in fact run off. When a father moves in and out with repeated separations and reunions, or when several boyfriends in succession live with a single mother and each one fathers a child, the household organization, roles, patterns of interaction, and relationship expectations can become highly confused.

It is important to ask about all men who have played a part in the lives of a mother and her children. If children have different fathers, and some have seemingly dropped out of the picture, it's important to ask specifically about the amount and dependability of contact and financial support. A mother may view a father as unreliable and never around, but a child may have some informal contact (e.g., at a grandmother's house). A therapeutic priority is to decrease the instability and to increase the reliability of contact and commitments to children wherever possible. If constraining barriers can be surmounted, I believe it is never too late for absent parents to become involved in supporting their children's growth and success.

Family Disorganization: Building Structure, Stability, and Leadership. Families reeling from the impact of multiple crises are likely to become disorganized. This underorganized pattern (Aponte, 1994) should be seen not as a preferred style or family type, but rather as the consequence of unremitting stress over time, wearing down a family's ability to function well. When families face daily environmental stresses, such as high crime, drugs, poor housing, health problems, and financial hardship, they must juggle their depleted resources to meet basic needs. Roles become poorly integrated, and family members have difficulty collaborating to structure daily life and to resolve the problems that accumulate. Frustration often boils over into disruptive behavior, extreme overreactions, and intense conflict, further splintering the family. A lack of security and consistency ensues, as family members may move in and out of households and go their separate ways. Yet amid this chaos is a deep longing for calm, security, and stability.

An all-or-none paradigm is evident in shifts between extreme rigidity and disorder. Having experienced so much upheaval, some families may become inflexible, fearing runaway change. An unspoken rule might be "Don't rock the boat," because the threat of "capsizing" again is so great. When families in crisis are overwhelmed and disorganized, the therapeutic setting must provide a safe haven and solid structure. The fear of lives flying out of control is a common source of "resistance" to change in therapy. Rather than stirring up anxiety, we need to provide reassuring calm and stability. Pushing too quickly for change may fuel fears of runaway change and loss of control. It's extremely important to work toward large changes in small, incremental steps that are carefully grounded. Although we cannot control our clients' lives (nor should we), we need to interrupt runaway processes or destructive interactional spirals to help families feel in control of the therapeutic process.

Family leadership, worn down by stress, is commonly erratic and ineffective. Limit setting and discipline are approached inconsistently or in an all-or-none fashion, without follow-through until a parent reaches a boiling point and explodes violently or threatens to send a misbehaving child away. A single parent may be unsure of how to provide both nurturance and discipline when these roles were formerly split in a two-parent family. Framing discipline as setting caring limits can be very helpful.

In many families, parents abdicate their position of authority. A mother and daughter may act like sisters; a father may avoid responsibility, acting like one of the kids. A child may be drawn into a parentified position to fill the void. For example, 14-year-old Leeza attended school irregularly, falling hopelessly behind in her work. Her parents often drank to excess in the evening; heated conflict led to her father's battering of her mother. He would then leave for several days, and her mother would stay in bed with the shades drawn, leaving Leeza to get her younger siblings off to school, clean the apartment, and take care of all household responsibilities.

Skews of overfunctioning–underfunctioning parents or siblings need to be rebalanced. It's important to put parents in charge and to support them in setting rules and limits. Older children can share responsibilities as long as parents do not abdicate leadership. Concrete guidelines, such as posting a chart of weekly chores and allocating them fairly among family members, can help to alleviate skews and to reinforce structure and follow-through. Weekly allowances or treats can reward children's efforts and build a sense of both personal autonomy and responsibility.

Assessing whether overwhelmed families are motivated poses the wrong question; rather, we need to ask how we can help them keep their heads above water to take on efforts for change. We should also be careful not to pile more responsibility on already overloaded parents. Inability to follow through reinforces their sense of deficiency and failure. It's important to acknowledge how difficult their position is. After just an hour of pandemonium in a session, or hearing about the myriad of problems they are facing, we can use our own overwhelmed reactions to identify with their predicament and applaud them for hanging in there all week."

A discouraged parent may seek help with several unruly children. If the therapist simply takes over, the parent's sense of incompetence is reinforced. We can empower parents by joining forces with them and backing them up to bolster their authority and leadership. We may need to take charge initially, but we should always model with the aim of increasing parents' competence and confidence to take over leadership themselves.

Family Fragmentation: Building Connection and Collaboration. Many overwhelmed families become fragmented, with members losing interest in one another and being left to fend for themselves. There is little time together; family members rarely share mealtime or enjoy pleasurable contact. Disengaged family patterns are seen commonly in abuse and neglect, with children showing serious conduct disorder. A depleted parent may show little concern about children's whereabouts and may be unaware of their drug or alcohol use. If children's feelings and perceptions are repeatedly ignored or rejected, they learn not to trust, to care about others, or even to feel. Families often become socially isolated and alienated, lacking positive supports. Parents may become so depleted that they take flight from responsibility, staying out all night or abusing alcohol or drugs themselves. Violence or threats of abandonment may come out of a sense of desperation when parents snap. It's important in such cases to help reduce the pileup of stress and frustration, to build supportive connections, and to structure in respite so that parents can replenish their energies.

Family Enmeshment: Strengthening Boundaries and Differentiation. In some families, members become enmeshed, with individual differences unacknowledged. As boundaries blur, thoughts, feelings, and identities are fused or distorted. Parents may confuse their own needs with those of their children. Inconsistent and unclear boundaries (common in borderline and eating disorders) can lead to intrusion and lack of privacy or violation in sexual abuse. Parents draw children into their marital affairs. Jenny, age 17, was hospitalized for self-destructive behavior after carving small crosses in her arms. Family assessment revealed her overinvolvement in her parents' intense marital conflict. When asked how it made her feel, she replied, "Caught in the crossfire."

All-or-none relationship patterns often lead family members to take flight from stifling overinvolvement by cutting off all contact. Family relationships may oscillate between pseudoautonomous distancing and falling back into overinvolvement and helpless dependence—a pattern particularly common in drug and alcohol abuse. When one child is embroiled in parental needs and conflicts, siblings may disengage themselves as a survival strategy. Jenny's brother "took the geographical cure" (as he put it)—abruptly leaving home, driving 500 miles to the north woods of Wisconsin, and living in a cabin off a dirt road with no telephone. When he returned, curious to "check out" the family therapy, he sat quietly through a session with a bemused smile. Later he confessed to me that he had been high on drugs, in order to keep "a safe distance." Intense, ambivalent attachments and loyalties cannot simply be resolved by physical separation. Family therapy, combined with individual work, helps to untangle members and to help them move together gradually toward more autonomy. Especially in cases where a child has been pulled in as an emotional mate or caregiver, it's crucial to strengthen generational boundaries and to work on marital issues.

Some families have become so disorganized, fragmented, and/or enmeshed that family life is chaotic and frighteningly out of control, as in the following case:

The Washingtons were referred for family therapy after two brothers, aged 14 and 15, were arrested for vandalism. Most recently, they had set their mother's bed on fire. It was learned that the mother had given her bedroom to her oldest son, Mark, 17, and appointed him "man of the house," after throwing the father out because of recurrent drunkenness and assaultive behavior. The mother's family-of-origin experience was also complicated by alcohol abuse, mental instability, and violence. Her sister had in fact "lost all control" and beaten her small child to death.

The therapist was understandably overwhelmed by the history and unsure of where to begin. It was important to identify and alter interactional patterns that reinforced vulnerability. When clear structure is lacking, things get out of control; anything can happen, from violence and murder to possible incest. Although the household was calmer and safer from violence without the father, the mother, who had relied on his "law and order" authority, felt unsure of her ability to be in charge. Furthermore, she held down a demanding job and was exhausted when she got home. Their apartment was in disarray. The mother slept on the sofa, while the 12-year-old sister was sleeping in the same room with her two "wild" brothers. Their living structure reflected and reinforced their sense of chaos.

It was crucial to shore up family stability, leadership, and boundaries. The therapist framed these objectives normatively, affirming the mother's position as head of the household and the healthy needs of all family members. It was suggested that the mother, as a hard-working single parent with "two shifts" of job and family demands, deserved to reclaim her own room, where she could close the door for respite. A separate space for the daughter was recommended, developmentally framed as a teenage girl's need for privacy. The family members were encouraged to look around their apartment and envision new ways of organizing it. At the next session, they sketched a floor plan and cut out pieces of paper to represent the furniture to be moved around. While they had fun doing this, it also gave them a sense of control in planning their living space. That week the daughter created a place for herself, clearing out a small room filled with junk. The eldest son moved back in with his brothers, helping to calm them down. Now that the family members were actively engaged in collaboration, they carried their tasks a step further: The kids all pitched in to fix up their own personal spaces with photos, posters, and the like. We can encourage families such as this one to make changes by facilitating their own creative solutions.

Communication Processes

Clarity. Families function best with communication clarity. Family vulnerability is heightened by pervasive unclarity: Everyone may talk at once, go off on different tangents, and not listen to others. Parents are inconsistent in words and deeds. Messages are distorted, and members think they can read minds, confusing one another's thoughts and feelings. Important issues remain murky (e.g., "Are Dad and Mom splitting up? What's going to happen to us?") when messages are vague or anxiety-producing topics are avoided.

Because family members have experienced so much confusion, inconsistency, and disappointment, it is crucial for us as therapists to be clear and consistent, especially in defining our relationship: what our role and commitment are to all family members, what they can expect of us, and what we will expect of them. It's important to keep sessions on a regular, predictable schedule and to make every effort to follow through on expectations. If we find we can't, acknowledge it and explain forthrightly what happened, owning responsibility.

Setting communication rules helps to bring order and focus. When family members talk over one another and constantly interrupt or shift their attention, a turn-taking rule in sessions is needed: "Only one person talks at a time. That way, when it's your turn to talk, everyone will be able to listen to you." Framing the rule in terms of the positive benefit to each member is more effective than issuing a critical warning not to interrupt others. A toy microphone might be passed around, like the "talking stick" used in tribal meetings; the person holding the microphone can talk while others listen.

Open Emotional Expression. A pileup of tensions in a family heightens emotional reactivity. Repeated negative interactions corrode family members' feelings and block mutual understanding. Members stop listening and just counterattack or withdraw. As therapists, we must be active and firm to interrupt cycles of blame, shouting, or cursing, and to help family members to handle frustration, disappointment, and anger in more constructive and respectful ways. When sensitive issues can be discussed more calmly, anxieties lessen and problems are tackled more effectively. Often blaming and scapegoating are fueled by self-blame, shame, and guilt, which should be explored. It is crucial to distinguish feelings from actions: Intense anger may be understandable, but acting on feelings in destructive ways is not acceptable. When harmful actions are denied or blamed on others, we must help members take responsibility for their own behavior, even when they feel provoked.

With persistent stress, a family may burn out, emotionally exhausted from the onslaught. Some members may try to maintain control and lower anxiety by prohibiting expression of thoughts and feelings that might be upsetting or endanger the family unit. They may avoid conflict out of catastrophic fears that it will escalate out of control into violence or abandonment, as in past experience. Yet when stresses mount and needs go unmet, there is a greater risk of periodic explosions: Conflict may be sealed over until it can be contained no longer and erupts like a volcano (again, in an all-or-none pattern). It's essential to understand catastrophic fears and to help family members express differences and hurts in ways that foster understanding and healing.

It is also important to help family members own and tolerate a range of feelings, especially in response to trauma and loss, while helping them to modulate the intensity of emotions. It's essential to set ground rules, so that family members feel safe to express concerns in sessions without fear of getting clobbered when they get home. Moreover, if emotions are too strong, they may remember little else that happened in a session or may carry away distorted perceptions. As therapists interrupt destructive interaction, members experience safe limits if they start to lose control. We need to teach family members ways to buffer conflict and reduce its intensity. We can help them notice signs of mounting tensions and interrupt their part in cycles before these spiral out of control. We may note how sensitive an issue is and encourage them to talk calmly about it, or have them take time out until they can do so. We can underscore valid points on each side and acknowledge concerns of all members. We might interrupt an intense interaction to explore how other relationships are affected. We can ask a father how conflict with his son is reminiscent of interactions he had with his own father. We can keep the focus on an issue and add other dimensions to it, while defusing tensions.

When the interaction in a session is volatile, it is crucial to track sessions to allow time at the end to process and calm an upsetting exchange, and to bring feelings under control in a cooling-down time. This gives the family members the experience of being able to open up a sensitive issue and yet contain it; the result is a greater sense of control over runaway processes. Often members bring up a highly charged issue just before the end of a session. It's important to acknowledge the importance or sensitive nature of the issue when discussion must wait until the next session, when there will be sufficient time to give it the attention it warrants. Often there is the catastrophic fear that Pandora's box has been opened and that feelings will fly wildly out of control. The tremendous anxiety generated can lead to destructive behavior. A dangerous situation, such as a threat of abuse or suicide, demands immediate attention.

In problem-saturated families, members can become so caught up in a quagmire of crisis and despair that they have no enjoyable time together. Encouraging pleasurable interaction is especially important in sessions and in tasks. For example, I might ask an estranged noncustodial father to plan with his son an activity they both enjoy, for a specific time in the coming week. I may need to nudge the conversation along from the father's hesitance ("I don't know what he'd like; he never seems interested in anything I suggest") or the child's self-protective indifference, and to actively encourage a dialogue that results in clear, concrete agreement on a plan, with approval of the custodial mother. I may also need to work with the mother on lingering anger at her ex-husband, to facilitate change that will benefit their children and ultimately the mother herself as well.

Collaborative Problem Solving. Action-oriented, concrete problem-solving approaches work best with overloaded families. Clear, reachable objectives should be defined, with stepwise progression to greater functioning. Families are likely to experience repeated failure if they hold vague, unrealistic expectations without taking steps to build a solid base. Problem solving should address the most pressing needs of the family, with a focus on the immediate future. A first priority may be addressing a family's concrete needs, such as adequate housing, day care, or job training. Again, small, manageable tasks should be tackled first; this fosters hope, allows family members to achieve success, and alters their expectations of failure from past experience. Each success builds more confidence in the ability to solve other, more complicated problems. It also builds trust in the therapeutic relationship and in family teamwork. Tasks should be designed to reduce stress and to strengthen family structure and interactions.

Therapists, like families themselves, can become flooded by the many problems the families are struggling with. We need to help family members apply triage to multiple problems, prioritize and focus their attention, and consider the timing in dealing most effectively with an issue. We can help families to anticipate setbacks or the upheaval if a new crisis hits, so that they are prepared and not discouraged. It's also valuable to help members realize that we are all human, that "stuff happens" and can interfere with plans, and that we can rebound. As noted throughout this book, a basic premise of resilience is that failure is not falling down, but staying down.

From Problems to Possibilities. From a family resilience perspective, it is not enough to reduce current stress and conflict; it is crucial to enhance families' problem-solving skills and their ability to buffer future stresses. The focus extends from solving presenting problems to preventing future ones. For example, we can ask family members how they might prepare for a threatened crisis or avert it altogether. We might also have them imagine the possibility that *no* crisis will occur over the coming week. What would it take for that to happen, and how could they celebrate? We want to encourage them to anticipate not only how things can go wrong, but how they can help them go right.

When family members are struggling to keep afloat, therapy, like learning to swim, empowers them by helping them develop their own resources. We therapists must sincerely communicate conviction in families' potential. Possibilities are generated as dilemmas are framed from several perspectives that expand rather than limit options, and as members gain new competence and confidence. It's easier to increase skills than to stop negative behavior. For instance, instead of trying to get a father to stop yelling, it's more effective to help him learn more caring ways to get his message across. Mastering the art of the possible means that we have to help families refocus from what cannot be changed—the damage that has been done—to their capacity to right themselves and move forward, as in the following case:

Crystal, age 14, was referred for individual therapy following her second attempt to run away from home. It was learned that she had been sexually abused by her grandfather when she was younger, and just recently by her mother's boyfriend, Rick. Her mother had ended this relationship after the incident, but Crystal angrily blamed her for not having protected her over the years. Her therapist, wishing to be supportive, joined in faulting the mother, only to find that after the session Crystal took a handful of pills in a suicide attempt.

Family therapy was begun, focusing on drawing out family resources to handle the current crisis. The mother was genuinely remorseful for not having been aware of any of the abuse or more tuned in to Crystal's distress. The therapist acknowledged the pain and regret, suggesting that perhaps they could learn from those experiences to approach this crisis in a new way. She credited the mother for ending her relationship with Rick, and thus demonstrating that Crystal's well-being came first. They focused on what might be done next, brainstorming about possible options. Crystal wanted to have Rick prosecuted. Her mother agreed to support her in pressing charges. The therapist enlisted Crystal's two older brothers to support Crystal and their mother through the ordeal of the legal maze and the trial ahead.

Over the next 3 months, the therapist tracked and commended the family's progress in doggedly pursuing the case. She supported the mother in remaining firm when Rick tried to get her to back down. The family members experienced a new solidarity in taking on this challenge and in their ultimate success at winning a conviction. Crystal threw her arms around her mother in the last family session, and thanked her mother and brothers: "You really came through for me this time. I feel like we're all really family for the first time."

Families are empowered when they gain access to their power. While acknowledging trauma and suffering that has occurred, we can put our weight on the side of hope—the potential that things can be changed for the better. We can emphasize the positive intentions, reinforce underutilized strengths, and recognize signs of progress.

The Interweaving of Key Resilience Processes

The following case illustrates the interweaving of belief systems, organizational processes, and communication processes in a family crisis situation and in therapeutic efforts.

Seven-year-old Mia was in individual therapy to recover from multiple traumas of abuse and neglect. Mia had recently been removed from her home after her baby sister was found dead in her crib. An investigation also found that Mia had been sexually abused by an uncle. Her mother, a single parent, had disappeared to avoid prosecution for negligence, signing over guardianship for Mia to the child's godmother, Darlene. Now living with Darlene's family, Mia was brought for help after she tried to kill herself by sticking her head in the oven. Although Mia was unable to talk about her experiences, she drew a picture of stick figures running away from a house with dark "monsters" in the window, explaining that this was the house of Casper the Friendly Ghost, who was friendly but very scary. The next session, she asked the therapist to help her erase the picture, insisting that it wasn't easy, but they must work hard at it.

Over the following weeks in therapy, Mia's creative stories and drawings continued to illuminate her pain and struggles to overcome her traumas.

Initial family assessment had focused on the family experiences Mia had left behind, but had not looked forward to helping her settle successfully in her new home. Structural aspects of her new family environment required immediate attention to assure security and stability. Caregiving roles, leadership, and responsibilities needed to be clear and physical boundaries firm. Although Darlene had assumed legal guardianship, the role of her husband, whom Mia called "Uncle" Frank, was ambiguous. In asking how daily life was structured, we learned that Darlene was at work until evening; "Uncle" Frank, unemployed and on disability, was at home with the children. Because she had been sexually abused by an uncle and abandoned by her mother, Mia's anxieties were heightened by this arrangement. The therapist clarified Mia's needs for security with Darlene and Frank, and helped them to clarify their roles and her ability to count on them. Learning that Mia was sleeping on the sofa, the therapist also encouraged them to create a space for her and to help her fit in with their own four children.

It was crucial to improve communication processes, as well as to strengthen the family structure. It was urgent to avert further self-destructive behavior by helping Mia verbalize her needs and concerns with her godmother and other family members. The therapist addressed Darlene and Frank's worry that Mia would try to hurt herself again. Not wanting to be negligent, they had become hypervigilant and yet felt unsure how to be helpful. The therapist commended their concern for Mia, as well as Darlene's difficult yet important legal commitment as guardian. She helped them allay Mia's anxieties by telling and showing her clearly that she would be well cared for and not abandoned. Darlene, as godmother, was encouraged to spent some quiet time with Mia at bedtime, talking about the day's activities and plans for the next day. This opened communication as it furthered stability and security.

Together they anticipated potential stresses and possible signs that Mia might be getting more upset, so that they could provide more support and tackle any problems (e.g., sibling rivalries) before they grew larger. Weekly family sessions sustained these efforts and continued to build everyone's trust and confidence in the new relationships.

Darlene then confided in the therapist that she knew where Mia's mother was, but had not told Mia for fear of upsetting her further. Because ambiguous loss complicates recovery, the therapist helped her to share this information in a sensitive way, and coached her to have Mia's mother write. Mia's mother's letter let her daughter know that she was getting help in a drug treatment program, that she loved Mia very much, and that she knew that her godmother would care well for her. Mia was encouraged to write back; she enclosed a drawing of a big heart with a tear that was being mended.

MASTERING PRACTICE CHALLENGES

Reaching Out to Families

Many multicrisis families become frustrated, wary, and mistrustful of well-intentioned "helpers" because of repeated negative interactions and unhelpful experiences with numerous systems (Kaplan, 1986). Family survival needs may lead members to guard against further dealings with professionals as problems become more chronic and entrenched. Nancy Boyd-Franklin (1989, 1993) emphasizes that many African American families and their communities have developd a healthy cultural suspicion of formal social service agencies and their providers. This skepticism can take many forms, from overt anger to missed sessions or lack of follow-through with agreed-upon plans. A discouraged family may protect itself by actions that express feelings of "Why bother? Nothing ever works out, and no one really cares." It's crucial to see this not as "resistance" intrinsic to a "hard-to-reach" family, but instead as an understandable, learned pessimism grounded in the disappointment of prior experience. As helping professionals, we need to anticipate this reaction and to be prepared to deal with it by making every effort to connect productively. It requires—and demonstrates—our perseverance to hang in with a reluctant family in order to gain trust and acceptance.

One rule of thumb is to include in therapy all family members whose participation can strengthen relationships and contribute to lower risk and vulnerability. For example, a mother may come for help, but may say that her substance-abusing partner is unwilling to come in or get help for his drinking. The best opportunities for involving a reluctant partner occur at the start of therapy. If we proceed with only the willing partner, problem interactions are likely to remain stuck or worsen. Individual coaching, especially with a person who is in a one-down position in a relationship, is unlikely to improve destructive interactional patterns or a partner's problem drinking. Also, putting one partner in charge of changing the other worsens power struggles and conflict. With individual intervention, the high probability of no change in the system heightens the risk for couple failure. Change may prove impossible, and separation may be for the best, but pessimistic forecasts should not deter us from first encouraging a collaborative effort to overcome problems.

Issues concerning blame, shame, and vulnerability are often a source of reluctance for men to take part in therapy, especially in cultures where pride,
authority, and invulnerability are intertwined in images of successful man-
hood. We can best enlist a father's active involvement in therapy as a caring
parent, underscoring his potential power and pride in helping his children
succeed.

In multicrisis families, siblings may keep to the edge of family life, where
they often become keen observers of the family drama. Yet they may fear
that any contact will pull them into quicksand. The involvement of higher-
functioning siblings in family therapy provides resources to more distressed
members and can benefit these siblings as well. Those who have distanced
themselves from embroilment in family problems can gain the ability to be
in contact with their family and still hold their own. We can strongly encourage them to come to family sessions and invite their comments and collaboration, yet also respect their boundaries, so that they that feel in control of
the extent of their involvement.

The unclear role of a live-in boyfriend in a family should be explored;
not only any heightened risks (e.g., substance abuse), but also his potential
strengths as a partner and support in parenting, should be assessed. When a
mother's past couple relationships have been unstable, children may express
anxieties in problem behavior that heightens risk of another breakup. Unclarity
also results in confusion for children around such issues as attachment, authority, and boundaries. Not including a live-in partner in the structure of
therapy reinforces a boundary around the single-parent family unit, making
it harder for couple and informal stepparent relationships to develop. We
might acknowledge the partners' uncertainty about their future relationship
commitment, yet encourage them to support each other and manage relationships with the children as they resolve presenting problems. By working
collaboratively, they can address problem areas common in reconstituted
families, and this can help to stabilize and solidify their relationship.

Crisis Intervention and Crisis Prevention

Some families seem to be in perpetual crisis, reeling from one traumatic event
to the next (Kagan & Schlosberg, 1989). Family members who are overwhelmed may think of therapy as an emergency room service, a lifeline in
times of crisis. Without a systemic frame and clear objectives, therapy too
will cast about in all directions, reeling from crisis to crisis. Each new crisis
interrupts focus on any one problem-solving effort. Therapists, like families
themselves, can get caught up in a reactive mode: We all become swept up
by the crisis and then focus on sweeping up in its aftermath. Yet many crises

can be anticipated. It's essential to get ahead of the next wave. If we structure initial family interviews sufficiently to enable us to obtain fuller information early on, we can anticipate problems and have a better chance of intervening in potentially dangerous situations before they get out of control. For instance, one therapist was relieved to learn initially that a mother's abusive boyfriend was in jail and out of the picture. However, 5 weeks later, the family was in crisis after the mother was battered once again by the boyfriend. She hadn't mentioned, and the therapist hadn't asked, when he was expected to be released; thus, the opportunity to think through planfully what she would do if he returned was missed.

Searching for Strengths Amid Persistent Crises

General Aims

With families flooded by problems, it is particularly challenging to resist the pull of pathology and to search for strengths. When families come for help in crisis, the problematic aspects of their lives stand out, and helping professionals may become as overwhelmed and discouraged as they are (Waters & Lawrence, 1993). We may become frustrated, pull back, and stop engaging with the families or thinking creatively about change. Our clients sense our loss of hope and commitment and feel worse about themselves, increasing the risk that they will give up and drop out of therapy. Gaining an appreciation of their healthy strivings gives us energy and hope to work with those strengths to overcome the chaos in their lives. When we underestimate our clients, we lose sight of their potential for mastery. There may be truly impossible cases, but, like my strength-oriented colleagues, that has rarely been my experience.

Even in the most troubled families, areas of competence can be found and enlarged as sources of pride and accomplishment. We are most effective when we encourage family members to develop options and skills rather than dwelling on their limitations. In the unfolding process of therapy, we face constant choices about what to pick up on. If we get caught up in a family's hopelessness and helplessness, therapy bogs down. Every maladaptive response also contains the seeds of healthy striving that can be cultivated. As Waters and Lawrence (1993) observe, parents may lose control and become abusive *because* they care so much and want so badly for a child to do better. We need continually to emphasize hope, caring, and small gains, to enable the parents to hang in and act on their best intentions. Although there is most often caring alongside abuse or neglect, there are some cases (e.g., families with seriously drug-addicted parents) where caring has been extinguished over time and cannot be revived. And yet we should not write off the possibility of change, but make a determined effort to support new beginnings.

The general aims of a strength-oriented approach with vulnerable families can be summarized as follows:

- Overcoming the cycle of suspicion, rejection, failure, and withdrawal
- Forging a trusting relationship through direct, honest, respectful communication
- Encouraging families to prioritize their many needs and aims
- Believing in family members' potential; giving them hope and confidence that they can improve their situation and overcome long-standing problems
- Increasing family members' ability to solve problems, avert crises, and advocate on their own behalf

To achieve these aims, we can draw on an array of techniques from strength-based family therapy approaches. The ultimate aim is to enable family members to take back control of their lives and regain belief in their competence and worth.

One of the hardest challenges for us as therapists is to align empathically with members of crisis-ridden families who are slow to change. We may also be drawn into villainizing men who have been abusive, or mothers who have failed to protect their children. While addressing problem behavior, we need to resist the pull to pathologize the person. We can gain empathy from seeing each person in the context of his or her relationships and life struggles: a single parent who is overwhelmed and undersupported; a wife whose trust has been shattered by past sexual abuse; a father who himself was abused and knows no other way to discipline children. Although viewing entrenched problems as constitutional and inevitable may relieve us of a sense of responsibility for therapeutic gridlock, we further erode our clients' sense of worth and life chances in doing so. We can open up possibilities for change by appreciating our clients' struggles and viewing therapeutic impasses as shared challenges, requiring courage, perseverance, and renewed teamwork.

Learning and Growth from Past Trauma

Often problems in one generation are repeated in the next. When a mother is worried that her 16-year-old daughter is sexually active and will get pregnant, a genogram may reveal that she herself became pregnant at 16. Although the immediate crises and chaos presented by a family can make history taking very challenging, learning about past conflicts and traumatic events—

particularly those occurring at the same nodal point in the life cycle a generation earlier—often sheds light on key issues in presenting problems.

In an integrative approach, the work is present- and future-focused, but is linked to each family's past. It is important to make connections and distinctions between past and present challenges and responses: As a child a person may have been powerless, but now as an adult he or she can learn from the past and take charge in dealing with current situations as a partner or parent. The therapeutic task is to make intergenerational patterns and linkages overt, and then to take lessons from painful past experience and seize the opportunity to do things differently with one's partner and children. It is helpful for children to hear stories of their parents' struggles as children, and for parents to gain empathy for their children's positions. Parents can be commended for caring enough about their children to take steps to prevent history from repeating itself. We can encourage them to act on their best intentions and their aching desire to create the strong bonds longed for in the past.

Recruiting Models and Mentors

Models and mentors can be found and recruited in even the most troubled family. In cases where parents are absent or limited by serious mental illness or substance abuse, it's crucial to enlist other members of the family system. Older siblings can be valuable resources, drawing on their abilities and talents to teach or assist younger children who are having difficulty. For instance, a teen doing well in math can help a faltering sibling; or older siblings can read with younger ones, building their relationship along with skills. Extended family members can also be valuable resources for resilience. The poet Maya Angelou tells a moving story from her childhood: Although dysfunction and disruption permeated her immediate household, every day after school she would go to the small store run by her Uncle Willie, where he would grill her on her homework. Uncle Willie was a man of humble means with little formal schooling; he was also lame and had a severe speech disability. Yet he valued education and became her mentor and champion. He prodded her to to do her best in her studies and to aim high in her life aspirations. She wrote a poem honoring him (Angelou, 1986), to encourage others to seek out their own Uncle Willies in their relationship networks and to serve as he did for others.

Creating Problem-Free Zones

Trained to think of therapy as the place to focus on problems, we need to be careful not to replicate a family's experience of life as nothing but a barrage of problems. It's important to encourage conversation about nonproblematic areas of life—to show interest in school and activities, highlights of the week, and moments of pleasurable interaction. It's amazing how faces will light up and conversation will become animated. We can also amplify areas of competence and success that instill hope and encourage family members to see beyond problems. When daily life is consumed by problems, we can help family members to structure problem-free zones: a family outing with problem talk off limits; a rule of no fighting at the dinner table or in the parents' bedroom.

In particular, respite from constant demands enables a parent to feel nurtured, to "refuel," and then to function more effectively. A single mother can be invited to pick times in the coming week for herself when she is "off cuty," and mobilize family members to ensure that Mom's time and space are honored. Calling upon extended family members to share a burden periodically can also relieve the constant stress.

Ending Therapy

When families present multiple and recurrent problems, it is difficult to determine not only where to begin, but also where to end therapy. Since the family members are likely to continue to experience high stress in their lives, their success should be defined not by the absence of problems, but by the family's having developed resilience to cope more effectively. What matters is that members have gained better relational resources to deal more successfully with the problems they will continue to face.

The end of therapy is likely to reactivate intense feelings of all other painful losses, most of which have been beyond family members' control. We should anticipate and explore upset and setbacks, and help families not to see them as signs of failure. "Termination" may stir up clients' memories of abandonment by parents, and beliefs that they were unlovable or drove the parents away. When a therapist or agency must end therapy before a family is ready, it's essential to clarify that it is not their fault and does not mean that we didn't care about them. In ending, it's important to convey what we liked best about each family member, the progress they have made, and the further gains we believe they are capable of making. If the family is transferred to another therapist, it is crucial to help them make a good connection. With vulnerable families, it 's helpful to plan toward ending and to gradually extend the length of time between sessions. This enables the family to experience control and predictability in the process and to become increasingly self-reliant, with the therapist still available to help them head off more serious difficulties and sustain their gains. A last session can be marked by a celebration that signifies all the family has accomplished.

Combined Therapeutic Modalities

Treatment models for substance abuse, violence, or sexual abuse typically employ a multimodality approach. Most experts in abuse strongly recommend individual or group intervention focused on stopping abusive behavior patterns as an immediate priority before couple or family therapy is begun (Trepper & Barrett, 1989). Support groups are valuable adjuncts to family counseling, helping families decrease isolation and develop a mutual support system. A weekly support group for overwhelmed single mothers is immensely beneficial in building confidence and competence. It's important to coordinate all approaches, with good communication among the professionals involved.

Outreach and Home Visits

When families are buffeted by stresses, therapeutic services need to be accessible and scheduled at convenient times. Therapists often need to go the extra distance, not only to engage family members, but also to sustain their efforts and gains over time. When an appointment has been missed, a reminder phone call for the next session communicates our investment and promotes continuity in the therapy process. Clients may be asked to phone in and leave a message of midweek progress. One therapist was frustrated and ready to give up working with a single mother who was unreliable in taking her psychotropic medication. Without it, she became neglectful of household and parenting responsibilities, and was in danger of losing custody of her children at an upcoming hearing. The therapist was encouraged to give her a strong, clear message that she must take her medications in order to function well enough to keep her children, and that he expected her to phone his office every morning over the next week, leaving a message that she had taken her medication. The therapist first had to overcome his own pessimism: he expressed his concern that this would only "foster her dependence" and his doubt that she would follow through anyway. However, she did call every day, and by the second week her improved functioning enabled her to keep on track herself with medication and parenting responsibilities.

Home visits indicate to family members that professionals are invested in them and that they are worth the effort. They can also provide a clear view of both the risks and the potential resources in the family's living arrangements, as in the following case:

> Jimmy Monroe, age 12, an only child, lived with his mother, Charlayne, and her long-time boyfriend, Al Stevens. Nine months earlier, Jimmy's

mother, in an acute psychotic episode, had tried to suffocate him with a pillow in the middle of the night. Jimmy had gone to live with an aunt while she was hospitalized and stabilized on medication, and was now again living at home. Charlayne failed to keep several appointments with Jimmy's new social worker, who then scheduled a home visit. As the worker approached the apartment, the front shade was suddenly pulled down and a light went off. No one answered her knocking.

In group supervision, the worker was encouraged to set up another home visit. This time Charlayne wearing a bathrobe and somewhat disheveled in appearance, opened the door. The worker showed her some of Jimmy's artwork, praising his creativity. Charlayne warmed a bit and offered some coffee. In the kitchen a man's voice could be heard. Sensing that they might presume her disapproval of a live-in boyfriend, the worker took the initiative, asking, "Oh, is that Mr. Stevens? Jimmy has told me he thinks the world of him." As Al entered the room hesitantly, the worker greeted him cordially and invited him to join their conversation. She began by orienting them to Jimmy's program and her role as a counselor. She explained her reason for meeting them: The program found that kids did best when their families were actively involved in supporting their success. She would set regular meetings to update them on Jimmy's progress, to respond to any concerns they or Jimmy might have, and to work together with them as a team. She answered their questions and let them know how to reach her. They were off to a good start. Charlayne thanked the worker for coming back, and Al offered to walk her to the bus stop, saying that the neighborhood could be a little rough toward dusk. She accepted his offer and took the opportunity to get to know him better.

After each session Al continued to walk the worker to the bus stop, at times bringing up concerns about Charlayne. He worked a night shift and worried about her night terror and difficulty sleeping; she often sat up with the TV on until his return and then slept most of the day. First, Charlayne's medication was adjusted to enable her to sleep more soundly through the night. Then they explored how Al might switch to a morning shift so that he could be home at night. The worker also encouraged his interest in spending more time with Jimmy. More regular dinnertime and weekend outings increased their sense of "family."

Conversations then explored future hopes and dreams and ways of moving toward them. Charlayne and Al wished to get a larger apartment on a safer block so that Jimmy could play outside, but they were financially strapped. Though Charlayne had daydreams of getting a job, she was unskilled, lacked transportation, and felt overwhelmed by the challenge. Together, the worker and family brainstormed about possibilities in the neighborhood. Charlayne astonished the worker only a month later by landing a part-time job in a nearby convenience store. Her functioning and sense of worth were enhanced by the job; as a result, she took better care of herself and Jimmy. Al and Charlayne playfully teased each other about ways to spend her new earnings. With remarkable progress by Jimmy and his family over the school year, monthly follow-up sessions were held to keep things on track. The family moved into a larger apartment, and Jimmy filled his new room with (what else?) Bulls posters.

Dogged persistence by a helping professional can be powerful in bringing about crucial structural and interactional changes in a family. In this case, the worker's supportive encouragement by her supervision group bolstered her ability to persevere.

Home visits do present challenges for therapists. Ground rules and a quiet setting for productive sessions need to be established, because the household environment is often stress-laden and chaotic. The first priority is to create a workable space and atmosphere, setting boundaries from intrusion. Enlisting family collaboration in this process sets the stage for therapeutic partnership. We might ask what space would work best for talking comfortably with minimal interruption; we can ask family members to take turns answering the phone or tending to a baby. Structuring a home session establishes a small island of calm in a sea of turmoil. This achievement is all the more profound because it takes place in the home unlike the artificial setting of a therapist's office, demonstrating that it is possible to gain more control over the bombardment of stresses in daily life.

Families and Foster Care: A Collaborative Systemic Approach

Although the child welfare system is committed in theory to maintaining children in their own homes, placement is a common option taken in practice. Poor minority children, especially from African American, Latino, and Native American families, are vastly overrepresented in out-of-home placement. Training of child welfare professionals in family systems concepts and methods would enable them to work more effectively to strengthen family capacities. Traditional dyadic models, which are focused too narrowly on the mother or primary caregiver, may neglect potential resources in the kin and community network. Workers trained to see family patterns and strengths through a systemic lens are less overwhelmed by the multiple problems and chaos. Family preservation programs can be most effective in preventing the need for placement, and in returning children to safe and stable home environments after temporary placement, when workers have adequate training in strength-oriented family systems approaches.

When placement is necessary, maintaining the continuity of key relationships should be a priority. Traditionally, foster care providers have been recruited by asking them to rescue or save children from dysfunctional families. This sets up parents and foster caregivers as adversaries, when what is most needed is collaboration for the sake of the children (Minuchin, 1995). Placement is further traumatizing when bonds to parents, siblings, and extended family members are abruptly severed. This issue is discussed further below.

Preventing Recidivism: Easing Transitional Stresses

Recidivism in foster care has been high. The transitional challenges when children return home after temporary placement require attention, as in the following case:

Eight-year-old Terrell was being seen in individual therapy for "separation anxiety" over the past 2 years, after he and three siblings were removed from their mother's custody because of cocaine dependence and neglect and were placed in foster care with their maternal grandmother. The parents, never legally married, separated at that time as well: The mother left the abusive relationship as part of her recovery efforts. Her long-term work with an individual therapist was successful; she was able to keep off drugs, maintained regular participation in Cocaine Anonymous, got off public assistance and into a job, and regained custody of her four children.

Planning and support services were needed to meet the transitional challenges. Instead, the mother's success brought termination of her therapy at the very time she most needed support: resuming parenting of four young children while managing a new full-time job. Moreover, no meetings were held to plan the changing role relations of grandparent and parent, or to buffer the emotional upheaval of the new separation and dislocation for the children. When the worker suggested meeting with the grandmother, the mother expressed strong reluctance. Still angry at her mother for having initiated the court-ordered transfer of the children, she had cut off all contact between the children and their grandmother (who had recently moved to an apartment on the same block to be near them) as soon as she regained custody. In regaining their mother, the children had now lost their grandmother, their caregiver for 2 years. Her proximity on the same block, with a prohibition against seeing her, fueled ambiguous loss and conflicted loyalties.

Six weeks after the return home, when the mother dropped off Terrell for his therapy, she mentioned to his therapist that she was about to quit her job because of the stress; she added vaguely that she might look for another job or maybe go back to school. She seemed overwhelmed and depleted, but when she was asked whether she'd like a new therapist for herself, she replied that she was too busy and didn't have time.

Called in as a consultant to a staff meeting at this point, I brought a family resilience perspective to the case. It was important to apply a systemic approach to guide intervention efforts. First, the original presenting problem—Terrell's separation anxiety—was intensified by the recent cutoff of the grandmother's contact. His siblings had also suffered this abrupt loss. To reduce the risk for further dysfunction, family interventions were needed to repair the strained relationship between the mother and grandmother.

Redefining and rebalancing caregiving roles were primary objectives. One aim would be to help the mother and grandmother shift from competition—a struggle over authority and competence—to collaboration—ways they could work together as a parenting team across households, with the mother in charge as primary parent. It would be crucial to reframe the grandmother's role—from rescuing the kids because the mother was deficient, to supporting her daughter's job efforts and maintaining her valuable bond with the grandchildren. For the mother, needing help was viewed as an indication that she'd "messed up" again, loaded with attributions of failure, blame, and shame. She was now having difficulty managing, and was at high risk of relapsing and losing her children once again. The rationale for backup caregiving and therapeutic support also needed to be reframed: to enable her to sustain her successful efforts in the face of an inherently difficult transition and the new set of job and family challenges. She and her children—and the grandmother—were all undergoing a stressful transition, a change in households and parenting roles, and demands in managing a new job.

The intervention focus was redirected from repairing past damage to helping the family master current and impending challenges in the precarious transition. Support to the mother was most urgent at this time. It was crucial to attend to her burdens to prevent the looming crisis: either collapsing under the strain or quitting her job without another means of support. To reduce the risk of further separation, loss, and upheaval for all family members, it was essential to shore up resources to manage parenting and financial demands. Instead of assigning the mother a new individual therapist and a separate meeting time (when she was already overloaded), it made more sense for the son's therapist to make time to meet with her when she brought him in. In discussing current stresses with her, the therapist learned that her work shift started at 5:00 A.M.—an untenable situation. Together, they brainstormed other job options, and the therapist coached her to press for a change of shift to reduce immediate pressures.

We also explored the father's potential contribution. He had never been contacted in the 2 years of his son's treatment, since the parents were unmarried and living apart. We learned that he was living in the community and saw the children almost weekly, although he contributed no financial support. This information surprised the staff members, who had written him off; this resource had been completely overlooked. He had a fairly steady construction job and, with ongoing investment in his children, could be brought into the picture and encouraged to contribute to the family's financial security. Here again, obtaining this help needed to be reframed from implying the mother's deficiency to making reasonable expectations of a caring father for support of his children.

It was important to put in place a model of sustaining care to provide intensive intervention during this stressful transition period, followed by monthly, ongoing support once higher functioning and stabilization of the family system were achieved. The dyadic view of parent/caregiver as one person, which reinforced dichotomous thinking about either mother *or* grandmother, was expanded to a collaborative model involving both, as well as the support of the noncustodial father. The goal was to build a caregiving network of relationships—a family full of resources.

As this case illustrates, simply reuniting children with their families without appropriate supports is a recipe for failure. It is advisable in the return of children to plan the transition period carefully, preparing children and caregivers in both households over at least several weeks. Parental visits should be well structured and gradually increased; emotional upheaval should be anticipated, troubleshooting for any potential crises. Posttransition structural changes (e.g., shifting role relations and child care arrangements) should also be planned to ensure children's safety and to buffer anticipated stresses. It is crucial not to dismiss the potential contributions of family members who may have been unable to provide care in the past. Images frozen in time need to be checked out and updated, recognizing the human capacity for change and growth.

Consistent, coordinated aftercare has been found to be the key to successful family efforts, such as the Homebuilders program. A range of services may be needed to enable families to function effectively, including substance abuse counseling; education, job, and housing referrals; parenting classes; and domestic violence counseling. The first few months is often a "honeymoon" period in family relationships while problems of basic survival predominate: maintaining income assistance, housing, health care, job training, and education. Traditional aftercare ends within 3–6 months. However, the time of highest risk is toward the end of the first year, with substance abuse relapses, the return of abusive partners, neglecting behavior, and disillusionment about family life. Sustaining care is essential to solidify gains and to prevent recurrence of serious problems. Extended contacts focus on keeping living situations stabilized and reducing family stress. Altering family interaction patterns also reduces the risk that other children and family members will become distressed.

Clear and Present Danger: Systemic Assessment

Family reunification is not a panacea. Child welfare workers struggle with an overriding dilemma: When is the risk of harm serious enough to remove children from the family home or to forbid their return? A careful systems assessment is required to determine when there is clear and present danger, as a case described in an article in *The New York Times* (July 26, 1996) graphically illustrates.

In a crime that convulsed the city of Chicago, Amanda Wallace wrapped an extension cord around the neck of her 3-year-old son, Joey; waved to him as he waved good-bye; and hanged him from a transom. His death became a lightning rod for critics of the state welfare system, resulting in the dismissal of three social workers and administrators who had insisted on returning Joey to his mother from foster care, even though psychiatrists had warned that his mother was mentally unstable and had a long history of violence. (Actually, a judge had ordered his return.)

Following her conviction, at the sentencing hearing to determine whether Amanda would receive the death penalty, the prosecution and defense argued over whether or not she was insane. In closing arguments, the defense counsel carried in three cardboard boxes containing just some of her records from mental hospitals, and reminded the court that she herself had been abused as a child. The prosecutor countered that "no one has mastered the abuse excuse" better than she had, and described her as "evil personified."

At the hearing, Amanda's older sister Evelyn testified that at age 11, when she (Evelyn) wet her bed, their mother punished her by whipping her with an extension cord. Amanda, then aged 2, watched as their mother placed

Evelyn on a stool, wrapped the cord around her neck, and looped it around a light bulb hanging from the ceiling. She then kicked away the stool, but Evelyn fell to the floor unhurt. Their mother also often whipped Amanda with extension cords and locked her in a dark closet for hours without food or water. Amanda soon began a lifelong pattern of self-destructive behavior: swallowing glass and nails, stabbing herself bloody with needles, and running away from home from age 7 onward. After setting her bed on fire in her first foster placement at age 8, she was shunted back and forth between mental institutions and foster homes.

During the sentencing hearing for her son's death, Amanda tried to bolt from the courtroom as the judge recited the details of Joey's last moments. Guards were ordered to take her to a holding cell, where she could hear the courtroom through a speaker. Moments later she tried to strangle herself with a jail shirt. The judge dismissed the incident, saying, "The court is satisfied that she is malingering as she so often does." He sentenced her to life in prison without parole.

Much could be learned from this case, which was doubly tragic for mother and son. Certainly, the court's vilifying and dehumanizing attitude toward the mother reflects the lack of human compassion toward vulnerable parents that is widespread throughout the welfare and court systems. Despite Amanda's thick file of incidents and treatments, it is doubtful that anyone ever meaningfully put together the fragmentary accounts of various episodes in her life to comprehend the devastating impact of her childhood abuse and the high risk it posed for parenting Joey on her own. A systemic assessment would have clarified the danger. It remains unclear how much help Amanda ever received or what potential family resources might have been drawn upon to make a difference. A parent skill building approach would have been insufficient here. More in-depth therapeutic work would have been required; Amanda's past trauma needed to be linked with the imperative to protect the son she truly loved from the very same abuses she had suffered.

Any decisions for out-of-home placement should be made without robbing a parent of humanity and dignity. We should make every attempt to involve key family members in making these decisions. A family council— much like a tribal council—can be convened, rallying the strongest resources in the extended family (e.g., a grandparent, an aunt and uncle, or a godmother), whose input could be invaluable for successful placement. Together with professionals, the family members can weigh and consider the various options, taking stock of kin and community resources. The collaborative process can reduce the sense that children are being removed by outside forces beyond family control, as well as the likelihood of arbitrary court decisions.

Involving key family members can promote their collaboration with a bio-logically unrelated foster family, their ongoing contact with children, and their investment in a successful placement experience.

Sustaining Vital Connections

We need to create a balanced service delivery system, in which family pres-ervation and out-of-home placement are seen as complementary, not mutu-ally exclusive, alternatives. We must shift from all-or-none thinking when children are placed out of the home to seeing foster and biological families as collaborative caregivers rather than adversaries (Minuchin, 1995). Assess-ment should determine not simply where children should live, but how they can be nurtured and protected from abuse *and* at the same time maintain some linkages with key family members, extended kin, and community, as well as with cultural traditions and spiritual sources of resilience. When out-of-home placement is required, we should find ways for children to sustain vital bonds through monitored contact with parents, visits with other rela-tives, phone calls, and letters. Even when direct contact efforts fail, it's im-portant for children to have photographs of family members and to hear sto-ries of their family history and cultural heritage. A piece of jewelry, a scarf, or a favorite shirt from a parent, older sibling, or grandparent can be a precious belonging. Older children can be encouraged to write letters and keep jour-nals or diaries to record their experiences and their memories, hopes, and dreams.

Building Therapeutic Partnerships

In work with multicrisis families, we must broaden the traditional view of therapy and of our role as therapists. When families have been beaten down, it's important to take an active, mobilizing position instead of waiting for family members to become "motivated." A pragmatic approach that includes cre-ativity, flexibility, and a variety of interventions is most effective. We may serve as facilitators, advocates, and allies, as well as models and nurturing mentors. We can draw from our own experiences and offer examples of others who have prevailed in similar straits to offer new perspectives and hope. A pri-mary goal of all intervention is to generalize the trusting relationship that develops to the family's social world.

Today there are more families in crisis, but fewer therapists and sessions for such families, due to funding cutbacks. In agencies working with multineed famillies, unrealistic expectations of staff members, case overload, and insuf-ficient resources can create an unhealthy work environment and result in burnout. A worker may come to feel as depleted as an overloaded, under-supported parent. Principles similar to those of resilience building with families apply to work systems: Provide adequate pay and resources, opportunities for professional growth, peer case consultation, staff involvement in decision making, recognition of workers' value, and opportunities to succeed. Such incentives sustain workers' personal investment and job commitment with very challenging caseloads. In a preventive approach, agencies can identify highly vulnerable families—those in precarious situations that lack resources and have been beset by numerous problems. Through outreach at moments of crisis, our job will be much easier than after serious symptoms have developed.

A collaborative approach is essential when overwhelmed family members wish for a therapist to solve their problems, or even to *become* the solution—that is, to assume the role of rescuer or to replace an absent parent. Many of us therapists have had early life training in assuming responsible roles in our families of origin to rescue or take care of other family members. Vulnerable clients may tug on our own inclinations to rescue them. Family members' distress may be so great that they wish we could move in with them and never leave. Our attempts to set limits may be miscontrued as not caring about them. We should keep mindful that their neediness may be great because their resources are drained or they are unprepared for responsibilities, especially when parents have lacked adequate parenting themselves. We may come to feel weighted down, as if we are sinking in quicksand along with them. Some warning signs we should heed include "forgetting" to return family members' calls or feeling relieved when they miss an appointment.

As therapists, we have to be clear about our own role and boundaries. While reaching out and actively engaging families, we need to model a relationship of caring and commitment with limits. Therapy can become skewed, burdensome, and unproductive: As we become overresponsible, family members become even less confident of their own ability to surmount their challenges. We do not serve our clients well—or care for ourselves—if we foster long-term dependence as their only lifeline. Families are empowered when we help them mobilize potential resources in their own kin networks and communities for support with urgent needs. We all do best under duress by strengthening real-life connections.

C·H·A·P·T·E·R   1·0

Reconnection and Reconciliation: Bridge over Troubled Waters

History, despite its wrenching pain,
Cannot be unlived, and if faced with courage,
Need not be lived again.
—MAYA ANGELOU "On the Pulse of the Morning"

I was often viewed as a resilient person, and came to see myself that way as well. I accepted the common belief that because I was resilient, I was able to "raise myself up" despite my family adversities. Like the resilient individuals from dysfunctional families in many case studies (Higgins, 1994; Wolin & Wolin, 1993), I followed the conventional wisdom and avoided contact with my family after leaving home. After college, I took the "geographical cure"—traveling halfway around the world, and returning to settle just halfway back, only going home for brief visits. Weekly phone calls were easier, since my father, who never quite got over the 1930s Depression, kept an egg timer next to the phone. At 3 minutes he'd announce, "Well, time's up!" and our conversation was over, even in midsentence.

Like many of my peers in young adulthood, I went into psychotherapy and focused on painful childhood experiences and my parents' shortcomings, which were catalogued and embroidered upon by the therapy. I increasingly thought of myself as resilient *despite* my family influence. It was only later that I came to realize that I'm resilient *because* of those challenges and because of the hidden strengths in my family that were not in my therapy story. Through those difficult childhood experiences, I emerged hardier than I might have if I had grown up in a placid, "ideal" environment.

Yet the dogma of family dysfunction and the linkage of resilience with disconnection from one's family continue to be dominant themes in U.S.

culture and the field of mental health. Lillian Rubin (1996), whose work I much admire, falls into this trap in her recent book *The Transcendent Child*. In her attempt to understand how she herself managed to triumph over childhood adversity in a "dysfunctional" family, she selects and interviews several other resilient individuals, whose stories she tells along with her own. Interestingly, as she notes, they all followed a similar pathway, distancing from their families of origin as a survival strategy. None have reconnected or reconciled over the years; their families have been left behind, cast in stone as damaged, pathetic, and destructive characters in their early life dramas, as they have moved on into other relationships. Such cutoffs are certainly understandable in cases of persistent strife, and may be the only option in extreme situations.

Yet in most cases disconnection is neither the necessary nor the optimal pathway for individual resilience. I take issue with the causal inference so often made—that is, the leap from description of common patterns of estrangement to the prescription that disconnection is essential for resilience. Individuals are encouraged by the recovery movement and by traditional clinical views of the family to push away from contact and to maintain fixed views of their families as hopelessly dysfunctional and their relationships as beyond repair. In the same fashion, individuals leave marriages and other significant relationships by casting off old partners, maintaining unremittingly negative views of them, and plunging into new relationships with the hope of starting afresh. Like our culture's mistaken view of resilience as simply putting our troubles behind us and moving on, these cut-and-run solutions may bring short-term relief, but leave long-term unresolved issues and a pessimism about resolving relational problems that we carry with us on our life journeys and transmit to the next generation. These disconnections leave a hole in our heart and in the fabric of our lives. We best achieve a sense of inner wholeness and a compassionate connectedness with the human community through reconciliation.

In my research with families of seriously disturbed young adults over 20 years ago, I was surprised by the strengths many so-called "dysfunctional" families showed in the midst of their adversities. Moreover, my experiences as a family therapist have convinced me that positive changes can occur even in the most troubled relationships and at any time in life. This closing chapter offers some guiding principles and case examples demonstrating the possibilities for reconnection and reconciliation. My encouragement of relational repair is based on the conviction (expressed throughout this book) that our resilience is best achieved through gaining new perspective on past adversity; appreciating the challenges and strengths, as well as the limitations, of those who may have hurt or failed us; and integrating the whole of this experience into our lives and relationships. The processes of reconnection and reconciliation are described, with their applications to the healing of family-of-origin wounds, couples on the brink of separation, and postdivorce family relationships. Difficult dilemmas in exoneration and forgiveness for past grievances are considered. Although forgiveness is not always possible, the opportunities for relational repair and growth are most often greater than anticipated. Throughout this discussion, I've chosen to speak from a personal voice as well as a professional one, and an inclusive "we" position, bridging therapists and clients as human beings struggling to come to terms with painful experiences from our past as we leave our legacies for the future.

History is essential to our ongoing understanding of ourselves, our families, and our culture. I believe that all of us have a deep need to be connected both to the larger society and to our own history, as Susan Griffin (1993) asserts:

> All history, including the histories of our families, is part of us, such that when we hear any secret revealed, a secret about a grandfather or an uncle, or a secret about the Battle of Dresden in 1945, our lives are made suddenly clearer to us, as the unnatural heaviness of unspoken truth is dispersed. For perhaps we are like stones—our own history and the history of the world embedded in us; we hold the sorrow deep within and cannot weep until that history is sung.

Lifting the "heaviness of unspoken truth" is part of the process of opening communication across the generations and in our social world. Opening our family histories and secrets to the light, despite the anxieties it can raise, can be powerfully healing (Imber-Black, 1995).

HEALING INTERGENERATIONAL WOUNDS

When most clinicians consider family-of-origin influences, the pathological bent remains strong, focused on uncovering sources of dysfunction in early childhood parenting and family-of-origin relationships. In individual psychodynamically oriented therapies, intergenerational dynamics in particular are usually presented as negative influences to be contained, avoided, or resolved through transference relationships with therapists. Intergenerational family therapists developed therapeutic approaches to facilitate awareness of covert transactional patterns and to encourage members to deal directly with one another, either within or between sessions; to work through unresolved conflicts and losses; and to test out, update, and alter negative introjects from the past (Framo, 1976; Paul & Grosser, 1991). The contextual family therapy approach of Boszormenyi-Nagy (1987), focused on multigenerational legacies of parental accountability and filial loyalty, aims toward the reconstruc-

tion and reunion of current extended family relationships through the resolution of grievances involving these legacies. The Bowen (1978) approach
fosters personal growth and relational healing through coaching methods that
help clients to increase both their differentiation and more genuine relatedness, while reducing anxiety and emotional reactivity. All efforts at reconnection and the healing of relational wounds can be facilitated by rebalancing our attention from negative family-of-origin influences to unrecognized
sources of strength and positive legacies (McGoldrick, 1995).

Seeing Others with Different Eyes;
Changing Ourselves in Relationships

We tend to see things not as *they* are, but as *we* are.

Roscoe, who grew up in a very troubled family (his mother was chronically depressed and his father was an alcoholic), came to think of his
family as toxic and his well-being as dependent on keeping as much distance as possible. He didn't want any contact, especially with his mother.
Even thoughts of her triggered inner turmoil. Altering this fixed view
was the key to change: "I began to understand that the only way my relationship with my mother could change was for me to see her with different eyes." With the support of his therapist, Roscoe began to develop
new relationships with his parents on a different basis; all have grown
and changed. They still have occasional problems, but are able to talk
about them and move through them.

In the work of reconnection and reconciliation, we need to see and hear
in new ways. The most important element is respectful, genuine curiosity
about the lives and perspectives of others. One of my psychology professors
at Berkeley, Neil Postman, offered a most valuable lesson: "Once you have
learned to ask questions—relevant, appropriate, and substantial questions—
you have learned how to learn, and no one can keep you from learning whatever you want or need to know."

In family-of-origin work toward reconciliation, the family evaluation
process surveys the entire nuclear and extended family field. A genogram
and timeline (McGoldrick & Gerson, 1985) diagram the network of relationships, important information, and nodal events to assist in exploring their
meaning and connections. Whereas traditional individual therapy is limited
by its reliance on the internalized images and perspectives of the client,
which are inherently partial and subjective, family therapists encourage an
individual to contact extended family members and others in order to clarify

obscured information and to gain new perspectives on key family members and relationships.

Opportunities can be seized to reconnect with our families at holiday gatherings and at events marking transitions, such as weddings, bar mitzvahs, graduations, and funerals. I recommend that clients actively plan and shape family gatherings, and that they encourage family historians and others to bring photos and memorabilia. One client, wishing to repair strained relationships in her family network, decided to organize a "No-Excuses Family Reunion." On the invitation, she drew message bubbles filled with possible excuses people might give for not attending: "I'm running in a marathon that weekend," "My cat is scheduled for surgery," "Nobody wants to see me anyway." Humor can work wonders.

Setting out to change others is usually doomed. Such failed attempts reinforce the frustration and hopelessness commonly experienced. As Bowen (1978) has advised, therapeutic efforts are most fruitfully directed at changing *oneself* in relation to other family members. Follow-through is essential to handle the anxiety generated by the process and by the system's initial self-correcting attempts that undermine change. To achieve success, we must deal with our own anxiety, keep from becoming reactive if initial responses are disappointing, and persist in our best efforts. Because of the recursive nature of human systems, if we change our own part in transactions, change by others is more likely to follow over time. Whatever the response, as our own perspective is enlarged by the process, we gain a more compassionate acceptance of others' strengths and limitations. As Monica McGoldrick (1995) observes, we would all like to be ourselves with our family members—to have them accept us as who we are. But we lose sight of the prerequisite: that we accept *them* for who *they* really are, and get past the anger, resentments, and regrets of not being an ideal family.

I once worked with Lydia, whose daughter, Amber, age 22, had run off with her boyfriend and cut herself off from the family 4 years earlier, after the death of her beloved father in an auto accident. The harder Lydia pursued Amber, the more she distanced herself, refusing any visit or phone contact. We considered the vicious cycle that had ensued: The mother's pain and frustration had fueled her reaction in guilt-inducing complaints that were self-defeating. Her daughter, further alienated, accused her mother of only needing Amber to meet her own needs, adding that her therapist agreed (although having never met the mother).

I worked with Lydia's long-standing pain at her double loss of husband and daughter, and her own efforts to move on with her life. Together, we tried to make meaning of Amber's flight—to see it less as a rejection of her mother, and more in developmental perspective (i.e., as an adolescent's reaction to the loss of her father and protective flight from a threatening mutual dependence with her mother). I helped Lydia sustain the hope of eventual reconciliation with her daughter, even in the face of repeated rebuffs. I encouraged her to write occasional letters and cards, sending news and photos. It was important to convey the caring yet undemanding message that she loved Amber and was keeping their connection alive and her door open. Lydia called me a year later to tell me that Amber had finally called and come home for a visit; the healing of their relationship was progressing.

The process of reconnection is advanced by redeveloping personal relationships with important family members, repairing cutoffs, detriangling from conflicts, and changing one's own part in emotionally charged vicious cycles. Humor can detoxify emotional situations. In attempting change, Bowen (1978) advised: Don't attack; don't withdraw; and don't defend. Clients often ask, "What else *is* there to do?" The "what else" lies at the heart of effective change: the ability to hold an assertive, centered position, and to express one's own thoughts, feelings, and concerns with respectful consideration of others. This must be accompanied by a genuine desire to understand their positions and to strive for a better relationship.

The use of photographs can help to connect family members, as they trigger storytelling about family members and their past. Letters can be another effective aid in reconnecting. In letters, we can carefully construct our messages without blame or defensiveness. Letters also allow an entire message to be conveyed and considered without immediate defensive reply and counterreaction. When a relationship has been strained for a long time, it's wise to proceed slowly, step by step, not expecting too much too soon. We can actively pursue a relationship, but cannot force one. At times, we may need to back off somewhat and renew efforts more gradually or take a different tack. Keeping a systemic perspective helps us to anticipate possible setbacks, understand them, and rebound undeterred.

Family History: Stories of Adversity and Resilience

When people have a fixed negative view of parental deficits, it's helpful to look back more broadly in the family history to gain a contextual evolutionary perspective and to search for examples of resilience in the face of life challenges. I encourage clients, as well as students, to explore their families' migration experiences, attending in particular to the trauma and losses their ancestors suffered and the resilience they forged to endure hardship and make their way in a new life. Some have little or no sense of their families' history. Many have learned, for the first time, how family members came to the United States or made other difficult life transitions. Several relatives have shared painful stories: stories of forced migration and cutoff in Native American families; accounts of slavery and racism endured by African American families; stories of Holocaust survivors; tales of Southeast Asians who suffered trauma and privation. Some family members came as political refugees; others fled their native lands to escape religious persecution or impoverished conditions. For most clients (or students), it is a new experience to search for resilience in these stories of trauma, loss, and dislocation. As they ask questions about the strengths that enabled their families to reorient and prevail, the stories themselves are enlarged. Reconnecting with the strengths of our ancestors can be empowering as we realize the heroism, perseverance, and inventiveness that enabled them to endure and surmount adversity.

THE PROCESS OF RECONCILIATION

All family relationships are bound to have occasional conflict, mixed feelings, or shifting alliances. When conflict has been intense and persistent, when ambivalence is strong, or when relationships have been cut off altogether, family therapy offers possibilities for reconciliation.

The potential for reconciliation is determined not so much by the severity of the break as by the depth of the will to be reconciled (Anderson, Hogue, & McCarthy, 1995). Reconciliation is not a hasty peace. Rather, it's a process of mutual reengagement, requiring a readiness on the part of each person to take the others seriously, to acknowledge violations to the relationship, and to experience the pain associated with this acknowledgment. Reconciliation is more than righting wrongs; it brings us to a deeper place of trust and commitment.

Respectful Confrontation

In seeking reconciliation, ways must be found to express anger and disappointment and yet to be respectful and considerate toward others, as the following case illustrates:

> In one Mexican American family, three young adult sons had all become estranged from their parents, but the mother's heart attack led them to come to their priest to seek help in mending their relationships. The sons

carried considerable anger toward their father for his long-standing harsh and abusive treatment when they failed to meet his expectations. However, they were reluctant at first to accept the recommendation of family counseling; they hesitated to confront him because they had been brought up never to show disrespect to their father. Distancing from the family had been their adaptive strategy. The family counselor, who was also Mexican American, acknowledged his own hesitation in opening up these wounds, since respect toward elders is such a strong value in Mexican culture. The therapeutic challenge was to face these sensitive issues in a respectful rather than an attacking way, with the goal of reconciliation.

The father, José, pained by his sons' estrangement, was quite open to family sessions to heal the wounds. With the counselor's facilitation, the sons talked about how it had felt to receive his harsh treatment and about their belief that they could never please him. The father hung his head, remaining silent. The therapist asked what was going through his mind. He said that he himself had suffered beatings and humiliation by his father, whom he had fled through immigration. José had never before talked about this experience and became tearful in acknowledging how he had turned into his father, driving his sons away. This led him to make a heartfelt apology. The sons were deeply moved by their father's account and his genuine remorse. Still, at the following session there was an uneasiness about how to move forward and what to do with lingering feelings about the past. The counselor noted that the family members' Catholic faith had been important to them, but that they hadn't gone to church all together in years. He asked whether this might be a resource. The mother suggested that they all go to mass the next Sunday and pray for guidance in healing their relationships. After the family attended the mass, the oldest son invited them all to his house for tamales (an old family tradition on Sundays), where José met his grandchildren for the first time. The healing had begun.

Weaving Disparate Parts into a Larger Whole

The process of reconciliation involves attempts to weave together two or more disparate views or experiences into a larger whole that holds and respects each in its place. The juxtaposition of elements of the traditional and the modern was one of the most startling images striking me in Third World countries like Morocco, where women cloaked from head to toe ride around town on motorbikes. These incongruous parts may not be synthesized in their lives, and may even remain jarring in their contrast; yet they come to be tolerated as part of a larger whole of their history and their ongoing experience, incorporating traditional and modern aspects. In our own family and social world, we may not be as aware of such incongruities. Yet as we struggle to know ourselves and our loved ones better, this bridging perspective can span ethnic or religious differences, can encompass both suffering and triumph, and can find joy in the midst of sorrow.

The ability to accept diverse aspects of a relationship as parts of a larger whole offers a path out of irreconcilable polarities (e.g., "How could my father have loved me if he hurt me so badly?" "Was it a loving or destructive romance?"). It requires a shift in our perspective from a split view to a larger, holistic perspective—from an "either–or" stance to a "both–and" position. A father may be both loving and harsh; a romantic relationship may be both passionate and destructive. We can then weigh and balance the various elements to make decisions about such relationships.

The Courage to Reach Out

Our families build our physical, emotional, and relational resilience through love and trust. I was most fortunate; despite my parents' persistent hardships and the toll these took on our lives, I never doubted their love and trustworthiness. In many families those resources have been depleted by hurtful actions, such as neglect, long-standing addictions, or physical, emotional, or sexual abuse. When an individual is harmed or violated by another family member, family transactions—powerful beliefs, patterns of organization, and communication processes—may allow the abuse to be denied or perpetuated. Individuals often distance and cut themselves off altogether from the family, finding that contact reactivates destructive interactional patterns and pain. Yet they carry disappointment, anger, and mistrust with them on their life journeys. Self-doubt and blame can permeate other relationships with partners and children.

Attempting reconciliation takes enormous courage because we may reenter relationships and reach out to others, only to find that they rebuff our efforts or still cannot be trusted. The work involves both risk and opportunity: the risk of reexperiencing hurt and no change; the opportunity to experience new relational possibilities. The challenge is to reconcile grievances and forgive injuries to the fullest extent possible. When others are unable to respond as we would wish, we have still gained in generosity and a sense that we've done all we could. This facilitates greater acceptance and enables us to embrace life with fuller integrity.

Even in cases of serious past injury or injustice, relationships can be reconciled and past emotional damage healed through work toward reconciliation, as Terry Hargrave (1994) has found in helping people achieve forgiveness by building love, justice, and trust. His approach involves four intertwined "stations" focused on insight, understanding, giving the opportunity for compensation, and the overt act of forgiving. This work can be painful and difficult. In the course of seeking understanding, we may get in touch with rage and sorrow, or a threatening image of an abuser. Yet when this work is carefully guided, it can be unexpectedly successful, precisely because it deals with a powerful vortex where past and future relationships can be changed simultaneously.

Exoneration and the Possibility of Forgiveness

In the process of reconciliation, exoneration involves the effort of a person who has experienced hurt or injustice to lift the load of culpability off the person(s) seen as responsible (Boszormenyi-Nagy, 1987; Hargreaves, 1994). Instead of subjecting the wrongdoer to endless condemnation, we can learn how patterns of injustice evolved, viewing them in social and historical context. The aim is to gain insight and understanding to appreciate the wrongdoer's situation, options, effort, and constraints. Traumatic events in the past are not erased, but our perceptions and feelings concerning them can be fundamentally altered.

Forgiveness goes beyond exoneration in requiring some specific action regarding the responsibility for the injustice that led to the hurt. When a relational injustice has occurred in a couple or family, it's reasonable to expect the wrongdoer to be held accountable. Forgiving can occur when the wrongdoer accepts responsibility for the injustice and resulting harm, and vows to refrain from further injustice. Forgiveness can also be accomplished by allowing the wrongdoer to compensate for past injustices by being trustworthy in significant ways in the future.

Exoneration is distinct from forgiveness. Exoneration by itself does not demand responsibility for the injustice or reestablishment of trust. Most often, this will limit future relationship possibilities. Yet this may be appropriate in cases where risk persists or the wrongdoer is unwilling to accept responsibility. Forgiveness demands that wrongs be acknowledged and trust restored after a relational hurt. Essentially, forgiving involves relationship transformation. Although forgiveness is enormously fruitful, it is not appropriate for every situation. If, for example, some form of abuse continues to be a threat, the abused person might run an unwise risk to pursue a forgiving relationship. In other cases, forgiveness is not possible because those harmed believe, justifiably, that there is no adequate compensation for the violation.

Can or should the traumatized forgive those who abused or were destructive? Forgiveness is extremely complex; different paths may be taken in varied situations. The process balances personal needs to maintain integrity and protection with efforts to tap family resources of love and trust that will strengthen the individual and bear fruit in other relationships. Reconciliation may involve forgiveness for the part of the relationship that was a violation. In many cases, one may not be able to forgive that part, but can forgive the person and heal the relationship. In doing so, one honors the hurtful experience while keeping it in its place so that it doesn't destroy the whole.

Truth Telling and Justice

In rebalancing our stories and legacies of our history to highlight (s)heroes and positive models, we must be careful not to tilt to the other extreme. We have to face the unpleasant as well as the affirmative side of the human story, including our own story as a nation and our own stories of our peoples. History in families, as in a society, is too easily written in the voice of its dominant members, with the experiences of the vulnerable silenced. In many cases, we must have the ugly facts in order to protect us from the official view of reality.

W. E. B. DuBois (1935/1964) wrote of his astonishment in the study of history at the recurrence of the idea that evil must be forgotten, distorted, skimmed over. We are taught to forget that George Washington was a slave owner and simply remember the things we regard as creditable and inspiring. "The difficulty, of course, with this philosophy is that history loses its value as an incentive and example; it paints perfect men and noble nations, but does not tell the truth" (p. 722).

Truth is at least half of justice when human rights have been violated, whether in a family, a community, or a nation. Recently, a Truth and Reconciliation Commission was formed in South Africa to gather facts and publish historical records about past atrocities during apartheid. Those who committed crimes must, at the very least, acknowledge their deeds publicly as a necessary condition of a plan for amnesty. Amnesty is then considered and offered on a case-by-case basis. In one situation, for instance, a police captain who had killed 13 women and children admitted and apologized for his actions to the victims' families, asking them "to consider" forgiving him. It was then the families' decision as to whether their forgiveness was possible (*New York Times*, October 27, 1996).

Compensation can often further a sense of justice. Yet in some cases, survivors may feel that horrific crimes are beyond compensation. Even when survivors are unable to forgive, telling and learning the truth about past atrocities is important for a brutalized individual, group, or society to bind up its wounds. It offers details about what happened and more catharsis for those who have suffered. Making sense of the senseless helps to render the horrific intelligible. The ambitious experiment in South Africa is fraught with dilemmas, as many perpetrators seeking amnesty have been accused of distorting or covering up facts to deny or minimize their role. For a just resolution, the full truth must be told.

Reviving trauma can initially increase pain and conflict, especially if the cold facts are brutal or shameful. Yet the ability to integrate painful experience and move on with life is furthered by the whole truth, including its comprehension within the context of its time and place. In the words of Martin Luther King, "the truth will set you free."

Forgive and Remember

Contrary to the popular saying "Forgive and forget," forgiveness does not necessarily mean that the slate is wiped clean or that harmful actions should be forgotten. The pain attached to past injustices does tend to fade with time if reconciliation and forgiveness are achieved, especially when love and trust are rebuilt. However, if we forget the damage that occurred, we may not learn from it to take the steps necessary to prevent such actions from happening again in the future. Trust is best restored not when family members (or a society) act as if no violation ever occurred, but rather when they remain mindful of the past and strive to relate differently. New terms for the relationship must be set to ensure that such damage never again occurs.

Forgiveness is often confused with forgetting, or forgiving the person is confused with forgiving the act. Understanding how past traumas contributed to parental vulnerabilities and limitations does not excuse violations. Family members must be held accountable for their motives, actions, and consequences. To explore possibilities, as therapists we might ask clients: "Are there any parts of the experience that can be forgiven? What might make it possible for you to forgive the person, if not the actions? Would it be possible to forgive the person if s/he made an effort to change and were able to acknowledge and apologize with genuine remorse? What if s/he were able to demonstrate some genuine interest in you and your well-being?"

Some regard forgiveness as a betrayal of their own ethical convictions. For example, a respected community leader may once have sexually abused one of his children. When a person abuses power, seriously harms another, and violates trust, it must be weighed quite seriously. Simiilarly, a man may only commit murder on one occasion—when he kills his former wife and her lover—but can or should his children forgive him because he has always been a good father to them? One could respond that killing their mother is not being a good father. Such difficult ethical concerns must be grappled with. As therapists we can try to help clients to gather information and weigh various perspectives in an attempt to make events, relationships, and actions comprehensible as they come to their own decisions.

In cases where there has been abuse, neglect, or other destructive behavior, therapists can strive to help clients reach a position of holding those family members accountable for their behavior, yet without blaming indictment. Therapy can attempt to foster an appreciation of the formative experiences that shaped the vulnerabilities and limitations of those individuals, and thereby to generate empathy for their experiences of suffering. We can encourage clients' refusal to spend their own lives immersed in accusation and bitterness. Above all, this entails a compassionate response to those who have suffered, and yet also to parents or other offenders for their hardship and suffering. In many cases, offenders also need therapists' help in forgiving themselves for past wrongs or shameful actions (Trepper & Barrett, 1989).

It should also be emphasized that the ability of resilient individuals and families to emerge from traumatic situations strong and healthy does not mean that brutalization or abuse is acceptable. Nor should it imply that others are weak and deficient if they are more deeply wounded and less hardy in recovery. Judith Herman (1992) has stressed the importance of "moral solidarity," with respect for those struggling with trauma, because they are most in need of hope and least in need of another reason to feel bad about themselves.

Creating Rituals for Healing and Reconciliation

Active involvement in meaningful rituals can be valuable in healing strained relationships after family trauma.

Raymundo, a trainee in our program, told of his powerful experience of a "family healing mass" held by a priest for him and members of his family of origin. The priest, who was also trained in family therapy as a pastoral counselor, first helped the family to construct a large genogram. Then, seated around a table with the genogram in the center, family members were encouraged to tell their stories of suffering—from drinking problems to intense conflict and abuse. The priest then asked for accounts of strength and heroism, to rebalance their stories and identify potential resources. He asked each to specify the relationship impasses they most hoped to heal, and to point to the relevant parts of the genogram. All family members were encouraged to contribute to this healing conversation from their own positions, expressing their pain and their hope. As each spoke in turn, the others were asked to listen attentively. One at a time, they were then asked whether they desired reconciliation, and whether they would be willing to own accountability for their part in problems and share in responsibility for improving relations. Each in turn affirmed a commitment to these vows and to working together in family therapy. In conclusion, the priest said a prayer for the family and touched each member's forehead with holy oil. For Raymundo and his family, this experience was quite profound and marked a turning point in their relationships.

Time *Can* Heal Old Wounds

Reconciliation between Aging Parents and Adult Children

Fitting the popular belief that "you can't teach an old dog new tricks," Americans carry the expectation that relationships between adults and their parents are cast in stone and unalterable. In my clinical work, I am grateful for my doctoral studies in human development, which focused on adult development and aging. Abundant research documents the potential for growth and change throughout middle and later life (Walsh, 1988b). As Bateson (1994) observes, in response to new circumstances, individuals reinvent themselves many times over. With life experience and the wisdom that comes with aging, people can and do change their ways, even after many years of destructive behavior. Moreover, as older adults seek to bring meaning and coherence to their lives, they attempt to come to terms with problematic and regrettable aspects of their relationships, and look for new opportunities to repair frayed bonds. This involves accepting what cannot be changed in the past, developing new perspectives on experiences, putting regrets in their place, and celebrating the successes.

At various phases in life cycle development, different issues come to the fore as others recede. As we change and grow through our life experience, our remembrance of the past and our current feelings about past events and relationships are altered by our ongoing experience. A conflict over autonomy and control that flared with burning intensity between an adolescent son and his father may no longer be relevant when the son is secure in his identity in midlife. Likewise, the impact of past traumatic events is altered with subsequent experience. A woman's mothering of a newborn is influenced less by her own early relationship with her mother than by the degree of resolution she has achieved in that relationship over time.

Adult development thus presents new possibilities for healing of old intergenerational wounds. In early and middle adulthood, such relationships continue to be renegotiated on an adult-to-adult basis. Rapprochement commonly occurs with such transitions as parenthood, when the younger generation directly experiences the challenges involved in child rearing and begins to gain empathy for their own parents. In fact, as we age, there are increasing numbers of things we find we need to learn from and can appreciate in our elders. We may discover that our parents, like Mark Twain's father, become wiser every year.

Yet time alone is not sufficient. Many relationships become frozen at an earlier point of conflict or cutoff, as if time stood still (McGoldrick, 1995). I was struck in my research interviews of troubled families that a traumatic loss 20 years earlier could still be as painful as if it had happened yesterday when it had not been dealt with. Caregiving for an aging parent can be complicated by an adult child's old anger and pain at not having received good care from that parent in childhood. Unresolved issues from the past can block the ability to see and respond to aging parents as persons facing their own ongoing challenges.

Charleen, a 35-year-old single parent, was furious with her father. He left a message on her answering machine to say that he would not come for Easter dinner at her home, because she wasn't planning to serve ham, and Easter was not the same without the traditional ham dinner her mother had always prepared. Charleen was incensed; he knew full well that she was a vegetarian and that she was going to great lengths to prepare a no-meat feast for their extended family. Charleen heard his refusal to attend as a ploy to control her, just as she had always felt controlled by him as a child. She would not give in to him and serve ham!

Charleen's therapist helped to calm her reactivity and, after hearing more about their past interactions, sought to help Charleen separate this incident from her childhood experience and to understand it in a more immediate context—particularly in light of her mother's death a year earlier. Charleen knew that her father had recently retired, but, busy with her own life, she knew little else about it. Her therapist encouraged her to call her brother, who was close to their father, and get his ideas on what might have triggered the father's abrupt behavior. She was surprised to learn that her father had been forced to retire. Just before his call to her, he had gone in to work for the last day and found that his name was already removed from the door, his office was cleared out, and his belongings were piled in the hallway.

This new information shifted Charleen's perspective in a fundamental way. She had framed the incident, as she usually saw their interactions, in the context of their old parent–child hierarchy—her father's need to exercise power and authority over her. Each time her childhood drama was reactivated, she rebelled angrily against feeling controlled and manipulated by him. Now she saw his recent actions in a new light: He was an aging man, recently widowed, in a life crisis of forced retirement. She went to see him and found him jolted by the cruel way in which he was let go and by the feeling that he had lost control over his own fate. His work world, his identity, his future security, and his dignity were suddenly shattered—and he was alone, missing his wife more than ever. For the first time, Charleen felt truly like an adult in relation to a parent in an older, aging generation, who was facing losses all around him. She could appreciate her father's urgent need to hold on to a part of himself and to maintain continuity with his past. She lovingly included her mother's recipe for ham in the Easter dinner preparations.

Repairing and Preventing Parent–Child Disconnections in Adolescence

In early adolescence, American children are socialized to make a rather crude break toward differentiation and autonomy. Our society encourages them not only to deidealize their parents (particularly their mothers), but to take a rather dim view of them, scrutinizing and finding fault with their every word and deed. As one of my colleagues (a mother herself) observed, "The danger of being thought stupid is that you begin to act that way." She described a "tongue-biting" dinner she attended with a friend, a man in his 40s, and his mother—a woman she knew to be funny, bright, and admirable. With her adult son, whose judgment was formed in adolescence and was never amended, the woman was not the person she was; instead, she became "Mom," nervous and cautious, unsure of what to say to him. Relying on an old formula for conversation, she asked, "Aren't you going to finish your vegetables?" She shriveled with instant regret as her son delivered a look across the table that could have melted lead.

Several years ago, I led groups for women that focused on the mother–daughter relationship and explored patterns and possibilities for growth-enhancing change. Each year the groups filled quickly. One year I thought it would be even more valuable to offer a group for women and their own mothers or daughters, much like a couple group, so that each could better understand the other and together define areas of change to work toward. I couldn't fill the group. Only a few women called; all were mothers at midlife who wanted to improve relationships with their young adult daughters. No daughters would come with their mothers. Yet these same young women were quite eager to come to a group composed of unrelated women where they could talk about their mothers, mostly in disappointing and depreciating ways. At least three issues contribute to such responses. The first is the overwhelmingly negative view of mothers our culture encourages, such that daughters want to seek distance from and to disidentify with them. Second, individuals in adolescence and young adulthood are encouraged to push away from intimate and dependent bonds with parents, especially their mothers. Third, adolescents and young adults have difficulty viewing their parents as persons, empathizing with their positions, or seeing their behavior in context. For example, a daughter of a mother in a traditional marriage may complain that her mother is overinvested in the daughter's career success to meet her own needs—trying to compensate for her life disappointments by living through her daughter. The daughter may need help in understanding her mother's position, contextualizing the gendered constraints in her historical time and social context that led her to sacrifice her identity and strivings to fulfill expectations as a good wife and mother. As a natural consequence, she came to live for and through her husband and children.

Consonant with the relational view of the Stone Center (Jordan et al., 1991), Kathy Weingarten (1994) challenges cultural and psychoanalytic assumptions that disconnection from relationships with mothers in adolescence is essential for healthy development to avoid overdependent and incestuous ties. This proscription against intimate connections silences the voices of mothers (and fathers), and denies young men and women the opportunity to know their parents as persons. Instead, Weingarten argues, fostering connectedness encourages adolescents to gain empathy for others as they differentiate their own positions. This better prepares them for a deeper mutuality with intimate partners and a caring interdependence in intergenerational relations through adulthood.

Healing Sibling Rivalries

Sibling relationships become increasingly valued over the life course. In many cases, such as the following, those relationships are blocked by old rivalries and grievances from childhood.

> Jimmy, age 34, sought therapy to improve his relationships with his siblings, who had been cut off from one another since the sudden death of both parents in an auto accident 2 years earlier. Old sibling rivalries had pitted them against one another since childhood. Their father had been fairly remote and their mother chronically depressed, with the siblings competing fiercely for the little attention they received. In an attempt at reconnection, Jimmy invited his siblings for dinner, but it was disastrous. His sister Carmen saw a treasured photo of their mother on the mantel and became furious with him for failing to make a copy for her, which he

had promised to do at their parents' funeral. Becoming defensive, Jimmy told her to get off his case. Carmen lashed out at him for being a "self-centered mama's boy." He called her a "spiteful old nag." Enraged, she grabbed the photo and tore it up; beside himself, he struck her, causing a nosebleed. The escalation continued in ensuing weeks as Carmen hired a lawyer to sue Jimmy for damages, and he refused to apologize, blamed the incident on her, and consulted a lawyer to countersue. His other siblings sided with his sister against him. Jimmy's wife was also becoming furious at his "childish" plans for revenge.

Old family triangles now entangled Jimmy's therapist. When she questioned Jimmy's proposed counterattack, he accused her of siding with his sister and wife against him, and threatened to stop therapy. The therapist clarified her position: She was not colluding with them against him; rather, she was trying to align with his better self. She knew him to be a decent and generous man, and she believed that deep down, he knew he had played a part in the conflict and might have some regrets. He put his head in his hands, sighed deeply, and nodded. They now more calmly reflected on the chain of events and the relational significance of the incident: keeping to himself (or, from his sister's perspective, withholding from her) the photo of their deceased mother, who hadn't been available when they had most needed her as children. Jimmy agreed that he needed to take responsibility for his own procrastination, since he knew how much the photo meant to Carmen. The therapist also helped him to see that no matter what his sister had done that had provoked him, he was accountable for his own violent reaction and harm to her. The therapist appealed to his better nature, urging him to apologize for his actions and to cease litigation, which would be self-defeating to his goal of improving his relationships with his siblings. She also urged him to find the negative of their mother's photo and to have enlarged copies made and framed for himself and all his siblings. A session with all siblings allowed each one to be heard and better understood. The therapist offered the idea that, in the spirit of reconciliation, they might plan a potluck dinner together, each contributing a favorite dish. At a follow-up session, Jimmy brought photos taken of them all together, celebrating their reunion.

Threatened Loss: Opportunity for Relational Recovery

Terminal illness and threatened loss can heighten the sense of preciousness of one's relationships, and can generate an urgent desire to make amends before it is too late.

Diane came to see me with a painful dilemma. She recounted that her 16-year-old son, Jason, had been fathered by a former boyfriend, Ron; Ron had left town when told of her pregnancy, saying that he wasn't ready for marriage or parenthood. In despair, she'd married Dwayne, a good friend who knew the child wasn't his but willingly accepted paternity. Her son had grown up believing that Dwayne was his biological father. Now Ron had called her from Arizona, saying that he had terminal cancer and wanted to see Jason before he died. We explored Diane's complex feelings in weighing her decision. On the one hand, she was enraged that Ron had abandoned her and their son. Over the years Ron had never seen Jason, expressed the slightest interest in him, or contributed to his support. What right did he have to disrupt their lives now? Furthermore, she worried that the news would be too upsetting for Jason and for her husband, and would risk shattering their stable "intact" family. She also feared that Jason would hate her for keeping the truth from him and living a lie all his life. Yet, on the other hand, she didn't want Jason to learn the truth somehow later on and hate her for denying him his only chance to know his birth father. After deep soul searching, she decided that Jason had a right to know about Ron and to meet him if he chose to do so.

Jason was initially disbelieving, then furious at everyone. However, as Diane and Dwayne hung in with their support and talked things through with him, Jason decided to go to meet his father. The visit was short but meaningful. Ron apologized for having been so scared and immature to have run out on Jason and his mother; a day had not passed without his thoughts of Jason. He was also ashamed that he had not sent money to Jason's mother for his support, because he'd been upset that Dwayne had so readily replaced him. He wanted Jason to know that he had just signed over his pension to Jason to help him through college; he knew that this wouldn't make up for the lost years, but wanted to do what he could now. After returning home, Jason was very grateful for his parents' trust in him. I applauded Diane and Dwayne for being generous in giving Jason and his father this opportunity. Through this process, contrary to Diane's fear of losing their "intact" family, they gained a fuller, truer family "intactness" in their incorporation of all three parents in Jason's life.

Healing and Reconciliation after a Death

"Death ends a life, but not a relationship, which struggles on in the survivor's mind, seeking some resolution which it may never find." This opening line in the film *I Never Sang for My Father* conveys the painful and protracted anguish so often experienced when relational wounds were not reconciled before a death. Much of my clinical work is involved in helping individuals find some resolution, often many years after a loss.

Lenore, age 43, came for therapy to explore unresolved issues centering around the loss of her mother when she was 9. She had just reached the age at which her mother had died, and she was experiencing a pervasive sense of emptiness in her life. Lenore had few memories of her mother, and had always believed that her mother had been cold and distant and had never loved her. I asked her to bring in old family photos; she had very few. Because her mother's health had slowly deteriorated over several years, she hadn't wanted to be photographed frail and in a wheelchair. In one photo, Lenore and several friends were in costumes for a school musical, with her mother behind them. I commented on how struck I was by her mother's fond gaze at her in the photo. She had never noticed that before, but could see it at once. She reported at our next session that she'd kept the photo with her all week, looking at it over and over, each time her eyes brimming with tears. She recalled that the photo was taken less than a year before her mother's death, when she was in great pain and limited in what she could do. Nevertheless, she had volunteered to make costumes for Lenore and her classmates. Now that Lenore cou ld see evidence of her mother's caring, new memories flowed out of the past darkness, and she began to revise her beliefs and stories to incorporate her mother's love. She came to think that her conviction that her mother hadn't cared about her had perhaps helped her to distance herself as her mother died; it had protected her from feeling an unbearable sadness in her loss.

Lenore also realized that she'd barely known her mother, since the mother had been ill for most of her childhood. I urged her to contact her mother's only surviving sister, still living in their hometown in the South, to learn more about her mother as a person. Her aunt sent photos of her mother growing up and invited her to visit. It was several months before Lenore overcame scheduling obstacles and anxieties to make the trip. There she saw her mother's childhood home, heard both poignant and funny stories about her mother's life, and learned how high-spirited she had been before her illness. Her aunt gave her a letter written by her mother shortly before her death, confiding that the hardest part about dying was not being able to be there for Lenore, and expressing her regret that the illness had robbed her of the strength to do all she might have for her. Lenore's enlarged view of her mother and their relationship, along with the new connection with her aunt and their hometown, were enormously healing. She felt more "full of life" and became more engaged in other relationships. Single with no children of her own, she was a talented school teacher, but she had a reputation for being cool and aloof. She brought her new "spiritedness" to her work and to connections with her students.

Through memory and inspiration, we carry on connections with loved ones who have died. Alice Walker (1983), describing her adult relationship with her own grown daughter, once said, "This great friendship of ours is pretty eternal. I often tell her that no matter what, I will always be with her. It's my sense that the real incarnation is not necessarily coming back as someone else but, just as you inherit your mother's brown eyes, you inherit part of her soul."

RECONCILIATION IN COUPLES ON THE BRINK OF SEPARATION OR DIVORCE

In every couple relationship, there are bound to be times of trouble and tensions that can lead to disconnection. For couples today there is a greater need to reconcile differences, in part because the diversity of our lives increases the risk for conflict (Anderson et al., 1995). More people marry across cultures, races, and religions, bringing different traditions to marriage. With rapid social changes, competing pressures of job and family, and new gender role relations, the values and challenges of couples today differ in many ways from those of their parents. We expect more from committed partnerships than ever before, and our expectations lead to greater frustration and disappointment when unrealistic dreams and incompatibilities collide. If each partner in a relationship learns to recognize the uniqueness of the other and to honor the differences, these can add to the richness of the relationship.

Couple therapists, for all our experience, cannot reliably predict which couples will stay together and which will ultimately split up. Often couples come to therapy hoping that we will tell them what they should do or confirm their view that their situation is hopeless. It may well be that relational conflict fuels symptoms, and that one partner feels relief when away from the other or invigorated by a secret affair. Often individuals consider leaving a relationship as their only option when they feel powerless in the relationship. Therapists should not simply accept clients' pessimism about the possibility for relationship change, or encourage them to walk away without assessing conjointly the possibilities for relational healing and considering the impact of a breakup (especially for children). Spouses considering divorce often frame their dilemma in a "take it or leave it" manner; they simply wonder whether to stay or to go. Such framing involves a presumption that "take it" means accepting the status quo, which may be intolerable. The partners may ruminate endlessly without fully exploring the potential gains and costs in either direction. Couple therapy can be valuable in helping both partners identify and communicate needed changes for them to reinvest in the relationship. Partners can be helped to reframe accusations and complaints in terms of their own needs and desires, and to clarify positive aims to work toward.

The possibility of reconciliation for a couple, as for a family-of-origin relationship, depends less on the severity of the break than on the depth of the will to reconcile. It requires a readiness to take the other person seriously, acknowledge the violations, and make amends for the pain suffered. It also means inviting and receiving the forgiveness inherent in the promise to be true to each other in good times and in bad.

Marriage is best seen not as an institution but as a work in progress. Rather than a static contract, it is a dynamic covenant. Because partners and circumstances inevitably change, all enduring relationships require regeneration, updating, and renegotiation of vows and mutual expectations (the relational "quid pro quo" discussed in Chapter 3). "Promising again" is an intentional, mutual renewal of vows requiring that each partner actively choose the other again for a committed relationship (Anderson et al., 1995). Such a ritual can occur at a transition or crisis when the customary ways of being together no longer work. Recommitment—including vows of needed change—is needed when promises have been broken or can't be kept in the form in which they were made. The act of "promising again" expresses the choice of hope over despair. The renewal promotes new life in the bond—a vital reconnection for sustaining and strengthening a relationship over its life course. Reconciliation does more than right wrongs; it can catalyze needed change, bringing partners to a deeper place of trust and commitment.

HEALING AND RECONCILIATION
AFTER SEPARATION AND DIVORCE

How families handle divorce processes over time are as important for recovery and adaptation as the fact of divorce itself. Perhaps more alarming than the current high divorce rate are the findings that within 2 years of divorce, nearly half of all children had not seen their fathers in the past year, and most fathers did not follow through with mandated child support (Furstenberg & Cherlin, 1991). However, divorce need not be an irreparable shattering of relationships and children's lives. Research finds that relationships between divorced parents and their children often improve when these are no longer embedded in ongoing marital conflict. In nearly half of postdivorce families, parents are able to work out an amicable coparenting relationship, and many former spouses are able to forge an informal kinship connection (Ahrons, 1994).

Divorce is rarely a quick and easy decision. It involves a complicated web of feelings and transactional processes over time—from the first consideration of separation, through failed attempts to reconcile and tangled legal proceedings, to transitional upheavals in the immediate aftermath, and on into varying postdivorce reconfigurations, which are further altered with remarriage or relocation. Unfortunately, the mistaken view of resilience as just putting our troubles behind us and moving on dovetails with our culture's "throwaway" mentality, with disposable razors, pens, and relationships. People commonly remarry with the attitude that they "messed up" with the first spouse and kids; this time they'll make a better choice and do things differently.

> Gary, age 45, began his first session by requesting my help "to get my wife—I mean my *life*—in order." He explained that his prior individual therapy had helped him realize that his 18-year marriage was hopelessly dysfunctional (even though the therapist had never met his wife or suggested the possibility of couple therapy). That had freed him to leave his marriage for a new, energizing affair. He mistakenly viewed resilience as simply putting the failed marriage behind him and bouncing right back into a new one, in which he could start fresh. He remarried immediately on the heels of a bitter divorce; the new couple had a baby within the year. His teenage kids refused to see him and sent back his birthday presents unopened. Gary blamed his "ex" for turning them against him. Their continuing stormy relationships, with constant sniping and disputes over visitation and support, were now seriously straining his current marriage. Why, he wondered, couldn't they just get on with their lives and accept the new realities?
>
> A session with Gary's older children and their mother, Cindy, revealed their rage that he could just cast them off and instantly create a new family to replace them. The oldest daughter was particularly upset that Gary was so doting on his new son—in fact, more involved than he had ever been with her or her siblings. Cindy was furious for having denied her own needs for so many years while Gary was building his career. His departure had been so abrupt that the whole family felt suddenly ripped apart. Moreover, Gary's refusal to talk about the past left the reasons for the breakup ambiguous and called into question their

perceptions of their shared history. Cindy tried in vain to make sense of it all—first blaming the other woman, and then blaming herself for not having met Gary's needs. If he could be so loving with a new wife and child, maybe it was their fault. They came to doubt their own lovability and their ability to trust men. It was crucial to heal the wounds of the breakup so that all of them could go on with their lives.

Overcoming Barriers to Postdivorce Reconciliation

Reconciliation does not necessarily mean reunion. It involves coming to terms with difficult and painful aspects of a relationship in order to integrate the experience and move ahead in life. Intense, mixed emotions are common in relationship endings. As researchers Connie Ahrons (1994) and Judith Stacey (1990) have found, many former partners are able to put old grievances in their place and to navigate new relationship territory. Hurts and hostilities can in most cases be reconciled to the extent that the ex-spouses can become collaborative parents to their children and can maintain cordial and respectful relations. It's crucial for them to clarify ambiguities that may fuel children's reunion fantasies: They will not be getting back together as a couple or a family unit, but they do care about each other and always will do their best to be there for the children.

The pain and ambivalent attachment can be so great that individuals swing back and forth between separation and reunion. Many heighten negativities and push their partners away, or get their partners to reject them, in order to make the break. Some get involved precipitously in new relationships to ease their transition. Although one spouse may have initiated legal proceedings, the other may have withdrawn from the relationship long before. A mutually reinforcing cycle of corrosive interactions tends to lead to divorce (Gottman, 1994; see Chapter 5, this volume). Repeated disconnections occur as spouses become increasingly detached. Flooding and negative attributions contribute to distancing and a negative recasting of the history of the relationship.

With divorce, a devaluing of the relationship and the other person commonly occurs; this loosens attachments, eases the pain of loss, and diminishes the sense of blame and shame. The adversarial legal system intensifies conflict and polarization. Divorce continues to hold stigmatizing implications of failure and inadequacy. Recent proposals to do away with "no-fault" laws and make divorce more difficult in order to save marriages would probably increase conflict and suffering still further. Studies show that children fare most poorly when families remain intact with high conflict or abuse, just as when such conflict persists after a divorce.

As divorce is acted upon, "divorce stories" take shape. Each person's narrative about the marriage and its breakdown influences relationships for years to come and for the next generation. Hetherington, Law, and O'Connor (1993) found that after divorce, the accounts given by ex-spouses were so different that "blind" raters could not match individuals who had been in the same marriage. The stories that people commonly construct can keep them trapped in a helpless, victimized position or an angry, accusatory stance. A person who feels depressed, enraged, or powerless over an undesired breakup or unforgivable actions by a former partner is more likely to try to punish the other through whatever means are available. After fighting over possessions, men commonly withhold child support payments as women withhold visitation in a vicious cycle of reactivity and mutual retaliation. Therapists and mediators can lay important groundwork at the time of divorce to prevent such avoidable fallout (Walsh et al., 1995).

Long-term follow-up studies show that children's successful postdivorce adaptation is enhanced when both parents can remain involved with their children and collaborate, to the fullest extent possible, in their rearing and financial support (Whiteside, 1998). Joint custody can facilitate continuing involvement; yet such arrangements require a high degree of mutual trust, cooperation, and communication. Without strong collaboration, children fare best in sole custody and a primary residence, while maintaining reliable contact with the noncustodial parent. An arrangement of "parallel parenting" is often more realistic than joint custody; in such an arrangement, each parent assumes authority and responsibility for his or her own parenting, with an agreement not to interfere with the other's parental rights or to involve children in coalitions against the other. Whatever the arrangement, clinicians can help to minimize hostilities and to increase mutual respect between parents, so that children can be assured of reliable, nonconflictual access to both parents. In cases where serious mental illness, addiction, abuse, or neglect precludes regular visitation with a noncustodial parent, children can fare quite well with a sole parent or guardian who has strong executive functioning and adequate financial support. Phone calls, letters, and carefully supervised visits should be arranged whenever possible with the other parent, as should contact with that parent's extended family.

There are many losses in divorce. Even if the partner or relationship was deeply disappointing or hurtful, divorce also involves the loss of the intact family unit and the hopes and dreams for the future of the relationships. The emotional divorce often lags behind the legal divorce, especially when continuing involvement in regard to children restimulates old attachments and conflicts. Ambiguous loss complicates griefwork. Unlike widowhood, in divorce the marriage is ended but the former partner lives on, moving into a separate life and other relationships. The ex-partners are no longer a couple, and yet they remain coparents to children for the rest of their lives. In my experience, the reigniting of such painful, complicated feelings of loss on contact fuels much postdivorce conflict and cutoff. One divorced man found it so upsetting to have to ring the doorbell of his former home to take his children out that he moved away and stopped seeing his children. Arranging pickups and dropoffs at school or other neutral places can ease such tensions.

The tendency to vilify an ex-spouse is as strong as the tendency to over-romanticize a new lover. The blame, shame, and guilt surrounding divorce, further inflamed by our adversarial legal system, often fuel brutal character assassinations that rationalize the divorce or a desired settlement. Many individuals are so hurt or bitter in the aftermath of divorce that they lose sight of the positive aspects of their former partners and their relationships, which connected them in the first place and may have yielded many good years. It takes maturity and generosity to resist joining in blaming indictments by well-intentioned family or friends. The actress Ingrid Bergman, in response to an interviewer's putdown of her ex-husbands, replied, "Please don't speak badly of my former husbands; they were wonderful men or I never would have married them."

It is vital to understand the hopes and dreams, the energies and sacrifices that were invested in a couple's relationship in order to understand relational disappointments. It's also important to consider the contribution of each family of origin to marital expectations. I asked Joel, recently divorced, when he had first considered divorce. He replied, "Even before the honeymoon." At the wedding, his father had congratulated him on finding a woman just like his mother—whom the father had constantly berated throughout their marriage. Joel remarked, "That was the kiss of death for my marriage."

An individual who is stuck in destructive, stereotypical victim–villain scenerios can be helped to revise such stories to include the many dimensions of the former partner and relationship, and thus to facilitate healing and reconciliation. A therapist can encourage such a person to review the history of the relationship, from courtship through the ups and downs of the marriage and its ending. It's also useful to gain clarifying information and perspectives from the ex-spouse, other important family members, and close friends, to comprehend more clearly how the marriage came apart. One woman, feeling inadequate for not having satisfied her ex-husband, learned from him a year later that he had left the marriage because he was gay and could no longer live a lie. Yet, because of the social stigma, he had not been able to acknowledge it openly at the time.

Adaptation is facilitated when both ex-partners can own their parts in the breakdown of a relationship over time. A therapist can pose questions that encourage them to rebalance their negative views to include positive aspects of each other and the relationship. Helping ex-partners to make meaning of their relationship and acknowledge their part in its ending can greatly facilitate the emotional resolution of the divorce, which is needed in order to move on with life without rancor or bitterness. A sense of dislocation, loss of security, and uncertainty about the future can all fuel anxiety. With a breakup, core beliefs and assumptions about oneself and the relationship are all reexamined (e.g., "Who am I if not in relation to you? How will we manage financially?"). A therapist's questions can also encourage future-oriented possibilities: "What strengths do you see the two of you having that could help to deescalate conflict? How might you set aside differences in order to collaborate in raising your children?" It's important to help the ex-partners accept what can't be changed and consider their possible options. With time and effort, many former spouses can transform a ruptured partnership into a caring kinship. One man, visiting his seriously ill ex-wife in the hospital, was unsure how to introduce himself when the doctor stopped by. His former wife said simply, "This is Sam; we were partners for many years, and now he's my good friend for life."

Transforming and Sustaining Extended Family Ties after Divorce

In conflictual divorces, the partners' families of origin commonly choose sides or are pushed to the margins, and are often at risk of losing precious contact with grandchildren. Yet active efforts can be made to avoid triangulations and to sustain extended family ties as they are transformed through divorce. We can strongly encourage clients to facilitate strong connections for their children and to consider the kinds of relationships they themselves would like to maintain with former in-laws and extended family members.

One source of discomfort concerns our language and categories to define these relations, other than jokingly referring to former in-laws as "outlaws." Recently, many years after my own divorce and remarriage, I was pleasantly surprised to hear my daughter's cousin on her father's side (my careful construction) still call me simply "Aunt Froma." I was delighted that she felt comfortable staying at our home for an overnight visit, yet I was awkward about whether I could still think of her as "my niece." And what should she call my husband? "Stepuncle" seemed as absurd as "ex-aunt." Many cultures don't have our problems with language and formality in regard to family reconfigurations; they value a wide variety and continuity of informal kin ties, and recognize that children's lives are nourished by having many brothers, sisters, aunts, uncles, cousins, grandparents, and godparents—whether "step" or otherwise. In turn, the lives of elders are enriched by these thick and over-lapping connections. We should worry less about proper kinship titles and forge as many linkages as possible.

Bridging the Old and the New in Remarriage

Over two-thirds of divorced individuals go on to remarry, and many bring unresolved issues into the new relationships that contribute to the 60% rate of divorce in remarriage. Researchers find that the biggest mistake in re-marriage is the misguided attempt to cut ties to the past, to seal a border around the new family unit, and to emulate an intact nuclear family model (Visher & Visher, 1993). Children are at higher risk of dysfunction when they are put into loyalty conflicts, cut off from biological parents, or expected to form an instant replacement bond with a stepparent. Fathers who cut off contact from their children in previous marriages often become blocked from developing relationships with stepchildren. Working through feelings of loss, guilt, and fears of attachment can facilitate both reconnection and new connections. It is also very helpful when subsequent partners under-stand children's need to maintain bonds with both biological parents, and when they are able not to be jealous of or threatened by a good relation-ship between the ex-partners. The resilience of stepfamilies and children is strongest when open boundaries and multiple connections across house-holds are encouraged.

THERAPIST, HEAL THY OWN RELATIONSHIPS: PERSONAL JOURNEYS AND REFLECTIONS

If therapists are to help clients overcome pessimism and anxiety about change in long-standing patterns, we must have a strong conviction that some change is possible in most cases. Such a conviction is difficult if we ourselves have given up on change in our own family relationships. Similarly, it may be dif-ficult to help partners repair their couple relationship while a therapist is currently going through a painful separation and unable to overcome similar impasses. However, therapists who have reached a good understanding and reasonable reconciliation following relational breakdown can often draw on their experience in helpful ways. Curiously, research has not attended to this connection between a therapist's own current state of relational resolution and the outcome of therapy with couples and families seeking reconciliation. In the hope that my own personal efforts at reconciliation may inspire others, I describe some of these experiences in this section.

Reconnecting with My Father and Learning His History

Although my early experiences as a family therapist and researcher convinced me that positive changes could occur in even the most troubled relationships, there was one nagging exception: my own relationship with my father, which I had given up on. I felt an uneasy dissonance between the professional and the personal—touting the strengths and possibilities for change in other families, but writing off my father as a hopeless case. For many years I carried disappointment, anger, and embarrassment about my father. He was a shy, unassuming man who walked with a limp. His adage was "Don't get your hopes up too high; then you'll never be disappointed." He made do with little and was looked down upon as a failure by others in our family and community who were impressed by social status. I received this view of him as the truth. Clearly, it was time to work on my own family relationships.

I was fortunate to be able to consult with Murray Bowen, and doubly blessed for the opportunity to process much of my work with my close friend and colleague Monica McGoldrick, who was also working on her family relationships at that time. We shored each other up, encouraging each other to keep hopeful and to persevere; our own deep friendship was a source of resilience for us both in our change efforts.

I had many opportunities to practice Bowen reconnection skills as I reengaged with my father. I had not seen him since my mother's death, 4 years earlier. When I phoned to tell him I wanted to fly out to visit him, instead of sounding pleased, he gruffly replied, "Well, don't expect me to pay for your airfare." I took a deep breath and assured him I didn't. Indicating no pleasure at the thought of my visit, he replied, "Well, my work is very heavy; I won't have much time to spend with you. And the apartment's a mess." I took a deeper breath and said, "That's OK; I thought I'd stay with a friend. [This was a break with the norm of a home stay.] I could meet you for dinner after work, if you're free." He retorted, "Oh, you mean you're *really* coming to see your friends." At this point, with my anger mounting, it would have been easy to chalk up another failed attempt and quit. Here I was, making this great effort, and there he was, unappreciative and hopeless. However, I tried not to get defensive or annoyed, and reasserted that my main wish was to see him. The call ended without an inkling of encouragement from him, but I went ahead with my plan. When my flight arrived at midday, my dad surprised me by being at the gate; he had taken a sick day so that we could spend time together.

It's very important to keep in mind that in efforts to reconnect, we must take the initiative and not get reactive if the immediate response is disappointing. And, as I have emphasized, it's crucial to try to understand the other person's position. I had been working toward this action for some time; my call caught my father unexpectedly and he reacted defensively, to protect his feelings. As I now came to realize, he had missed me terribly. I tried to put myself in his place: Why was I calling now? Did I want something from him? Was I just being "polite" and really motivated to visit my friends? He was aware of my discomfort with him over the years, and had lost hope that I genuinely cared about him and might actually want to see him.

My efforts to reconnect with my father reaped benefits far beyond my expectations. Over the next few years, our relationship deepened with each contact, yet not without occasional friction. He was a quiet man who didn't like to talk about problems or painful subjects. It took my genuine interest in hearing more about his life, and my doggedly persistent urging over many visits, for him to share stories of his childhood and reveal the suffering he had endured and his remarkable comebacks.

My father and his family were famous for telling little about themselves or their past. My father never wanted to talk about his limp; my mother gathered it was caused by a sports injury in adolescence. I seized an opportunity to learn more at a family wedding, cornering my uncle, who had had enough champagne to open up. I was astonished to learn that my father had fallen from his high chair as an infant, breaking his hip. He had undergone surgery three times by the age of 8; each time, he was encased for many months in a plaster cast from waist to foot. Each time, when the cast was removed, his hip had slipped out of place again. This ordeal forced him to spend his childhood at home, unable to walk freely or play. With tremendous perseverance by his parents (who used up their entire modest savings), his leg was finally repaired, although by then it was shorter than the other. He started school at the age of 11, where, although he was bright, the young children in his first-grade class made fun of him. Awkward and embarrassed, he left school at 14 and completed his GED on his own. He then enrolled in a local college, working for a pharmacist to put himself through school. After 3 years, the college went bankrupt and closed, a casualty of the Great Depression. His boss praised my father's hard work and promised to give him the pharmacy at retirement, if he would continue to work for very little pay through those hard times. When my parents married, they were struggling financially, yet hopeful for the future. Despite their best efforts, the pharmacy folded in 1939 and my father's dreams were once again dashed. My parents then started over, moving to a new community where my uncles gave my father a small, failed business to try his hand at. They both worked hard; I was born; and just as they seemed to be doing well, a fire in our apartment building wiped out everything they had. It could be said that I was born into adversity, but we also had good fortune: The night of the fire, I was in the hospital having my tonsils out, which saved all our lives.

I pieced together much of this story as my father and I continued our journey of reconciliation. Putting his life into perspective fundamentally altered my view of him and my feelings toward him. My anger and disappointment melted as a compassionate understanding of his life emerged. He was no longer a failure in my eyes, but instead a hero, who had struggled valiantly to overcome the many hardships and cruel disappointments in his life. He was a loner, an oddball, never quite comfortable in social situations or the company of more financially successful relatives. Yet in many ways he was the strongest, most resilient one in his family. He met his life's misfortunes with courage; tested repeatedly, he always rose to meet the challenge.

While I was growing up, my father worked 7 days a week, 12 hours a day—except for the occasional Sunday drive we took, when he put up a sign: "Open every day but not today." He managed to build our small house himself, along with a neighboring carpenter and electrician, who traded services with him. My mother also worked very hard as a music teacher, yet always made time for community service projects. My father worked until, at 70, he could no longer stand on his feet all day. Then, living only on Social Security, he got up each day and did full-time volunteer office work for his men's organization to raise money for hospitals serving children with disabilities. In clearing out his apartment at his death, I found many service awards, which in his modesty he had never mentioned.

I had never understood my father until I was able to put his life together and gain a sense of coherence. In the early phase of reconciliation, I experienced tremendous sadness at "time lost," as I regretted all those years when my disappointment and shame at my father's deficits had blinded me to his strengths and blocked our relationship. Those last precious years of discovery and reconnection are a continual wellspring of love and inspiration in my life.

As Monica McGoldrick (1995) reminds us, there are few pure saints or sinners in real families. If we look for redeeming qualities in family members who are seen only as villains or failures, we will begin to see them. Following the wisdom of Native Americans, we may have to believe in the possibilities in order to see them. In the same way, if we can believe that even the most troubled relationships have the potential for change and growth, we are more likely to act in ways that indeed foster reconnection and reconciliation.

Seizing the Opportunity

My mother had been cut off from her family after leaving the Catholic Church, and then converted to Judaism when she married my father. Although we received annual Christmas cards from her brother, I had only met him once briefly, as a child; he had turned a cold shoulder when my mother sought his support during hard times. Shortly before my mother's death, when I was 27 and eager to know her better in what little time we had, she shared a secret she had kept even from my father: She had been a nun for 17 years. She died before I could ask the many questions I was left with.

Several years later, in the usual holiday card from my uncle, he mentioned that he was looking forward to a family reunion. However, he offered no details or invitation. Overcoming my initial anger and identification with my mother's painful exclusion, I decided to take a risk and write back to express my interest and ask if I might attend. He replied immediately with a gracious invitation. I learned that the reunion was in honor of the retirement of Sister Honoria as Mother Superior of her order. She was my mother's cousin and had been her closest confidante through her teen years and early adulthood: as best friends, they had entered the convent together at the age of 16. This was an opportunity I couldn't miss.

I also learned that there were other relatives going to the reunion from Chicago—relatives I didn't even know lived in my city. Flying to the reunion together, I found myself more anxious than I had anticipated; these newfound cousins were friendly, yet conversation was superficial and awkward, with no mention of my mother. At the reunion, everyone greeted me warmly, but still no one spoke of my mother. I felt strangely as if I had somehow landed in this family all by myself.

My family therapy tools of the trade saved the day, relieving my anxiety and making connections. I first pored over old photographs, eager to hear about the whole cast of characters. Then I sat down at the kitchen table with paper and pencil and began to sketch a genogram, asking questions as I drew. Soon family members gathered around, curious and eager to add their pieces or make corrections, and stories began to flow. As I brought up my desire to hear stories of my mother, they dug out photos of my mother in her nun's habit; they too had been carrying the secret, unsure whether I knew. Over the next 2 days, relatives kept coming up to me with more stories and questions. I encouraged them to talk with one another, to put together partial accounts, and to contact others who couldn't be there to "fill in the blanks" and send me any more recollections that might come to them. I promised to draw up a complete family genogram (and sent it to everyone several months later with a New Year's greeting).

At the reunion, I invited Sister Honoria to go for a walk. She too had hoped for a chance for us to talk. My first question concerned my desire to understand why my mother had become a nun. I learned that my maternal grandmother, a deeply religious French Canadian Catholic, had hoped that my mother's brother, whom she favored, would become a priest. When he left the seminary after a year to marry his sweetheart, my mother seized the opportunity to gain her mother's favor by entering the convent.

As I learned about this hidden phase in my mother's life, the discordant parts in my understanding of my mother as a person became more coherent. A gifted musician, she became a highly admired teacher, organist, and choir director. But she experienced her deep personal spirituality, humanity, and love of life as increasingly at odds with her hierarchical, ascetic, and clois-tered environment. With great anguish, she came to the courageous decision to leave the order for the real world. In that time and place, such a decision was shame-laden and unforgivable. After she left the convent, her mother refused to see her; she died within the year, and my mother was not informed of it until after the funeral. This loss of reconciliation was a deep sadness my mother carried secretly all her life. I now understood the sorrow I had seen in her eyes, the sadness that could find no comfort.

Reaching Out to Widen the Circle

At the family reunion, I felt particularly anxious when I saw my mother's cousin Alma. I had a dark memory of her from childhood, the only time my mother and I visited her. Having married well, she lived in luxury. She received us coldly; my mother said afterward that she thought she was too good for us. Picking up my mother's embarrassment, I took this to mean that it was my father's fault for being the wrong religion and not a financial success. Seeing her again, I felt intimidated and wary, although she warmed up to me and invited me to visit her.

After the reunion, I kept meaning to visit Alma, but I found myself put-ting it off. When many months had passed, I finally pushed myself to call and visit. I felt trepidation as I approached the house, which looked just as I re-membered from childhood. Alma greeted me warmly and had a large box of old photographs waiting for me. As she shared memories over the photos, her tears came. She confessed that she had been very jealous of my mother as a child. Her own father, a lumberjack, had disappeared on a logging job and was presumed dead, although his body was never found. Her mother, left penniless, was forced to work long hours in a laundry and sent Alma to live with my mother's family. Sealing over her losses and grief, she became aloof and resentful of the loving bond she saw daily between my mother and her father. It was the reactivation of that old pain that had triggered her de-fensive coldness when my mother and I had last visited her. I hugged her with a new affection when this visit ended, treasuring the many photos and new perspectives she gave me.

Three weeks later, another relative called to tell me that Alma had died in her sleep. I realized that because of my busy schedule and my procrastination, we had nearly missed this transforming connection. Learning from this experience, I now urge my clients and students not to put off acting on good intentions to transform painful experiences and heal wounded relationships. This is especially urgent with elders and those with life-threatening illness. Yet all of our lives are unpredictable, and we should never take time for granted in any relationship. A key to relational resilience is active initiative—seizing the opportunities before us and creating the new relational possibilities we yearn for.

Naming: Bridging the Divide

Naming is often a way of making connections across the generations and in joining families by marriage. In my own family, naming became a way for my mother to weave together the disparate threads of her life and identity. Her mother, a devout Catholic, named my mother and her brother Mary and Joseph. After Joe left the seminary, my mother not only took his place by entering the convent; she even took his name, becoming Sister Josephine. When she eventually left the religious order to lead a "normal" life, she held on to that part of her identity by calling herself Mary Jo. (Recently I noted that the same year my mother came out into the world, Katharine Hepburn portrayed Jo in a film version of *Little Women*.) When she married my father and converted to Judaism, she became known as Jo. To bridge the cultural and religious divide and to win the approval of her new mother-in-law, she named me after my father's maternal grandmother, Frimid. (My middle name, Carolyn, is her own mother's name.) Only when I reached adulthood did I learn that Froma (Frimid) is derived from the Jewish name Fruma, meaning "pious" or "spiritual." My name would thus have had special meaning for my mother. Although she chose a secular life, she remained a deeply spiritual person (and even became temple organist and later, B'nai B'rith president).

WHAT CAN BE LEARNED?: LESSONS FOR THE FUTURE

Another important key in resilience is learning from adversity. What can be learned from trauma and tragedies? What is their legacy? In one of the most painful and enduring photo images of the Vietnam War, 9-year-old Phan Thi Kim Phuc was running naked, her arms outstretched, screaming in agony and terror as napalm seared her body. She endured a score of surgical operations and became a political symbol of the horror of war. By her mid-30s, she felt she was finally living a "normal, happy life" with her husband and small son in a one-room apartment in an Asian neighborhood in Toronto. In an act of reconciliation nearly 25 years after her ordeal, she went to Washington, D.C., to lay a wreath at the Vietnam Veterans' Memorial on Veterans' Day 1996. Speaking before a large audience who greeted her with standing ovations, she told them:

> "I have suffered a lot from both physical and emotional pain. Sometimes I could not breathe. But God saved my life and gave me faith and hope. Even if I could talk face to face with the pilot who dropped the bombs, I would tell him, 'We cannot change history, but we should try to do good things for the present and for the future to promote peace.'" (Quoted in Sciolino, 1996, p. A1)

When a tragedy occurs, history need not repeat itself. As Phan Thi Kim Phuc has shown, we can be victimized and yet not assume an identity as victims. This first victimization may be beyond our control; avoiding the trap of a victimized life stance is within our power. Instead, we can forge resilience by rising up above the trauma, pulling out strength from deep inside us that galvanizes our determination to make changes for the better.

History tends to be written by the most powerful, to support their privilege and legitimize their actions. We need to expand the power of history to people who have been unjustly or brutally treated and marginalized, either within their families or by societies, so that all of us are empowered to use our understanding of the past to inform and inspire our best actions in the present and the future.

Spirit with a Broken Heart

In the powerful video documentary *The West* (Ives, Abramson, & Kantor, 1996), Albert White Hat, a Lakota Indian, tells of his struggle to come to terms with the genocidal atrocities committed against his tribe over the last 150 years, which churned inside his entire being:

> I grew up with a lot of the older people, listened to the stories. The stories were inside of me. I went into a boarding school system and they killed those stories in that system. I came to be ashamed of who I am, what I am.
>
> In the late '60s I returned to the culture, let my hair grow, and started speaking the language. I did the Vision Quest for 5 years; I fasted. One of those times, it was a beautiful night, the stars were out, it was calm, and around midnight I got up and I prayed and sat there a while. Then all of a sudden I had these flash-

backs—of Sand Creek, Wounded Knee—and every policy, every law that was imposed on us by the churches hit me one at a time and how it affected my life. And as I sat there I got angrier and angrier, till it turned to hatred. And I looked at this whole situation, the whole history, and there was nothing I could do. It was too much. The only thing I could do, to me, was: When I come off that hill I'm going to grab a gun and I'm going to start shooting; and then maybe my grandfathers will honor me if I go that route.

I got up and I turned around and faced the East and it was beautiful; there was dawn light. Right above that blue light in the darkness was the sliver of the moon in the morning. And I wanted to live. I wanted to live and be happy. I feel I deserve it. But the only way I was going to do that was if I forgive. And I cried that morning because I had to forgive.

Since then I work every day on that commitment. Now, I don't know how many people feel that way, but every one of us, if you're a Lakota, you have to deal with this at some point in your life. You have to address that and you have to make a decision. If you don't, you're going to die on the road someplace, either from being too drunk or from putting a bullet in your head. So this isn't history; it's still with us. What has happened in the past will never leave us. The next 100 years it will be with us. And we have to deal with it every day.

As Albert White Hat came to realize, if we are consumed by accusatory rage, it can enslave our present and our future to past horrors, and preclude our having a decent life.

Despite family therapists' adherence to systems principles of circularity, the passage of time moves forward. We are all drawn to the wish-fulfilling fantasy of a time machine that will allow us to go back to the past, so that we can repair it or change it. We may not be able to recover the past in that way, but we can alter our perspectives on that past and can vow to live and relate differently. History need not repeat itself. The therapeutic task is to make the covert linkages overt between events and feelings in the past and those in the present, and then to draw upon the best resources within us and our legacies. As children in our families of origin, we had little control over traumatic events; as adults and parents, we have the power and opportunity to do better—with our own children, with others in our lives, and in compassion toward the human community. Our future will be promising if we can come to understand our lives and take up our responsibilities to all living things.

References

Ahrons, C. (1994). *The good divorce: Keeping your family together when your marriage comes apart*. New York: HarperCollins.

Ahrons, C., & Rogers, R.H. (1989). *Divorced families: Meeting the challenges of divorce and remarriage*. New York: Wiley.

American Association of University Women (AAUW), Educational Foundation. (1992). *How schools shortchange girls*. Washington, DC: Author.

Anderson, B., Kiecolt-Glaser, J., & Glaser, R. (1994). A biobehavioral model of cancer stress and disease course. *American Psychologist, 49,* 389–404.

Anderson, C. M. (1986). The all-too-short trip from positive to negative connotation. *Journal of Marital and Family Therapy, 12,* 351–354.

Anderson, C. M., Reiss, D., & Hogarty, G. (1986). *Schizophrenia and the family*. New York: Guilford Press.

Anderson, C. M., & Stewart, S. (1994). *Flying solo: Women at midlife and beyond*. New York: Norton.

Anderson, H., & Goolishian, H. (1988). Human systems as linguistic systems. *Family Process, 27,* 371–393.

Anderson, H., Hogue, D., & McCarthy, M. (1995). *Promising again*. Louisville, KY: Westminster.

Anderson, S., Piantanida, M., & Anderson, C. (1993). Normal processes in adoptive families. In F. Walsh (Ed.), *Normal family processes* (2nd ed.). New York: Guilford Press.

Angelou, M. (1986). *Poems: Maya Angelou*. New York: Bantam Books.

Angelou, M. (1992, January). *On the pulse of morning*. Inaugural poem, Washington, DC.

Anthony, E. J. (1987). Risk, vulnerability, and resilience: An overview. In E. J. Anthony & B. Cohler (Eds.), *The invulnerable child*. New York: Guilford Press.

Antonovsky, A. (1979). *Health, stress, and coping*. San Francisco: Jossey-Bass.

Antonovsky, A. (1987). *Unraveling the mystery of health*. San Francisco: Jossey-Bass.

Antonovsky, A., & Sourani, T. (1988). Family sense of coherence and family adaptation. *Journal of Marriage and the Family, 50,* 79–92.

Aponte, H. (1994). *Bread and spirit: Therapy with the new poor*. New York: Norton.

Baltes, M. (1996). *The many faces of dependency in old age*. New York: Cambridge University Press.

Bank, S. (1997). *The sibling bond* (rev. ed.). New York: Basic Books.

Barnard, C. P. (1994). Resiliency: A shift in our perception? *American Journal of Family Therapy, 22,* 135–144.

Barnett, R. C., & Rivers, C. (1996). *She works/he works.* San Francisco: HarperSanFrancisco.

Bateson, G. (1979). *Mind and nature: A necessary unity.* New York: Dutton.

Bateson, M. C. (1989). *Composing a life.* New York: Atlantic Monthly Press.

Bateson, M. C. (1994). *Peripheral visions.* New York: HarperCollins.

Beavers, J., Hampson, R., Hulgus, Y., & Beavers, W. R. (1986). Coping in families with a retarded child. *Family Process, 25,* 365–378.

Beavers, W. R. (1986). *Successful marriages.* New York: Norton.

Beavers, W. R., & Hampson, R. B. (1990). *Successful families: Assessment and intervention.* New York: Norton.

Beavers, W. R., & Hampson, R. B. (1993). Measuring family competence: The Beavers systems model. In F. Walsh (Ed.), *Normal family processes* (2nd ed.). New York: Guilford Press.

Beck, A., Rush, A. J., Shaw, B. F., & Emery, G. (1987). *Cognitive therapy of depression.* New York: Guilford Press.

Becker, E. (1973). *The denial of death.* New York: Free Press.

Bellah, R., Madsen, R., Sullivan, W., Swidler, A., & Tipton, S. (1985). *Habits of the heart: Individualism and commitment in American life.* Berkeley: University of California Press.

Berg, I. (1997). *Family-based services: A solution-focused approach.* New York: Norton.

Bernard, J. (1982). *The future of marriage.* New Haven, CT: Yale University Press.

Bernardin, J. (1997). *The gift of peace.* Chicago: Loyola Press.

Bernheim, K., & Lehman, A. (1985). *Working with families of the mentally ill.* New York: Norton.

Billingsley, A. (1992). *Climbing Jacob's ladder: The enduring legacy of African American families.* New York: Simon & Schuster.

Borden, W. (1992). Narrative perspectives in psychosocial intervention following adverse life events. *Social Work, 37,* 153–141.

Boss, P. (1987). Family stress. In M. B. Sussman & S. K. Steinmetz (Eds.), *Handbook of marriage and the family.* New York: Plenum Press.

Boss, P. (1991). Ambiguous loss. In F. Walsh & M. McGoldrick (Eds.), *Living beyond loss: Death in the family.* New York: Norton.

Boss, P., Caron, W., Horbal, J., & Mortimer, J. (1990). Predictors of depression in caregivers of dementia patients: Boundary ambiguity and mastery. *Family Process, 29,* 245–254.

Boszormenyi-Nagy, I. (1987). *Foundations of contextual family therapy.* New York: Brunner/Mazel.

Bowen, M. (1978). *Family therapy in clinical practice.* New York: Jason Aronson.

Bowlby, J. (1988). *A secure base: Parent–child attachment and healthy human development.* New York: Basic Books.

Boyd-Franklin, N. (1989). *Black families in therapy: A multi-systems approach.* New York: Guilford Press.

Boyd-Franklin, N. (1993). Race, class, and poverty. In F. Walsh (Ed.), *Normal family processes* (2nd ed.). New York: Guilford Press.

Braverman, L. (1989). The myths of motherhood. In M. McGoldrick, C. Anderson, & F. Walsh (Eds.), *Women in families: A framework for family therapy.* New York: Norton.

Bronfenbrenner, U. (1979). *The ecology of human development.* Cambridge, MA: Harvard University Press.

Brooks, R. B. (1994). Children at risk: Fostering resilience and hope. *American Journal of Orthopsychiatry, 64,* 545–553.

Bruner, J. (1986). *Actual minds, possible worlds.* Cambridge, MA: Harvard University Press.

Brunner, E. (1984). *Revelation and reason.* Raleigh, NC: Stevens Book Press.

Bussell, D., & Reiss, D. (1993). Genetic influences on family process. In F. Walsh (Ed.), *Normal family processes* (2nd ed.). New York: Guilford Press.

Burton, L. (1990). Teenage childbearing as an alternative life-course strategy in multigeneration black families. *Human Nature, 1,* 123–143.

Butler, K. (1997, March–April). The anatomy of resilience. *Family Therapy Networker,* pp. 22–31.

Byng-Hall, J. (1995). *Rewriting family scripts: Improvisation and systems change.* New York: Guilford Press.

Campbell, T. (1986). The family's impact on health: A critical review. *Family Systems Medicine, 4,* 135–328.

Campbell, T., & Patterson, J. (1995). The effectiveness of family interventions in the treatment of physical illness. *Journal of Marital and Family Therapy, 21,* 545–583.

Carter, B. (1996). *Love, honor, and negotiate.* New York: Pocket Books.

Carter, B., & McGoldrick, M. (Eds.). (1998). *The expanded life cycle: Individual, family, community.* Needham Heights, MA: Allyn & Bacon.

Cederblad, M., & Hanson, K. (1996). Sense of coherence—A concept influencing health and quality of life in a Swedish psychiatric at-risk group. *Israeli Journal of Medical Science, 32,* 194–199.

Central Conference of American Rabbis. (1992). *Gates of prayer for weekdays and at a house of mourning: A gender-sensitive prayerbook.* New York: Author.

Chase-Lansdale, L., & Brooks-Gunn, J. (1991). Children having children: Effects on the family system. *Pediatric Annals, 20,* 467–481.

Children's Defense Fund. (1992). *Helping children by strengthening families: A look at family support programs.* Chicago: Family Resource Coalition.

Cohler, B. (1987). Adversity, resilience, and the study of lives. In E. J. Anthony & B. Cohler (Eds.), *The invulnerable child.* New York: Guilford Press.

Cohler, B. (1991). The life story and the study of resilience and response to adversity. *Journal of Narrative and Life History, 1,* 169–200.

Coleman, S. (1991). Intergenerational patterns of traumatic loss: Death and despair in addict families. In F. Walsh & M. McGoldrick (Eds.), *Living beyond loss: Death in the family.* New York: Norton.

Coles, R. (1997). *The moral intelligence of children.* New York: Random House.

Combrinck-Graham, L. (1985). A developmental model for family systems. *Family Process, 24,* 139–150.

Comer, J. (1997). *Waiting for a miracle.* New York: Viking.

Coohey, C., & Marsh, J. (1995). Promotion, prevention, and treatment: What are the differences? *Research on Social Work Practice, 5,* 524–538.

Coontz, S. (1997). *The way we really are: Coming to terms with America's changing families.* New York: Basic Books.

Cousins, N. (1979). *The anatomy of an illness as perceived by the patient.* New York: Norton.

Cousins, N. (1989). *Head first: The biology of hope.* New York: Dutton.

Cowan, P. A., Cowan, C. P., & Schulz, M. S. (1996). Thinking about risk and resilience in families. In M. Hetherington & E. A. Blechman (Eds.), *Stress, coping, and resilience in children and families.* Mahwah, NJ: Erlbaum.

Csikszentmihalyi, M. (1996). *Creativity: Flow and the psychology of discovery and invention.* New York: HarperCollins.

Dallos, R. (1991). *Family belief systems, therapy, and change.* Philadelphia: Open University Press.

DeFrain, J. (1991). Learning about grief from normal families: SIDS, stillbirth, and miscarriage. *Journal of Marital and Family Therapy, 18,* 215–323.

Delany, S., & Delany, A. E., with Hearth, A. H. (1993). *Having our say: The Delany sisters' first 100 years.* New York: Dell.

de Shazer, S. (1985). *Keys to solution in brief therapy.* New York: Norton.

DeSilva, C. (Ed.). (1996). *In memory's kitchen: A legacy from the women of Terezin.* New York: Jason Aronson.

Doherty, W. (1996). *The intentional family.* Reading, MA: Addison-Wesley.

Dohrenwend, B. S., & Dohrenwend, B. P. (Eds.). (1981). *Stressful life events and their contexts.* New York: Prodist.

Doka, K. (1998). *Living with life-threatening illness.* San Francisco: Jossey-Bass.

Dossey, D. (1993). *Healing words: The power of prayer and the practice of medicine.* New York: Harper.

Dugan, T., & Coles, R. (Eds.). (1989). *The child in our times: Studies in the development of resiliency.* New York: Brunner/Mazel.

Dunst, C. (1995). *Key characteristics and features of community-based family support programs.* Chicago: Family Resource Coalition.

Dunst, C., Trivette, C., & Deal, A. (1988). *Enabling and empowering families.* Brookline, MA: Brookline.

Edelman, M. W. (1992). *The measure of our success.* Boston: Beacon Press.

Elder, G., Caspi, A., & Nguyen, T. V. (1985). Resourceful and vulnerable children: Family influences in hard times. In R. K. Silbereisen & K. Eyferth (Eds.), *Development in context.* New York: Springer.

Epstein, N., Bishop, D., Ryan, C., Miller, I., & Keitnor, G. (1993). The McMaster model: View of healthy family functioning. In F. Walsh (Ed.), *Normal family processes* (2nd ed.). New York: Guilford Press.

Erikson, K. T. (1976). *Everything in its path: Destruction of community in the Buffalo Creek flood.* New York: Simon & Schuster.

Fadiman, A. (1997). *The spirit catches you and you fall down.* San Francisco: Ferrer.

Falicov, C. J. (Ed.). (1988). *Family transitions: Continuity and change over the life cycle.* New York: Guilford Press.

Falicov, C. J. (1995). Training to think culturally: A multidimensional comparative framework.. *Family Process, 34,* 373–388.

Falicov, C. J. (1998). *Latino families in therapy: A guide to multicultural practice.* New York: Guilford Press.

Falloon, I., Boyd, J., & McGill, C. (1984). *Family care of schizophrenia.* New York: Guilford Press.

Family Resource Coalition. (1996). *Guidelines for family support practice.* Chicago: Author.

Felsman, J. K., & Vaillant, G. (1987). Resilient children as adults: A 40-year study. In E. J. Anthony & B. Cohler (Eds.), *The invulnerable child.* New York: Guilford Press.

Figley, C. (1989). *Helping traumatized families.* San Francisco: Jossey-Bass.

Figley, C. (1995). *Compassion fatigue.* San Francisco: Jossey-Bass.

Fisher, L., Ransom, D., & Terry, (1993).

Fowers, B., Lyons, E. M., & Montel, K. H. (1996). Positive illusions about marriage: Self-enhancement or relationship enhancement? *Journal of Family Psychology, 10,* 192–208.

Framo, J. (1976). Family of origin as a therapeutic resource in marital and family therapy: You can and should go home again. *Family Process, 15,* 193–210.

Frankl, V. (1984). *Man's search for meaning.* New York: Simon & Schuster. (Original work published 1946)

Freedman, J., & Combs, G. (1996). *Narrative therapy.* New York: Norton.

Furstenberg, F., & Cherlin, A. (1991). *Divided families.* Cambridge, MA: Harvard University Press.

Ganong, L., & Coleman, M. (1995). *Remarried family relationships.* Thousand Oaks, CA: Sage.

Garbarino, J. (1997). *Raising children in a socially toxic environment.* San Francisco: Jossey-Bass.

Garmezy, N. (1974). Vulnerability research and the issues of primary prevention. *American Journal of Orthopsychiatry, 41,* 101–116.

Garmezy, N. (1987). Stress, competence, and development: Continuities in the study of schizophrenic adults, children vulnerable to psychopathology, and the search for stress-resistant children. *American Journal of Orthopsychiatry, 57,* 159–174.

Garmezy, N. (1991). Resiliency and vulnerability to adverse developmental outcomes associated with poverty. *American Behavioral Scientist, 34,* 416–430.

Garmezy, N., & Rutter, M. (Eds.). (1983). *Stress, coping, and development in children.* New York: McGraw-Hill.

Geertz, C. (1986). Making experiences, authoring selves. In V. Turner & E. Bruner (Eds.), *The anthropology of experience.* Chicago: University of Chicago Press.

Gergen, K. (1989). Understanding, narration, and the cultural construction of the self. In J. Stigler, R. Shweder, & G. Herdt (Eds.), *Cultural psychology*. Cambridge, England: Cambridge University Press.

Gleick, J. (1987). *Chaos: Making a new science*. New York: Viking.

Goldner, V. (1985). Feminism and family therapy. *Family Process, 24*, 31–47.

Goldner, V. (1988). Gender and generation: Normative and covert hierarchies. *Family Process, 27*, 17–31.

Goldstein, M., & Kopeikin, H. (1981). Short- and long-term effects of combining drug and family therapy. In M. Goldstein (Ed.), *New developments in interventions with families of schizophrenics*. San Francisco: Jossey-Bass.

Goleman, D. (1995). *EQ: Emotional intelligence*. New York: Bantam.

Gonzalez, S., Steinglass, P., & Reiss, D. (1989). Putting the illness in its place: Discussion groups for families with chronic medical illness. *Family Process, 28*, 69–87.

Gottman, J. (1993). A theory of marital dissolution and stability. *Journal of Family Psychology, 7*, 57–75.

Gottman, J. (1994). *Why marriages succeed or fail*. New York: Simon & Schuster.

Gottman, J. (1998). *Raising an emotionally intelligent child*. New York: Simon & Schuster.

Green, R.-J., & Werner, P. D. (1996). Intrusiveness and closeness–caregiving: Rethinking the concept of family enmeshment. *Family Process, 35*, 115–136.

Griffin, S. (1993). *A chorus of stones*. New York: Anchor.

Griffith, J., & Griffith, M. (1994). *The body speaks*. New York: Basic Books.

Griffith, J., & Griffith, M. (1998). *Sacred encounters*. Manuscript in preparation.

Grinker, R. R., & Spiegel, J. (1945). *Men under stress*. Philadelphia: Blakiston.

Guerney, B. (1991). Marital and family enrichment research: A decade review and look ahead. In A. Booth (Ed.), *Contemporary families*. Minneapolis: National Council on Family Relations.

Hadley, T., Jacob, T., Miliones, J., Caplan, J., & Spitz, D. (1974). The relationship between family developmental crises and the appearance of symptoms in a family member. *Family Process, 13*, 207–214.

Haley, J. (1976). *Problem-solving therapy*. San Francisco: Jossey-Bass.

Haley, J. (1980). *Leaving home*. New York: McGraw-Hill.

Hare-Mustin, R. (1987). The problem of gender in family therapy theory. *Family Process, 26*, 15–33.

Hargrave, T. (1994). *Families and forgiveness*. New York: Brunner/Mazel.

Harris, I. B. (1996). *Children in jeopardy: Can we break the cycle of poverty?* New Haven, CT: Yale Child Study Center.

Harway, M. (1996). *Treating the changing family: Handling normative and unusual events*. New York: Wiley.

Hatfield, A., & Lefley, H. (Eds.). (1987). *Families of the mentally ill: Coping and adaptation*. New York: Guilford Press.

Hauser, S., Vierya, M., Jacobson, A., & Wertlieb, D. (1985). Vulnerability and resilience in adolescence: Views from the family. *Journal of Adolescence, 5*, 81–100.

Hawley, D. R., & DeHaan, L. (1996). Toward a definition of family resilience: Integrating life-span and family perspectives. *Family Process, 35,* 283–298.

Helmreich, W. B. (1992). *Against all odds: Holocaust survivors and the successful lives they made in America.* New York: Simon & Schuster.

Herbert, T. B., & Cohen, S. (1993). Stress and immunity in humans: A meta-analytic review. *Psychosomatic Medicine, 55,* 364–379.

Herman, J. (1992). *Trauma and recovery.* New York: Basic Books.

Hess, G., & Handel, G. (1959). *Family worlds: A psychological approach to family life.* Chicago: University of Chicago Press.

Hetherington, E. M. (1989). Coping with family transitions: Winners, losers, and survivors. *Child Development, 60,* 1–14.

Hetherington, E. M., Law, T., & O'Connor, T. (1993). Divorce: Challenges, changes, and new chances. In F. Walsh (Ed.), *Normal family processes* (2nd ed.). New York: Guilford Press.

Higgins, G. O. (1994). *Resilient adults: Overcoming a cruel past.* San Francisco: Jossey-Bass.

Hill, R. (1949). *Families under stress.* New York: Harper.

Hochschild, A. (1989). *The second shift: Working parents and the revolution at home.* New York: Viking Penguin.

Hochschild, A. (1997). *Time bind.* New York: Holt.

Hoffman, L. (1990). Constructing realities: An art of lenses. *Family Process, 29,* 1–12.

Holmes, T. H., & Masuda, M. (1974). Life change and illness susceptibility. In B. S. Dohrenwend & B. P. Dohrenwend (Eds.), *Stressful life events: Their nature and effects.* New York: Wiley.

Holtzworth-Monroe, A., & Jacobson, N. (1991). Behavioral marital therapy. In A. Gurman & D. Kniskern (Eds.), *Handbook of family therapy* (Vol. 2). New York: Brunner/Mazel.

Imber-Black, E. (1988). *Families and larger systems.* New York: Guilford Press.

Imber-Black, E. (1995). *Secrets in families and family therapy.* New York: Norton.

Imber-Black, E., Roberts, J., & Whiting, R. (Eds.). (1988). *Rituals in families and family therapy.* New York: Norton.

Institute for Health and Aging. (1996). *Chronic care in America: A 21st century challenge.* Princeton, NJ: Robert Wood Johnson Foundation.

Ives, S., Abramson, J., & Kantor, M. (Producers). (1996). *The West* [Videocassettes, 9 vols.]. Alexandria, VA: PBS Home Video.

Jackson, D. D. (1977). Family rules: Marital quid pro quo. In P. Watzlawick & J. Weakland (Eds.), *The interactional view.* New York: Norton.

Jackson, P., with Delehanty, H. (1995). *Sacred hoops: Spiritual lessons of a hardwood warrior.* New York: Hyperion Books.

Jordan, D. (1996). *Family first: Winning the parenting game.* New York: HarperCollins.

Jordan, J. (1992, April). *Relational resilience.* Paper presented at Stone Center Colloquium Series, Wellesley College, Wellesley, MA.

Jordan, J., Kaplan, A., Miller, J. B., Stiver, I., & Surrey, J. (1991). *Women's growth in connection: Writings from the Stone Center.* New York: Guilford Press.

Kagan, J. (1984). *The nature of the child.* New York: Basic Books.

Kagan, R., & Schlosberg, S. (1989). *Families in perpetual crisis.* New York: Norton.

Kagan, S., & Weissbourd, B. (1994). *Putting families first.* San Francisco: Jossey-Bass.

Kaminer, W. (1992). *I'm dysfunctional, you're dysfunctional.* Reading, MA: Addison-Wesley.

Kaplan, L. (1986). *Working with multiproblem families.* New York: Lexington Books.

Kaplan, L., & Girard, J. (1994). *Strengthening high-risk families.* New York: Lexington Books.

Karpel, M. (1986). *Family resources: The hidden partner in family therapy.* New York: Guilford Press.

Kaufman, J., & Zigler, E. (1987). Do abused children become abusive parents? *American Journal of Orthopsychiatry, 57,* 186–192.

Kazak, A. (1989). Families of chronically ill children: A systems and social ecological model of adaptation and challenge. *Journal of Consulting and Clinical Psychology, 57,* 25–30.

Keller, H. (1968). *Midstream: My later life.* New York: Greenwood. (Original work published 1929)

Kleinman, A. (1988). *Illness narratives: Suffering, healing, and the human condition.* New York: Basic Books.

Kluckhohn, F. R. (1960). Variations in the basic values of family systems. In N. W. Bell & E. F. Vogel (Eds.), *The family.* Glencoe, IL: Free Press.

Kobasa, S. (1985). Stressful life events, personality, and health: An inquiry into hardiness. In A. Monat & R. Lazarus (Eds.), *Stress and coping* (2nd ed.). New York: Columbia University Press.

Kobasa, S., Maddi, S., & Kahn, R. (1982). Hardiness and health: A prospective study. *Journal of Personality and Social Psychology, 37,* 1–11.

Kotlowitz, A. (1991). *There are no children here.* New York: Doubleday.

Laird, J. (1989). Women and stories: Restorying women's self-constructions. In M. McGoldrick, C. Anderson, & F. Walsh (Eds.), *Women in families.* New York: Norton.

Laird, J. (1993). Lesbian and gay families. In F. Walsh (Ed.), *Normal family processes* (2nd ed.). New York: Guilford Press.

Laird, J., & Green, R.-J. (Eds.). (1996). *Lesbians and gays in families and family therapy.* San Francisco: Jossey-Bass.

Lamb, M. E. (Ed.). (1997). *The role of the father in child development* (3rd ed.). New York: Wiley.

Landau-Stanton, J. (1986). Competence, impermanence, and transitional mapping: A model for systems consultation. In L. C. Wynne, S. McDaniel, & T. Weber (Eds.), *Systems consultation.* New York: Guilford Press.

Landau-Stanton, J. (1993). *AIDS, health, and mental health: A primary sourcebook.* New York: Brunner/Mazel.

Langsley, D. G., & Kaplan, D. M. (1968). *The treatment of families in crisis.* New York: Grune & Stratton.

Lavee, Y., McCubbin, H. I., & Olson, D. H. (1987). The effect of stressful life events and transitions on family functioning and well-being. *Journal of Marriage and the Family, 49,* 857–873.

Lazarus, R., & Folkman, S. (1984). *Stress, appraisal, and coping.* New York: Springer.

Leach, P. (1994). *Children first.* New York: Knopf.

Lee, S. (Director). (1994). *Crooklyn* [Film]. New York: 40 acres and a mule.

Lefley, H. P. (1996). *Family caregiving in mental illness.* Thousand Oaks, CA: Sage.

Lewis, J., Beavers, W. R., Gossett, J., & Phillips, V. (1976). *No single thread: Psychological health in family systems.* New York: Brunner/Mazel.

Lidz, T. (1963). *The family and human adaptation.* New York: International Universities Press.

Lifton, R. J. (1979). *The broken connection: On death and the continuity of life.* New York: Simon & Schuster.

Lifton, R. J. (1993). *The Protean self: Human resilience in an age of fragmentation.* New York: Basic Books.

Luthar, S. S., & Zigler, E. (1991). Vulnerability and competence: A review of research on resilience in childhood. *American Journal of Orthopsychiatry, 61,* 6–22.

Markman, H., & Notarius, C. (1994). *We can work it out: Making sense of marital conflict.* San Francisco: Jossey-Bass.

Markman, H., Renick, M. J., Stanley, S., & Floyd, F. (1992). The prevention of divorce and marital distress. *Journal of Consulting and Clinical Psychology, 60.*

Masten, A. S., Best, K. M., & Garmezy, N. (1990). Resilience and development: Contributions from the study of children who overcome adversity. *Development and Pychopathology, 2,* 425–444.

McAdoo, H. (Ed.). (1996). *Black families* (3rd ed.). Thousand Oaks, CA: Sage.

McCubbin, H., McCubbin, M., McCubbin, A., & Futrell, J. (Eds.). (1995). *Resiliency in ethnic minority families: Vol. 2. African-American families.* Madison: Center for Excellence in Family Studies, University of Wisconsin.

McCubbin, H., McCubbin, M., Thompson, E., & Fromer, J. (Eds.). (1995). *Resiliency in ethnic minority families: Vol. 1. Native and immigrant families.* Madison: Center for Excellence in Family Studies, University of Wisconsin.

McCubbin, H., & Patterson, J. M. (1983). The family stress process: The Double ABCX model of adjustment and adaptation. In H. McCubbin, M. Sussman, & J. M. Patterson (Eds.), *Social stress and the family: Advances in family stress theory and research.* New York: Haworth Press.

McFarlane, W. (1991). Family psychoeducational treatment. In A. Gurman & D. Kniskern (Eds.), *Handbook of family therapy* (Vol. 2). New York: Brunner/Mazel.

McGoldrick, M. (1995). *You can go home again: Reconnecting with your family.* New York: Norton.

McGoldrick, M., Almeida, R., Hines, P., Garcia-Preto, N., Rosen, E., & Lee, E. (1991). Mourning in different cultures. In F. Walsh & M. McGoldrick (Eds.), *Living beyond loss.* New York: Norton.

McGoldrick, M., Anderson, C., & Walsh, F. (Eds.). (1989). *Women in families: A framework for family therapy.* New York: Norton.

McGoldrick, M., & Gerson, R. (1985). *Genograms in family assessment.* New York: Norton.

McGoldrick, M., Giordano, J., & Pearce, J. (Eds.). (1996). *Ethnicity and family therapy* (2nd ed.). New York: Guilford Press.

McGoldrick, M., & Walsh, F. (1983). A systemic view of history and loss. In M. Aronson & L. Wolberg (Eds.), *Group and family therapy.* New York: Brunner/Mazel.

McGoldrick, M., & Walsh, F. (1991). A time to mourn: Death and the family life cycle. In F. Walsh & M. McGoldrick (Eds.), *Living beyond loss: Death in the family.* New York: Norton.

McGoldrick, M., & Walsh, F. (1998). Death and loss through the family life cycle. In B. Carter & M. McGoldrick (Eds.), *The expanded family life cycle* (3rd ed.). Needham Heights, MA: Allyn & Bacon.

Mead, M. (1972). *Blackberry winter.* New York: William Morrow.

Meth, R., & Pasick, R. (1990). *Men in therapy: The challenge of change.* New York: Guilford Press.

Minuchin, P. (1995). Foster and natural families: Forming a collaborative network. In L. Combrinck-Graham (Ed.), *Children in families at risk.* New York: Guilford Press.

Minuchin, P., Colapinto, J., & Minuchin, S. (1998). *Working with families of the poor.* New York: Guilford Press.

Minuchin, S. (1974). *Families and family therapy.* Cambridge, MA: Harvard University Press.

Minuchin, S. (1992). *Family healing: Strategies for hope and understanding.* New York: Macmillan.

Minuchin, S., Montalvo, B., Guerney, B., Rosman, B., & Schumer, F. (1967). *Families of the slums.* New York: Basic Books.

Mitford, J. (1978). *The American way of death.* New York: Touchstone. (Originally published 1963)

Moos, R., & Moos, B. S. (1976). A typology of family social environments. *Family Process, 15,* 357–371.

Murphy, L. (1987). Further reflections on resilience. In E. J. Anthony & B. Cohler (Eds.), *The invulnerable child.* New York: Guilford Press.

Murphy, L., & Moriarty, A. E. (1976). *Vulnerability, coping, and growth: From infancy to adolescence.* New Haven, CT: Yale University Press.

Napier, A. (1988). *The fragile bond: In search of an equal, intimate, and enduring marriage.* New York: Harper & Row.

National Commission on Children. (1993). *Strengthening and supporting families.* Washington, DC: National Commission on Children.

National Institute of Mental Health (NIMH). (1993). *The prevention of mental disorders: A national research agenda.* Washington, DC: U.S. Government Printing Office.

National Network for Family Resiliency. (1996). *Understanding resiliency* [Online]. Available: http://www.agnr.umd.edu/users/nnfr/pub_under.html

Neugarten, B. (1976). Adaptation and the life cycle. *The Counseling Psychologist, 6,* 16–20.

Nichols, M., & Schwartz, R. (1995). *Family therapy: Concepts and methods* (3rd ed.). Needham Heights, MA: Allyn & Bacon.

Olson, D. H. (1993). Circumplex model of marital and family systems. In F. Walsh (Ed.), *Normal family processes* (2nd ed.). New York: Guilford Press.

Olson, D. H., Fournier, D. G., & Druckman, J. M. (1986). *PREPARE, PREPARE-MC and ENRICH inventories.* St. Paul, MN: PREPARE/ENRICH, Inc.

Olson, D. H., McCubbin, H., Barnes, H., Larsen, A., Muxen, M., & Wilson, M. (1989). *Families: What makes them work?* (rev. ed.). Newbury Park, CA: Sage.

Olson, D. H., Russell, C. S., & Sprenkle, D. H. (Eds.). (1989). *Circumplex Model: Systemic assessment and treatment of families.* New York: Haworth Press.

Ooms, T., & Preister, S. (Eds.). (1988). *Strengthening families: Using family criteria in policymaking and program evaluation. A consensus report of the Family Criteria Task Force.* Washington, DC: Family Impact Seminar.

Parsons, T., & Bales, R.F. (1955). *Family, socialization, and interaction processes.* Glencoe, IL: Free Press.

Patterson, G. (1983). Stress: A change agent for family process. In N. Garmezy & M. Rutter (Eds.), *Stress, coping, and development in children.* New York: McGraw-Hill.

Patterson, G. R., Reid, J., Jones, R., & Conger, R. (1975). *A social learning approach to family interaction.* Eugene, OR: Castalia.

Patterson, J. M., & Garwick, A. W. (1994). Theoretical linkages: Family meanings and sense of coherence. In H. McCubbin, E. Thompson, A. Thompson, & J. Fromer (Eds.), *Sense of coherence and resiliency: Stress, coping, and health.* Madison: Center for Excellence in Family Studies, University of Wisconsin.

Paul, N., & Grosser, G. (1991). Operational mourning and its role in conjoint family therapy. In F. Walsh & M. McGoldrick (Eds.), *Living beyond loss: Death in the family.* New York: Norton.

Penn, P. (1985). Feed forward: Future questions, future maps. *Family Process, 24,* 299–310.

Pearlin, L., & Schooler, C. (1978). The structure of coping. *Journal of Health and Social Behavior, 19,* 2–21.

Piotrkowski, C., & Hughes, D. (1993). Dual-earner families in context: Managing family and work systems. In F. Walsh (Ed.) *Normal family processes* (2nd ed.). New York: Guilford Press.

Pipher, M. (1997). *The shelter of each other: Rebuilding our families.* New York: Ballantine.

Pittman, F. (1987). *Turning points: Treating families in transition and crisis.* New York: Norton.

Prest, L. A., & Keller, J. F. (1993) Spirituality and family therapy. *Journal of Marital and Family Therapy, 19,* 137–148.

Rabinow, P. (1977). *Reflections on fieldwork in Morocco.* Berkeley: University of California Press.

Rando, T. (1984). *Grief, dying, and death: Clinical interventions for caregivers.* Champaign, IL: Research Press.

Rapaport, R. (1962). Normal crises, family structure, and mental health. *Family Process, 2,* 68–71.

Reiss, D. (1981). *The family's construction of reality.* Cambridge, MA: Harvard University Press.

Reiss, D., & Oliveri, M. (1980). Family paradigm and family coping: A proposal for linking the family's intrinsic adaptive capacities to its responses to stress. *Family Relations, 29,* 431–444.

Rodham Clinton, H. (1996). *It takes a village.* New York: Simon & Schuster.

Rolland, J. (1994). *Families, illness, and disability: An integrative treatment model.* New York: Basic Books.

Rosen, E. (1998). *Families facing death* (2nd ed.). San Francisco: Jossey-Bass.

Rubin, L. B. (1994). *Families on the faultline.* New York: HarperCollins.

Rubin, L. B. (1996). *The transcendent child: Tales of triumph over the past.* New York: Basic Books.

Rutter, M. (1985). Resilience in the face of adversity: Protective factors and resistance to psychiatric disorder. *British Journal of Psychiatry, 147,* 598–611.

Rutter, M. (1987). Psychosocial resilience and protective mechanisms. *American Journal of Orthopsychiatry, 57,* 316–331.

Sandmeier, M. (1994). *Original kin: The search for connection among adult sisters and brothers.* New York: Plume.

Satir, V. (1988). *The new peoplemaking.* Palo Alto, CA: Science & Behavior Books.

Scharff, D., & Scharff, J. S. (1987). *Object relations family therapy.* New York: Jason Aronson.

Schorr, L. (1988). *Within our reach: Breaking the cycle of disadvantage.* New York: Anchor.

Schumm, W. (1985). Beyond relationship characteristics of strong families: Constructing a model of family strengths. *Family Perspective, 19,* 1–9.

Schwartz, P. (1994). *Love between equals.* New York: Free Press.

Schwartz, R. (1997, March–April). Don't look back. *Family Therapy Networker,* pp. 40–47.

Sciolino, E. (Nov. 11, 1996). A painful road from Vietnam to forgiveness. *New York Times,* A1, A8.

Seligman, M. (1990). *Learned optimism.* New York: Random House.

Seligman, M. (1995). *The optimistic child.* Boston: Houghton Mifflin.

Shange, N., & Shabalala, J. (1995). *Nomathemba.* Performance, Steppenwolf Theatre, Chicago.

Simeonsson, R. (1995). *Risk, resilience, and prevention: Promoting the well-being of all children.* Baltimore: Paul H. Brookes.

Simon, R. (1997, March–April). Systems therapy NBA style. *Family Therapy Networker,* pp. 49–61.

Skinner, H., Santa Barbara, J., & Steinhauer, P. (1983). The family assessment measure. *Canadian Journal of Community Mental Health, 2,* 91–105.

Skolnick, A. (1991). *Embattled paradise: The American family in an age of uncertainty.* New York: Basic Books.

Sluzki, C. (1983). Process, structure, and world views in family therapy: Toward an integration of systemic models. *Family Process, 22,* 469–476.

Speck, R., & Attneave, C. (1973). *Family networks.* New York: Pantheon.

Spiegel, D. (1993). *Living beyond limits.* New York: Random House.

Stacey, J. (1990). *Brave new families: Stories of domestic upheaval in late twentieth century America.* New York: Basic Books.

Stacey, J. (1996). *In the name of the family: Rethinking family values in the postmodern age.* Boston: Beacon.

Stanton, M. D. (1977). The addict as savior: Heroin, death, and the family. *Family Process, 16,* 191–197.

Steinberg, L., Lamborn, S. D., Dornbusch, S. M., & Darling, N. (1992). Impact of parenting practices on adolescent achievement: Authoritative parenting, school involvement, and encouragement to succeed. *Child Development, 63,* 1266–1281.

Steinglass, P., & Horan, M. (1988). Families and chronic medical illness. In F. Walsh & C. Anderson (Eds.), *Chronic disorders and the family.* New York: Haworth Press.

Stierlin, H. (1974). *Separating parents and adolescents.* New York: Jason Aronson.

Stinnett, N., & DeFrain, J. (1985). *Secrets of strong families.* Boston: Little, Brown.

Stinnett, N., Knorr, B., DeFrain, J., & Rowe, G. (1981). How strong families cope with crises. *Family Perspective, 15,* 159–166.

Swadener, B. B., & Lubeck, S. (Eds.). (1995). *Children and families "at promise": Deconstructing the discourse of risk.* Albany: State University of New York Press.

Taggart, S. (1994). *Living as if: Belief systems in mental health practice.* San Francisco: Jossey-Bass.

Tannen, D. (1994). *You just don't understand.* New York: Ballantine.

Taylor, S. E. (1989). *Positive illusions: Creative self-deception and the healthy mind.* New York: Basic Books.

Trepper, T., & Barrett, M. J. (1989). *Systemic treatment of incest: A therapeutic handbook.* New York: Brunner/Mazel.

Vaillant, G. (1995). *Adaptation to life* (rev. ed.). Cambridge, MA: Harvard University Press.

Visher, E., & Visher, J. S. (1993). Remarriage families and stepparenting. In F. Walsh (Ed.), *Normal family processes* (2nd ed.). New York: Guilford Press.

Visher, E., & Visher, J. S. (1996). *Therapy with stepfamilies.* New York: Brunner/Mazel.

Walker, A. (1983). *The color purple.* New York: Washington Square Press.

Walker, G. (1991). *In the midst of winter.* New York: Norton.

Wallerstein, J., & Blakeslee, S. (1989). *Second chances: Men, women, and children a decade after divorce.* New York: Ticknor & Fields.

Walsh, F. (1978). Concurrent grandparent death and birth of schizophrenic offspring: An intriguing finding. *Family Process, 17,* 457–463.

Walsh, F. (1983). The timing of symptoms and critical events in the family life cycle. In H. Liddle (Ed.), *Clinical implications of the family life cycle.* Rockville, MD: Aspen.

Walsh, F. (1985). Social change, disequilibrium, and adaptation in developing countries: A Moroccan example. In J. Schwartzman (Ed.), *Families and other systems.* New York: Guilford Press.

Walsh, F. (1987a). The clinical utility of normal family research. *Psychotherapy, 24*, 496–503.

Walsh, F. (1987b). Family relationship patterns in schizophrenia. In R. R. Grinker, Sr., & M. Harrow (Eds.), *Clinical research in schizophrenia: A multi-dimensional approach*. Springfield, IL: Charles C Thomas.

Walsh, F. (1989). Reconsidering gender in the 'marital quid pro quo.' In M. McGoldrick, C. Anderson, & F. Walsh (Eds.), *Women in families: A framework for family therapy*. New York: Norton.

Walsh, F. (1991). Promoting healthy functioning in divorced and remarried families. In A. Gurman & D. Kniskern (Eds.), *Handbook of family therapy*. New York: Brunner/Mazel.

Walsh, F. (1993). Conceptualization of normal family processes. In F. Walsh (Ed.), *Normal family processes* (2nd ed.). New York: Guilford Press.

Walsh, F. (1995a). From family damage to family challenge. In R. Mikesell, D. D. Lusterman, & S. McDaniel (Eds.), *Integrating family therapy: Handbook of family psychology and systems therapy*. Washington, DC: American Psychological Association.

Walsh, F. (1995b). Families and mental illness: What have we learned? In B. Abosh (Ed.), *Mental illness and the family*. Toronto: University of Toronto Press.

Walsh, F. (1999). Beliefs, spirituality, and transcendence: Keys to family resilience. In M. McGoldrick (Ed.), *Re-visioning family therapy: Race, culture, and gender in clinical practice*. New York: Guilford Press.

Walsh, F. (1998b). Families in later life: Challenges and opportunities. In B. Carter & M. McGoldrick (Eds.), *The expanded family life cycle*. Needham Heights, MA: Allyn & Bacon.

Walsh, F. (Ed.). (1999). *Spiritual resources in family therapy*. New York: The Guilford Press.

Walsh, F., & Anderson, C. M. (1988). Chronic disorders and families: An overview. In F. Walsh & C. Anderson (Eds.), *Chronic disorders and the family*. New York: Haworth Press.

Walsh, F., Jacob, L., & Simons, V. (1995). Facilitating healthy divorce processes: Therapy and mediation approaches. In N. Jacobson & A. Gurman (Eds.), *Clinical handbook of couple therapy*. New York: Guilford Press.

Walsh, F., & McGoldrick, M. (1991). Loss and the family: A systemic perspective. In F. Walsh & M. McGoldrick (Eds.), *Living beyond loss: Death in the family*. New York: Norton.

Walsh, F., & Olson, D. H. (1989). Utility of the Circumplex Model with severely dysfunctional families. In D. Olson, D. Sprenkle, & C. Russell (Eds.), *The Circumplex Model: Systemic assessment and treatment of families*. New York: Haworth Press.

Walsh, F., & Scheinkman, M. (1989). (Fe)male: The hidden gender dimension in models of family therapy. In M. McGoldrick, C. Anderson, & F. Walsh (Eds.), *Women in families: A framework for family therapy*. New York: Norton.

Waters, D., & Lawrence, E. (1993). *Competence, courage, and change*. New York: Norton.

Watzlawick, P., Beavin, J., & Jackson, D. (1967). *Pragmatics of human communication*. New York: Norton.

Weakland, J., Fisch, R., Watzlawick, P., & Bodin, A. (1974). Brief therapy: Focused problem-resolution. *Family Process, 13,* 141–168.

Weil, A. (1994). *Spontaneous healing*. New York: Knopf.

Weingarten, K. (1994). *The mother's voice: Strengthening intimacy in families*. New York: Guilford Press.

Werner, E. E. (1993). Risk, resilience, and recovery: Perspectives from the Kauai longitudinal study. *Development and Psychopathology, 5,* 503–515.

Werner, E. E., & Smith, R. S. (1982). *Vulnerable but invincible: A study of resilient children*. New York: McGraw-Hill.

Werner, E. E., & Smith, R. S. (1992). *Overcoming the odds: High risk children from birth to adulthood*. Ithaca, NY: Cornell University Press.

West, C. (1995). *Race matters*. Cambridge, MA: Harvard University Press.

Weston, K. (1991). *Families we choose: Lesbians, gays, and kinship*. New York: Columbia University Press.

Whitaker, C., & Keith, D. (1981). Symbolic-experiential family therapy. In A. S. Gurman & D. Kniskern (Eds.), *Handbook of family therapy*. New York: Brunner/Mazel.

White, M., & Epston, D. (1990). *Narrative means to therapeutic ends*. New York: Norton.

Whiteside, M. (1998). The postdivorce co-parental alliance. *Journal of Marital and Family Therapy, 24,* 3–24.

Wiesel, E. (1995). *All rivers run to the sea: Memoirs*. New York: Knopf.

Wilson, W. J. (1987). *The truly disadvantaged*. Chicago: University of Chicago Press.

Wilson, W. J. (1996). *When work disappears: The world of the urban poor*. New York: Random House.

Wolin, S., & Bennett, L. (1984). Family rituals. *Family Process, 23,* 401–420.

Wolin, S., & Wolin, S. (1993). *The resilient self: How survivors of troubled families rise above adversity*. New York: Villard.

Wood, B. (1985). Proximity and hierarchy: Orthogonal dimensions of family interconnectedness. *Family Process, 24,* 487–507.

Worden, W. J. (1996). *Children and grief: When a parent dies*. New York: Guilford Press.

Wortman, C., & Silver, R. (1989). The myths of coping with loss. *Journal of Counseling and Clinical Psychology, 57,* 349–357.

Wright, L., Watson, W. L., & Bell, J. M. (1996). *Beliefs: The heart of healing in families and illness*. New York: Basic Books.

Wuerffel, J., DeFrain, J., & Stinnett, N. (1990). How strong families use humor. *Family Perspective, 24,* 129–142.

Wyman, E., Cowen, W., Work, W., & Parker, G. (1991). Developmental and milieu correlates of resilience in urban children who have experienced major life stress. *American Journal of Community Psychology, 19,* 405–426.

Wynne, L., McDaniel, S., & Weber, T. (Eds.). (1986). *Systems consultation*. New York: Guilford Press.

Zacks, E., Green, R.J., & Marrow, J. (1988). Comparing lesbian and heterosexual couples on the circumplex model: An initial investigation. *Family Process, 27,* 471–484.

I·N·D·E·X